D0180322

The New
SHORT STORY
THEORIES

THE NEW
SHORT STORY THEORIES

Edited by Charles E. May

OHIO UNIVERSITY PRESS
ATHENS

Ohio University Press, Athens, Ohio 45701
© 1994 by Ohio University Press
Printed in the United States of America
All rights reserved

10 09   5

Ohio University Press books are printed on acid-free paper ∞

Library of Congress Cataloging-in-Publication Data

The New short story theories / edited by Charles E. May.
    p.   cm.
    Includes bibliographical references.
    ISBN 0–8214–1087–3 (pbk.)
    1. Short story.   I. May, Charles E. (Charles Edward), 1941–   .
PN3373.N44   1994
808.3'1—dc20   94–7037
                                                                  CIP

This book is dedicated with abiding love to my wife Patricia.
I can't imagine life without her.

Contents

Preface

WHEN *Short Story Theories* was published in 1976, the first essay was entitled "The Short Story: An Underrated Art." I am happy to say that such an essay is no longer necessary, for in the past decade the short story has enjoyed a "renaissance" of interest. More serious writers are experimenting with the form, more publishers are willing to take a chance on short-story collections, and more critics are seriously discussing the short story. The most basic reason for this revival of interest is that a new generation of writers has appeared since the first edition of *Short Story Theories*—writers such as Raymond Carver, Tobias Wolff, Ann Beattie, Bobbie Ann Mason, and Mary Robison—who have found the short story to be particularly appropriate for their vision and talents.

There are some indications that the first edition of this book played a small role in the renewed critical interest in the form. Susan Lohafer, in the introduction to her own anthology, *Short Story Theory at a Cross-roads,* calls *Short Story Theories* "the first, if not the biggest, move toward a forum for theory." I am grateful to all the students and teachers who have used the book over the years and thus have kept it in print for so long.

This second edition is eighty percent new. I have retained some basic pieces such as Poe's Hawthorne review and Brander Matthews' extension and formalization of Poe's theories, for it is impossible to talk about the nature of the short story without considering Poe's ideas. In fact, I have added some additional Poe pieces—excerpts from early reviews, from the famous "Philosophy" essay, and from his prose poem *Eureka*—because I believe that his contribution to understanding the nature of the form is still underestimated. I also have retained the essays by Jarrell, Bowen, and Gordimer, for I think they make important suggestions about the basic characteristics of the form. All the rest are new to this edition, and most of them have appeared since the first publication of *Short Story Theories*.

As the Table of Contents suggests, the organization of the items in this new edition has a rationale. The overall movement is a circular one from general considerations on the nature of "story" to cognitive considerations on the nature of "storyness." All the essays in between deal in some fashion with the more specific literary genre that has come to be known as the short story. The "Early Formalist Theory" section could also be called "The Poe Tradition," just as "The Modern Short Story" section might be called "The Chekhov Tradition"; for the two most significant "beginnings" of the form are marked by the contributions of those two masters. Sections III and IV include suggestions about the definition of the form and provide a framework for its historical development. Section VI will probably be seen as the most arbitrary grouping, for it could have included many more authors, or many different authors, than it does. Difficulty in securing reprint permission accounts for some omissions; my own personal choice accounts for the rest.

The annotated bibliography has, of course, been updated. I have retained some of the older items which, in my opinion, have historical and critical interest. One of the truest indicators of the revived interest in the short story is the large number of books and essays on the form that have appeared since the first edition of *Short Story Theories*. By collecting these essays and references together in one convenient place, I hope that many more teachers, students, and admirers of the short story will be stimulated to continue the ongoing dialogue about this once underrated form.

Although a number of critics and scholars have shown an enthusiastic interest in the short story since the first edition of *Short Story Theories* appeared, I wish to particularly express my appreciation to Susan Lohafer and Mary Rohrberger. In the books and articles they have written, the conferences they have organized and sponsored, and the journals and collections they have initiated and edited, they have done a remarkable and exciting job of encouraging serious study of the form. I am very proud to call them my colleagues.

Acknowledgments

Baldeshwiler, Eileen. "The Lyric Short Story: The Sketch of a History." *Studies in Short Fiction,* 6 (1969). Copyright 1969 by Newberry College. Reprinted by permission of *Studies in Short Fiction.*

Bowen, Elizabeth. "The Faber Book of Modern Short Stories." From *Collected Impressions.* New York: Alfred A. Knopf, 1950. Copyright 1950 by Elizabeth Bowen. Reprinted by permission of Curtis Brown & John Farquharson for the Estate of Elizabeth Bowen.

Carver, Raymond. "On Writing." From *Fires,* copyright © 1983 by Raymond Carver. Reprinted with permission of Capra Press, Santa Barbara.

Chekhov, Anton. *Letters on the Short Story, Drama, and Other Literary Topics.* New York: Dover Publications. Reprinted by permission of Dover Publications, Inc.

Cortázar, Julio. "Some Aspects of the Short Story." Translated by Aden Hayes. *The Arizona Quarterly,* Spring 1982. Copyright 1982 by Arizona Board of Regents. Originally appeared in *Cuadernos Hispanoamericanos,* 255 (1971). Reprinted by permission of Instituto de Cooperacion IberoAmericana and Arizona Board of Regents.

Éxjenbaum, B. M. *O. Henry and the Theory of the Short Story.* Translated by I. R. Titunik. Reprinted by permission of Michigan Slavic Publications.

Ferguson, Suzanne C. "Defining the Short Story: Impressionism and Form." *Modern Fiction Studies* 28 (1982). Copyright 1982, by Purdue Research Foundation, West Lafayette, Indiana. Reprinted with permission.

Good, Graham. "Notes on the Novella." *Novel: A Forum on Fiction,* 10 (Spring 1977). Copyright *Novel* Corp. © 1977. Reprinted with permission.

Gordimer, Nadine. "South Africa." First published as part of "The International Symposium on the Short Story." *Kenyon Review*—Original

Series, Fall 1969, Vol. XXX, 1968. Reprinted with permission of the *Kenyon Review* and the author. Copyright 1968 by Kenyon College.

Harris, Wendell. "Vision and Form: The English Novel and the Emergence of the Short Story." *Victorian Newsletter,* No. 47, 1975. Reprinted with permission of *The Victorian Newsletter.*

Jarrell, Randall. "Stories." © 1962 by Randall Jarrell. From *Sad Heart at the Supermarket* published by Atheneum Publishers. Permission granted by Rhoda Weyr Agency, New York.

Lohafer, Susan. "A Cognitive Approach to Storyness." From *Short Story,* Spring, 1990. Reprinted with permission of *Short Story.*

Marler, Robert F. "From Tale to Short Story: The Emergence of a New Genre in the 1850's." *American Literature* 44: 2 Copyright 1974, Duke University Press, Durham, NC. Reprinted with permission.

May, Charles. "Chekhov and the Modern Short Story." In *A Chekhov Companion,* edited by Toby Clyman. Copyright 1985 by Greenwood Press, an imprint of Greenwood Publishing Group, Inc. Reprinted with permission.

May, Charles. "The Nature of Knowledge in Short Fiction." *Studies in Short Fiction,* 21 (1984), 327–38. Copyright 1984 by Newberry College. Reprinted with permission of *Studies in Short Fiction.*

Pasco, Allan H. "On Defining Short Stories." *New Literary History,* 22 (Spring 1991). Reprinted with permission of the author and The Johns Hopkins University Press.

Penn, William S. "The Tale as Genre in Short Fiction." *Southern Humanities Review,* 15 (1981). Reprinted with permission of the author.

Pratt, Mary Louise. "The Short Story: The Long and the Short of It." *Poetics.* Vol 10 (1981). Reprinted with permission of Elsevier Science Publishers B.V. and the author.

Shadbolt, Maurice. "New Zealand." First published as part of "The International Symposium on the Short Story: Part Two." *Kenyon Review*—Original Series, Issue 1, Vol. XXXI, 1969. Reprinted with permission of the *Kenyon Review* and the author. Copyright 1969 by Kenyon College.

Stierle, Karl-Heinz. "Story as Exemplum: Exemplum as Story." In *New Perspectives in Germany Literary Criticism,* edited by Richard Amacher and Victor Lange. Translated by David Wilson, et. al. Princeton University Press, 1979. Copyright 1979 by Princeton University Press. Reprinted with permission of Princeton University Press.

Van Dijk, Teun A. "Story Comprehension: An Introduction." *Poetics,* Vol. 9. Reprinted with permission of Elsevier Science Publishers B.V. and the author.

Introduction

THE FIRST EDITION of *Short Story Theories* was created to stimulate debate about the short story as a genre; this second edition has been extensively revised to reflect some of that debate and to provide a fairly complete source book for future study of the form. In one way or another the essays in this collection (supplemented by the references in the annotated bibliography) assert, deny, examine, debate, or at least allude to every theoretical issue that has been raised about the short story since Poe argued that it was a unique narrative form.

Critics, teachers, students, and writers who read these essays and consult some of the additional items in the bibliography will, of course, find their own stimuli for debating and extending the ideas included here. I have suggested my own notions about the short story in various other places and thus, beyond the audacity of including two of my own essays, have no desire to insist on those ideas any further in this introduction. However, since the pieces included here reflect my own choices, I would be remiss if I did not justify those choices by commenting briefly on what I consider to be the crucial issues they raise.

It seems to me the first issue about which we need to come to some understanding—if for no other reason than to call a truce on it—is the issue of definition. Suzanne Ferguson says that in the first edition of *Short Story Theories* there is no single characteristic or cluster of characteristics that the commentators claim absolutely distinguishes the short story from other fictions. She argues that length alone is not a sufficient determiner if all characteristics besides length that may be posited for the short story may also be posited for the novel.

The short story's adjacency to the novel has indeed always been one of the central problems in coming to an understanding of the characteristics of the form. Mary Louise Pratt pushes this issue of "adjacency" to extremes, insisting that the relationship between the novel and the short story is "asymmetrical," that the short story is secondary to and dependent on the novel—which is, historically, the dominant, normative genre. Thus, Pratt claims, because the short story cannot be defined except by comparison to the novel it must therefore be dependent on the novel. Like Ferguson and Good, Pratt reminds us that shortness cannot be an intrinsic property of anything, but can only be seen as relative to something else. However, one might note, this has never been a stumbling block for generic discussions of the novel; for some reason, the "longness" of the novel has been seen as an intrinsic characteristic.

In contrast to these skeptics about generic characteristics of the short story, there are those critics who believe that either the shortness of the form or its historical traditions, or both, have resulted in properties of the short story that distinguish it from the novel. Poe was, of course, the first to make this case; and indeed the case he makes depends on both the issue of shortness and the issue of historical ancestry. First of all, when Poe referred to the short prose tale—which he claimed was different from and superior to long narrative—he meant short fiction within the tradition of the romance, a form which, regardless of length, practically all critics, even Graham Good, agree is different in content and conventions from the novel. Furthermore, Poe's notion of unity and singleness of effect was indebted to the kinds of transformations being worked on the romance, fairy tale, folktale form by the German romantics. As can be seen in Good's helpful summary, the theories of the novella by Goethe, Tieck, and Schlegel were central in influencing Irving, Hawthorne, and Poe's innovations in short fiction.

Poe's theories about the difference between the novel and the short story became more solidified in criticism at the turn of the century by Brander Matthews, who argued that the difference between the two forms was not a mere difference in length, but a difference in kind. Although Matthews may have gone too far with some of his formulas and therefore helped create an entire industry of how-to books on the short story during this period, he is probably right to insist that the difference between the novel and the short story or even the mere anecdote and the short story has something to do with what he calls "neatness of construction" and "polish of execution." Matthews' emphasis, as it was for Poe, is on "plot" understood as pattern or unified plan, not a mere anecdotal series of events. As opposed to the novel, Matthews suggests that the short story focuses only on those details that are "bound" to the preestablished plan, not on details that provide either a cross section of life or fidelity to the external world.

One of the best-known arguments for the difference between the short story and the novel in the twentieth century is that of B. M. Éjxenbaum, the Russian formalist critic of the 1920s who claimed a fundamental distinction between big and small narrative forms. Consistent with Poe's "Philosophy of Composition"—in which he emphasized beginning with the end of a work and then creating a formal pattern that inevitably leads up to that end—Éjxenbaum argues that the short story amasses all its weight on its conclusion. This emphasis on "closure" in the short story—also suggested by Chekhov's intuition that he must focus on the end of a short story and "artfully" concentrate there an impression of the total work—becomes a central characteristic of the form as argued by later critics such as Susan Lohafer and John Gerlach.

Julio Cortázar also argues for a basic difference between the novel and the short story, using a metaphoric comparison between photography and motion pictures to make his point. Believing there are certain constants that hold true for all short stories, Cortázar claims that the short story's significant element is the act of choosing a real or imaginary happening that has the mysterious property of illuminating something beyond itself. He insists that, like the photograph, the short story is a paradoxical form which cuts off a fragment of reality in such a way that the fragment acts like an explosion that opens up a more ample reality. This notion of the short story illuminating something beyond itself Cortázar relates to the short story's technique of compression and intensity; he says (as Poe did before him) that "intensity" results from the elimination of all intermediary ideas or situations, while "tension" results from the atmosphere created by the unity of bound details in the story.

The difference between those critics and writers who doubt that a definition of the short story is possible and those critics and writers who argue for such a definition revolves around two different concepts of generic definition. The nay-sayers insist on a positivist definition that includes characteristics common to all examples of the short story that will sufficiently distinguish it from the novel. The pro-definition group is more inclined to adopt Ludwig Wittgenstein's "family resemblance" theory. Instead of trying to find exclusionary characteristics common to all hypothetical examples of the form, they are interested in locating a network of similarities and relationships within examples of the form. As long as they can find some characteristics that are shared by hypothetical examples of the short story, they do not need to find a definition that satisfies necessary and sufficient conditions to distinguish one genre from the novel. They believe that as long as prototypical members of the genre have a high degree of resemblances to each other, such a group of "family resemblances" are useful for the interpretation of individual members of the genre, for discussion of the historical development of the genre, and for heuristic discussion about the epistemological and aesthetic implications of these characteristics.

Allan Pasco is the most emphatic proponent of this group in this collection; he believes that the work of defining a genre succeeds when the definition corresponds to general practice and understanding; he is therefore not concerned with finding a single touchstone for the form but rather looks for clusters of traits common to it. The best that a generic definition can do, says Pasco, is to draw attention to the dominant aspects of a genre, which may indeed include elements that one can find in other genres.

Although I have been accused of insisting on a single exclusionary trait characteristic of the short story, particularly by Norman Friedman in his essay in *Short Story Theory at a Crossroads,* I include myself in the "family resemblance" group. In my own essay on the nature of knowledge in short fiction, I offer suggestions for relating the shortness of the form to the typical kind of experience embodied in the form; I also argue that the tradition of the short story as descended from myth, folktale, fable, and romance forms, drives it toward focusing on eternal values rather than temporal ones and sacred/unconscious reality rather than profane/everyday reality.

On the assumption that a useful definition of the short story can be made up of family resemblances, clusters of qualities, dominant characteristics, I would like to call attention to some of these characteristics suggested by the essays in this book. I begin with the essay by Karl-Heinz Stierle, in many ways the most dense and demanding piece in this collection, because he raises basic issues about the story form related to the nature of the short story. He, too, agrees with the Wittgenstein approach, arguing that when we use the word "story" we should not ask what basic common idea underlies all stories, but rather examine the "use" of the word, that is, all the contexts in which the word is used and the activities these contexts reveal. The basic problem of story, reminds Stierle, is: How can a narrative text, which is, after all, an account of a series of events, one thing after another, be transformed into a systematic text, that is, something that has meaning?

Stierle is, of course, not the first to raise this issue. "It is astonishing how little attention critics have paid to story considered in itself," C. S. Lewis once lamented. Whereas forms of fiction in which the story exists for the delineation of character have been discussed abundantly, Lewis notes, those forms in which everything exists for the sake of the story have been given little serious attention. As E. M. Forster points out in his chapter on story in *Aspects of the Novel,* this is as true of long forms as of short ones. Even as we agree that the "fundamental aspect of the novel is its story-telling aspect," we voice our assent, says Forster, sadly: "Yes—oh, dear, yes—the novel tells a story."

Both Forster and Lewis suggest that the problem lies with the sense of time. Forster notes that in addition to the time sense in daily life there is something else, something not measured by minutes or hours, but by intensity, something called value. Story, qua story, however can only deal with the time sense. Story, the "naked worm of time," is an atavistic form which presents an appearance both "unlovely and dull," says Forster, yet writers flout it at their peril. As soon as fiction is "completely delivered from time it cannot express anything at all."

Gertrude Stein, Forster notes, offers an instructive example of a writer who tried to "emancipate fiction from the tyranny of time" and inevitably failed. The problem is, says Forster, one cannot abolish story unless one abolishes the sequence between sentences, which in turn cannot be done unless one abolishes the order of words in a sentence, which then necessitates abolishing the order of letters or sounds in the words. A narrative that attempts to destroy the time sense and only express the sense of value "becomes unintelligible and therefore valueless."

Forster's distinction between narrative's double allegiance to time and value corresponds to C. S. Lewis's distinction between story and theme in fiction. The central problem, says Lewis, is that for stories to be stories, they must be a series of events; yet at the same time it must be understood that this series is only a net to catch something else. And this "something else," which, for want of a better word, we call theme, is something "that has no sequence in it, something other than a process and much more like a state or quality." Thus, the basic internal tension of all fiction is the tension between story and theme, a situation which suggests that the means of fiction are always at war with its end.

Jonathan Culler has discussed this conflict as the tension between what the formalists and structuralists have called "story" and "discourse." Whereas "story" refers to a sequence of events, independent of the way they are manifested in an actual work of fiction, "discourse" refers to the discursive presentation of the events. Culler says that this tension creates a kind of double logic that perhaps governs all narrative. On the one hand, a piece of fiction presents its plot as a sequence of events prior to and independent of the given perspective of the events in a particular story, while on the other hand, the story's very claim to significance and meaning suggests that the events are justified by their appropriateness to a thematic structure. One crucial implication of this double logic, suggests Culler, is that events in a piece of fiction are not "givens" existing prior to the discourse but rather products of the requirements of the discourse itself. In other words, the end or meaning of the work—its overall pattern understood as theme, *dianoia,* meaning—precedes the presentation of its specific details.

If the means by which a syntagmatic sequence gives rise to a paradigmatic theme is a central issue for understanding the nature of narrative in general, then it seems clear that short fiction—which has from its beginning been closely tied to its exemplary nature, its emphasis on meaning, and thus its formal patterning—is more emphatically enmeshed in what Culler calls narrative's double logic than the novel, which places its main emphasis on character, temporal sequence, and verisimilitude.

Both Randall Jarrell and Teun A. Van Dijk, although from radically different perspectives, also emphasize the basic nature of story. Jarrell's interest lies in the basic psychological function stories serve. Like Bruno Bettleheim in his study of fairy tales, Jarrell sees stories functioning much the way Freud argued that dreams did; that is, either as wish fulfillment or an expression of the repetition compulsion, demonstrating that we take pleasure in repeating over and over until we can bear it all that we found unbearable.

Many writers and readers of short stories have suggested that the means by which stories work depends more on their pattern than on their ostensible content. Human beings need to hear stories the same way they need to experience religion, says Canadian writer Hugh Hood. "Story is very close to liturgy, which is why one's children like to have the story repeated exactly as they heard it the night before. The scribe ought not to deviate from the prescribed form. That is because the myths at the core of story are always going on. . . . Myth exists to give us this reassurance of the persistence of some of the fundamental forms of human action."

This notion of the story as liturgy is also suggested by Indries Shah in his discussion of the Sufi teaching story. Such stories do not teach by concept, but rather by some more intuitive method of communication, by rhythm, or as the structuralists would say, by a deep structure that lies beneath the conscious level of concept. We must go back to an early stage to prepare ourselves for the story, says Shah, a stage in which we regard the story as "a consistent and productive parallel or allegory of certain states of mind. Its symbols are the characters in the story. The way in which they move conveys to the mind the way in which the human mind can work." Such teaching stories, claims Shah, depend on an ancient and irreplaceable method of "arranging and transmitting a knowledge which cannot be put in any other way."

Van Dijk, summarizing the interests that cognitive psychologists and specialists in artificial intelligence have in the basic nature of story, is, like Stierle, concerned with the links between syntax and semantics, that is, between the narrative sequence and its thematic meaning. Stories are appealing for discourse study precisely because of their double logic; that is, even as they are about human action in temporal sequence, at the same time they are artificially patterned like play or game to create meaning.

Van Dijk's "macrostructures" suggests that narrative discourse is understood by readers in "chunks" dominated by a macroproposition—a concept related to the notion of patterns of motifs suggested by the Russian formalist Boris Tomashevsky and the transformation of narrative sequence into spatial pattern outlined by Northrop Frye and Joseph Frank. As both Stierle and Van Dijk point out, the very fact that the structure of narrative can be schematized means that stories take on meaning when they involve a syntagmatic unfolding of paradigmatic poles, that is, when the temporal sequence of events of story is transformed by the reading process into sets (or chunks) of thematic units or motifs that can then be read paradigmatically. As Van Dijk points out, we only accept as stories those action discourses which have a specific narrative structure, that is, a point.

Roman Jakobson, of course, has discussed this basic transformation of the syntagmatic into the paradigmatic or mere sequence into meaning. In his famous essay, "Linguistics and Poetics," Jakobson refers to the selection/combination or metaphor/metonymy dichotomy he discussed in more detail in *Fundamentals of Language*. In any discourse, Jakobson reminds us, one selects a noun and comments on it by means of a related verb. "Both chosen words combine in the speech chain. The selection is produced on the base of equivalence, similarity and dissimilarity, synonymity and antonymity, while the combination, the build up of the sequence, is based on contiguity. The poetic function projects the principle of equivalence from the axis of selection into the axis of combination." Chiding literary critics for paying so much attention to the principle of metaphor in poetry and ignoring the principle of metonymy in prose, Jakobson notes that prose is often ignored because the verbal devices are unostentatious and seem transparent, and the parallelisms are less obvious. He reminds us that Vladimir Propp in his study on fairy tales and Claude Lévi Strauss in his studies on myth have shown that a syntactic approach can lay bare the laws of prose plots. The basic issue Jakobson raises here is the same one raised by Stierle: How can a syntagmatic series of events, one after another, result in a paradigmatic meaning?

Susan Lohafer is also interested in Van Dijk's concept of macrostructures, for she wishes to examine how serial, temporal, linear pieces of text are combined into sets of general propositions, that is, how readers chunk text into meaningful units. As Frye pointed out years ago, the way we possess a sequence of events from the past is not in their temporal structure, but rather in how those macrostructures or chunks of thematic motifs that readers recognize and reorganize create a meaningful spatial form. Lohafer's basic hypothesis, much like Poe's emphasis on beginning with the end of a narrative and Éjxenbaum's insistence on the importance of the ending of short stories, is that the idea of storyness is tied more directly to closure than to any set of story components.

As Frank Kermode reminds us, "Endings are always faked, as are all other parts of a narrative structure that impose metaphor on the metonymic sequence." Any time authors arrange a narrative sequence to reflect meaning and anytime readers make use of the processes of repetition and metaphor to reconstruct a syntagmatic flow into paradigmatic or metaphoric sets, endings must be "faked." For this faking of an ending is the very act that makes meaning out of the "one damned thing after another" of mere story; such faking thus constitutes the essence of narrative art.

Stierle points out the concept of the wholeness of a work (one of Poe's major points) can only exist if the events are already past and one has a complete view of them. In other words, because the teller has the conclusion of the story in mind as he begins the discourse, he is able to have some rhetorical end or purpose in mind that controls the selection and description of those story events. As Stierle says, the basic rule underlying the unity of the whole is the purpose of the whole.

And the closer the narrative text comes to emphasizing that purpose, the closer it is to being a systematic text. Stierle notes that although it is conceivable that a story could be told in such a way that there is nothing in it but the characteristic features of the category to which it usually belongs, stories usually have a narrative surplus the purpose of which is to enhance probability by presenting realistic details. However, the more important the case the less there will be of such details. What this suggests is that the process of deriving systematic texts from narrative texts—that is, meaning from a mere series of events—involves stripping away the irrelevant and moving more and more toward compression, thus focusing on the obsessive core of the story. It follows that the primary way that short stories "mean" anything is to become more and more compressed, more and more formally unified, more and more restricted only to those details that are relevant to the systematic theme or purpose underlying the narrative.

A number of short-story writers and critics have commented on the implications of shortness, compression, and intensity for a story's thematic significance. Once again, Poe is the first to suggest that the compression and intensity of the short story suggests an undercurrent of significance. For Poe, the way the form creates this sense of significance, as Pasco reminds us, is by depth of implication rather than by multiplicity. Precisely because it is short and highly unified, the short story tends toward the universal, having an affinity for the formalistic, the epitome, the essential truth or idea or image that rises above time and negates chronological progression. Maurice Shadbolt is only one of many short-story writers who agree, claiming that the short story attempts to produce an "hallucinatory point in which time past and time future seem to coexist with time present."

Stierle reminds us that there are two different ways in which narrative texts produce systematic texts—by means of the fable and the exemplum. By fable, Stierle means roughly the same thing Robert Marler means by tale; by exemplum, he means roughly the same time Marler means by the short story. For although fable and exemplum "mean" in quite different ways—the fable presenting the general *as* the particular, while in the exemplum the general appears *in* the particular—at a certain historical point (roughly the end of the eighteenth or the beginning of the nineteenth centuries), it became less easy to determine the meaning lying beyond the events depicted in the story. As Stierle points out, when history freed itself from a moral-philosophic system in the late eighteenth century, it left the paradigmatic and entered into the syntagmatic sphere of endless interconnections.

The whole history of the development of the short story can be seen as the constant interplay between the exemplary nature of the story and its "realistic" presentation of characters in time with a consciousness of their own. As Graham Good points out, this transition not only takes place with Boccaccio, it also takes place in the early nineteenth century with the German romantics. Robert Marler suggests that this transition also takes place in the mid nineteenth century with the shift from the tale form of Poe to the short story form created by Herman Melville. Using "Bartleby" as his example, Marler argues that when characters in short fictions take on a consciousness of their own, undergoing internal changes, and when the form eschews supernaturalism and rejects symbols not at first functional in the story's natural order, these two forces conspire to push meaning beneath the surface, where because of its indistinctness, it gives the impression of being inexplicable.

Of course the movement toward so-called realism, by which the tale form moves further and further away from its fable nature continues in the next basic shift in the historical development of the short story—the development of the so-called modern story with Chekhov, Joyce, and others. Increasingly, as Stierle points out, the ego—with all its contradictions that produce endless reflections—replaces history. If one's perspective changes from moment to moment, there cannot be a story of a whole life. Since each moment is basically only itself separated from all others, one's existence breaks up into a succession of discontinuous moments. What makes history impossible is what makes story possible.

This is of course Nadine Gordimer's central point about the short story's particular relevance to the modern condition. She notes, like Pratt and Good, the adjacency of the short story and the novel. But she suggests a general dissatisfaction of writers with the novel as a means of "netting ultimate reality," suggesting that the short story is better equipped to capture reality at a time when we are "drawing nearer to the mystery of life." According to Gordimer, the strongest convention of the novel, prolonged coherence of tone, is false to the nature of whatever can be grasped of human reality. The art of the short-story writer is "the art of the only thing one can be sure of—the present moment." "A discrete moment of truth is aimed at—not *the* moment of truth, because the short story doesn't deal in cumulatives."

Suzanne Ferguson's essay is primarily motivated by her desire to account for the persistent notion that the "modern" short story since Chekhov differs from the tale or sketch that precedes him. She identifies this shift from tale to modern short story with impressionism and argues that the same sort of thing happens with the novel; it is just that the short story by its shortness manifests this impressionism more than the novel, which still bears many similarities to the realistic novel that preceded it. This is a worthwhile point, for it suggests that whereas there can be no purely impressionistic novel, there can be purely impressionistic short stories. It might also suggest that the short narrative form is, and has always been, more amenable to the characteristics of what Ferguson calls "impressionism" and what many others call "modernism" (which some argue began with the romantics at the beginning of the nineteenth century) than the novel is: e.g., foregrounding of point of view, emphasis on inner experience, reliance on metaphor, rejection of chronological time, use of formal economy, and foregrounding of style.

Ferguson reinforces many of the points made by Stierle when she suggests that the less we are occupied with verisimilitude, physical action, and extended characterization—as we are in the novel—the more obvious it is that what binds the narrative into a whole is what readers perceive as the governing theme, the author's intention, or, in older stories, what we called the moral. Whereas in realistic fiction, most prominently represented by the novel, the interplay of character and event is crucial, in the modern short story, the reader's recognition of theme is equivalent to the recognition that it is a story indeed.

Wendell Harris makes many of the same points in his description of the rise of the short story in England in the 1890s. Whereas the great Victorian novels depended on shaping individuals by socioeconomic pressures and individual choices and presented the interconnectedness of things in a social and temporal way, the short story depends on forces outside socioeconomic ones. Harris argues, as have many others, that the short story portrays the individual, moment, or scene detached from the great social and historical continuum which the English novel had made its own.

The most famous expression of this notion is Frank O'Connor's intuition that the short story has always been detached from any concept of a normal society, remaining by its very nature remote from the community— romantic, individualistic, and intransigent; consequently, always in the short story there is a sense of outlawed figures wandering about the fringes of society. Similarly, Elizabeth Bowen says the short story places human beings alone on that stage which, inwardly everyone is conscious of occupying alone and that, in this regard, exempt from the novel's often forced conclusiveness, the short story may more nearly "approach aesthetic and moral truth."

It is important to remember, however, that this aesthetic and moral truth does not result from the short story's imitation of external reality, but rather from the story's own compression, pattern, and intensity. Danforth Ross in his study of the American short story says that the major contribution that Poe makes to the form is that he brings "tension," long a characteristic of poetry, to story. Whereas Irving's tales meander, Poe attempted to present a story as a dramatist does in a play. In an article in 1943, Gorham Munson agrees: "Poe aimed not at a transcription of actuality, but at a patterned dramatization of life." For this, says Munson, he needed a "storyable incident," an anecdote in the Jamesian sense of something that "oddly happened," an anecdote with a hard nugget of "latent value." Even Somerset Maugham, whose story preference was for one that could be told in a drawing room or smoker, insisted on stories as a "dramatisation" of life, not simply a transcription. V. S. Pritchett has said much the same. In spite of the work of Flaubert and James, the length, inclusiveness, and shapelessness of the novel creates a "bemusing effect." "The short story, on the other hand, wakes the reader up. Not only that; it answers the primitive craving for art, the wit, paradox and beauty of shape, the longing to see a dramatic pattern and significance in our experience, the desire for the electric shock."

This means that the short story must be more rigorously conceived than the novel; it must tend, says Herbert Gold to "control and formalize experience" and strike hot like the lyric poem." Because of the subjectivity of the form, Herschell Brickell has noted, it requires technical accomplishment. "The whole thing is delicate and subtle, a matter of nuances, and the style itself must have both beauty and exactness, must partake of the esthetic and the functional, if the full effect is to be achieved." British short-story writer Elizabeth Taylor has suggested that the short story by its lyrical nature, its sustaining of one mood throughout, can give an impression of "perfection" and give the feeling of "being lifted into another world, instead of rather sinking into it, as one does with longer fiction." The German short story writer Martin Walser also sees the short story as a form that presents not reality but "transcendence of reality," a counterpoint to reality.

I could go on for some time citing critics and short-story writers who are convinced that both the historical tradition and the generic shortness of the short story result in a number of basic characteristics of the form. However, the preceding should be sufficient to suggest that such "family resemblances" do exist and that the question of their historical and generic relationship is worth further examination. I make the following tentative suggestions about those historical/generic relationships: In their very shortness, short stories have remained close to the original source of narrative in myth, folktale, fable, and fairy tale. They, therefore, are more apt to focus on basic desires, dreams, anxieties, and fears than novels are and thus are more aligned with the original religious nature of narrative. Short stories are therefore more apt to embody a timeless theme and are thus less dependent on a social context than novels. Consequently, short stories are more likely to identify characters in archetypal terms and are more patterned and aesthetically unified than novels are. For this reason, short stories are more dependent on craftsmanship and exhibit more authorial control than novels, making them closer to poetry and thus more "artistic."

Many readers will not agree with all of these characteristics of the short story, finding it easy to point out exceptions to any one of them in one story or another. But no matter. The purpose of my comments here is simply to draw attention to some of the most common remarks about the short story and suggest some of their implications and connections. Everything is, as it should be, up for debate and disagreement.

PART ONE

Basic Issues
of Story

Stories

RANDALL JARRELL

I

STORY, THE DICTIONARY tells one, is a short form of the word *history*, and stands for *a narrative, recital, or description of what has occurred;* just as it stands for a *fictitious narrative, imaginative tale; Colloq. a lie, a falsehood.*

A story, then, tells the truth or a lie—is a wish, or a truth, or a wish modified by a truth. Children ask first of all: "Is it a *true* story?" They ask this of the storyteller, but they ask of the story what they ask of a dream: that it satisfy their wishes. The Muses are the daughters of hope and the stepdaughters of memory. The wish is the first truth about us, since it represents not that learned principle of reality which half-governs our workaday hours, but the primary principle of pleasure which governs infancy, sleep, daydreams—and certainly, many stories. Reading stories, we cannot help remembering Groddeck's "We have to reckon with what exists, and dreams, daydreams too, are also facts; if anyone really wants to investigate realities, he cannot do better than to start with such as these. If he neglects them, he will learn little or nothing of the world of life." If wishes were stories, beggars would read; if stories were true, our saviors would speak to us in parables. Much of our knowledge of, our compensation for, "the world of life" comes from stories; and the stories themselves are part of "the world of life." Shakespeare wrote:

> *This is an art*
> *Which does mend nature, change it rather, but*
> *The art itself is nature . . .*

and Goethe, agreeing, said: "A work of art is just as much a work of nature as a mountain."

In showing that dreams sometimes both satisfy our wishes and punish us for them, Freud compares the dreamer to the husband and wife in the fairy tale of The Three Wishes: the wife wishes for a pudding, the husband wishes it on the end of her nose, and the wife wishes it away again. A contradictory family! But it is this family—wife, husband, and pudding— which the story must satisfy: the writer is, and is writing for, a doubly- or triply-natured creature, whose needs, understandings, and ideals—whether they are called id, ego, and super-ego, or body, mind, and soul—contradict one another. Most of the stories that we are willing to call works of art are compounds almost as complicated as their creators; but occasionally we can see isolated, in naked innocence, one of the elements of which our stories are composed. Thomas Leaf's story (in Hardy's *Under the Greenwood Tree*) is an example:

> "Once," said the delighted Leaf, in an uncertain voice, "there was a man who lived in a house! Well, this man went thinking and thinking night and day. At last, he said to himself, as I might, 'If I had only ten pound, I'd make a fortune.' At last by hook or by crook, behold he got the ten pounds!"
>
> "Only think of that!" said Nat Callcome satirically.
>
> "Silence!" said the tranter.
>
> "Well, now comes the interesting part of the story! In a little time he made that ten pounds twenty. Then a little after that he doubled it, and made it forty. Well, he went on, and a good while after that he made it eighty, and on to a hundred. Well, by-and-by he made it two hundred! Well, you'd never believe it, but—he went on and made it four hundred! He went on, and what did he do? Why, he made it eight hundred! Yes, he did;" continued Leaf, in the highest pitch of excitement, bringing down his fist upon his knee, with such force that he quivered with the pain; "yes, and he went on and made it A THOUSAND!"
>
> "Hear, hear!" said the tranter. "Better than the history of England, my sonnies!"
>
> "Thank you for your story, Thomas Leaf," said grandfather William; and then Leaf gradually sank into nothingness again.

Every day, in books, magazines, and newspapers, over radio and television, in motion-picture theaters, we listen to Leaf's story one more time, and then sink into nothingness again. His story is, in one sense, better than the history of England—or would be if the history of England were not composed, among other things, of Leaf's story and a million like it. His story, stood on its head, is the old woman's story in *Wozzeck*. "Grandmother, tell us a story," beg the children. "All right, you little crabs," she answers.

> Once upon a time there was a poor little girl who had no father and mother because everyone was dead and there was no one left in the whole world. Everyone was dead, and she kept looking for someone night and day. And since there was no one on earth, she thought she'd go to heaven. The moon looked at her so friendly, but when she finally got to it, it was just a piece of rotted wood. So she went on to the sun, and when she got there, it was just a dried-up sunflower. And when she got to the stars, they were just little gold flies stuck up there as if they'd been caught in a spider web. And when she thought she'd go back to earth, it was just an upside-down pot. And she was all alone. And so she sat down and cried. And she's still sitting there, all alone.

The grandmother's story is told less often—but often enough: when we wake into the reality our dream has contradicted, we are bitter at returning against our wishes to so bad a world, and take a fierce pleasure in what remains to us, the demonstration that it is the worst of all possible worlds. And we take pleasure also—as our stories show—in repeating over and over, until we can bear it, all that we found unbearable: the child whose mother left her so often that she invented a game of throwing her doll out of her crib, exclaiming as it vanished: "Gone! gone!" was a true poet. "Does I 'member much about slavery times?" the old man says, in *Lay My Burden Down;* "well, there is no way for me to disremember unless I die." But the worst memories are joyful ones: "Every time Old Mistress thought we little black children was hungry 'tween meals she would give us johnnycake and plenty of buttermilk to drink with it. There was a long trough for us they would scrub so clean. They would fill this trough with buttermilk and all us children would sit round the trough and drink with our mouths and hold our johnnycake with our hands. I can just see myself drinking now. It was so good. . . ." It is so good, our stories believe, simply to remember: their elementary delight in recognition, familiarity, mimesis, is another aspect of their obsession with all the likenesses of the universe, those metaphors that Proust called essential to style. Stories want to *know:* everything from the first blaze and breathlessness and fragrance to the last law and structure; but, too, stories don't want to know, don't want to care, just want to *do as they please.* (Some great books are a consequence of the writer's losing himself in his subject, others are a consequence of his losing himself in himself. Rabelais' "do what

you please" is the motto of how many masterpieces, from Cervantes and
Sterne on up to the present.) For stories vary from a more-than-Kantian
disinterestedness, in which the self is a representative, indistinguishable
integer among millions—the mere *one* or *you* or *man* that is the subject
of all the verbs—to an insensate, protoplasmic egotism to which the self
is the final fact, a galaxy that it is impractical to get out of to other gal-
axies. Polarities like these are almost the first thing one notices about fiction. It is as much haunted by the chaos which precedes and succeeds
order as by order; by the incongruities of the universe (wit, humor, the
arbitrary, accidental, and absurd—all irruptions from, releases of, the unconscious) as by its likenesses. A story may present fantasy as fact, as the
sin or *hubris* that the fact of things punishes, or as a reality superior to
fact. And, often, it presents it as a mixture of the three: all opposites meet
in fiction.

The truths that he systematized, Freud said, had already been discovered by the poets; the tears of things, the truth of things, are there in
their fictions. And yet, as he knew, the root of all stories is in Grimm, not
in La Rochefoucauld; in dreams, not in cameras and tape recorders. Turgenev was right when he said, "Truth alone, however powerful, is not
art"—oxygen alone, however concentrated, is not water; and Freud was
right, profoundly right, when he showed "that the dream is a compromise
between the expression of and the defence against the unconscious emotions; that in it the unconscious wish is represented as being fulfilled; that
there are very definite mechanisms that control this expression; that the
primary process controls the dream world just as it controls the entire unconscious life of the soul, and that myth and poetical productions come
into being in the same way and have the same meaning. There is only one
important difference: in the myths and in the works of poets the secondary elaboration is much further developed, so that a logical and coherent
entity is created." It is hard to exaggerate the importance of this difference, of course; yet usually we do exaggerate it—do write as if that one
great difference had hidden from us the greater similarities which underlie it.

II

A baby asleep but about to be waked by hunger sometimes makes little
sucking motions: he is dreaming that he is being fed, and manages by
virtue of the dream to stay asleep. He may even smile a little in satisfaction. But the smile cannot last for long—the dream fails, and he wakes.

This is, in a sense, the first story; the child in his "impotent omnipotence" is like us readers, us writers, in ours.

A story is a chain of events. Since the stories that we know are told by men, the events of the story happen to human or anthropomorphic beings—gods, beasts, and devils, and are related in such a way that the story seems to begin at one place and to end at a very different place, without any essential interruption to its progress. The poet or storyteller, so to speak, writes numbers on a blackboard, draws a line under them, and adds them into their true but unsuspected sum. Stories, because of their nature or—it is to say the same thing—of ours, are always capable of generalization: a story about a dog Kashtanka is true for all values of dogs and men.

Stories can be as short as a sentence. Bion's saying, *The boys throw stones at the frogs in sport, but the frogs die not in sport but in earnest,* is a story; and when one finds it in Aesop, blown up into a fable five or six sentences long, it has become a poorer story. Blake's *Prudence is a rich, ugly old maid courted by Incapacity* has a story inside it, waiting to flower in a glass of water. And there is a story four sentences long that not even Rilke was able to improve: *Now King David was old and stricken in years; and they covered him with clothes, but he got no heat. Wherefore his servants said unto him, Let there be sought for my lord the king a young virgin: and let her stand before the king and let her cherish him, and let her lie in thy bosom, that my lord the king may get heat. So they sought for a fair damsel throughout all the coasts of Israel, and found Abishag a Shunamite, and brought her to the king. And the damsel was very fair, and cherished the King, and ministered to him: but the king knew her not. . . . .* The enlisted men at Fort Benning buried their dog Calculus under a marker that read: *He made better dogs of us all,* and a few days ago I read in the paper: *A Sunday-school teacher, mother of four children, shot to death her eight-year-old daughter as she slept today, state police reported. Hilda Kristle, 43, of Stony Run, told police that her youngest daughter, Suzanne, "had a heavy heart and often went about the house sighing."*

When we try to make, out of these stories life gives us, works of art of comparable concision, we almost always put them into verse. Blake writes about a chimney sweep:

> *A little black thing among the snow*
> *Crying "'weep! 'weep!" in notes of woe!*
> *"Where are thy father & mother, say?"*

"They are both gone up to the church to pray.

"Because I was happy upon the heath,
And smil'd among the winter's snow
They clothed me in the clothes of death,
And taught me to sing the notes of woe.

"And because I am happy & dance & sing,
They think they have done me no injury,
And are gone to praise God & his Priest & King,
Who make up a Heaven of our misery—"

and he has written enough. Stephen Crane says in fifty words:

In the desert
I saw a creature naked, bestial,
Who, squatting upon the ground,
Held his heart in his hands
And ate of it.
I said, "Is it good, friend?"
"It is bitter—bitter," he answered;
"But I like it
Because it is bitter
And because it is my heart."

These are the bones of stories, and we shiver at them. The poems one selects for a book of stories have more of the flesh of ordinary fiction. A
truly representative book of stories would include a great many poems:
during much of the past people put into verse the stories that they intended to be literature.

But it is hard to put together any representative collection of stories. It
is like starting a zoo in a closet: the giraffe alone takes up more space than
one has for the collection. *Remembrance of Things Past* is a story, just as
Saint-Simon's memoirs are a great many stories. One can represent the
memoirs with the death of Monseigneur, but not even the death of Ber-
gotte, the death of the narrator's grandmother, can do that for *Remembrance of Things Past*. Almost everything in the world, one realizes after
a while, is too long to go into a short book of stories—a book of short
stories. So, even, are all those indeterminate masterpieces that the nineteenth century called short stories and that we call short novels or novelettes: Tolstoy's *The Death of Ivan Ilyich, Hadji Murad, Master and Man;*
Flaubert's *A Simple Heart;* Mann's *Death in Venice;* Leskov's *The Lady*

Macbeth of the Mzinsk District; Keller's *The Three Righteous Comb-Makers;* James's *The Aspern Papers;* Colette's *Julie de Carneilhan;* Kleist's *Michael Kohlhaas;* Joyce's *The Dead;* Turgenev's *A Lear of the Steppes;* Hoffmannsthal's *Andreas;* Kafka's *Metamorphosis;* Faulkner's *Spotted Horses;* Porter's *Old Mortality;* Dostoievsky's *The Eternal Husband;* Melville's *Bartleby the Scrivener, Benito Cereno;* Chekhov's *Ward No. 6, A Dreary Story, Peasants, In the Ravine.*

And there are many more sorts of stories than there are sizes. Epics; ballads; historical or biographical or autobiographical narratives, letters, diaries; myths, fairy tales, fables; dreams, daydreams; humorous or indecent or religious anecdotes; all those stories which might be called specialized or special case—science fiction, ghost stories, detective stories, Westerns, True Confessions, children's stories, and the rest; and, finally, "serious fiction"—Proust and Chekhov and Kafka, *Moby-Dick, Great Expectations, A Sportsman's Notebook.* What I myself selected for a book of stories was most of it "serious fiction," some of it serious fiction in verse; but there was a letter of Tolstoy's, a piece of history and autobiography from Saint-Simon; and there were gipsy and German fairy tales, Hebrew and Chinese parables, and two episodes from the journal of an imaginary Danish poet, the other self of the poet Rainer Maria Rilke. There are so many good short narratives of every kind that a book of three or four hundred pages leaves almost all of their writers unrepresented. By saying that I was saving these writers for a second and third book I tried to make myself feel better at having left them out of the first. For I left out all sagas, all ballads, all myths; a dozen great narrators in verse, from Homer to Rilke; Herodotus, Plutarch, Pushkin, Hawthorne, Flaubert, Dostoievsky, Melville, James, Leskov, Keller, Kipling, Mann, Faulkner—I cannot bear to go on. Several of these had written long narratives so much better than any of their short ones that it seemed unfair to use the short, and it was impossible to use the long. Hemingway I could not get permission to reprint. Any anthology is, as the dictionary says, a bouquet—a bouquet that leaves out most of the world's flowers.

My own bunch is named *The Anchor Book of Stories,* and consists of Franz Kafka's *A Country Doctor;* Anton Chekhov's *Gusev;* Rainer Maria Rilke's *The Wrecked Houses* and *The Big Thing* (from *The Notebooks of Malte Laurids Brigge*); Robert Frost's *The Witch of Coös;* Giovanni Verga's *La Lupa;* Nicolai Gogol's *The Nose;* Elizabeth Bowen's *Her Table Spread;* Ludwig Tieck's *Fair Eckbert;* Bertolt Brecht's *Concerning the Infanticide Marie Farrar;* Lev Tolstoy's *The Three Hermits;* Peter Taylor's *What You Hear from 'Em?;* Hans Christian Anderson's *The Fir Tree;* Katharine Anne Porter's *He;* a Gipsy's *The Red King and the Witch;*

Anton Chekhov's *Rothschild's Fiddle;* the Brothers Grimm's *Cat and Mouse in Partnership;* E. M. Forster's *The Story of the Siren; The Book of Jonah;* Franz Kafka's *The Bucket-Rider;* Saint-Simon's *The Death of Monseigneur;* Isaac Babel's *Awakening;* five anecdotes by Chuang T'zu; Hugo von Hofmannsthal's *A Tale of the Cavalry;* William Blake's *The Mental Traveller;* D. H. Lawrence's *Samson and Delilah;* Lev Tolstoy's *The Porcelain Doll;* Ivan Turgenev's *Byezhin Prairie;* William Words-worth's *The Ruined Cottage;* Frank O'Connor's *Peasants;* and Isak Dine-sen's *Sorrow-Acre.*

I disliked leaving out writers, but I disliked almost as much having to leave out some additional stories by some of the writers I included. I used so many of the writers who "came out of Gogol's *Overcoat*" that *The Overcoat* was in a sense already there, but I wished that it and *Old-World Land-owners* had been there in every sense; that I could have included Chekhov's *The Bishop, The Lady with the Dog, Gooseberries, The Darling, The Man in a Shell, The Kiss, The Witch, On Official Business,* and how many more; that I could have included Kafka's *The Penal Colony* and *The Hunter Gracchus;* and that I could have included at least a story more from Lawrence, Tolstoy, Verga, Grimm, and Andersen. With Turgenev's masterpiece all selection fails: *A Sportsman's Notebook* is a whole greater and more endearing than even the best of its parts.

III

There are all kind of beings, and all kinds of things happen to them; and when you add to these what are as essential to the writer, the things that don't actually happen, the beings that don't actually exist, it is no wonder that stories are as varied as they are. But it seems to me that there are two extremes: stories in which nothing happens, and stories in which everything is a happening. The Muse of fiction believes that people "don't go to the North Pole" but go to work, go home, get married, die; but she believes at the same time that absolutely anything can occur—concludes, with Gogol: "Say what you like, but such things do happen—not often, but they do happen." Our lives, even our stories, approach at one extreme the lives of Prior's Jack and Joan:

> *If human things went Ill or Well;*
> *If changing Empires rose or fell;*
> *The Morning past, the Evening came,*
> *And found this couple still the same.*
> *They Walked and Eat, good folks: What then?*

Why then they Walk'd and Eat again:
They soundly slept the Night away:
They did just Nothing all the day . . .
Nor Good, nor Bad, nor Fools, nor Wise;
They wou'd not learn, nor cou'd advise:
Without Love, Hatred, Joy, or Fear,
They led—a kind of—as it were;
Nor Wish'd, nor Car'd, nor Laugh'd, nor Cry'd:
And so They liv'd; and so They dy'd.

Billions have lived, and left not even a name behind, and while they were alive nobody knew their names either. These live out their lives "among the rocks and winding scars/ Where deep and low the hamlets lie/ Each with its little patch of sky/ And little lot of stars"; soundly sleep the Night away in the old houses of Oblomov's native village, where everybody did just Nothing all the day; rise—in Gogol's Akaky Akakyevich Bashmachkin, in the *Old-World Landowners,* to a quite biblical pathos and grandeur; are relatives of that Darling, that *dushechka,* who for so many solitary years "had no opinions of any sort. She saw the objects about her and understood what she saw, but could not form any opinion about them"; sit and, "musing with close lips and lifted eyes/ Have smiled with self-contempt to live so wise/ And run so smoothly such a length of lies"; walk slowly, staring about them—or else just walk— through the pages of Turgenev, Sterne, Keller, Rabelais, Twain, Cervantes, and how many others; and in Chuang T'zu disappear into the mists of time, looming before us in primordial grandeur: "In the days of Ho Hsu the people did nothing in particular when at rest, and went nowhere in particular when they moved. Having food, they rejoiced; having full bellies, they strolled about. Such were the capacities of the people."

How different from the later times, the other pages, in which people "wear the hairs off their legs" "counting the grains of rice for a rice-pudding"! How different from the other extreme: the world of Svidrigaylov, Raskolnikov, Stavrogin, where everything that occurs is either a dream told as if it were reality, or reality told as if it were a dream, and where the story is charged up to the point at which the lightning blazes out in some nightmare, revelation, atrocity, and the drained narrative can begin to charge itself again. In this world, and in the world of *The Devil, The Kreutzer Sonata, The Death of Ivan Ilyich,* everything is the preparation for, or consummation of, an Event; everyone is an echo of "the prehistoric, unforgettable Other One, who is never equalled by anyone later." This is the world of Hofmannsthal's *A Tale of the Cavalry,* where even the cow being dragged to the shambles, "shrinking from the smell of blood and the fresh hide of a calf nailed to the doorpost, planted its hooves firm on the ground, drew the reddish haze of the sunset in through dilated nostrils, and, before the lad could drag her across the road with stick and rope, tore away with piteous eyes a mouthful of the hay which the sergeant had tied on the front of his saddle." It is the world of Nijinsky's diary: "One evening I went for a walk up the hill, and stopped on the mountain . . . 'the mountain of Sinai.' I was cold. I had walked far. Feeling that I should kneel, I quickly knelt and then felt that I should put my hand in the snow. After doing this, I suddenly felt a pain and cried with it, pulling my hand away. I looked at a star, which did not say good evening to me. It did not twinkle at me. I got frightened and wanted to run, but could not because my knees were rooted to the snow. I started to cry, but no one heard my weeping. No one came to my rescue. After several minutes I turned and saw a house. It was closed and the windows shuttered . . . I felt frightened and shouted at the top of my voice: 'Death!' I did not know why, but felt that one must shout 'Death!' After that I felt warmer . . . I walked on the snow which crunched beneath my feet. I liked the snow and listened to its crunching. I loved listening to my footsteps; they were full of life. Looking at the sky, I saw the stars which were twinkling at me and felt merriment in them. I was happy and no longer felt cold . . . I started to go down a dark road, walking quickly, but was stopped by a tree which saved me. I was on the edge of a precipice. I thanked the tree. It felt me because I caught hold of it; it received my warmth and I received the warmth of the tree. I do not know who most needed the warmth. I walked on and suddenly stopped, seeing a precipice without a tree. I understood that God had stopped me because He loves me, and therefore said: 'If it is thy will, I will fall down the precipice. If it is thy will, I will be saved.'"

This is what I would call pure narrative; one must go to writers like Tolstoy and Rilke and Kafka to equal it. In the unfinished stories of Kafka's notebook, some fragment a page long can carry us over a whole abyss of events: "I was sitting in the box, and beside me was my wife. The play being performed was an exciting one, it was about jealousy; at that moment in the midst of a brilliantly lit hall surrounded by pillars, a man was just raising his dagger against his wife, who was slowly retreating to the exit. Tense, we leaned forward together over the balustrade; I felt my wife's curls against my temples. Then we started back, for something moved on the balustrade; what we had taken for the plush upholstery of the balustrade was the back of a tall thin man, not an inch broader than the balustrade, who had been lying flat on his face there and was now slowly turning over as though trying to find a more comfortable position. Trembling, my wife clung to me. His face was quite close to me, narrower than my hand, meticulously clean as that of a waxwork figure, and with a pointed black beard. 'Why do you come and frighten us?' I exclaimed. 'What are you up to here?' 'Excuse me!' the man said, 'I am an admirer of your wife's. To feel her elbows on my body makes me happy.' 'Emil, I implore you, protect me!' my wife exclaimed. 'I too am called Emil,' the man said, supporting his head on one hand and lying there as though on a sofa. 'Come to me, dear sweet little woman.' 'You cad,' I said, 'another word and you'll find yourself lying down there in the pit,' and as though certain that this word was bound to come, I tried to push him over, but it was not so easy, he seemed to be a solid part of the balustrade, it was as though he were built into it, I tried to roll him off, but I couldn't do it, he only laughed and said: 'Stop that, you silly little man, don't wear out your strength prematurely, the struggle is only beginning and it will end, as may well be said, with your wife's granting my desire.' 'Never!' my wife exclaimed, and then, turning to me: 'Oh, please, do push him down now.' 'I can't,' I exclaimed, 'you can see for yourself how I'm straining, but there's some trickery in it, it can't be done.' 'Oh dear, oh dear,' my wife lamented, 'what is to become of me?' 'Keep calm,' I said, 'I beg of you. By getting so worked up you're only making it worse, I have another plan now, I shall cut the plush open here with my knife and then drop the whole thing down and the fellow with it.' But now I could not find my knife. 'Don't you know where I have my knife?' I asked. 'Can I have left it in my overcoat?' I was almost going to dash along to the cloakroom when my wife brought me to my senses. 'Surely you're not going to leave me alone now, Emil,' she cried. 'But if I have no knife,' I shouted back. 'Take mine,' she said and began fumbling in her little bag, with trembling fingers, but then of course all she produced was a tiny little mother-of-pearl knife."

One of the things that make Kafka so marvellous a writer is his discovery of—or, rather, discovery by—a kind of narrative in which logical analysis and humor, the greatest enemies of narrative movement, have themselves become part of the movement. In narrative at its purest or most eventful we do not understand but are the narrative. When we understand completely (or laugh completely, or feel completely a lyric empathy with the beings of the world), the carrying force of the narrative is dissipated: in fiction, to understand everything is to get nowhere. Yet, walking through Combray with Proust, lying under the leaves with Turgenev and the dwarf Kasyan, who has ever wanted to get anywhere but where he already is, in the best of all possible places?

In stories-in-which-everything-is-a-happening each event is charged and about to be further charged, so that the narrative may at any moment reach a point of unbearable significance, and disintegrate into energy. In stories-in-which-nothing-happens even the climax or denouement is liable to lose what charge it has, and to become simply one more portion of the lyric, humorous, or contemplative continuum of the story: in Gogol's *The Nose* the policeman seizes the barber, the barber turns pale, "but here the incident is completely shrouded in a fog and absolutely nothing is known of what happened next"; and in *Nevsky Avenue,* after Schiller, Hoffman, and Kuntz the carpenter have stripped Lieutenant Pirogov and "treated him with such an utter lack of ceremony that I cannot find words to describe this highly regrettable incident," Pirogov goes raging away, and "nothing could compare with Pirogov's anger and indignation. Siberia and the lash seemed to him the least punishment Schiller deserved . . . But the whole thing somehow petered out most strangely: on the way to the general, he went into a pastry-cook's, ate two pastries, read something out of the *Northern Bee,* and left with his anger somewhat abated"; took a stroll along Nevsky Avenue; and ended at a party given by one of the directors of the Auditing Board, where he "so distinguished himself in the mazurka that not only the ladies but also the gentlemen were in raptures over it. What a wonderful world we live in!"

One of these extremes of narrative will remind us of the state of minimum excitation which the organism tries to re-establish of the baby asleep, a lyric smile on his lips, the other extreme resembles the processes of continually increased excitation found in sex and play.

Story as Exemplum
—Exemplum as Story

On the Pragmatics and Poetics of Narrative Texts

KARL-HEINZ STIERLE

I fancy that something like an Ariadne thread has been found, that leads one out of all sorts of half-understood intricacies, once one resolutely defines speech as action. —K. Bühler, *Sprachtheorie*, p. 52.

I

To BEGIN WITH, a few remarks concerning the methods we shall use in approaching this subject.

If one understands texts as a permanent rendering of continuous speech actions, then the most common frame of reference as regards the constitution of texts must be a theory of action.[1] At the beginning of his *Philosophische Untersuchungen,* Wittgenstein makes the far-reaching observation that speech occurs in actions.[2] This is only a short step away from the idea that speech occurs as an action. It is characteristic of actions that the impulses of which they consist are orientated towards a particular meaning, which in principle is easy enough to understand. The object of this understanding, however, is not simply the relation between action and meaning, but the schema of action through which it is conveyed, and which transcends the individual action and indeed is the prime influence on it. For Max Weber, such "types of courses of action" are the actual subject of sociology. "Within social activities one can perceive real regularities, i.e., courses of action, in a typically, homogeneously *intended sense,* that are repeated by the same doer and/or are spread amongst many doers. Sociology is concerned with these *types* of courses of action, in contrast to history as the causal accounting of important, i.e., fateful, individual contingencies."[3] Actions, insofar as they are based on such a schema, are conventional—they stand within a cultural and social frame of reference which endows them with a "meaning" that extends beyond mere rational expediency. This conventional aspect of actions is their "sign." F. de Saussure, for whom linguistics counted as part of a science which he called *sémiologie,* and which he regarded as "science qui étudie la vie des signes au sein de la vie sociale,"[4] saw the meaning structure of conventional actions in the context of these "signs": "considérant les rites, les coutumes etc. . . . comme des signes" (p. 35).

If Saussure's concept of semiology might be called "action as speech," when we come to consider texts the term might be reversed to "speech as action." Texts can be understood in two ways—as speech and as action. W. Kamlah and P. Lorenzen, in their *Logische Propädeutik,* use the terms "Handlungsverstehen" (action understanding) and "Redeverstehen" (speech understanding) in order to differentiate between the two approaches.[5] Understanding a text as action is based on understanding a text as speech. The correlatives of this form of understanding have been aptly described by J. L. Austin[6] as "the act of saying" and its reification, the "act by saying" (or perlocutionary act).[7] Both levels follow their own rules in the composition of the text, and it is only their interaction that brings about the complexity of the concrete text structure itself. The "act of saying" might be called the object of the text, and coincides with those aspects of the text that remain identical when it is translated into other languages. It is what has long been known, somewhat unsubtly, as *content.* The "act of saying" culminates in the object's becoming a text, captured by an "act by saying" which divides it up in accordance with the possibilities of a given vocabulary, and sticks it together again on a new level, in accordance with the rules of a given syntax. As regards the concrete text, there is an interaction between the structures that go to make up these two acts.

Austin's distinction between the "act of saying" and the "act by saying" presupposes two different theoretical frames of reference. That of the "act of saying"—in its extra-syntactical consistency—might be called *text-semeiotic,* and that of the "act by saying," *text-pragmatic.*[8] The latter might be joined to a third frame of reference—*text-poetic.* As regards the schemata of pragmatic speech actions, Ch. Morris[9] distinguishes between their "primary use" and their "secondary use"; an essential object of the text-poetic is the "secondary use" of schemata of pragmatic speech actions and their liberation from the pragmatic context—whether this be for the purpose of reflecting them (a simple example, a kind of linguistic "minimal art," would be P. Handke's[10] arrangement of a football team as a "poem"), or in order to make possible an illusory identification with an implied reader. A borderline case of our text-poetic would be speech actions without pragmatic correlatives, as in concrete writing in which speech action is enclosed in itself, and the criteria of its composition have first to be deciphered.[11]

As far as text-pragmatic is concerned, A. Jolles' studies of the "simple forms"[12] of literature are of immediate significance. By "simple forms," Jolles means those forms which, so to speak without the aid of the writer, occur in the language itself and arise out of the language" (p. 10). They are determined by their "Bündigkeit" (p. 22)—the arrangement of a distinct coherence of linguistic "gestures." According to Jolles, the simple form itself is not something one actually comes across in the text. The concrete form is what he calls "vergegenwärtigt" (p. 264)—"realized." Out of the interaction of constant and variable elements of these "realizations" there emerges the inherent schema of the simple form. However, Jolles does not stop at tracing the realized back to the simple form. He also asks—and herein lies the pragmatic side of his approach—about the "Geistesbeschäftigung" (spiritual occupation) which manifests itself through the simple form and in the realized form. The term "Geistesbeschäftigung" is certainly linked with ideological presuppositions which must be put on one side if anything is to be gained from Jolles' account. This "Geistesbeschäftigung" he calls "Arbeit der Sprache" (work of language) (p. 16), but for him work is typologically confined to that of the farmer, the mechanic, and the priest. What these people do is performed once more in speech, and is preserved in speech as a simple form. Jolles' sentimental conception of a thus-constituted "division of labor," with little or no regard for economic or social history, has as little attraction as his restriction to a system of simple forms which, in the guise of primal forms of linguistic behavior, are supposed to correspond to primal forms of human activity. The question of the pragmatic, extra-syntactic forms cannot be narrowed down a priori. Historic change, which implies a change in society and its modes of communication, results in the emergence of new schemata of linguistic action, together with new possibilities for their poetic development and variation; in the context of text-pragmatic and text-poetic, these possibilities cannot be discussed in isolation, but must be related to their historical position.

The simple forms that Jolles describes are almost exclusively *narrative.* Narrative forms have an exceptional degree of self-containment, which at the same time allows a good deal of variation. Jolles' work shows the par-

ticular relevance of the pragmatic aspect of texts to the constitution of the
story as a text. The essential distinction between the forms lies in the way
the narrative is put together, and the way in which differently expressed
interests correspond to the object presented—interests from which the
speech action emerges as the force that captures the narrative cohesion.
Here Jolles is demonstrating something that has frequently been overlooked in subsequent narrative theory. Weinrich,[13] for instance, with his
distinction between "discussed and narrated world," proceeds from a typical "speech situation of narrative" (p. 48). The great number of possible
narrative approaches are traced back to a single one, from which all others
are supposed to be deducible. The narrator is defined as one particular
prototype: "The prototype of the *narrator,* with which literature continually confronts us in its stories within stories, is the storyteller. We have a
quite definite conception of him: he is old rather than young; in fairytales
he is the kind uncle or—if it is a woman—the kind aunt or grandmother.
He does not stand up, but is seated—in an armchair, on a sofa, or by the
fireplace. His hour is evening, after work. He likes to interrupt his story
in order to have a puff on his pipe or cigar (rarely a cigarette!). His
movements are slow; he takes his time, looking at his audience one after
the other, or he gazes thoughtfully up at the ceiling. His gestures are spar-
ing, his expression reflective rather than animated. He is *quite relaxed"*
(p. 49). Weinrich regards storytelling as a kind of primal phenomenon.
But the story of the accused describing the details of a crime, the story the
parson inserts in his sermon, the story the newspaper puts on its front
page, the story the historian reports on, the eyewitness account the policeman notes down—these are all speech actions that cannot be deduced
from Weinrich's picture of a narrator. The fact that something is to be
narrated does not tell us all we need to know about the speech situation. It
is this situation which in fact determines the narration. The composition
of narrative texts is independent of the use that is made of them, and so it
is independent of their position in any particular linguistic or nonlinguis-
tic context. It would be possible to examine the word *story,* together with all
its connotations, as Wittgenstein has examined the word *game.* Instead of
asking what basic, common idea underlies all games, he investigates the use
of the word—i.e., the contexts in which the word occurs, and the activities
revealed in these contexts. At one point in his *Philosophische Untersuchungen,* Wittgenstein, anticipating Chomsky, differentiates between "Ober-
flächengrammatik" (surface grammar) and "Tiefengrammatik" (depth
grammar).[14] What on the surface seems to suggest agreement proves in
its deeper structure to stretch further and further apart. "The indescribable diversity of all our daily language games does not enter into our con-

sciousness, because the clothes of our language make everything the same"
(p. 261).

Despite this diversity, the category of narrative texts is unmistakably
separated from that of systematic texts by the narrative schema that underlies them all. A. C. Danto, in his "Analytical Philosophy of History"[15]
defines this as follows:

(1) x is F at t-1
(2) H happens to x at t-2
(3) x is G at t-3. (p. 236)

This formula describes the basic structure of narrative. The subject of the
story takes on the predicate F at the time of t-1, and the predicate G at t-3.
F and G denote a change. Between the two conditions the story tells us H
during the period of t-2. (1) and (3) represent the thing to be explained,
and (2) is the explanation. In this sense, Caesar's "veni, vidi, vici" could be
taken as an example of a minimal, irreducible story. Between the times of
t-1 (*veni*) and t-3 (*vici*) lies the period t-2 with its *vidi,* which is so effective precisely because of the witty, impressive way in which it reduces the
long period to a mere nothing.

For Danto history is certainly an illustration of a process which upsets
the balance of a situation and, after a series of changes, creates a new situation which forms a contrast to the first. However, Danto makes it quite
clear that it is not the subject which determines its form of organization,
but the form of organization which primarily gives rise to the subject.
What constitutes this form is *contrasts* and the way in which they are
conveyed. At this point we must differentiate between *system* and *process*—
a difference inherent in language itself. According to L. Hjelmslev, language as a system is determined by the correlatives either-or, and as a
process by both-and.[16] The basic difference between language as a process
and language as a system, between the syntagmatic and the paradigmatic
perspectives, occurs again on the level of texts as the difference between
systematic and narrative texts.

The mode of narration follows the both-and construction, the sequent
poles of which determine the scope of the story. The narrative schema
makes possible a syntagmatic unfolding of paradigmatic poles, which can
"act out" their parts as they are embodied in the text. There is one class of
poles that has an especially important part: such contrasts as life-death,
young-old, inexperienced-experienced, which have a fixed, sequent relation (what Hjelmslev calls "determinations"). On these narrative contrasts depend all other contrasts.

A story does not take shape solely through its narrative schema, but also through the implementation of the schema on the different levels of the text. The task of describing this implementation as a speech action and of tracing it back to its context is fulfilled by the text-pragmatic and the text-poetic respectively. If one wishes to extract a story out of the narrative schema formulated by Danto there would have to be a whole series of transformations which we do not have time to go through in detail here. One might call the dimension arising out of the narrative schema, the *disposition* of the story. In this, the narrative schema is subject to a thematic situation. What lies between story disposition and story is the actual composition of the story. This might be regarded as analogous to the different "situations" of a printing-block.

The pragmatic connection between story disposition and story can be illustrated by a simple example. There is a whole collection of pragmatically determined story dispositions—namely, the paragraphs of the penal code. From every premise one can deduce stories, or at least incomplete halves of stories. Alternatively, there are stories that can be reduced to the premises of paragraphs in the penal code,[17] though they, too, are incomplete and in need of a conclusion. This is provided by the conclusion of the paragraph, in accordance with the given pragmatic context. The story can end only with the conclusion of the paragraph—a story the poles of which are offense and punishment. T-1 and t-3, offense and punishment, are named by the paragraph; t-2, in between, is implicitly presumed in the paragraph—namely, the judgment. Obviously under these conditions there must be two separate modes of narration in court (*diegesis* and *narratio* in classical rhetoric). In his narration the accused will take care not to allow a story to unfold. The accuser, on the other hand, will set out to arrange the "facts" as a story. It will be one of those stories which, as it comes under the premise of a paragraph, will be only "half a story," i.e., the first half. This is the kind of story we mean when we use such phrases as "a likely story," "telling stories" etc. It is no accident that Wilhelm Schapp's book is called *In Geschichten verstrickt*[18] (Entangled in Stories), and it is no accident that the last horizon in these stories is the "*Weltgeschichte im christlichen Sinne*" (p. 202)—a world history coordinated with a world court.

II

The transition from paragraphs of the penal code to the story that is implicit in them, is a transition from the systematic to the narrative text. It is conceivable that the story could be narrated in such a way that it contained nothing but the characteristic features of that category of stories to be associated with the particular paragraph. In the sphere of juridical narration, this would mean that the more serious the case, the less would be told. In other spheres there is normally a narrative surplus, which, however, has another pragmatic function: namely, to enhance probability by means of realistic detail.

It would seem that the borderland between systematic and narrative texts contains much that will help us to understand the way in which "stories" are constituted as texts. This territory was closely explored by Lessing in his *Abhandlungen über die Fabel.*[19] The fable and the exemplum are minimal narrative forms arising from minimal systematic texts such as maxims, proverbs, and moral precepts. Lessing shows step by step how a narrative text can be extracted from the systematic text that is its subject:

"The weaker is generally a prey to the stronger. This is a generalization that brings to my mind a series of things, one of which is always stronger than the next, and which can therefore destroy one another in the descending order of their various strengths. A series of *things!* Who will enjoy spending his time thinking about the dreary idea of a *thing* without alighting upon this or that *definite thing* whose qualities will conjure up a clear picture for him? And so here, too, instead of a series of *indefinite* things I will assume a series of *definite, real* things. I could seek out a series of states or kings in history; but how many people are so conversant with history that, the moment I named my states or kings, they could recall the size and power these states and kings had in relation to one another? I should have made my sentence only a little more conceivable, and I should like to make all of it as conceivable as possible! I hit on the idea of animals; and why shouldn't I be allowed to choose a series of animals—especially if they are well-known animals? A cock, a marten, a fox, a wolf: we know these animals; we only have to hear their names to know which is the weaker and which the stronger. So now my sentence reads: the marten eats the cock, the fox the marten, the wolf the fox. It *eats?* But perhaps it isn't eating. This is not yet definite enough for me. And so I say: it *ate.* And now, you see, my sentence has become a fable!" (p. 16).

What brings about the transformation of the general into the particular is the effect. Through this, a moral statement is to be made vivid and "conceivable." Thus the sum total of a moral statement is translated into the sum total of an *action:* "An action is what I call a series of changes which together make up a whole. This unit of the whole rests on the conformity of all the parts to a single purpose. The purpose of the fable—that for which the fable has been devised—is the moral precept" (pp. 24 f.). The "purpose," i.e., the pragmatic connection, determines the constitution of the narrative text—the manner in which the narrative schema is put together.

Lessing's idea of the "unit of the whole" has implications for the tense of his narrative. The chronologically arranged whole of the "action" can be a whole only if one has a complete view of it. And this means that the story has to be in the past. The preterite here, as in all narrative texts, is the tense denoting completeness of action, i.e., its state of being past. Käte Hamburger, who cannot see the connection between completeness and "pastness," has, in her book *Die Logik der Dichtung,*[20] developed a series of imaginary problems out of the difference between the role of the preterite in texts of fiction and non-fiction. For her the narrative as fiction has, to a certain degree, no narrator. What is presented here is "a fictional reality with an existence of its own, which *as fiction is just as independent of a narrator as is a 'real' reality*" (p. 112). As the fictional narrative, according to Hamburger, is not narrated, it is also not in the past but in a fictional present. In fiction, "the grammatical form of the imperfect (loses) its function of informing us about the past state of the facts conveyed" (p. 64). But in fact she is overlooking the particular function of the preterite: that right up to the penultimate sentence of the narrative text it denotes an already completed situation which, precisely because it is a "whole," is the determining factor in the style of text construction. The preterite always denotes this all-embracing completeness. In this it differs from the present tense and has a special (cataphoric) quality in that it makes possible a "whole" that may extend over a period of time.

Exemplum and fable coincide insofar as they constitute a narrative completeness relating to a systematic completeness. The style and method, of course, are different, with the fable approaching closer to the borders of the systematic text. At one point in his thesis, Lessing deals with the difference between fable and exemplum. In the "inner probability" (p. 45) that is uninfluenced by the factual nature of the real case, Lessing—in contrast to Aristotle—sees an advantage that fables have over historical examples, with regard to the power of conviction (p. 45). Lessing's idea of the "inner probability" distinguishing the fable from the exemplum is not altogether apposite. It conceals the programmatic improbability of the fable and hence what really separates fable and exemplum from each other.[21] Every improbability in a fable has a particular function: it is a sign of the allegoric intention underlying the "genre." In the fable, the general appears *as* the particular; in the exemplum, it appears *in* the particular. In the first case, the general is represented, in the second it is implied. If one draws a difference between "blind" and thematic implications, the exemplum makes a theme of those implications that give rise to the whole of the underlying moral precept. What the exemplum implies is this moral precept, and the medium through which it makes itself explicit is the story, or the history. The exemplum is a form of expansion and reduction all in one—expansion as regards its underlying maxim, reduction as regards a story from which is extracted and isolated that which the speech action of the exemplum needs in order to take on a concrete form. As far as the direction of the text composition is concerned, there is no doubt. The basic rule underlying the unity of the whole is the "purpose" of the exemplum—the moral precept.

In his book *Die Rechtsmetaphysik der Göttlichen Komödie*,[22] Hugo Friedrich interprets the exemplum as the embodiment of a moral type: "The story refers to something lying beyond the events it depicts—a moral type freed from time" (pp. 28 f.). He is concerned particularly with Dante, in whose work the exemplum contracts to a great and memorable exemplary figure, thus changing its status. It is in these exemplary figures as transformations of the exemplum that the architectural structure of Dante's symbolic world is to be seen. But the exemplum, in this basic structure, does not denote moral types so much as moral relations. It is the relations between good and evil, cleverness and naiveté, power and impotence, or illusion and disillusionment, that emerge from the narrative range of the exemplum. This is composed of the three elements of situation, decision, outcome. The resultant tripartition is shaped by the pragmatic context in which the exemplum is to be placed. In accordance with what in fact is its rhetorical aim, the exemplum is set in a pragmatic situation that is inconclusive and demands a decision. The pragmatic situation and the ultimate situation of the exemplum are isomorphic. Insofar as the given situation and the exemplum are isomorphic, the outcome for the exemplum can be interpreted as an anticipation of the outcome for one's own situation. The exemplum, in fact, shows what it will lead to if one makes a particular decision in a particular situation. It is this form of parallelism that gives the exemplum its power of persuasion in the matter of action or nonaction. The fact that the exemplum can be understood as anticipating the outcome of an isomorphic but still incomplete situation, is based on certain deep-lying premises concerning the story-comprehension out of which the exemplum arises. The ideas which Aristotle expressed in his *Rhetorica* on the difference between fable and exemplum, are valuable evidence of this:

"Fables are suitable for addresses to popular assemblies; and they have one advantage—they are comparatively easy to invent, whereas it is hard to find parallels among actual past events. You will in fact frame them just as you frame illustrative parallels: all you require is the power of thinking out your analogy, a power developed by intellectual training. But while it is easier to supply parallels by inventing fables, it is more valuable for the political speaker to supply them by quoting what has actually happened, since in most respects the future will be like what the past has been."[23]

What happens in history is by nature not unique but recurrent. One could therefore say that history in the Aristotelian sense is not unique but recurrent. And so the exemplum indicates a unit of situation and outcome which, because it is recurrent, is of general significance. This is why the Aristotelian exemplum really does have an anticipatory character, for it enables one to assess a still inconclusive situation in the light of earlier experience, and so to take a reasoned decision that is not merely the result of a rhetorical sophism. Quintilian[24] also advised his rhetor to have as many exempla as possible at the ready. Quintilian had in mind the juridical case in particular, and the testimonial value that a skilfully chosen example might have. The exemplum has—or appears to have—the higher authority of detachment and impartiality. Here the authority is no longer that of the recurrent but of the completed past, which lends it greater exemplary validity. In both cases—Aristotle and Quintilian—history is shown in a particular perspective, which Cicero described in a slogan that has lasted right up to the present: "historia magistra vitae."[25] This maxim draws attention to the connection, extending beyond the scope of any single lesson, between history and moral philosophy—a connection that establishes the frame within which the exemplum as a "simple form" has its own position. The maxim offers us, to a certain degree, the perspective through which history first becomes visible. History itself is shaped from a moral-philosophical standpoint and appears separated from the historical continuum, bearing its own meaning within itself. History is a macroexemplum. The criteria by which events may be translated into history are those of moral philosophy, which find their expression in the context of a "story." What occurs during the translation of events into history is repeated during the translation of history into exempla, except that here the moral-philosophical substrata undergo a new compression. The "Umwegstruktur"[26] (digressive structure) that is peculiar to history as a "macroexemplum," is lost in this second translation. The exemplum as a minimal narrative unit relates to the minimal systematic unit of the moral-philosophical precept in such a way that they virtually form a compound. "Solum quod facit ad rem est narrandum"[27] runs one of the exemplary rules of Humbert de Romance. The "res" here is the moral precept.

The historical process, as Antiquity understood it and as it underlies the "simple form" of the exemplum, might be described by a term of modern linguistics as "paradigmatic." Wherever history takes on a concrete form, it does so in a manner related to its subsumption under categories of the moral system. Only if a history has its place in the moral system and stands surety for one of that system's precepts, can it assume an exemplary character; only then can it claim the right to be extracted from the continuum of mere events or from the digressiveness of history as a "macroexemplum," and placed in its new paradigmatic context. As a result of this process, the exemplum dispenses with the difference between "mythology, legend, poetry on the one hand, and real history on the other" (Friedrich, p. 28). "What is given in a continual and many-sided tradition is regarded as an event" (p. 28). The drive to gain systematic control of the ever-expanding surfeit of noteworthy material, and the insatiable gathering and sorting of traditional material into a paradigmatic moral system, increased in the Middle Ages and the Renaissance until it became a kind of obsession which is difficult for us to understand today. "It is as if history, pulped and shredded, returned again to the primal force of its boundless material—as is manifested in the encyclopedias of the twelfth and thirteenth centuries, as elsewhere, in which norms and types are no longer capable of mastering the material of experience and history" (Friedrich, p. 32).

With the reactions of the Christian Middle Ages, however, the exemplum changes its character. Now it is seen as a *figura* and enters into a figure typology[28] that determines the frame of reference for all figures, and in this respect it can be read on two levels—the paradigmatic and the syntagmatic. As history is at one and the same time "magistra vitae" and the story of Christ, so, too, does the exemplum relate both to its paradigmatic classification in the context of the moral-philosophical system and, as a figure, to the proclamation and fulfillment of the story of Christ.

R. Koselleck[29] connects the disappearance of the exemplum since the late eighteenth century with a changed conception of history, the underlying experience of which could no longer be that of the "magistra vitae." The adherence to the continuum of events, which is integral to this new conception of history, can be termed "syntagmatic." As history frees itself from the clutches of the moral-philosophic system, it goes out of the paradigmatic and into the syntagmatic sphere of endless interconnections which continually overlap but can never be conclusively defined. Only now does history as such appear as the quintessence of all "stories" that touch on the factual. With Voltaire, the two possibilities of historical orientation still co-exist. History is narrated (a) in the syntagmatic framework of world history, and (b) in the paradigmatic framework of a collection of exempla for the never-changing condition of human baseness.[30]

So long as the story as an exemplum is related to a moral-philosophical system, the narrative schema will continue to appear fixed, as it were, by outside influences. But this foreignness is not confined to narrative texts. The relation between "case" and penal code, between exemplum and moral precept, is not exceptional. It merely illustrates with particular clarity a more or less prominent determinant of every story. It is characteristic of all stories that there is a specific imbalance of narrative expansion, due to the particular pragmatic context to which the story belongs. As with the exemplum, the paradigmatic conception of history comes closest to the sphere of systematic texts, so history seeks in its syntagmatic context to minimize the "foreignness." Its aim is to represent things "as they actually were." But, ultimately, instead of removing the foreignness, it can only achieve the illusion of having removed it. This is precisely what Roland Barthes, in an essay on *Le discours de l'histoire*,[31] describes as history-writing's pretension to reality, with which an implicit ideology covers itself. The writing of any story presupposes an interest that needs to be theorized.

III

The idea of poetic autonomy has, with some exceptions, so far prevented literary critics from seeking out the pragmatic forms underlying poetic forms, and from working out the connection between the latter and their pragmatic correlatives. Once one is aware of this connection, one realizes that a critical treatment of pragmatic speech actions is the great source for the origin of poetic forms. An analytic attitude towards the pragmatic form entails a change of focus, to which there corresponds a speech action that is in direct opposition to a speech action as manifested by the pragmatic form. A pragmatic speech action does not become concrete in its context, but as regards its final purpose it arranges itself, so to speak, spontaneously. An act of attentiveness is necessary, an "intentio obliqua," to give a concrete form to the "intentio recta" of the pragmatic speech action as such. If the pragmatic form turns out to be the shortest way to the fulfillment of an intention, the release of the pragmatic form entails the possibility of provoking this intention through the manner of its presentation, and calling into question its pragmatic stylistic principle. Flaubert acts rather in this manner when, in *Bouvard et Pécuchet,* he makes the speech action "popular scientific representation" the subject of a quotation which inexorably brings to light its ideological implications and ridicules it simply by the manner of its repetition. This example illustrates the possibilities of the "secondary use" of pragmatic speech actions, which enables a problem to be made implicitly conceivable without going beyond the confines of the thing that is criticized—in contrast to explicit criticism, which takes place on the level of a metalanguage and is therefore bound to enter into an abstract relationship with the object of the criticism.

Following the transformation of the exemplum into its problematical situation means tracing the reversal of "story as exemplum" to "exemplum as story." But before the end of the eighteenth century, when for historical and philosophical reasons the exemplum as a simple form faded out, there were two instances of a paradigmatic accomplishment of this reversal: first in the stories of Boccaccio, and then in Montaigne's essays.

Of the medieval narrative forms that Boccaccio subsumes under the new "genre" of the short story, the exemplum—as H.-J. Neuschäfer has shown in his comprehensive study *Boccaccio und der Beginn der Novelle*[32]—is pre-eminent. A simple instance of Boccaccio's method of handling the speech action of the exemplum is the way he deals with the exemplum of the good friend—in the collection *Disciplina clericalis*.[33] Neuschäfer has made a perspicacious comparison between the exemplum and the story that proceeds from it. He shows that the example of the generous man, who unhesitatingly gives his bride to his friend who falls in love with her, becomes problematical in the story because "the characters are no longer there merely as the vehicle for an idea, but have a consciousness of their own" (p. 45). And so the clarity of the exemplum is obscured in particular through the fact that in Boccaccio's story the bride is not simply an object but is conscious, is horrified by the demand made on her, and so sets off a whole chain of ever-widening complications, which quite undermine the exemplarity of the exemplum. As the ideal conception of generosity is now confronted with problems and resistance, opposed as it is by existing factors of reality, Neuschäfer goes so far as to state "that the story throws direct doubts on the meaning of the exemplum" (p. 47). This is certainly an "overexposure" of the story's intention, for the exemplary element is not completely lost, but simply complicated and made into an object for reflection. "Santissima cosa adunque è l'amistà" is still the last word even here.[34] Neuschäfer himself refers to Boccaccio's "peculiar method" of "so to speak applying the brake and catching up the uncertainties of his story at a particular point" (p. 48). Boccaccio's "critique" involves explaining "blind implications" on the level of the text itself. As he makes a particularity out of the exemplum which is to illustrate a generality, he lays bare the purely formal side of this claim to particularity. And so he passes beyond the exemplum in the direction of a story whose surplus of determinants makes it impossible for it to be reduced to a simple moral precept or, in this case, a moral idea.

There is a fundamental difference between the case that is offered for judgment and the example that is meant directly or indirectly to inspire imitation. As speech actions they appeal to two quite different modes of thought. The "one-sided emphasis on *one* standpoint," which Neuschäfer sees as the "characteristic of the mediaeval exemplum" (p. 54), can easily be explained in terms of the intention immanent in the exemplum—an appeal for *imitatio*.

The explanation of "blind implications"—i.e, such implications as are not taken up thematically—will result in one's calling into question the priority of the generality that gave rise to the exemplum. What this secondary level of narrative allows is primarily a change of attitude, from "imitation" to "judgment." Through this change of attitude, which the secondary narrative represents, the exemplum becomes a case, or a story demonstrating the case. The link between case and story has been convincingly drawn by A. Jolles. His definition of the case coincides exactly with what we have termed the attitude of "judging." "In the case, the form results from the criterion used as a measure during the evaluation of actions, but in the realization the question concerns the value of the norms. The existence, validity, and range of different norms are considered, but this consideration contains the question: where lies the weight, and according to which norm is one to evaluate?" (p. 190). The case is the form of the uncertainty itself: "The strange thing about the case form is the fact that although it asks the question, it cannot give the answer; it imposes on us the duty of deciding, but it doesn't contain the decision itself—what is realized in it is the weighing, but not the result of the weighing" (p. 191). Jolles' account of the original connection between case and story is directly confirmed by the fact that Boccaccio himself had a predilection for using the term in referring to his stories. Thus at the end of the fourth day, Dioneo looks back on the "infortunati casi d'amore"[35] which the company had learned about that day. Or at the beginning of the eighth story on the second day, when the narrator intervenes, reference is made, not without a smile, to the coming story and the "vari casi della bella donna."[36]

The problematic exemplum does not, of course, coincide simply with that speech action which, as a "case," has its firm position in the context of law. The *casus* as a problematic case has a particularly complex relation to the norm of the law; the communication of case and legal norm presupposes a high degree of discernment on the part of the presiding judge. If we want to find out the particular link between the short story and the case and exemplum, we had best go back to an examination of the structure of discernment, as provided by Kant's *Kritik der Urteilskraft*. For Kant, *discernment* is "the abitity to realize the particular as contained in the general."[37] Discernment "with regard to a conception through which an object is conveyed, needs and indeed demands the concurrence of two powers of conception: the imagination (for the perception and combination of the manifold) and intellect (for the definition that will cover this combination)" (p. 137). In this regard there is one category of judgment that is particularly relevant—that in which there is no definition that corresponds to the conception. Kant calls this category *judgments of taste*. "As there is no definition of the object as a basis for the judgment, it can only exist in the subsumption of the imagination itself (with a conception through which an object is given), on condition that the intellect proceeds from perception to definitions" (p. 137). The object of the judgment of taste, produced by the imagination itself, is "esthetic ideas" (p. 167). "But by esthetic idea I mean that conception by the imagination which stimulates much thought, without any definite idea—i.e., definition—being adequate to express it, and which consequently no language can fully encompass or make intelligible" (p. 168). The relation between the esthetic idea and the definition is determined by the fact that "a host of feelings and secondary conceptions is stirred up for which there is no expression" (p. 170). "In a word, the esthetic idea is a conception of the imagination associated with a given definition—a conception which is linked to such a multiplicity of partial conceptions in its free application that no expression denoting a particular definition can be found for it; a conception, then, that makes one think much that is indefinable in addition to what one thinks about a definition, and it is the feeling for the indefinable that animates the faculty of cognition and provides a spiritual link with language, as mere letters" (p. 171). It is precisely this confirmation of discernment, which transcends the limits of legally fixed norms and is no longer definable but, as a reflection, i.e., a search for definitions, remains inconclusive, that forms the intentional correlative which distinguishes the poetic speech action "short story" from the pragmatic speech actions "case and exemplum." What is demanded of the reader is not a real but a "specimen" judgment. The pragmatic structure becomes a tentative pragmatic structure; the reader no longer merely accepts a part that is assigned to him—he *plays* a part.

When the exemplum is exposed to a "multiplicity of partial conceptions," it loses its generality and tends towards the individual case. "The place of the legal typicality is taken by a unique case, which can be problematical precisely because of its uniqueness; for only the particular and the unique, not the general and what is always so, raises problems" (Neuschäfer, p. 43). However, this uniqueness is not absolute. It is true that the complexity of the moral situation can no longer be resolved by an underlying moral precept, and thus retains its uniqueness; but the Boccaccio short story, as a story, still retains its exemplary structure, insofar as it illustrates a narrative arrangement that forms the basis of a large number of stories. What always happens in the *Decameron* is that on each evening the narrative arrangement is explained that is to be the meeting point of the stories to be told the following day. And so in spite of their "uniqueness," the stories generally stand within a common paradigmatic frame which must be taken into account when we are confronted with each individual story. If the exemplum used to be nothing more than the narrative transposition of a moral precept, in Boccaccio the story is told in three different "situations," which in their interrelation move ever farther away from the paradigmatic center-point. This gradated narrative expansion is what is special about Boccaccio's stories. The reader first learns about the narrative arrangement. This is outlined in the "argument" that precedes each story and "summarizes" the story—i.e., fixes on an element of the constitutional process of the narrative text, from the standpoint of which the narrative expansion can be analyzed.

In Boccaccio's *Decameron,* the (fictional) narrators are identical with the (fictional) audience. Narrator and audience as constituent implications in the story itself become explicit in the overall framework, and so are directly conceivable. If one proceeds from the fact that the intended use of a text prescribes the rules that direct its composition, then from the narrator-audience society pictured in the framing story, one can derive the poetics of the story arising out of the pragmatic element of the exemplum. The new mode of presentation of the story is made into a theme, as denoting the self-evidence of the society made explicit in the framing story. Perhaps the idea of maturity can give the clearest description of this self-awareness. What Neuschäfer says of Boccaccio's characters also— indeed, especially—applies to the little society of the framing story, i.e., that "they are not mere objects" of some superhuman power, or one-sided representatives of a superordinate idea, but are independent "subjects" who are capable of discussing and judging the given data for themselves (p. 61). This maturity has a Utopian character. The little company that flees from the fear of the plague in Florence, to live together for a few days in complete and undisturbed harmony, anticipates the reconciliation between nature and reason that was a continual subject of discussion right up to Schiller's letters on the esthetic upbringing of man. Reasonable nature and natural reason are the factors that govern the conduct of this ideal society. The two together form the basis for that liberality of judgment that each individual in this society must maintain, both in narrating and in listening, if he is to have a feeling for the multiplicity of human appearances and for the inexhaustible residue of cases that lie outside the established norms.

In this framing story, Neuschäfer sees, above all, the "intention to confront us with human nature in its very inconsistency" (p. 134). He feels that this inconsistency can be ironed out only from case to case through a "compromise" (p. 64). "One can say that in the stories of the Decameron human nature is revealed for the first time with all its own uncertainties, and that this is the first attempt to present it in its inconsistency, and that the framework of the stories, with Miseria and Dignitas, circumscribes those two poles which for Boccaccio denoted the absolute extremes of its possibilities" (p. 134 ff.). For Neuschäfer, the polarity of Miseria and Dignitas represents Boccaccio's final word. But this reveals only the medieval Boccaccio. It leaves out what lies between the lines—the liberating laugh, the superior smile, the reconciliation of nature and reason in anticipation of the ideal, emancipated society. It is this very force of anticipation—which makes possible the cheerful composure of the members of this society—that stands out in such stark contrast to the terror of the plague in Florence.

The reader of the *Decameron* is not identical to the audience evoked in the framing story. But he does not stand in a direct relation to the narratives either. However, his perspective is mapped out. It lies in the process of *identification* with that ideal society in which—if only exceptionally and for a short time—nature and reason are reconciled. And so he becomes a partner in this foretaste of a mature society, from the standpoint of which the new "genre" of the short story first takes on its real meaning.

IV

In R. Koselleck's essay *Historia magistra vitae,* which is a "dissolution of the topic against the background of the violent history of modern times," Montaigne's attitude plays only a minor role. This appears to be a borderline example of that skeptical view of history which amounts to the doctrine that there is nothing to learn from history. "Even the fact that one could learn nothing from history was, after all, a definite experience, an historical lesson, which could make the knower more discerning, cleverer, or—to use Burckhardt's terms—wiser" (p. 200). The process of "dissolving the topic"—this is Koselleck's thesis—starts off with the eighteenth century and with certain specific premises. "Up until the eighteenth century, the use of this expression remained an infallible indication of the constancy—taken for granted—of human nature, whose activities lend themselves to the provision of repeatable proofs of moral, theological, or political doctrines" (p. 197). However misguided it might be to regard Montaigne as the precursor of dissolution of the paradigmatic dimension of history set off in the eighteenth century as a result of a new experience of history, this certainly does not mean to say that his skeptical attitude towards the exemplum has no place in history. The position occupied by Montaigne's skepticism can be described, in terms used by Roland Barthes, as *degré zéro*[38] of history. Where Montaigne makes his attitude most clear, history finds itself an equal distance away from both the syntagmatic and the paradigmatic level. Thus past faith in the consistency of history is abandoned, along with Christian faith in the salvationary orientation of history. But under this premise it is just as impossible to reach a decision concerning the statement that something can be learned from history as it is to reach one on the opposite, and yet implicitly confirmatory, statement that nothing is to be learned from history. Montaigne's concern is with the suspense that has become a principle of representation itself. In Montaigne, the vast number of historically viewed stories neither fulfill their traditional paradigmatic function, nor take on any syntagmatic relationship, nor bear their own value within themselves. But this very inconclusiveness gives room for reflection, though this will no longer arrive at a goal that can be reified as a "doctrine." It is true that the "historiens" give a picture of "homme en général de qui je cherche la connaissance," but if here this picture is to be found "plus vif et plus entier qu'en nul autre lieu," then this is only as "la diversité et vérité de ces conditions internes en gros et en détail, la variété des moyens de son assemblage et des accidents qui le menacent."[39] But Montaigne is not concerned solely with the endless diversity of events, which continually reveals the endless diversity of "homme en général" and thus makes the whole concept increasingly problematical, but his interest lies even more with the higher level of the relation between events and history, i.e., the manner in which the diverse approaches of the historians first compose the history. Two things may be regarded as exemplary: one, a form of representation that makes a theme of the multiplicity of communications between events and history, "qui nous représente la diversité même des bruits qui courent et le différent rapport qu'on lui faisoit" (II, 10, p. 459); two, a manner of representation, the excellence of which is attributable not so much to the "histoire" itself as to the discernment of the historian.

In the one case, the events withdraw behind the "diversité" of the evidence guaranteeing them; in the other, they withdraw behind the perfection of a well-grounded but therefore only "probable conception." As such problematic stories are continually set in a state of suspense, they are drawn into the sphere of reflection, which is continually made concrete as a speech action of suspense. To the extent that the "final purpose" becomes problematic, the speech action can take as its subject only its own movement. This priority of speech action over its purpose is shown clearly by Montaigne himself when he chooses as the title of his work the mode of treatment that he intends to use: *Les Essais*. The essay is at one and the same time a pragmatic and a poetic speech action. As pragmatic, it is a reflection on the possibility of knowing "homme en général"; as poetic, it takes as its subject this very reflection, in the unforeseeability and inconclusiveness of its movement. When, in the essay "De l'exercitation" (II, 6), Montaigne says of himself "Je peins principalement mes cogitations, subjecte informe, qui ne peut tomber en production ouvragère" (p. 416), with "peindre" and "cogitations" he is denoting this very bipartition.

Montaigne's view of history is a view of stories, and his view of stories is a view of exempla. It is only because stories are presented to him as exempla that he can in turn reduce them to stories that are no longer exemplary representatives of something general but, as they represent only themselves, become components of an immeasurable "diversité" of what is actually possible. However, the process of this reduction does not simply lead back to the original state of the story before it was given the status of an exemplum. The stories from which exempla were traditionally extracted were already designed for this purpose. They were macro-exempla which could also be read as a series of micro-exempla. If a story is taken out of its context and raised to the level of an exemplum and then in a second reproduction is withdrawn from its exemplarity, it will express an ambiguity which was not built into the original context of the story. The "meaning" of the story will no longer be fixed, and can be only tentatively grasped by a reflective process:

"Et combien y ay-je espandu d'histoires qui ne disent mot, lesquelles qui voudra esplucher un peu ingenieusement, en produira infinis Essais. Ny elles, ny mes allegations ne servent pas tousjours simplement d'exemple, d'authorité ou d'ornement. Je ne les regarde pas seulement par l'usage que j'en tire. Elles portent souvent, hors de mon propos, la semence d'une matiere plus riche et plus hardie, et sonnent à gauche un ton plus delicat, et pour moy qui n'en veux exprimer d'avantage, et pour ceux qui rencontreront mon air" (*Considération sur Cicéron*, I, 40, p. 289).

The course that Boccaccio took from the exemplum, through the problematic exemplum, to the short story was determined by the fact that in the narrative process itself he unfolded the "blind implications" of the exemplum, thus challenging its clarity. Montaigne, however, through his process of reduction, liberates the "blind implications" by making them the subject of a study that is fully aware of the inexhaustibility of its subject.

Exemplum and maxim are complementary. The exemplum is an exemplum with reference to a maxim; the maxim can take on a concrete form only through the perspective of an exemplum. The parallel in Montaigne is the complement of the *problematic* exemplum and the *problematic* maxim, i.e., reflection. It is only in the light of this complementary structure that the construction of Montaigne's essays can be understood. This fact has long been obscured by a misconception that the actual relevance of the essays must be found in the "artistic" self-presentation of the later essays. Even Hugo Friedrich makes this a point of his book on Montaigne, therein following Villey[40] and especially Burckhardt's conception of the Renaissance as an era of discovery of individuality;[41] he sets out to "give expression basically only to the dominant ideas of the middle and later periods, i.e., those which frequent repetition guarantees to be an integral part of his spiritual organism."[42] The reference of the ego to itself seems in this context to guarantee the unity: "His writing, which judged from the standpoint of systematization appears to be a ramble without a destination, proves to be the organic radiation of an ego that can remain completely occupied by itself." But if one replaces this very isolated theme of self-presentation back in the general framework of the essays, it becomes clear that the theme is only the logical development of problems that were already the subject of the earliest essays.

For the link between problematic exemplum and problematic maxim, from which Montaigne's essays proceed, the introductory essay "Par divers moyens on arrive à pareille fin" offers a model which is continually developed in the essays that follow.[43] The title of the essay is itself a maxim, but of so general a nature that one cannot gauge any idea of the mode of treatment from it. Here to a certain extent the maxim only denotes a form of its own absence, for it sets up as a theme something that directly contradicts the traditional clarity and finality of maxim and exemplum— namely, *diversité*. The essay itself also begins with a maxim or at least a pseudomaxim: "La plus commune façon d'amollir les coeurs de ceux qu'on a offensez, lors qu'ayant la vengeance en main, ils nous tiennent à leur mercy, c'est de les esmouvoir par submission à commiseration et à pitié" (I, 1, p. 27). This introductory maxim is an illustration of the titular maxim, insofar as it is a qualification of the original maxim and makes it something to be reflected upon. Parallel to the "la plus commune façon" with which it is introduced, there is in the very next sentence a qualifying "toutesfois," which brings into play the contrasting possibility: "Toutes-fois la braverie, et la constance, moyens tous contraires, ont quelquesfois servi à ce mesme effect." To illustrate this latter possibility, he then offers three examples: Edward Prince of Wales captures a town that he intends to punish, and after all pleas for mercy have done nothing but increase his wrath, he is so impressed by the sight of three of his enemies heroically defending themselves that his wrath disappears and he pardons them and all the other inhabitants of the town. Scanderbeg forgives a soldier because he defiantly faces him with his sword drawn at the ready. Emperor Conrad pardons the women of Weinsberg, who with cunning and with courage try to rescue their menfolk. To these three examples of anger suddenly appeased by courage, Montaigne adds a personal reflection of his own:[44] with him, pity and courage would be equally successful, but pity would be more natural for him. The confession is at once qualified, as it is contrasted with the Stoic standpoint, according to which pity is nothing but a "passion vitieuse." Montaigne returns to his examples and tries to systematize them: weak natures lapse into pity, "femmes, enfants, le vulgaire" (amongst whom Montaigne counts himself with ironic self-debasement); admiration of fearless virtue is the sign of "une âme forte et inployable." But this is again followed by a qualifying "toutesfois." Also with "âmes moins généreuses," "étonnement" and "admiration" may be equally effective. On the one hand, Pelopidas is pardoned by the people of Thebes because he confesses his crime and begs for mercy; but, on the other, Epaminondas, who arrogantly challenges everyone, is also released by the people. Finally, Dionysius, who wishes to make a "tragique exemple" of his enemy, finds that the imperturbability of the latter threatens to have an influence on the attitude of his army, and so has to have him killed in secret. Following on directly from this new collection of examples comes a reflection that does away with all tendencies to systematize and defines the Montaigne view of mankind: "Certes, c'est un subject merveilleuse-ment vain, divers, et ondoyant, que l'homme. Il est malaisé d'y fonder jugement constant et uniforme" (p. 29). Following this reflection come the contradictory exempla of Pompey, who pardoned a town because of the greatness and virtue of a single citizen, and the guest of Sylla who sacrificed himself for nothing—and these put the titular maxim in reverse. In the light of these new examples it ought to read: "Par pareils moyens on arrive à diverses fins." What is here only the implicit enigma and in-calculability of human conduct becomes explicit in the last exemplum, which Montaigne sets "directement contre mes premieres exemples" (p. 30) and which is of especial significance if only because it is by far the most expansive example in the essay.[45] Alexander, who after a long period of siege has captured the town of Gaza, takes prisoner the commander, whose heroism is evinced by the most astonishing deeds of valor. The imperturbability of the commander, whom he confronts with the prospect of an agonizing death, so enrages Alexander that he has him tortured to death on the spot. In ever wilder rage, he has the whole town razed to the ground. What is vital in this anti-exemplum, which again calls into question the titular maxim, is the inherent incalculability of human conduct. What happens between the time t-1, when the commander is taken prisoner, and t-3, when he is put to death—i.e., the period t-2—can no longer be comprehended. And so the story falls into two sections, and what lies between them does not occur on the level of the story but on the level of the narrator's conjectures. At this vital point, there is mention only of possibilities, which take the place of any definite answer. Thus the "explanation" is offered only in the form of a threefold question: "Seroit-ce que la hardiesse luy fut si commune que, pour ne l'admirer point, il la respectast moins? Ou qu'il l'estimast si proprement sienne qu'en cette hauteur il ne peust souffrir de la veoir en un autre sans le despit d'une passion envieuse, ou que l'impetuosité naturelle de sa cholere fust incapable d'opposition?"

It is the vital middle section, which binds together the situation and the outcome and thus constitutes the "meaning" of the exemplum, that in Montaigne becomes problematic. Whereas in the classic exemplum the link between situation and solution was indisputable and had only to be taken note of, now the link itself has become a puzzle, and is therefore an interesting subject of psychological and moral cogitation. With this change of orientation, the frame of reference is removed, which is essential if an exemplum is actually to be an example. The change of status of the exemplum in Montaigne's essay involves its no longer setting an example for actions, but an example for *re*actions. The spontaneity and unforeseeability of the reactions captures the essence of human mystery and unfathomableness. The human enigma becomes the theme. As reactions, the "exemplary" actions in this essay are no longer the responsibility of the subject. If traditional forms of exemplum presupposed the possibility of a decision—as is implied by the moral category of responsibility—the reactions in Montaigne's exempla are conditioned by the irreducible complexity of the character and the dramatic moment. This means that the exemplum loses its representative function and is directed back to a story the meaning of which is no longer obvious, but is a starting point for purely subjective and constantly renewed conjecture.

While the early essays are generally problematic chains of self-cancelling exempla with occasional reflections, in the later essays the "simple form" of the historic exemplum fades further and further into the background. The authenticity of the exemplum, which was the traditional foundation of its authority, itself becomes questionable in the same proportion as the supposed exemplarity of the example is open to question. The best exempla are now those that are most obvious, taken from one's own experience and authenticated by it. "La vie de César n'a point plus d'exemples que la notre pour nous" (III, 13, p. 1205). This turning away from "exemples étrangers et scholastiques" (III, 13, p. 1214) arises out of the discovery of the self as an inexhaustible source of exempla, backed by the authority of experience. Thus the ego replaces history as the quintessence of authenticated stories. But just as in Montaigne "historia" cannot be "magistra vitae," so neither can the ego itself become "magistra vitae." As it (the ego) presents itself with all its endless contradictions and inconsistencies, it induces not learning—for this presupposes something dependable—but endless reflection. The examples in Montaigne—even the examples from his own life—have the paradoxical function of being examples for the particular and not for the general. This new meaning of "exemple" in Montaigne is illustrated in the essay "De l'experience" (III, 13). The problematic relation between the general and the particular is considered here with reference to the incongruity of laws and human conduct. Even the subtlest refinement of the laws is still bound to be inadequate in view of the immeasurable diversity of human actions. At this point Montaigne continues: "La multiplication de nos inventions n'arrivera pas à la variation des exemples" (p. 1196). The exemplum here is the individual case, which cannot be subsumed and to which even the widest diversification of the laws cannot do justice, because finally it conforms only to itself.

Ultimately for Montaigne the impossibility of exempla implies the impossibility of stories and hence even of one's own life-story. Montaigne begins his essay "Du repentir" (III, 2) with a basic idea that sets up the program for a life-story and at the same time demonstrates its impossibility. The first sentence leads one to expect a biography: "Les autres forment l'homme: je le récite" (p. 899). But in the reflections that follow immediately afterwards, the conditions that would make such a story possible are done away with. The world is nothing but an incessant fluctuation, and the things in it fluctuate in two ways—by themselves and through the movement of the whole. Consistency is only a borderline case of this fluctuation: "La constance mesme n'est autre chose qu'un branle plus languissant." And so even the representation cannot be certain of the object it is representing: "Je ne puis asseurer mon object; il va trouble et chancelant, d'une yvresse naturelle." The fluctuation of the object also corresponds to the impermanence of the perspective in which it appears— a perspective that changes from one moment to the next: "Je le prens en ce point, comme il est, en l'instant que je m'amuse à luy." Out of this arises the program of a representation that is the program of an "anti-story," insofar as from the story are extracted the integrant elements that first enable it to be meaningfully split up. "Je ne peints pas l'estre. Je peints le passage: non un passage d'aage en autre, ou, comme dict le peuple, de sept en sept ans, mais de jour en jour, de minute en minute." But not only does the story break up into ever smaller segments deter- mined by an ever decreasing unit of time: the story itself continually has to be adjusted, since it changes from hour to hour as it comes under ever new perspectives. "Il faut accommoder mon historie à l'heure. Je pourray tantost changer, non de fortune seulement, mais aussi d'intention." Thus the representation of one's own life is "un contrerolle de divers et muables accidens et d'imaginations irresolues et, quand il y eschet, contraires: soit que je sois autre moymesme, soit que je saisisse les subjects par autres cir- constances et considerations. Tant y a que je me contredits bien à l'adven- ture, mais la vérité, comme disoit Demades, je ne la contredy point" (p. 900). However, this "vérité" is no longer that of a "récit," but that of an essay: "Si mon ame pouvoit prendre pied, je ne m'essaierois pas, je me re- soudrois; elle est tousjours en apprentissage et en espreuve." What makes the "histoire" impossible makes the essay possible. What was revealed by the Alexander exemplum in Essay I, 1—the disintegration of the story— has itself become the object of reflection. The radicality with which this occurs is of theoretic significance, and does not simply reflect the difficulties of writing a biography. In his reflections, just as when he is actually speak- ing about himself, Montaigne is not solely concerned with himself; refer- ences to the authenticity of one's own existence also have a philosophic significance, and this is strikingly revealed by the fact that the essay which follows these programmatic introductory reflections—"Du repentir"— makes astonishingly little reference to the problems of self-representa- tion—a fact which until now has constantly been overlooked. The "*pro- gramme* of self-representation" has generally been separated both from the closely related reflections on the impossibility of the life-story and from the actual subject of the essay itself, repentance. Thus E. Auerbach, for in- stance, in the Montaigne chapter of his *Mimesis*,[46] does not even consider the link between the "programme" and the essay. But it is only through this link that the actual philosophic intention of the introduction becomes apparent. To understand this, it is necessary to return once more to Montaigne's contrast between *être* and *passage* (je ne peints pas l'estre. Je peints le passage). Set against the timeless substance, *l'être,* is the *passage—* a time structure that is not to be understood as a directed process or as a transition, but as a skipping from one moment of time to another in accordance with a basic principle of unforeseeability. The temporality of man appears as something discontinuous. Just as there is no constituent connection between moments of time, and each moment is basically only itself and separated from all others, so one's own existence breaks up into a succession of discontinuous moments of existence, which make up the ego in its immeasurable diversity throughout an extent of time. The unity of the person can be captured only in the unity of the moment. But the ever decreasing reduction of the moment of time must still remain illusory because this unity is not to be found in even the smallest moment, for the simple reason that the ego is already contradictory in itself. This contrariness is manifested in the synchronism of the individual moment just as much as in the diachronism of the sequent moments. From now on we can see that "pendre le passage," apparently intended only as an illumination of the subjective individual, is in fact related to a quite different intention—namely, the refutation of the Christian demand for repentance. Repentance, "le repentir," has a time structure of its own. It involves a qualitative differentiation in the sequence of moments of existence, in such a manner that the present moment is privileged and stands out from the rest of the sequence so far, in that it enables us not only to view the past as it was, but also as it should have been. Present repentance and the combining of past moments of existence into the story of a lapse are mutually constituent factors. Thus the confessions of Augustine, for instance, are a story that can be composed only from the privileged standpoint of the present moment with its superior insight. For Montaigne, however, this elevation of the present self, which is indispensable for the possibility of repentance, is naive and blind to perspectives, and cannot take responsibility for the relativity of the most immediate, i.e., the present moment. Once this relativity is recognized, the task must be not to judge the moments of past existence from the standpoint of the present, but to leave them alone in their wholeness and so enhance one's awareness of the diversity of one's own self. Seen in this perspective, the possibility of composing a story and the possibility of repentance appear equally illusory.

As Montaigne lights the way from exemplum to story and thence to the dissolution of the story, he shows that the problem is one of the pre-

mises under which stories become possible in the first place. The problem
of the constitution of stories is an example of the wider problem of the
relation between the general and the particular, which in Montaigne's
eyes represents the overall problem of cognition. If Descartes' *Discours de
la méthode* is in principle a reply to Montaigne's principled problematic
view of cognition, the philosophy of history in the eighteenth century is a
reply, however tortuous, to Montaigne's problematic view of the story—a
reply which sought to counter his atomization of the moments of a story
with a philosophic legitimization of historic construction. But despite
Montaigne's skeptical argument against the possibility of historic construction, the philosophy of history remains as far from conclusion as the
theory and practice of "stories." The modern novel has taken up Montaigne's ideas in earnest, and has set itself the task of bringing about the
poetic speech action of the "impossible story."

NOTES

1. The claim is that the study of literature, as the systematic study of texts,
has its place in the framework of the active sciences. Under this premise, the
adaptation of theoretical concepts integral to the active sciences may provide substantial stimuli for the study of literature. The following essay, however, makes
only a very limited allowance for this. It is first and foremost an attempt to apply
the concept of the speech action, which is attracting increasing attention in modern philology, philosophy of language, and sociology, to texts and not merely to
minimal speech utterances. For the concept of speech action, see especially J. L.
Austin, *How to Do Things with Words* (Harvard University Press, 1962); K.
Bühler, *Sprachtheorie* (1934), (2nd ed., Stuttgart, 1965); J. Frese, "Sprechen als
Metapher für Handeln," in *Das Problem der Sprache. 8. Deutscher Kongress für
Philosophie* (Munich, 1967); A. Gehlen, *der Mensch* (1940), (8th ed., Frankfurt,
1966), esp. chapter on "Handlung und Sprache"; J. Habermas, "Vorbereitende
Bemerkungen zu einer Theorie der kommunikativen Kompetenz," in Habermas-
Luhmann, *Theorie der Gesellschaft oder Sozialtechnologie* (Frankfurt, 1971); W.
Kamlah, P. Lorenzen, *Logische Propädeutik* (Mannheim, 1967), esp. II, 2: "Sprache
und Rede"; K. Lorenz, *Elemente der Sprachkritik* (Frankfurt, 1970), N. Luh-
mann, "Sinn als Grundbegriff der Soziologie," in Habermas-Luhmann, *Theorie
der Gesellschaft oder Sozialtechnologie* (Frankfurt, 1971); B. Malinowski, "The
Problem of Meaning in Primitive Languages," in Ogden and Richards, *The
Meaning of Meaning* (1923); G. H. Mead, *Mind, Self and Society* (Chicago,
1934); K. L. Pike, *Language in Relation to a Unified Theory of the Structure of
Human Behavior,* 2nd ed. (The Hague, 1967); S. J. Schmidt, "Sprachliches und
sociales Handeln. Überlegungen zu einer Handlungstheorie der Sprache," in
Linguistische Berichte 2 (1969); J. R. Searle, *Speech Acts. An Essay in the Phi-
losophy of Language* (London, 1969); L. Wittgenstein, *Philosophische Untersu-*

chungen (Frankfurt, 1967); D. Wunderlich, "Die Rolle der Pragmatik in der Linguistik," in *Der Deutschunterricht* (1970), *Heft* 4.

2. L. Wittgenstein, p. 24: "The word '*Sprachspiel*' (language game) is meant to bring out the fact that speaking a language is part of an activity or a form of life."

3. Max Weber, *Wirtschaft und Gesellschaft,* 2 vols., ed. J. Winckelmann (Cologne, 1964), I, 20.

4. F. de Saussure, *Cours de linguistique générale* (Paris, 1968), p. 33.

5. Kamlah, Lorenzen, p. 57.

6. J. L. Austin, *How to Do Things with Words* (Oxford, 1965), pp. 101 ff.

7. For our purposes it is unnecessary to consider Austin's second category of speech actions, the "illocutionary acts" (acts in saying), which related to the special case of definite, explicit, linguistically normalized acts.

8. Ch. Morris, *Signification and Significance* (Cambridge, 1964), p. 44: "Pragmatics is the aspect of semeiotics concerned with the origins, uses and effects of signs." For Morris, semantics, syntactics, and pragmatics stand on one level; together they form the sphere of semeiotics. Our suggestion is that only syntactics and semantics be subsumed under semeiotics, and pragmatics be set up as an opposing field on its own. In *Linguistische Berichte,* there is a report by H. Schnelle on a discussion of Morris' schema that took place during the 1970 colloquy in Jerusalem on Pragmatics in Natural Languages.

9. Ch. Morris, *Signs, Language and Behavior* (New York: Braziller, no date), p. 94. Cf. also the fundamental observations on "Endzweck und Selbstzweck des Handelns," in Gehlen, *Urmensch und Spätkultur* (Bonn, 1956), pp. 33 ff.

10. P. Handke, *Die Aufstellung des I. FC Nürnberg vom Jan. 27, 1968, "Die Innenwelt der Aussenwelt der Innenwelt,"* ed. Suhrkamp (Frankfurt, 1969).

11. Only this type of text, which is constituted purely on the text surface, is dealt with in M. Bense's text theory, which purchases its conciseness at the price of an arbitrary narrowing down of its subject matter. See M. Bense, *Einführung in die informationstheoretische Ästhetik,* in *Rowohlts Deutsche Enzyklopädie* (Hamburg, 1969).

12. A. Jolles, *Einfache Formen* (Darmstadt, 1958).

13. H. Weinrich, *Tempus. Besprochene und erzählte Welt* (Stuttgart, 1964).

14. P. 203.

15. A. C. Danto, *Analytical Philosophy of History* (Cambridge, 1968).

16. L. Hjelmslev, *Prolegomena to a Theory of Language,* revised English edition (Madison, 1963), p. 36: "This is what is behind the distinction between process and system: in the process, in the text, is present a both-and, a conjunction or co-existence between the functives entering therein, in the system is present an either-or, a disjunction or alternation between the functives entering therein." For remarks on this statement, see A. Greimas, *Du Sens* (Paris, 1970), esp. the chapter "Éléments d'une grammaire narrative."

17. From another standpoint A. Jolles has also referred to this connection: "We see how a rule, a legal paragraph, merges into an event; an event comes into

existence, and as it is captured by language, it takes on a gestalt." Instead of "event," we should prefer the term "story" here.

18. W. Schapp, *In Geschichten verstrickt* (Hamburg, 1963).

19. G. E. Lessing's *Collected Works*, ed. P. Rilla (Berlin, 1955), vol. IV.

20. Käte Hamburger, *Die Logik der Dichtung* (Stuttgart, 1968).

21. On the function of the improbable in fables, see the author's "Poesie des Unpoetischen. Über La Fontaines Umgang mit der Fable," in: *Poetica*, 1 (1967).

22. H. Friedrich, *Die Rechtsmetaphysik der Göttlichen Komödie* (Frankfurt, 1942).

23. *The Works of Aristotle*, vol. XI, *Rhetorica*, transl. by W. R. Roberts (Oxford, 1946), II, 20.

24. Quintilian, *Institutio oratoria*, X.I.34, ed. H. E. Butler, The Loeb Classical Library, in 4 vols., IV, p. 22: "(. . .) ex cognitione rerum exemplorumque, quibus imprimis instructus esse debet orator, ne omnis testimonia expectet a litigatore, sed pleraque ex vetustate diligenter sibi cognita sumat, hoc potentiora, quod ea sola criminibus odii et gratiae vacant."

25. Cicero, *De oratore II*, c. 9, 36.

26. I have taken the term from H. Blumenberg, "Wirklichkeitsbegriff und Wirklichkeits-potential des Mythos," in *Poetik und Hermeneutik*, IV.

27. Quoted by Friedrich, p. 28.

28. See the fundamental essay by E. Auerbach, "Figura," in *Archivum Romanicum*, XXII (1938), pp. 436–89.

29. R. Koselleck, "Historia Magistra Vitae. Über die Auflösung des Topos im Horizont neuzeitlich bewegter Geschichte," in *Natur und Geschichte, Karl Löwith zum 70. Geburtstag* (Stuttgart, 1967), pp. 196–218.

30. See the author's Einleitung zu Voltaire, *Aus dem Philosophischen Wörterbuch*, Sammlung Insel (Frankfurt, 1967).

31. R. Barthes, "Le Discours de l'Histoire," in *Information sur les Sciences Sociales* (1967), p. 73: "Comme on le voit, par sa structure même et sans qu'il soit besoin de faire appel à la substance de contenu, le discours historique est essentiellement idéologique, ou pour être plus précis, imaginaire, s'il est vrai que l'imaginaire est le langage par lequel l'énonçant d'un discours (entité purement linguistique) 'remplit' le sujet d'énonciation (entité psychologique ou idéologique)."

32. H.-J. Neuschäfer, *Boccaccio und der Beginn der Novelle* (Munich, 1969). On the relation between exemplum and story, see also W. Pabst, *Novellentheorie und Novellendichtung*, 2nd ed. (Heidelberg, 1967), and S. Battaglia, *Giovanni Boccaccio e la riforma della narrativa* (Naples, 1969).

33. Boccaccio, *Il Decameron*, ed. Ch. S. Singleton, 2 vols. (Bari, 1955), *Giornata de cima, novella ottava*, I, 275–91.

34. I, 290.

35. I, 325.

36. I, 143.

37. I. Kant, *Kritik der Urteilskraft*, ed. K. Vorländer (Hamburg, 1959), intro-

duction, p. 15. On Kant's theory of the example, see G. Buck, *Lernen und Erfahrung* (Stuttgart, 1967).

38. R. Barthes, *Le degré zéro de l'écriture* (Paris, 1969), p. 67. Barthes has transferred the linguistic term ("on sait que certains linguistes établissent entre les deux termes d'une polarité . . . l'existence d'un troisième terme, terme neutre ou terme zéro") to the new field of "écriture."

39. Montaigne, *Essais,* II, 10, *Des Livres,* ed. A. Thibaudet, Bibliothèque de la Pléiade (Paris, 1950), p. 458.

40. P. Villey, *Les sources et l'évolution des essais de Montaigne,* 2 t. (Paris, 1908), t.2, *l'évolution des Essais,* p. 43: "Il n'est personne qui n'ait été surpris de tous ces petits chapitres, si grêles, qui ouvrent le premier livre. On s'étonne qu'ils puissent être de la même main qui a écrit l'essai 'De la vanité' ou celui 'De l'expérience.' Ces chapitres-là coûtent peu à Montaigne, il n'y met rien du sien. N'importe qui les multiplierait à l'infini, car ils n'ont aucune personnalité."

41. J. Burckhardt, *Die Kultur der Renaissance in Italien, Ges. Werke,* III (Darmstadt, 1962). See especially the second part "Entwicklung des Individuums" and the notes on the "Vollendung der Persönlichkeit."

42. H. Friedrich, *Montaigne* (Bern, 1949), p. 8. But the perspective of this important representation extends far beyond its program.

43. On this essay, see also the interpretation by Friedrich, pp. 181–86. As I have subsequently discovered, the following account largely coincides with that of Friedrich.

44. This reflection is added in the second edition (1588).

45. The exemplum of Alexander's anger is added in the 1588 edition. The conjectures on the reasons for Alexander's conduct, which conclude the text, are extended by two new possibilities in the posthumous edition of 1595. Here the conclusion is the depiction of the destruction of Thebes.

46. E. Auerbach, *Mimesis,* 2nd ed. (Bern, 1959), pp. 271 ff.

The Tale as Genre
in Short Fiction

W. S. PENN

THE STORY IS, according to Wallace Stegner, "the most formal of all prose forms, the most difficult," and it is "different from the novel in kind as well as duration."[1] To prove the first half of Stegner's statement is not my concern here. What is my concern, as well as my assumption, is that the short story has genres of its own invention, and, thus, that the terms we use to talk about it should be derived from the story form itself, not imported from other prose forms such as the novel or the novella.

What is a genre? The word has been used in two basic ways: first, as an indication of class—poem, short story, or novel; and second, as an indication of the mode of the member of the class—myth, romance, tragedy, realism, or irony. But if we use the word in both these ways, then we again make ourselves subject to the same kind of confusion that exists when we speak about stories as if they were derived from novels.[2] Even after presenting a useful and intelligent theory of modes in *Anatomy of Criticism,* Northrop Frye begins to crumble beneath the sheer weight of the existing confusion between mode and genre. If we retreat slightly, we can discover a third indicator of genre, that of structure.

Jonathan Culler in *Structuralist Poetics* says, "The function of genre conventions is essentially to establish a contract between writer and reader so as to make certain relevant expectations operative. . . ."[3] Whether or not one is a structuralist, or calls oneself such, should not matter in recognizing that Culler is basically right in his use of the word "contract." However, there are two levels on which we might use this term, and the first level is actually a preliminary expectation, rather than a contract. This is the expectation a potential reader derives from such things as reviews, the dustjacket, previous knowledge of the particular author, or thumbing through a volume in the bookstore. This expectation indicates the class of the work of literature: Novel, Poem, or Story. The second and more important level is the set of expectations derived from the opening paragraph of a story, and, in retrospect, from the relation of the title to that opening. This level is the reader's first real contract with the writer, since it indicates the structure of the story as well as the mode and the kind of language it will use.

In order to distinguish between the what-a-thing-is, the expectations generated by the contract, and the how-a-thing-is, the degrees of satisfaction or dissatisfaction with those expectations, we have two general categories of conditions: mode and tropical convention. By "mode" I mean the five ideal models developed by Northrop Frye in the first essay of *Anatomy,* "Historical Criticism: Theory of Modes"—Myth, Romance, the High Mimetic, the Low Mimetic, and Irony. Tropical convention, on the other hand, requires that we establish a vertical scale of literary "tropes," ranging from the convention of "pure" allegory through metaphor to the convention of "pure" symbol. This scale is neither fixed nor intended to imply a hierarchy from bad to good. Its movement might be likened to the movement of language in "achieving its inner freedom," which is a movement, according to Cassirer, through the stages of "mimetic, analogical, and symbolic expression."[4] By "mimetic" Cassirer means that the process of signification is a one-step process from word to thing, that "word" means (or is) "thing." However, for our purposes, it might be better to view these stages as synecdochic, metaphoric, and metonymic, always remembering that each stage is an indication of relation to the other two stages, a matter of degree and not exclusion. Using these two conditions, we are thus able, first, to distinguish between the structures of thematic presentation (modes), and, second, to discern the manner by which the writer allows, and in which the reader accomplishes, understanding and interpretation of the language (tropical convention). As we shall see, modes are often mixed in the story, any two of them existing equally side by side. However, with tropical conventions we can postulate our first trigram which is schematized thus:

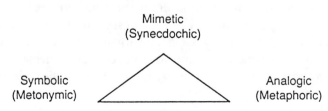

Mimetic
(Synecdochic)

Symbolic
(Metonymic)

Analogic
(Metaphoric)

The "manner in which the writer allows" interpretation implies that there is a discoverable author behind the work. That the reader usually and automatically seeks this discoverable author is a fact Tolstoi, among others, took for granted.[5] But how do we discover the author when all we have are the words? As the genres of the story class become increasingly difficult to understand, and as writers attempt to move themselves further into the background of the work or to remove themselves altogether, we are cast into a search for the moral relation of the author to the world at large, while at the same time we know that this moral relation can, if presented by an easily detectable author in the form of clear statement (as is often the case with Solzhenitsyn), destroy the pleasure we take in reading. Therefore, we need a way of perceiving this relation which can account for most, if not every kind of story. Again we turn to Culler, to his chapter, "Poetics of the Lyric": "The poetic persona is a construct, a function of the language of the poem, but it nonetheless fulfills the unifying role of the individual subject, and even poems which make it difficult to construct a poetic persona rely for their effects on the fact that the reader will try to construct an enunciative posture."[6] If we substitute "story" for "poem" in Culler's definition of the function of the persona, we can, I think, discover a distinction which is useful for discussing all kinds of stories, ranging from Tale to Metafiction (and beyond).

Thus, "enunciative posture" in relation to the story means the detectable or intuited moral relation of the implied author to both the world at large as well as to the world he or she creates in the story. Within that understood frame exists a second set of limits, which we will call the "narrative posture." This second posture is the moral position of the interior narrators to their world, ranging from the ostensible teller of the story (such as Conrad's Marlow) to any individual character who speaks within the story, and including such things as the narrator's person and point-of-view. Although these two postures are often highly related and sometimes confused, using them has the advantages of allowing us to indicate the source of our interpretation, as well as to speak of the reliability or unreliability of either (or both) posture(s). This way, we can avoid simply harping upon our tastes: we can say, to pick on Solzhenitsyn, that "Matryona's House" is unconvincing in its enunciative posture because that posture is didactically one-dimensional, expressed as the implied author's determination to preach not what can be discovered to be true (except in isolation), but only what the author wants to convey as message; and that enunciative posture prevents the existence of any believable narrative posture within the story.

With the term enunciative posture, we have presumed that all writing communicates something about the implied author to a reader (even Nathalie Sarraute, one of the writers Robbe-Grillet often refers to in *For a New Novel,* postulates this communication process in the preface to her novel, *Tropisms*). With the presumption of communication, we may as well add the postulate that all genres of the short story communicate as if told or spoken. The difference between genres is one of degree.

Roland Barthes asserts that "writing is a hardened language which leads an independent existence. . . ."[7] We are able to agree without much effort that written language bears something of the character of inscription. However, Barthes' statement ignores two of the central characteristics of language in the story: first, within written language there are widely varying degrees of hardness, and, second, none of the language in a story leads an independent existence; almost everything we say about stories, from posture to the interestedness of language, is a description of dependence.

In order to understand this dependence most clearly, we might pick an example of the story which varies widely from the genre of the tale, such as William Gass' "Order of Insects." Here, I think, we find that we have very little interest in the discoverable author behind the work; we feel as though we are overhearing a mind or a solitary persona thinking to herself. Further, without an active interest in the enunciative posture (which interest always exists, nonetheless, at least passively), we listen to this anonymous woman's voice and find ourselves concerned with what her words mean, not with how her words characterize a person. In other words, since the voice is disembodied, our energy is focused on deciphering the highly symbolic language.

Within a story, then, words that can be associated with the voice of the implied author differ greatly from those written as if spoken by a disembodied, anonymous persona, and both of these kinds of words differ from those written as if told to an implied audience by a narrator such as Conrad's Marlow. Thus, calling written language "hardened" in relation to spoken language simply acknowledges the already implicit character of writing and even ignores much of the problem of reading. Once a word is read and the reader passes on from it, the character of the read-word becomes increasingly more fluid, receding, as it does, into the reader's memory. It is the awareness of this increasing fluidity which forces story writers to jog the reader's memory by repeating a phrase, a word, an analogy or metaphor, if they wish the reader to make a connection between what is being read and what has been read five or six pages before. Therefore, the taxonomy of language as written or spoken becomes, for the critic of the story, not false but inadequate for his purposes. He must pay attention to how the word was written or spoken and who wrote it or said it; he must pay attention to source and degree.

A large amount of banter travels to and fro between writers and theorists about the oral traditions of literature, focusing on the oral roots of poetry. But poetry alone cannot claim to be related to this tradition, this nature, since all classes of literature produce varying sensations of oralness in the reader's mind. The level of oration, then, indicates the relative degree of the reader's sense that he is being told a story, and, combined with other distinctions such as posture, will enable us to describe our sense of both the reader's and the writer's experiences of story-telling techniques—of how stories are told. These degrees range from a very high level of oration (the legend or tale) to the story in which the oral sense is subdued, erased, or disembodied, and these degrees can be schematized in the following manner:

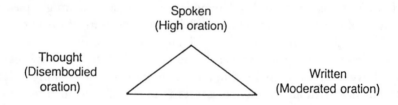

Finally, the levels of oration lead us to our last broad distinction, that of the kind of language used. Northrop Frye, among others, believes that the lyric poem uses "disinterested" language.[8] Since his description of disinterested language seems to be equivalent to what Cassirer called symbolic and we called metonymic language (see above), and since we know that the use of language varies tremendously within all classes of literature, we may suppose that the language of the story becomes increasingly disinterested as the genre approaches the level of disembodied oration. Thus, we can lay a trigrammatic structure over that of the level of oration:

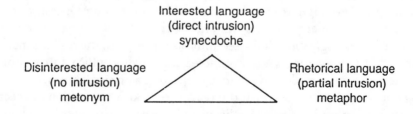

By interested language, we mean the language which directly signifies one thing, one meaning (in its purest form); and, on the highest level of oration, this allows for the implied author, or the author himself, to intrude to suggest how the reader is to take things. By rhetorical language, we mean that the implied author uses, and is discoverable by means of, isolated words which modify (adjectives, adverbs, or metaphors). By disinterested, then, we mean a highly symbolic language which addresses the reader intellectually or philosophically or abstractly, allowing several levels of interpretation, but forbidding the positive discovery of the implied author (Borges and Gass are different but adequate examples), forbidding the discovery, that is, by means of the language alone.

We have reached the point, now, where we can posit the main trigram of the short story. Again, we must remember that the vectors connecting each genre flow both ways, in order to prevent the scheme from becoming static. Thus, we have three genres, all in an active relationship to each other in this fashion:

Tale

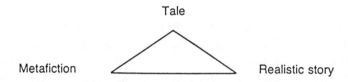

Metafiction   Realistic story

In discussing *Wuthering Heights,* Frye says:

> The shape of the plot is different: instead of manoeuvering around a central situation, as Jane Austen does, Emily Bronte tells her story with linear accents. . . . a form which we shall here call the romance. Here again, we have to use the same word in several different contexts, but romance seems on the whole better than tale, which appears to fit a somewhat shorter form [my emphasis.][9]

That Northrop Frye submits to the predominant confusion of the term "romance" is disappointing after such an intriguing first essay on modes. There is no more reason to use the same word in the same context—within the context of the novel—than to use Wittgenstein's "bububu."

However, this is slightly beside our point here, where we are concerned only with the first point of the story's trigram. This point is the genre of story called the tale, which is most often viewed wrongly as a derivative of the indescribable beast called the "romance." Tale, in this essay, by no means implies that the story's predominant mode is "romance." Indeed, many tales depend equally upon the interrelationship of two or more modes.

Linear accents are the sense the reader has of the historical nature of a work of literature, of how the events reflect backwards and forwards in chronological time, beyond the actual limits of the story. Thus, "the larger the scheme of a novel becomes, the more obviously its historical nature appears."[10] To adapt this statement to the genre of the tale, we might say that in order to enlarge its scheme, the tale emphasizes—begins and ends with—the diachronic background of historical time and events, against which the particular plot of events is placed.

Hawthorne's "My Kinsman, Major Molineux" begins:

> After the kings of Great Britain had assumed the right of appointing the colonial governors, the measures of the latter seldom met with the ready and general approbation which had been paid to those of their predecessors, under the original charters. . . . These remarks may serve as a preface to the following adventures, which chanced upon a summer's night, not far from a hundred years ago.[11]

These remarks are not merely prefatory but serve a definite and wholly conventional function: they place the tale against a broad ground of historical time and event and allow the particular tale to be synecdochally associated with, in this case, the "puberty" of a young country. (We might also note, out of curiosity, that Hawthorne uses the very same structure in "The Custom-House" and the opening of *The Scarlet Letter*, which he originally conceived of as a long tale.) By the author's use of this convention of the tale, Robin's quest for identity is directly related to the world of historical time and socio-political events. Were we to edit the first section of "My Kinsman," and begin it with, "It was near nine o'clock of a moonlight evening. . . ," we would move the tale slightly down the trigrammatic vector toward "realistic story," and the synecdochal associations mentioned above would then be made more metaphorically (analogically) by the reader.

Further, once we understand the convention of the opening of Hawthorne's tale, we can speak of its ending as being insincere (even though Frye claims that terms such as "insincere" are ways of laundering criticism), but insincere structurally, in that the tale would be more perfect in structure if it ended prior to the dream-coda which burdens the actual end of it. That is, the tale begins against a historical ground and returns to that same ground, which is continuous in time, with "On swept the tumult, and left a silent world behind." The coda which follows this sentence (often set apart by asterisks) contradicts the reader's sense of possible endings, adds nothing to the theme, and does not provide a significant aid to the reader's naturalization or interpretation of the tale's meaning.

In terms of posture, we might understand the contradiction even better. "My Kinsman" has a one-dimensional enunciative posture: the implied author who seems to be saying that it is tough to grow up whether you are a lad or a young country, and that things are not always what they seem on the surface. This posture, in this case, aligns with the historical grounding of the tale in time, psyche, and social action, and emphasizes broad historical process. The narrative posture, on the other hand, is essentially two-dimensional: Robin, "every-boy," speaks questions which are answered ambiguously by "Other"—by narrators who are not individualized, but are all aspects of the same problem to Robin. At the tale's end, the two dimensions tend to align with each other: Robin is at the point of breaking through the confusing appearances, of becoming individualized in the face of on-going history, of encountering himself in relation to the process of time and change. When the coda is added to the tale, the postures change radically and this alignment is wedged apart. Robin is no longer "everyboy," but just plain Robin; and the voice of the "Other" is transmuted into the kindly voice of the implied author who seems to desire the certainty that we have read the tale properly. The insincerity, therefore, is the confusion of the two sets of postures.

Similarly, Flaubert's "The Legend of St. Julian the Hospitaller" begins with the sense of broad history stretching out behind the tale we are about to "hear." Of course, the enunciative posture is implied for the reader in the title as well as in the opening of the tale, a saint's life which, in being re-told, may have a purpose different from the usual saint's life; and the diachronic historicity is lent emphasis by the use of the French medieval word, "hospitaller." But, unlike Hawthorne's coda, Flaubert's emphasizes the oral nature of this tale, and the last paragraph of "St. Julian" is therefore an important key to the meaning; "I am telling this tale," Flaubert suggests in this paragraph, "as an allegory of an aesthetic experience, rather than a religious one."

Further, the enunciative posture of Flaubert's tale coincides with the narrative posture, and this coincidence not only prevents the insincerity noted in Hawthorne's tale, but also tends to generate and justify the interested use of language in "St. Julian." This language is the use of archaisms and of a diction which is directly bold, extreme, yet simple. Phrases such as "he took unto himself a wife of high lineage" and "the little creatures dropped about him in multitudes" carry in them a Biblical, epochal sense. However, Flaubert's language, though simple, is not simply allegorized by the reader; the reader always has the sense that this or that word or phrase means something, but the interpretation of thematic levels is not explicitly directed by the enunciator, as it is in Hawthorne's tale.

So far, we have spoken of the historical ground of the tale. Frank Kermode, in *The Sense of an Ending,* provides two useful terms which can be adapted for the discussion of time: epoch and chronos.[12] Because of the established ground, the tale generally does not shift backwards against the flow of its own historicity (epoch). If time does change, it is the chronos which shifts forwards toward the possible ending created by the epoch, and this shift occurs most frequently at the tale's end in an effort to re-orient the chronos to the epoch, to bring the particular events into structural agreement with the broader background. Thus, we may think of epoch as "the implied fatefulness of time," as the seasonal cycles which relate every season in its nature to all seasons. Against the backdrop of this fatefulness exists the chronos, the "'passing time'" of the characters or events within the tale which, "according to Revelation, 'shall be no more.'"[13]

Not every work of literature which can be called a tale will fit as nicely into the schemata which have been set up thus far. If we combine the relationships of time, language, and posture, we discover that the fourth measure of the tale—the level of oration—divides into two possible categories. Some of Twain's or Poe's tales, or those of less known writers such as George Washington Harris, Augustus B. Longstreet, or T. B. Thorpe, tend to emphasize the narrative posture over the enunciative, to have a less defined epoch and a more immediate chronos, and to use a language that is rhetorical in its portrayal of regional or local dialect. Yet they certainly have the high level of oration of the tale. These tales, less concerned with portraying themes which transcend regional, national, or historical bounds, are more limited in their scope and seem to be interested in regional variations on local types or themes. In order to provide this sense of limitation, they use individualized narrators in one of two ways: they use a first-person narrator to report the ostensible tale of another narrator, or they use one third-person narrator (often the disguised embodiment of the enunciator) to preface the tale of the first-person narrator.

Since both kinds of tale depend on the reader's sense of a high level of oration, it seems reasonable to make our distinction between the two methods of oral presentation. This might be done by calling one the "radical" oral and the other the "exponential" oral. The radical oral is the kind found in the tales of Hawthorne and Flaubert. The exponential oral, on the other hand, is the kind we find in Harris' "Rare Ripe Garden Seed" or Twain's "Baker's Blue-jay Yarn."

For example, in Twain's tale, the enunciative posture exists less in the historical ground and more in the embodied, first-person narrator who introduces Baker's yarn and who is, then, present as an exponent of Baker's story. Thus, rather than setting the tale against the broad epochal ground, this narrator establishes both our attitude toward the tale and the kind of language the tale will use. Towards the end of his lengthy prefatory remarks, in which he recounts the discussion of himself by two ravens, the first narrator of Twain's tale says:

> Animals talk to each other, of course. There can be no question about that; but I suppose there are few people who can understand them. I never knew but one man who could. I knew he could, however, because he told me so himself. . . . This (man) was Jim Baker.[14]

After this, the exponent becomes not only the reporter of Jim Baker's yarn, but the listener, the "you" to whom Jim Baker tells his story. Also, since this enunciative-exponent exists only to introduce and then present, in a continuous quotation, the narrative posture, we are prevented from comparing or contrasting the dimensions of the enunciative and narrative postures. For the enunciative posture is not meant to have any real dimension. In addition, because the speaker never changes (only his diction and syntax change) the two postures never separate, and therefore do not have to re-align at the end of the tale.

We might, as we did with Hawthorne's "My Kinsman," edit out the prefatory remarks of the first narrator, and begin Twain's tale with Jim Baker's first words. By doing so and then contrasting what we have cut away, we can see that where Hawthorne's tale lost its ground of epochal history, Twain's loses only the embodied exponent of credibility, the first-person enunciator. Therefore, because it is narrowed in scope of time, Twain's tale depends for its breadth of effect on an expansion of detail, partly descriptive and partly in the use of dialect (which may or may not seem irrelevant to the development of theme). Thus, the language of the exponential oral is less interested than that of the radical oral since the emphasis is on the dialect of the narrator and not on that of the enunciator. Indeed, the tropical convention of the language, while synecdochal in many places, becomes increasingly metaphoric—like the language of the jays, it is "no mere commonplace language, . . . but rattling, out-and-out booktalk—and bristling with metaphor."[15]

If we examine the structure of this tale further, we can see how it contrasts with the structure of Hawthorne's and Flaubert's. Instead of a movement from epoch into the chronos of events and then back outwards to epoch, we find a continual narrowing in Twain's tale from a prefatory, chronological anecdote, down to the introduction of Jim Baker; then the prefatory remarks of Jim Baker (still reported by the enunciative-exponent) down to the anecdote of the Blue-jay. What we are interested in, in Twain's tale, is not the relation of the chronos (events) to epoch, but rather the comparison of Jim Baker's diction to the exponent's diction and the analogic relation of Jim Baker's detailed anecdote to the exponent's sketchy anecdote. Thus we can see that, unlike Hawthorne or Flaubert, Twain makes even the structure of his tale an analogue. Because of this, the reader's sense at the end of Twain's tale is not of the continuous relation of events to history, not of linear accents, but of the contained reflexive relations between two independent and anecdotal events. To summarize the difference more simply, the purer tale does not shift backwards against the flow of its events or theme, but Twain's does—at least thematically.

Nonetheless, the distinction between the radical oral and exponential oral should be understood as a distinction of kind and not of genre, since Twain's highly oral yarn is closer to the tale than to the realistic story. Still, without intending a value judgment, we might say that the voice which is unembodied in the tale, the voice of Time, of History, of God-the-author (enunciated by the implied author) is a purer form of the tale. For the exponential oral cuts or begins to cut away the background of epoch, replacing it with the first- or third-person narrator who prefaces the themes of the tale; it begins to mix its modes intentionally; and it forces the reader to use more than one tropical convention to interpret its meaning. These changes, then, indicate the beginnings of a movement away from the pure tale toward the realistic story. We are able to see what people call the "tall" tale as the result of writers' playing with convention. The tale which was stamped with verité or truth by the characters' existence in historical time moves toward the analogic structure and is lent reality by the exponent's claim to authority through the expansion or accretion of detail and the use of metaphoric language.

Historically, the earliest genre of the story—that most difficult and formal of prose forms—is the tale. However, this does not mean that a traditional tale cannot be written in the late twentieth century. Nor does it mean that a combination of elements from different genres could not be used by the story writer. What it means is that generic theory must evolve—grow or completely change—along with the development of new genres. The description of the tale as a genre of the story is only a beginning; yet, as long as we are able to describe the genre, structure, enunciative and narrative postures, mode, and tropical convention, the beginning is a valid one.

NOTES

1. Wallace Stegner, "Teaching the Short Story," in *Davis Publications in English* (Davis: University of California, Davis Press, Fall, 1965), No. 2, p. 3.

2. See Wayne C. Booth, *The Rhetoric of Fiction* (Chicago, 1961), pp. 36 ff.

3. Jonathan Culler, *Structuralist Poetics* (Ithaca, New York, 1976), p. 147.

4. Ernst Cassirer, *The Philosophy of Symbolic Forms: Language* (New Haven & London 1973), pp. 186–97.

5. George P. Elliott, *Conversions: Literature and the Modernist Deviation* (New York, 1973), p. 124.

6. Culler, p. 170.

7. *Ibid,* p. 133.

8. Northrop Frye, *Anatomy of Criticism* (Princeton, New Jersey, 1971), p. 4.

9. *Ibid,* p. 304.

10. *Ibid,* p. 306.

11. James H. Pickering, *Fiction 100* (New York, 1974), p. 419.

12. Frank Kermode, *The Sense of an Ending* (New York, 1970), pp. 44 ff. I have altered Mr. Kermode's terms slightly.

13. *Ibid,* p. 47.

14. Mark Twain, "The Blue-jay Yarn," *American Literature: Tradition and Innovation,* ed. Harrison T. Meserole, Walter Sutton, and Brom Weber (Lexington, Massachusetts, 1974), p. 2136.

15. *Ibid,* p. 2136.

PART TWO

Early Formalist Theories

Poe on
Short Fiction

EDGAR ALLAN POE

Review of Twice-Told Tales

WE SAID A FEW hurried words about Mr. Hawthorne in our last number, with the design of speaking more fully in the present. We are still, however, pressed for room, and must necessarily discuss his volumes more briefly and more at random than their high merits deserve.

The book professes to be a collection of *tales,* yet is, in two respects, misnamed. These pieces are now in their third republication, and, of course, are thrice-told. Moreover, they are by no means *all* tales, either in the ordinary or in the legitimate understanding of the term. Many of them are pure essays; for example, "Sights from a Steeple," "Sunday at Home," "Little Annie's Ramble," "A Rill from the Town Pump," "The Toll-Gatherer's Day," "The Haunted Mind," "The Sister Years," "Snow-Flakes," "Night Sketches," and "Foot-Prints on the Sea-Shore." We mention these matters chiefly on account of their discrepancy with that marked precision and finish by which the body of the work is distinguished.

Of the essays just named, we must be content to speak in brief. They are each and all beautiful, without being characterised by the polish and adaptation so visible in the tales proper. A painter would at once note their leading or predominant feature, and style it *repose.* There is no attempt at effect. All is quiet, thoughtful, subdued. Yet this repose may exist simultaneously with high originality of thought; and Mr. Hawthorne has demonstrated the fact. At every turn we meet with novel combinations; yet these combinations never surpass the limits of the quiet. We are soothed as we read; and withal is a calm astonishment that ideas so apparently obvious have never occurred or been presented to us before. Herein our author differs materially from Lamb or Hunt or Hazlitt—who, with vivid originality of manner and expression, have less of the true novelty of thought than is generally supposed, and whose originality, at best, has an uneasy and meretricious quaintness, replete with startling effects unfounded in nature, and inducing trains of reflection which lead to no satisfactory result. The Essays of Hawthorne have much of the character of Irving, with more of originality, and less of finish; while, compared with the Spectator, they have a vast superiority at all points. The Spectator, Mr. Irving, and Mr. Hawthorne have in common that tranquil and subdued manner which we have chosen to denominate *repose;* but, in the case of the two former, this repose is attained rather by the absence of novel combination, or of originality, than otherwise, and consists chiefly in the calm, quiet, unostentatious expression of common-place thoughts, in an unambitious, unadulterated Saxon. In them, by strong effort, we are made to conceive the absence of all. In the essays before us the absence of effort is too obvious to be mistaken, and a strong under current of *suggestion* runs continuously beneath the upper stream of the tranquil thesis. In short, these effusions of Mr. Hawthorne are the product of a truly imaginative intellect, restrained, and in some measure repressed, by fastidiousness of taste, by constitutional melancholy and by indolence.

But it is of his tales that we desire principally to speak. The tale proper, in our opinion, affords unquestionably the fairest field for the exercise of the loftiest talent, which can be afforded by the wide domains of mere prose. Were we bidden to say how the highest genius could be most advantageously employed for the best display of its own powers, we should answer, without hesitation—in the composition of a rhymed poem, not to exceed in length what might be perused in an hour. Within this limit alone can the highest order of true poetry exist. We need only here say, upon this topic, that, in almost all classes of composition, the unity of effect or impression is a point of the greatest importance. It is clear, moreover, that this unity cannot be thoroughly preserved in productions whose perusal cannot be completed at one sitting. We may continue the reading of a prose composition, from the very nature of prose itself, much longer than we can persevere, to any good purpose, in the perusal of a poem. This latter, if truly fulfilling the demands of the poetic sentiment, induces an exaltation of the soul which cannot be long sustained. All high excitements are necessarily transient. Thus a long poem is a paradox. And, without unity of impression, the deepest effects cannot be brought about. Epics were the offspring of an imperfect sense of Art, and their reign is no more. A poem *too* brief may produce a vivid, but never an intense or enduring impression. Without a certain continuity of effort—without a certain duration or repetition of purpose—the soul is never deeply moved. There must be the dropping of the water upon the rock. De Beranger has wrought brilliant things—pungent and spirit-stirring—but, like all immassive bodies, they lack *momentum,* and thus fail to satisfy the Poetic Sentiment. They sparkle and excite, but, from want of continuity, fail deeply to impress. Extreme brevity will degenerate into epigrammatism; but the sin of extreme length is even more unpardonable. *In medio tutissimus ibis.*

Were we called upon, however, to designate that class of composition which, next to such a poem as we have suggested, should best fulfil the demands of high genius—should offer it the most advantageous field of exertion—we should unhesitatingly speak of the prose tale, as Mr. Hawthorne has here exemplified it. We allude to the short prose narrative, requiring from a half-hour to one or two hours in its perusal. The ordinary novel is objectionable, from its length, for reasons already stated in substance. As it cannot be read at one sitting, it deprives itself, of course, of the immense force derivable from *totality.* Worldly interests intervening during the pauses of perusal, modify, annul, or counteract, in a greater or less degree, the impressions of the book. But simple cessation in reading, would, of itself, be sufficient to destroy the true unity. In the brief tale, however, the author is enabled to carry out the fullness of his intention, be it what it may. During the hour of perusal the soul of the reader is at the writer's control. There are no external or extrinsic influences—resulting from weariness or interruption.

A skilful literary artist has constructed a tale. If wise, he has not fashioned his thoughts to accommodate his incidents; but having conceived, with deliberate care, a certain unique or single *effect* to be wrought out, he then invents such incidents—he then combines such events as may best aid him in establishing this preconceived effect. If his very initial sentence tend not to the outbringing of this effect, then he has failed in his first step. In the whole composition there should be no word written, of which the tendency, direct or indirect, is not to be the one preestablished design. And by such means, with such care and skill, a picture is at length painted which leaves in the mind of him who contemplates it with a kindred art, a sense of the fullest satisfaction. The idea of the tale has been presented unblemished, because undisturbed; and this is an end unattainable by the novel. Undue brevity is just as exceptionable here as in the poem; but undue length is yet more to be avoided.

We have said that the tale has a point of superiority even over the poem. In fact, while the *rhythm* of this latter is an essential aid in the development of the poet's highest idea—the idea of the Beautiful—the artificialities of this rhythm are an inseparable bar to the development of all points of thought or expression which have their basis in *Truth*. But Truth is often, and in very great degree, the aim of the tale. Some of the finest tales are tales of ratiocination. Thus the field of this species of composition, if not in so elevated a region on the mountain of Mind, is a table-land of far vaster extent than the domain of the mere poem. Its products are never so rich, but infinitely more numerous, and more appreciable by the mass of mankind. The writer of the prose tale, in short, may bring to his theme a vast variety of modes or inflections of thought and expression—(the ratiocinative, for example, the sarcastic, or the humorous) which are not only antagonistical to the nature of the poem, but absolutely forbidden by one of its most peculiar and indispensable adjuncts; we allude, of course, to rhythm. It may be added here, *par parenthèse* that the author who aims at the purely beautiful in a prose tale is laboring at great disadvantage. For Beauty can be better treated in a poem. Not so with terror, or passion, or horror, or a multitude of such other points. And here it will be seen how full of prejudice are the usual animadversions against those *tales of effect*, many fine examples of which were found in the earlier numbers of Blackwood. The impressions produced were wrought in a legitimate sphere of action, and constituted a legitimate although sometimes an exaggerated interest. They were relished by every man of genius; although there were found many men of genius who condemned them without just ground. The true critic will but demand that the design intended be accomplished, to the fullest extent, by the means most advantageously applicable.

We have very few American tales of real merit—we may say, indeed, none, with the exception of "The Tales of a Traveller" of Washington Irving, and these "Twice-Told Tales" of Mr. Hawthorne. Some of the pieces of Mr. John Neal abound in vigor and originality; but in general, his compositions of this class are excessively diffuse, extravagant, and indicative of an imperfect sentiment of Art. Articles at random are, now and then, met with in our periodicals which might be advantageously compared with the best effusions of the British Magazines; but, upon the whole, we are far behind our progenitors in this department of literature.

Of Mr. Hawthorne's Tales we would say, emphatically, that they belong to the highest region of Art—an Art subservient to genius of a very lofty order. We had supposed, with good reason for so supposing, that he had been thrust into his present position by one of the impudent *cliques* which beset our literature, and whose pretensions it is our full purpose to expose at the earliest opportunity; but we have been most agreeably mistaken. We know of few compositions which the critic can more honestly commend than these "Twice-Told Tales." As Americans, we feel proud of the book.

Mr. Hawthorne's distinctive trait is invention, creation, imagination, originality—a trait which, in the literature of fiction, is positively worth all the rest. But the nature of originality, so far as regards its manifestation in letters, is but imperfectly understood. The inventive or original mind as frequently displays itself in novelty of *tone* as in novelty of matter. Mr. Hawthorne is original at *all* points.

It would be a matter of some difficulty to designate the best of these tales; we repeat that, without exception, they are beautiful. "Wakefield" is remarkable for the skill with which an old idea—a well-known incident— is worked up or discussed. A man of whims conceives the purpose of quitting his wife and residing *incognito,* for twenty years, in her immediate neighborhood. Something of this kind actually happened in London. The force of Mr. Hawthorne's tale lies in the analysis of the motives which must or might have impelled the husband to such folly, in the first instance, with the possible causes of his perseverance. Upon this thesis a sketch of singular power has been constructed.

"The Wedding Knell" is full of the boldest imagination—an imagination fully controlled by taste. The most captious critic could find no flaw in this production.

"The Minister's Black Veil" is a masterly composition of which the sole defect is that to the rabble its exquisite skill will be *caviare.* The *obvious* meaning of this article will be found to smother its insinuated one. The *moral* put into the mouth of the dying minister will be supposed to convey the *true* import of the narrative; and that a crime of dark dye (having reference to the "young lady"), has been committed, is a point which only minds congenial with that of the author will perceive.

"Mr. Higginbotham's Catastrophe" is vividly original and managed most dexterously.

"Dr. Heidegger's Experiment" is exceedingly well imagined, and executed with surpassing ability. The artist breathes in every line of it.

"The White Old Maid" is objectionable, even more than the "Minister's Black Veil," on the score of its mysticism. Even with the thoughtful and analytic, there will be much trouble in penetrating its entire import.

"The Hollow of the Three Hills," we would quote in full, had we space;—not as evincing higher talent than any of the other pieces, but as affording an excellent example of the author's peculiar ability. The subject is commonplace. A witch subjects the Distant and the Past to the view of a mourner. It has been the fashion to describe, in such cases, a mirror in which the images of the absent appear; or a cloud of smoke is made to arise, and thence the figures are gradually unfolded. Mr. Hawthorne has wonderfully heightened his effect by making the ear, in place of the eye, the medium by which the fantasy is conveyed. The head of the mourner is enveloped in the cloak of the witch, and within its magic folds there arise sounds which have an all-sufficient intelligence. Throughout this article also, the artist is conspicuous—not more in positive than in negative merits. Not only is all done that should be done, but (what perhaps is an end with more difficulty attained) there is nothing done which should not be. Every word *tells,* and there is not a word that does *not* tell. . . .

In the way of objection we have scarcely a word to say of these tales. There is, perhaps, a somewhat too general or prevalent *tone*—a tone of melancholy and mysticism. The subjects are insufficiently varied. There is not so much of *versatility* evinced as we might well be warranted in expecting from the high powers of Mr. Hawthorne. But beyond these trivial exceptions we have really none to make. The style is purity itself. Force abounds. High imagination gleams from every page. Mr. Hawthorne is a man of the truest genius. We only regret that the limits of our Magazine will not permit us to pay him that full tribute of commendation, which, under other circumstances, we should be so eager to pay.

The Brief Article

From "Watkins Tottle and Other Sketches," *Southern Literary Messenger,* June 1836.

It is not every one who can put "a good thing" properly together, although, perhaps, when thus properly put together, every tenth person you meet may be capable of both conceiving and appreciating it. We cannot bring ourselves to believe that less actual ability is required in the composition of a really good "brief article," than in a fashionable novel of the usual dimensions. The novel certainly requires what is denominated a sustained effort—but this is a matter of mere perseverance, and has but a collateral relation to talent. On the other hand—unity of effect, a quality not easily appreciated or indeed comprehended by an ordinary mind, and a *desideratum* difficult of attainment, even by those who can conceive it— is indispensable in the "brief article," and not so in the common novel. The latter, if admired at all, is admired for its detached passages, without reference to the work as a whole—or without reference to any general design—which, if it even exist in some measure, will be found to have occupied but little of the writer's attention, and cannot, from the length of the narrative, be taken in at one view, by the reader.

Totality of Interest

From a review of *Zinzendorff, and Other Poems* by L. H.. Sigourney, *Southern Literary Messenger,* January 1836.

In poems of magnitude the mind of the reader is not, at all times, enabled to include in one comprehensive survey the proportions and proper adjustment of the whole. He is pleased—if at all—with particular passages; and the sum of his pleasure is compounded of the sums of the pleasurable sensations inspired by these individual passages during the progress of perusal. But in pieces of less extent—like the poems of Mrs. Sigourney—the pleasure is *unique,* in the proper acceptation of that term—the understanding is employed, without difficulty, in the contemplation of the picture *as a whole*—and thus its effect will depend, in a very great degree, upon the perfection of its finish, upon the nice adaptation of its constituent parts, and especially upon what is rightly termed by Schlegel, the *unity or totality of interest.*

Unity of Plot

From a review of *Night and Morning: A Novel* by Edward Bulwer-Lytton, *Graham's Magazine,* April 1841.

The word *plot,* as commonly accepted, conveys but an indefinite meaning. Most persons think of it as simple *complexity;* and into this error even so fine a critic as Augustus William Schlegel has obviously fallen, when he confounds its idea with that of the mere *intrigue* in which the Spanish dramas of Cervantes and Calderon abound. But the greatest involution of incident will not result in plot; which, properly defined, is *that which no part can be displaced without ruin to the whole.* It may be described as a building so dependently constructed, that to change the position of a single brick is to overthrow the entire fabric. In this definition and description, we of course refer only to that infinite perfection which the true artist bears ever in mind—that unattainable goal to which his eyes are always directed, but of the possibility of attaining which he still endeavors, if wise, to cheat himself into the belief. The reading world, however, is satisfied with a less rigid construction of the term. It is content to think that plot a good one, in which none of the *leading* incidents can be *removed* without *detriment* to the mass. . . .

Without excessive and fatiguing exertion, inconsistent with legitimate interest, the mind cannot comprehend at one time, and in one survey, the numerous individual items which go to establish the whole. Thus the high ideal sense of the *unique* is sure to be wanting:—for, however absolute in itself be the unity of the novel, it must inevitably fail of appreciation. We speak now of that species of unity which is alone worth the attention of the critic—the unity or totality *of effect.*

Mystery

From a review of *Barnaby Rudge* by Charles Dickens, *Graham's Magazine,* February 1842.

We have given, as may well be supposed, but a very meagre outline of the story, and we have given it in the simple or natural sequence. That is to say, we have related the events, as nearly as might be, in the order of their occurrence. But this order would by no means have suited the purpose of the novelist, whose design has been to maintain the secret of the murder, and the consequent mystery which encircles Rudge, and the actions of his wife, until the catastrophe of his discovery by Haredale. The *thesis* of the novel may thus be regarded as based upon curiosity. Every point is so arranged as to perplex the reader, and whet his desire for elucidation. . . .

Now there can be no question that, by such means as these, many points which are comparatively insipid in the natural sequence of our digest, and which would have been comparatively insipid even if given in full detail in a natural sequence, are endued with the interest of mystery; but neither can it be denied that a vast many more points are at the same time deprived of all effect, and become null, through the impossibility of comprehending them without the key. . . . But the reader may easily satisfy himself of the validity of our objection. Let him *re-peruse Barnaby Rudge,* and, with a pre-comprehension of the mystery, these points of which we speak break out in all directions like stars, and throw quadruple brilliance over the narrative—a brilliance which a correct taste will at once declare unprofitably sacrificed at the shrine of the keenest interest of mere mystery.

The Philosophy of Composition

Charles Dickens, in a note now lying before me, alluding to an examination I once made of the mechanism of *Barnaby Rudge,* says—"By the way, are you aware that Godwin wrote his *Caleb Williams* backwards? He first involved his hero in a web of difficulties, forming the second volume, and then, for the first, cast about him for some mode of accounting for what had been done."

I cannot think this the *precise* mode of procedure on the part of Godwin—and indeed what he himself acknowledges, is not altogether in accordance with Mr. Dickens' idea—but the author of *Caleb Williams* was too good an artist not to perceive the advantage derivable from at least a somewhat similar process. Nothing is more clear than that every plot, worth the name, must be elaborated to its *dénouement* before any thing be attempted with the pen. It is only with the *dénouement* constantly in view that we can give a plot its indispensable air of consequence, or causation, by making the incidents, and especially the tone at all points, tend to the development of the intention.

There is a radical error, I think, in the usual mode of constructing a story. Either history affords a thesis—or one is suggested by an incident of the day—or, at best, the author sets himself to work in the combination of striking events to form merely the basis of his narrative—designing, generally, to fill in with description, dialogue, or autorial comment, whatever crevices of fact, or action, may, from page to page, render themselves apparent.

I prefer commencing with the consideration of an *effect.* Keeping originality *always* in view—for he is false to himself who ventures to dispense with so obvious and so easily attainable a source of interest—I say to myself, in the first place, "Of the innumerable effects, or impressions, of which the heart, the intellect, or (more generally) the soul is susceptible, what one shall I, on the present occasion, select?" Having chosen a novel, first, and secondly a vivid effect, I consider whether it can best be wrought by incident or tone—whether by ordinary incidents and peculiar tone, or the converse, or by peculiarity both of incident and tone—afterward looking about me (or rather within) for such combinations of event, or tone, as shall best aid me in the construction of the effect.

I have often thought how interesting a magazine paper might be written by any author who would—that is to say, who could—detail, step by step, the processes by which any one of his compositions attained its ultimate point of completion. Why such a paper has never been given to the world, I am much at a loss to say—but, perhaps, the autorial vanity has had more to do with the omission than any one other cause. Most writers—poets in especial—prefer having it understood that they compose by a species of fine frenzy—an ecstatic intuition—and would positively shudder at letting the public take a peep behind the scenes, at the elaborate and vacillating crudities of thought—at the true purposes seized only at the last moment—at the innumerable glimpses of idea that arrived not at the maturity in full view—at the fully matured fancies discarded in despair as unmanageable—at the cautious selections and rejections—at the painful erasures and interpolations—in a word, at the wheels and pinions—the tackle for scene-shifting—the step-ladders and demon-traps—the cock's feathers, the red paint and the black patches, which, in ninety-nine cases out of the hundred, constitute the properties of the literary *histrio*.

I am aware, on the other hand, that the case is by no means common, in which an author is at all in condition to retrace the steps by which his conclusions have been attained. In general, suggestions, having arisen pell-mell, are pursued and forgotten in a similar manner.

For my own part, I have neither sympathy with the repugnance alluded to, nor, at any time, the least difficulty in recalling to mind the progressive steps of any of my compositions; and, since the interest of an analysis, or reconstruction, such as I have considered a *desideratum,* is quite independent of any real or fancied interest in the thing analyzed, it will not be regarded as a breach of decorum on my part to show the *modus operandi* by which some one of my own works was put together. I select "The Raven," as the most generally known. It is my design to render it manifest that no one point in its composition is referrible either to accident or intuition—that the work proceeded, step by step, to its completion with the precision and rigid consequence of a mathematical problem.

Let us dismiss, as irrelevant to the poem *per se,* the circumstance—or say the necessity—which, in the first place, gave rise to the intention of composing a poem that should suit at once the popular and the critical taste.

We commence, then, with this intention.

The initial consideration was that of extent. If any literary work is too long to be read at one sitting, we must be content to dispense with the immensely important effect derivable from unity of impression—for, if two sittings be required, the affairs of the world interfere, and every thing like totality is at once destroyed. But since, *ceteris paribus,* no poet can afford to dispense with *any thing* that may advance his design, it but remains to be seen whether there is, in extent, any advantage to counterbalance the loss of unity which attends it. Here I say no, at once. What we term a long poem is, in fact, merely a succession of brief ones—that is to say, of brief poetical effects. It is needless to demonstrate that a poem is such, only inasmuch as it intensely excites, by elevating, the soul; and all intense excitements are, through a psychal necessity, brief. For this reason, at least one half of the *Paradise Lost* is essentially prose—a succession of poetical excitements interspersed, *inevitably,* with corresponding depressions—the whole being deprived, through the extremeness of its length, of the vastly important artistic element, totality, or unity, of effect.

It appears evident, then, that there is a distinct limit, as regards length, to all works of literary art—the limit of a single sitting—and that, although in certain classes of prose composition, such as *Robinson Crusoe,* (demanding no unity,) this limit may be advantageously overpassed, it can never properly be overpassed in a poem. Within this limit, the extent of a poem may be made to bear mathematical relation to its merit—in other words, to the excitement or elevation—again in other words, to the degree of the true poetical effect which it is capable of inducing; for it is clear that the brevity must be in direct ratio of the intensity of the intended effect:—this, with one proviso—that a certain degree of duration is absolutely requisite for the production of any effect at all.

Eureka

To the few who love me and whom I love—to those who feel rather than to those who think—to the dreamers and those who put faith in dreams as in the only realities—I offer this Book of Truths, not in its character of Truth-Teller, but for the Beauty that abounds in its Truth; constituting it true. To these I present the composition as an Art-product alone,—let us say as a Romance; or, if I be not urging too lofty a claim, as a Poem.

What I here propound is true:—therefore it cannot die:—or if by any means it be now trodden down so that it die, it will "rise again to the Life Everlasting."

Nevertheless, it is as a Poem only that I wish this work to be judged after I am dead.

E. A. P.

My general proposition, then, is this:—*In the Original Unity of the First Thing lies the Secondary Cause of All Things, with the Germ of their Inevitable Annihilation.* . . .

I now assert—that an intuition altogether irresistible, although inexpressible, forces me to the conclusion that what God originally created—that Matter which, by dint of his Volition he first made from his spirit, or from Nihility, could have been nothing but Matter in its utmost conceivable state of—what?—of *Simplicity?* . . .

Let us now endeavor to conceive what Matter must be when, or if, in its absolute extreme of *Simplicity.* Here the Reason flies at once to Imparticularity—to a particle—to *one* particle—a particle of *one* kind—of one character—of *one* nature—of *one* size—of *one* form—a particle therefore, "*without form and void*"—a particle positively a particle at all points—a particle absolutely unique, individual, undivided, and not indivisible only because He created it, by dint of his Will, can by an infinitely less energetic exercise of the same Will, as a matter of course, divide it.

Oneness, then, is all that I predicate of the originally created Matter; but I propose to show that this *Oneness is a principle abundantly sufficient to account for the constitution, the existing phenomena, and the plainly inevitable annihilation of at least the material Universe.* . . .

This constitution has been effected by *forcing* the originally and therefore normally *One* into the abnormal condition of *Many.* An action of this character implies reaction. A diffusion from Unity, under the conditions, involves a tendency to return into Unity—a tendency ineradicable until satisfied. . . .

Unless we are to conceive that the appetite for Unity among the atoms is doomed to be satisfied *never;*—unless we are to conceive that what had a beginning is to have no end—a conception which cannot *really* be entertained, however much we may talk or dream of entertaining it—we are forced to conclude that the repulsive influence imagined, will, finally—under pressure of the *Uni-tendency collectively* applied, but never and in no degree *until,* on fulfillment of the Divine purposes, such collective application shall be naturally made—yield to a force which, at that ultimate epoch, shall be the superior force precisely to the extent required and thus permit the universal subsidence into the inevitable, because original and therefore normal, *One.* . . .

Every atom, of every body, attracts every other atom, both of its own and of every other body, with a force which varies inversely as the squares of the distance between the attracting and attracted atom. . . . Does not so evident a brotherhood among the atoms point to a common parentage? Does not a sympathy so omniprevalent, so ineradicable, and so thoroughly irrespective, suggest a common paternity at its source? . . . In a word, is it not because the atoms were, at some remote epoch of time, even *more than together*—is it not because originally, and therefore normally, they were *One*—that one in all circumstances—at all points—in all directions— by all modes of approach—in all relations and through all conditions— they struggle *back* to this absolutely, this irrelatively, this unconditionally *one?* . . .

In Divine constructions the object is either design or object as we choose to regard it—and we may take at any time a cause for an effect, or the converse—so that we can never absolutely decide which is which. . . .

The pleasure which we derive from any display of human ingenuity is in the ratio of *the approach* to this series of reciprocity. In the construction of *plot,* for example, in fictitious literature, we should aim at so arranging the incidents that we shall not be able to determine, of any one of them, whether it depends from any one other or upholds it. In this sense, of course *perfection of plot* is really or practically unattainable— but only because it is a finite intelligence that constructs. The plots of God are perfect. The Universe is a plot of God. . . .

The sense of the symmetrical is an instinct which may be depended upon with an almost blindfold reliance. It is the poetical essence of the Universe—*of the Universe* which, in the supremeness of its symmetry, is but the most sublime of poems. Now symmetry and consistency are convertible terms:—thus Poetry and Truth are one. A thing is consistent in the ratio of its truth—true in the ratio of its consistency. *A perfect consistency, I repeat, can be nothing but an absolute truth.* We may take it for granted, then, that man cannot long or widely err if he suffer himself to be guided by his poetical, which I have maintained to be his truthful, in being his symmetrical, instinct. . . .

The cycles of the Universe are perpetual—the Universe has no conceivable end. Had an end been demonstrated, however, from so purely collateral a cause as an ether, Man's instinct of the Divine *capacity to adapt,* would have rebelled against the demonstration. We should have been forced to regard the Universe with some sense of dissatisfaction as we experience in contemplating an unnecessarily complex work of human art. Creation would have affected us as an imperfect *plot* in a romance, where the *dénoument* is awkwardly brought about by interposed incidents external and foreign to the main subject; instead of springing out of the bosom of the thesis—out of the heart of the ruling idea—instead of arising as a result of the primary proposition—as inseparable and inevitable part and parcel of the fundamental conception of the book. . . .

The Philosophy of
the Short-Story

BRANDER MATTHEWS

THE DIFFERENCE between a Novel and a Novelet is one of length only: a
Novelet is a brief Novel. But the difference between a Novel and a Short-
story is a difference of kind. A true Short-story is something other and
something more than a mere story which is short. A true Short-story
differs from the Novel chiefly in its essential unity of impression. In a far
more exact and precise use of the word, a Short-story has unity as a Novel
cannot have it.[1] Often, it may be noted by the way, the Short-story fulfils
the three false unities of the French classic drama: it shows one action, in
one place, on one day. A Short-story deals with a single character, a single
event, a single emotion, or the series of emotions called forth by a single
situation. Poe's paradox[2] that a poem cannot greatly exceed a hundred
lines in length under penalty of ceasing to be one poem and breaking into
a string of poems, may serve to suggest the precise difference between the
Short-story and the Novel. The Short-story is the single effect, complete
and self-contained, while the Novel is of necessity broken into a series of
episodes. Thus the Short-story has, what the Novel cannot have, the
effect of "totality," as Poe called it, the unity of impression.

Of a truth the Short-story is not only a chapter out of a Novel, or an
incident or an episode extracted from a longer tale, but at its best it
impresses the reader with the belief that it would be spoiled if it were
made larger, or if it were incorporated into a more elaborate work. The
difference in spirit and in form between the Lyric and the Epic is scarcely
greater than the difference between the Short-story and the Novel; and
the "Raven" and "How we brought the good news from Ghent to Aix"
are not more unlike the "Lady of the Lake" and "Paradise Lost," in form
and in spirit, than the "Luck of Roaring Camp," and the "Man without a

Country," two typical Short-stories, are unlike "Vanity Fair" and the "Heart of Midlothian," two typical Novels.

Another great difference between the Short-story and the Novel lies in the fact that the Novel, nowadays at least, must be a love-tale, while the Short-story need not deal with love at all. Although there are to be found by diligent search a few Novels which are not love-tales—and of course "Robinson Crusoe" is the example that swims at once into recollection—yet the immense majority of Novels have the tender passion either as the motive power of their machinery or as the pivot on which their plots turn. Although "Vanity Fair" was a Novel without a hero, nearly every other Novel has a hero and a heroine; and the novelist, however unwillingly, must concern himself in their love-affairs. . . .

While the Novel cannot get on easily without love, the Short-story can. Since love seems to be almost the only thing which will give interest to a long story, the writer of Novels has to get love into his tales as best he may, even when the subject rebels and when he himself is too old to take any delight in the mating of John and Joan. But the Short-story, being brief, does not need a love-interest to hold its parts together, and the writer of Short-stories has thus a greater freedom; he may do as he pleases; from him a love-tale is not expected.[3]

But other things are required of a writer of Short-stories which are not required of a writer of Novels. The novelist may take his time; he has abundant room to turn about. The writer of Short-stories must be concise, and compression, a vigorous compression, is essential. For him, more than for any one else, the half is more than the whole. Again, the novelist may be commonplace, he may bend his best energies to the photographic reproduction of the actual; if he show us a cross-section of real life we are content; but the writer of Short-stories must have originality and ingenuity. If to compression, originality, and ingenuity he add also a touch of fantasy, so much the better.

In fact, it may be said that no one has ever succeeded as a writer of Short-stories who had not ingenuity, originality, and compression; and that most of those who have succeeded in this line had also the touch of fantasy. But there are not a few successful novelists lacking, not only in fantasy and compression, but also in ingenuity and originality; they had other qualities, no doubt, but these they had not. If an example must be given, the name of Anthony Trollope will occur to all. Fantasy was a thing he abhorred; compression he knew not; and originality and ingenuity can be conceded to him only by a strong stretch of the ordinary meaning of the words. Other qualities he had in plenty, but not these. And, not having them, he was not a writer of Short-stories. Judging from his essay on

Hawthorne, one may even go so far as to say that Trollope did not know a good Short-story when he saw it.

I have written "Short-stories" with a capital S and a hyphen because I wished to emphasize the distinction between the Short-story and the story which is merely short. The Short-story is a high and difficult department of fiction. The story which is short can be written by anybody who can write at all; and it may be good, bad, or indifferent; but at its best it is wholly unlike the Short-story. In "An Editor's Tales" Trollope has given us excellent specimens of the story which is short; and the narratives which make up this book are amusing enough and clever enough, but they are wanting in the individuality and in the completeness of the genuine Short-story. Like the brief tales to be seen in the British monthly magazines and in the Sunday editions of American newspapers into which they are copied, they are, for the most part, either merely amplified anecdotes or else incidents which might have been used in a Novel just as well as not.

Now, it cannot be said too emphatically that the genuine Short-story abhors the idea of the Novel. It neither can be conceived as part of a Novel, nor can it be elaborated and expanded so as to form a Novel. A good Short-story is no more the synopsis of a Novel than it is an episode from a Novel. A slight Novel, or a Novel cut down, is a Novelet: it is not a Short-story. Mr. Howells's "Their Wedding Journey" and Miss Howard's "One Summer" are Novelets,—little Novels, Mr. Anstey's "Vice Versa," Mr. Besant's "Case of Mr. Lucraft," Hugh Conway's "Called Back," Mr. Julian Hawthorne's "Archibald Malmaison," and Mr. Stevenson's "Strange Case of Dr. Jekyll and Mr. Hyde" are Short-stories in conception although they are without the compression which the Short-story requires. . . .

It is to be noted as a curious coincidence that there is no exact word in English to designate either *vers de société* or the Short-story, and yet in no language are there better *vers de socité* or Short-stories than in English. It may be remarked also that there is a certain likeness between *vers de société* and Short-stories: for one thing, both seem easy to write and are hard. And the typical qualifications of each may apply with almost equal force to the other: *vers de société* should reveal compression, ingenuity, and originality, and Short-stories should have brevity and brilliancy. In no class of writing are neatness of construction and polish of execution more needed than in the writing of *vers de société* and of Short-stories. The writer of Short-stories must have the sense of form, which has well been called "the highest and last attribute of a creative writer." The construction must always be logical, adequate, harmonious.

Here is a weak spot in Mr. W. H. Bishop's "One of the Thirty Pieces,"
the fundamental idea of which—that fatality awaits every successive pos-
sessor of every one of the coins paid to Judas for his betrayal of Jesus—has
genuine strength, not fully developed in the story. But other of Mr.
Bishop's stories—the "Battle of Bunkerloo," for instance—are admirable
in all ways, conception and execution having an even excellence. Again,
Hugh Conway's, "Daughter of the Stars" is a Short-story which fails from
sheer deficiency of style: here is one of the very finest Short-story ideas—
the startling and fascinating fantasy that by sheer force of will a man
might have been able to draw down from the depths of the sky a lovely
astral maid to share his finite human life—ever given to any mortal, but
the handling is at best barely sufficient. To do justice to the conception
would tax the execution of a poet. We could merely wonder what the tale
would have been had it occurred to Hawthorne, to Poe, or to Theophile
Gautier. An idea logically developed by one possessing the sense of form
and the gift of style is what we look for in the Short-story.

But, although the sense of form and the gift of style are essential to the
writing of a good Short-story, they are secondary to the idea, to the conception, to the subject. Those who hold, with a certain American novelist,
that it is no matter what you have to say, but only how you say it, need not
attempt the Short-story; for the Short-story, far more than the Novel
even, demands a subject. The Short-story is nothing if there is no story to
tell;—one might almost say that a Short-story is nothing if it has no
plot,—except that "plot" may suggest to some readers a complication and
elaboration which are not really needful. But a plan—if this word is less
liable to misconception than "plot"—a plan a Short-story must have,
while it would be easy to cite Novels of eminence which are wholly
amorphous—for example, "Tristram Shandy."

Whatever its length, the Novel, so Mr. Henry James told us not long
ago, "is, in its broadest definition, a personal impression of life." The
most powerful force in French fiction today is M. Emile Zola, chiefly
known in America and England, I fear me greatly, by the dirt which masks
and degrades the real beauty and firm strength not seldom concealed in
his novels; and M. Emile Zola declares that the novelist of the future will
not concern himself with the artistic evolution of a plot: he will take *une
histoire quelconque,* any kind of a story, and make it serve his purpose,—
which is to give elaborate pictures of life in all its most minute details.

It is needless to say that the acceptance of these stories is a negation of
the Short-story. Important as are form and style, the subject of the Short-
story is of more importance yet. What you have to tell is of greater inter-

est than how you tell it. . . . As a Short-story need not be a love-story, it
is of no consequence at all whether they marry or die; but a Short-story in
which nothing happens at all is an absolute impossibility.

Perhaps the difference between a Short-story and a Sketch can best be
indicated by saying that, while a Sketch may be still-life, in a Short-story
something always happens. A Sketch may be an outline of character, or
even a picture of a mood of mind, but in a Short-story there must be
something done, there must be an action.[4] Yet the distinction, like that
between the Novel and the Romance, is no longer of vital importance in
the preface to the "House of the Seven Gables," Hawthorne sets forth the
difference between the Novel and the Romance, and claims for himself
the privileges of the romancer. Mr. Henry James[5] fails to see this difference. The fact is, that the Short-story and the Sketch, the Novel and the
Romance, melt and merge one into the other, and no man may mete the
boundaries of each, though their extremes lie far apart. With the more
complete understanding of the principle of development and evolution in
literary art, as in physical nature, we see the futility of a strict and rigid
classification into precisely defined genera and species. All that is needful
for us to remark now is that the Short-story has limitless possibilities: it
may be as realistic as the most prosaic novel, or as fantastic as the most
ethereal romance.

The Short-story should not be void or without form, but its form may
be whatever the author please. He has an absolute liberty of choice. It may
be a personal narrative, like Poe's "Descent into the Maelstrom" or Mr.
Hale's "My Double, and how he Undid me"; it may be impersonal, like
Mr. Frederick B. Perkins's "Devil-Puzzlers" or Colonel J. W. De Forest's
"Brigade Commander"; it may be a conundrum, like Mr. Stockton's insol-
uble query, the "Lady or the Tiger?" it may be "A Bundle of Letters," like
Mr. Henry James's story, or "A Letter and a Paragraph," like Mr. Bunner's;
it may be a medley of letters and telegrams and narrative, like Mr. Aldrich's
"Margery Daw"; it may be cast in any one of these forms, or in a combination of all of them, or in a wholly new form, if haply such may yet be
found by diligent search. Whatever its form, it should have symmetry of
design. If it have also wit or humour, pathos or poetry, and especially a
distinct and unmistakable flavour of individuality, so much the better.[6]
But the chief requisites are compression, originality, ingenuity, and now
and again a touch of fantasy. Sometimes we may detect in a writer of
Short-stories a tendency toward the over-elaboration of ingenuity, toward
the exhibition of ingenuity for its own sake, as in a Chinese puzzle. But

mere cleverness is incompatible with greatness, and to commend a writer as "very clever" is not to give him high praise. From this fault of super-subtlety, women are free for the most part. They are more likely than men to rely on broad human emotion, and their tendency in error is toward the morbid analysis of a high-strung moral situation.

The more carefully we study the history of fiction the more clearly we perceive that the Novel and the Short-story are essentially different—that the difference between them is not one of mere length only, but funda-mental. The Short-story seeks one set of effects in its own way, and the Novel seeks a wholly distinct set of effects in a wholly distinct way. We are led also to the conclusion that the Short-story—in spite of the fact that in our language it has no name of its own—is one of the few sharply defined literary forms. It is a *genre,* as M. Brunetière terms it, a species, as a naturalist might call it, as individual as the Lyric itself and as various. It is as distinct an entity as the Epic, as Tragedy, as Comedy. Now the Novel is not a form of the same sharply defined individuality; it is—or at least it may be—anything. It is the child of the Epic and the heir of the Drama; but it is a hybrid. And one of the foremost of living American novelists, who happens also to be one of the most acute and sympathetic of Ameri-can critics, has told me that he has often distracted by the knowledge of this fact even while he was engaged in writing a novel.

In the history of literature the Short-story was developed long before the Novel, which indeed is but a creature of yesterday, and which was not really established in popular esteem as a worthy rival of the drama until after the widespread success of the Waverley Novels in the early years of the nineteenth century. The Short-story also seems much easier of accom-plishment than the Novel, if only because it is briefer. And yet the list of the masters of the Short-story is far less crowded than the list of the mas-ters of the longer form. There are a score or more very great novelists recorded in the history of fiction; but there are scarcely more than half a score Short-story writers of an equal eminence.

From Chaucer and Boccaccio we must spring across the centuries until we come to Hawthorne and Poe almost without finding another name that insists upon enrolment. In these five hundred years there were great novelists not a few, but there was no great writer of Short-stories. A little later than Hawthorne and Poe, and indeed almost contemporaneous with them, are Mérimée and Turgenef, whose title to be recorded there is none to dispute. Now at the end of the nineteenth century we find two more that no competent critic would dare to omit,—Guy de Maupassant and Rudyard Kipling.

NOTES

1. In a letter to a friend, Stevenson lays down the law with his usual direct-ness: "Make another end to it? Ah, yes, but that's not the way I write; the whole tale is implied; I never use an effect when I can help it, unless it prepares the effects that are to follow; that's what a story consists in. To make another end, that is to make the beginning all wrong. The denouement of a long story is nothing, it is just 'a full close,' which you may approach and accompany as you please—it is a coda, not an essential member in the rhythm; but the body and end of a short-story is bone of the bone and blood of the blood of the beginning." *Vailima Letters,* Vol. I, p. 147.

2. See his essay on "The Philosophy of Composition," to be found in the sixth volume of the collected edition of his works, prepared by Messrs. Stedman and Woodberry.

3. In an essay on "The Local Short-story" contributed to the *Independent* for March 11, 1892, Colonel T. W. Higginson points out the disadvantages the novel-ist labours under when he knows that his work is to be published in instalments; and he declares that this possible serial publication "affords the justification of the short-story. For here, at least, we have the conditions of perfect art; there is no sub-division of interest; the author can strike directly in, without preface, can move with determined step toward a conclusion, and can—O highest privilege!—stop when he is done. For the most perfect examples of the short-story—those of De Maupassant, for instance—the reader feels, if he can pause to think, that they must have been done at a sitting, so complete is the grasp, the single grasp, upon the mind. This completeness secures the end; they need not be sensational, because there is no necessity of keeping up a series of exciting minor incidents; the main incident is enough. Around the very centre of motion, as in a whirl-wind, there may be a perfect quiet, a quiet which is formidable in its very response. In De Maupassant's terrific story of Corsican vengeance, "Une Ven-detta," in which the sole actor is a lonely old woman who trains a fierce dog so that he ultimately kills her enemy, the author simply tells us, at the end, that this quiet fiend of destruction went peacefully home and went to sleep. *Elle dormit bien, cette nuit-là.* The cyclone has spent itself, and the silence it has left behind it is more formidable than the cyclone."

4. This difference is considered briefly by Mr. F. B. Perkins in the character-istically clever preface to the volume of his ingenious Short-stories, which takes its title from the first and best—"Devil-Puzzlers" (New York: G. P. Putnam's Sons).

5. In the narrow but suggestive biography of Hawthorne contributed to Mr. John Morley's "English Men of Letters."

6. In a chatty and somewhat uncritical paper on the "Rise of the Short-story" contributed by Mr. Bret Harte to the "International Library of Famous Litera-ture" and published also in the *Cornhill Magazine* for July, 1899, we find the assertion that the secret of the American Short-story is "the treatment of charac-

teristic American life, with absolute knowledge of its peculiarities and sympathy with its methods, with no fastidious ignoring of its national expression, or the inchoate poetry that may be found hidden even in its slang; with no moral determination except that which may be the legitimate outcome of the story itself; with no more elimination than may be necessary for the artistic conception, and never from the fear of the fetish of conventionalism." This is cleverly phrased; but it is open to the obvious objection that it is not so much an adequate definition of the Short-story as a form as it is a defence of the special kind of Short-story Mr. Bret Harte himself had chosen to write.

O. Henry and
the Theory of
the Short Story

B. M. ÉJXENBAUM
Translated by I. R. Titunik

THE NOVEL AND THE short story are forms not only different in kind but also inherently at odds, and for that reason are never found being developed simultaneously and with equal intensity in any one literature. The novel is a syncretic form (whether its development be directly from collections of stories or complicated by the incorporation of manners-and-morals material); the short story is a fundamental, elementary (which does not mean primitive) form. The novel derives from history, from travels; the story—from folklore, anecdote. The difference is one of essence, a difference in principle conditioned by the fundamental distinction between *big* and *small* form. Not only individual writers but also individual literatures cultivate either the novel or the short story.

The story must be constructed on the basis of some contradiction, incongruity, error, contrast, etc. But that is not enough. By its very essence, the story, just as the anecdote, amasses its whole weight *toward the ending*. Like a bomb dropped from an airplane, it must speed downwards so as to strike with its war-head full-force on the target. I am speaking, of course, of the story of action, leaving aside stories of the sketch or *skaz*[1] type, typical, for instance, of Russian literature. Short story is a term referring exclusively to plot, one assuming a combination of two conditions: *small* size and *plot impact* on the ending. Conditions of this sort produce something totally distinct in aim and devices from the novel.

An enormous role is played in the novel by techniques of retardation [*texnika tormoženija*] and of linking and welding together disparate materials, by skill in deploying and binding together episodes, in creating diverse centers, in conducting parallel intrigues, and so on. With that sort of structuring, the ending of the novel is a point of let-up and not of intensification. The culmination of the main line of action must come somewhere *before the ending*. Typical for the novel are "epilogues"— false endings, summations setting the perspective or informing the reader of the *Nachgeschichte* of the main characters (cf. *Rudin. Vojna i mir* [*War and Peace*]). It is only natural, then that surprise endings should be a very rare occurrence in the novel (if encountered, then most likely testifying to the influence of the short story); big form and multiformity of episodes preclude that sort of construction. The short story, on the contrary, gravitates expressly toward maximal unexpectedness of a finale concentrating around itself all that has preceded. In the novel there must be a descent of some kind after the culmination point, whereas it is most natural for a story to come to a peak and stay there. The novel is a long walk through various localities with a peaceful return trip assumed; the short story—a climb up a mountain the aim of which is a view from on high.

Tolstoj could not end *Anna Karenina* with Anna's death. He had to write an entire extra section, however difficult that might have been with the novel largely centered on Anna's fate. Otherwise the novel would have had the appearance of a drawn-out story rigged with completely superfluous characters and episodes. The logic of the form required a continuation. It was a sort of *tour de force*—to kill-off the main heroine before the fate of the other personages had been decided. There is good reason why heroes usually do manage somehow or other to hang on till the end (the supporting roles fall by the wayside) or manage to save themselves after having been a hairsbreadth from death. What helped Tolstoj was the parallelism of the construction—Levin's competing with Anna from the very beginning in an effort to occupy the central position. Quite on the other hand, Puškin in *Belkin Tales* aims expressly at making the ending of the story coincide with the high point of the plot and at creating the effect of a surprise denouement (cf. "*Metel'*" [The Snowstorm], "*Grobovščik*" [The Coffin-maker]).

The story is a problem in posing a single equation with one unknown; the novel—a problem involving various rules and soluble with the aid of a whole system of equations with various unknowns in which the intermediary steps of posing are more important than the final answer. The story is a riddle; the novel something on the order of a charade or a rebus.

The story, precisely as *small form* (short story), has nowhere been so consistently cultivated as in America. Until the middle of the nineteenth century, American literature, in the minds both of its writers and readers, was merged with English literature and largely incorporated into it as a "provincial" literature. Washington Irving, in the preface to his sketch of English life (*Bracebridge Hall*), says not without bitterness: "It has been a matter of marvel . . . that a man from the wilds of America should express himself in tolerable English. I was looked upon as something new and strange in literature; a kind of demisavage, with a feather in his hand, instead of on his head; and there was a curiosity to hear what such a being had to say about civilized society."[2] Nevertheless, he himself acknowledges that he had been brought up on English culture and literature, and his sketches have, unquestionably, very close affinity to the tradition of English manners-and-morals sketch-writing: "Having been born and brought up in a new country, yet educated from infancy in the literature of an old one, my mind was early filled with historical and poetical associations, connected with places, and manners and customs of Europe; but which could rarely be applied to those of my own country . . . England is as classic ground to an American, as Italy is to an Englishman; and old London teems with as much historical association as mighty Rome."[3] True, in his first book of sketches there are attempts to use American material ("Rip Van Winkle," "Philip of Pokanoket"); "Philip of Pokanoket" begins with Irving expressing regret that "those early writers, who treated of the discovery and settlement of America, have not given us more particular and candid accounts of the remarkable characters that flourished in savage life."[4] However, the very type of sketches he wrote remained traditional in manner and language; there was nothing "American" about them in the contemporary meaning of the word.

The thirties and forties bring out with full clarity the tendency of American prose to develop the short story genre. At this very same time English literature cultivates the novel. By mid-century various types of magazines had begun to play a sizable role both in England and America and to increase in numbers. But it is characteristic that primarily the big novels of Bulwer-Lytton, Dickens, Thackeray were printed in the English magazines, while the main position in American magazines was held by short stories. This, incidently, is a good illustration to support the contention that the development of the short story in America cannot be regarded as a simple consequence of the appearance of magazines. In this instance, as in many others, there is no simple causality. The consolidation of the short-story genre was associated with, not engendered by, the propagation of magazines.

It was only natural that American criticism at this period should have shown special interest in the story and, coupled with it, a marked indisposition toward the novel. The views of Edgar Allan Poe, whose stories themselves testify to the consolidation of the genre, are especially noteworthy and revealing in this connection. His article on the tales of Nathaniel Hawthorne reads as a sort of treatise on the specific characteristics of story structure. "There has long existed in literature," writes Poe, "a fatal and unfounded prejudice, which it will be the office of this age to overthrow—the idea that the mere bulk of a work must enter largely into our estimate of its merit. I do not suppose even the weakest of the Quarterly reviewers weak enough to maintain that in a book's size or mass, abstractly considered, there is anything which especially calls for our admiration. A mountain, simply through the sensation of physical magnitude which it conveys, does indeed affect us with a sense of the sublime, but we cannot admit any such influence in the contemplation even of 'The Columbiad.'"[5] Poe further develops his own particular theory which consists in the fact that, in terms of artistry, the "rhymed poem," not exceeding in length what can be read in an hour, stands highest of all: "the unity of effect or impression is a point of greatest importance." The long poem, from Poe's point of view, is a paradox: "Epics were the offspring of an imperfect sense of Art, and their reign is no more." Closest of all to the poem, as the ideal type, stands the "prose tale." For prose Poe considers it possible to increase the time limit, "from the very nature of prose itself," to two hours of reading aloud (in other words, up to 32 printed pages). As for the novel, he considers it "objectionable" because of its size, to begin with: "as it cannot be read at one sitting, it deprives itself, of course, of the immense force derivable from totality."[6]

Finally, Poe passes on to a characterization of the story genre itself: "A skilful literary artist has constructed a tale. If wise, he has not fashioned his thoughts to accommodate his incidents; but having conceived, with deliberate care, a certain unique or single *effect* to be wrought out, he then invents such incidents—he then combines such events as may best aid him in establishing this preconceived effect. If his very initial sentence tend not to the outbringing of this effect, then he has failed in his first step. In the whole composition there should be no word written, of which the tendency, direct or indirect, is not to the one pre-established design. And by such means, with such care and skill, a picture is at length painted which leaves in the mind of him who contemplates it with a kindred art, a sense of the fullest satisfaction. The idea of the tale has been presented unblemished, because undisturbed; and this is an end unattainable by the novel."[7] Poe has said of his own stories that he was in the habit of writing them from back to front—the way the Chinese write their books.

Poe thus ascribes particular importance in a story to a central effect to which all the details must gravitate and to a finale which must account for everything which preceded. An awareness of the particular importance of the final impact runs throughout the cultivation of the story in America, whereas for the novel—especially the Dickens or Thackeray type of novel— the finale plays the role not so much of a dénouement as of an epilogue. Stevenson wrote a friend of his in 1891 apropos of one of his stories: "What am I to do? . . . Make another ending to it? Ah, but that's not the way I write; the whole tale is implied; I never use an effect, when I can help it, unless it prepares the effects that are to follow; that's what a story consists in. To make another end, that is to make the beginning all wrong. The dénouement of a long story is nothing; . . . it is a coda, not an essential member in the rhythm; but the body and the end of a short story is bone of the bone and blood of the blood of the beginning."[8]

Such is the general conception of the specific characteristics of the story in American literature. All American stories, beginning with Edgar Allan Poe, are more or less constructed on these principles. Hence—the particular attention paid to the unexpected in the finale and, connected with it, a story structured on the basis of a riddle or an error which holds back the significance of the plot mainspring until the very end. This kind of story is at first completely serious in character; in the case of some writers, the effect of the unexpected is vitiated by moralistic or sentimental tendencies, but the principles of construction remain the same. This is so, for instance, in the case of Bret Harte: the posing of the riddle is usually more interesting than its solution. Take his story "An Heiress of Red Dog." There you have a riddle or even two riddles at its basis: why did the old man will his money to that particular, plain and ignorant woman and why was she so stingy about making use of it? But the solution is disappointing. The first riddle remains entirely unsolved, and the solution to the second one—the old man had forbidden her to give the money to anyone with whom she fell in love—seems insufficient, feeble. The same impression is produced by the sentimental-moralistic solutions of such pieces as "The Fool of Five Forks," "Miggles," "The Man Whose Yoke Was Not Easy." Bret Harte seems almost afraid to give the finale point in order not to forego the sentimental naiveté with which he imbues the tone of his narrator.

Stages in the evolution of every genre can be observed when the genre, once utilized as an entirely serious or "high" one, undergoes regeneration, coming out in parodic or comic form. Such was the case with the lyric poem, the adventure novel, the biographical novel, and so forth. Local and historical conditions bring about the most diverse variations, of course, but the process itself, as a sort of *sui generis* law of evolution, maintains its effect: an initially serious treatment of the *fable*,[9] with its painstaking and detailed motivation, gives way to irony, joke, parody; motivational connections grow slack or are laid bare as conventions, and the author himself steps to the forefront, time and again destroying the illusion of genuiness and seriousness; the plot construction takes on the character of a play on the *fable,* while the *fable* turns into riddle or anecdote. It is in this way that the regeneration of a genre comes about—a transition from one set of possibilities and forms to another.

The American story passed through its first stage of development in the hands of Irving, Edgar Allan Poe, Hawthorne, Bret Harte, Henry James and others, changing in style and construction but remaining serious and "high." The appearance in the eighties of the humorous stories of Mark Twain,[10] who switched the story over onto the track of anecdote and who augmented the role of the narrator-humorist, was therefore an entirely natural and logical consequence. This affinity with the anecdote is in some instances even pointed out by the author himself. Take, for example, "About Magnanimous-Incident Literature," where Mark Twain says: "All my life, from boyhood up, I have had the habit of reading a certain set of anecdotes. . . . Many times I wished that the charming anecdotes had not stopped with their happy climaxes, but had continued the pleasing history of the several benefactors and beneficiaries. This wish rose in my breast so persistently that at last I determined to satisfy it by seeking out the sequels of those anecdotes myself."[11] Three anecdotes with special "continuations" or "sequels" follow.

The novel retreats to the background and continues to exist primarily in the form of the dime detective novel. In connection with this, a fashion for parodies develops. Among Bret Harte's works, alongside his own unsuccessful novels, there is a series of parodies on novels by others which, in the form of condensed sketches (*Condensed Novels*), illustrates the manner of various writers—Cooper, Miss Braddon, Dumas, Brontë, Marryat, Hugo, Bulwer-Lytton, Dickens, and others. It is no wonder that Poe so vehemently attacked the novel—the principle of structural unity serving his point of departure discredits big form in which different centers and parallel lines are inevitably constructed and descriptive material brought to the fore, etc. In this regard Poe's critical essay apropos of Dickens' novel *Barnaby Rudge* is very significant. Among other things, Poe criticizes Dickens for inconsistencies and factual errors, seeing the reason for this in "the present absurd fashion of periodical novel-writing . . . [whereby] . . . our author had not sufficiently considered or determined upon *any* particular plot when he began the story . . . ."[12]

Novels come on the scene which, by their entire character, are manifestly oriented toward the story (with their small number of personages, their one, central effect consisting in some secret, etc.). Such a work is, for example, Hawthorne's *The Scarlet Letter,* the remarkable structure of which American theoreticians and historians of literature are forever pointing out. The novel has only three characters, bound to one another by a single secret which is disclosed in the last chapter ("Revelation"). There are no parallel intrigues, no digressions or episodes; there is complete unity of time, place and action. This is something different in principle from the novels of Balzac or Dickens, writers who take their origin not from the story but from sketches of manners and morals or so-called physiological sketches.

In sum, characteristic for American literature is that type of story built on the principle of structural unity with centralization of basic effect and strong accentuation on finale. Until the eighties this kind of story kept changing with its type, now approaching the sketch, now moving away from it, but maintaining a serious—moralistic, sentimental, psychological or philosophical—character. Beginning in the eighties, the American story takes a decided step in the direction of the anecdote, bringing the narrator-humorist to the fore or introducing elements of parody and irony. The feature of the surprise finale takes on the character of a play on the plot scheme and on the reader's expectations. Structural devices are purposely laid bare in their purely formal meaning, motivation becomes simpler, psychological analysis disappears. It is on this foundation that the stories of O. Henry are developed, stories in which the principle of approximation to the anecdote is carried, it would seem to the limit.

TRANSLATOR'S NOTES

1. There is no direct correspondence in English for this Russian term, nor is there a precise, established definition of it, as a technical literary term, in Russian. Éjxenbaum's own understanding of it changed somewhat over the years of his concern with the problem. The following definition from his article "*Leskov i sovremennaja proza*" [Leskov and contemporary prose] (in *Literatura: Teorija. Kritika. Polemika.* Leningrad, 1926) is probably the one he had in mind here: "By *skaz* I mean that form of narrative prose which, in its lexicon, syntax and selection of intonations, reveals an orientation toward the oral speech of a narrator. . . . a form which fundamentally departs from written discourse and makes the narrator as such a real personage. . . . It signalizes, on the one hand, a shift of center of gravity from the *fable* to the verbal fabric (and by that same token, from the 'hero' to the telling of this or that happening, incident, etc.) and, on the other, liberation from the traditions connected with the culture of the printed

word [*pis'menno-pečatnaja kul'tura*] and a return to oral, living language . . ."
(pp. 214–15). What is at issue here, in other words, is a shift of structural focus
or organizing center from 'narrated event' to 'speech event.' For a detailed analysis of *skaz* derived from Éjxenbaum's point of view, see H. McLean, "On the Style
of a Leskovian *Skaz,*" *Harvard Slavic Studies,* II, Cambridge, 1954, pp. 297–322.
Èjxenbaum is too preoccupied here with 'action plots' to deal with the fact that O.
Henry may also be regarded a *skaz* writer, as Evgenij Zamjatin correctly points
out in a somewhat erratic, very brief, but extremely interesting article, "*O'Genri*"
(sic) (in *Lica* [Personas], New York, 1955, pp. 149–154). For the term 'fable'
(Russian *fabula*) see note 15.

   2. *The Works of Washington Irving,* New York, 1908, Vol. II, p. 9.

   3. *Ibid.,* p. 10.

   4. *Ibid.,* Vol. I, p. 406.

   5. *The Works of E. A. Poe,* edited by John H. Ingram, London, 1901, Vol. IV,
p. 227.

   6. *Ibid.,* p, 215.

   7. *Ibid.,* p. 216.

   8. *The Letters of Robert Louis Stevenson,* edited by Sir Sidney Colvin, New
York, 1925, Vol. III, p. 287.

   9. The terms *fable* and *sujet* (Russian *fabula* and *sjužet*), key terms in Russian formalist analyses of prose fiction, are adopted and explained in René Wellek and Austin Warren's *Theory of Literature* (New York, 1949): "The Russian
formalists distinguish the 'fable,' the temporal-causal sequence which, however it
may be told, is the 'story' or story-stuff, from the 'sujet,' which we might translate
as 'narrative structure.' The 'fable' is the sum of all the motifs, while the 'sujet' is
the artistically ordered presentation of the motifs (often quite different)," (p. 226).

   10. "About Magnanimous-Incident Literature" came out actually somewhat
earlier, in 1878. See Note 2.

   11. *The Writings of Mark Twain,* New York and London, 1911, Vol. XX,
p. 326.

   12. E. A. Poe, *op. cit.,* p. 121.

PART THREE

Issues of
Definition

The Short Story

THE LONG AND
THE SHORT OF IT

MARY LOUISE PRATT

IN TOKYO THESE DAYS, according to folklorist V. Hrdličkova (1969), there are two types of professional oral storytelling: *kodan*, the telling of long, serious, mainly historical narratives, and *rakugo*, the telling of short, humorous anecdotes. The two genres are performed in different theatres, with different gestures, props, mannerisms, and different training programs for apprentices. One, *kodan*, at the moment is in serious decline; *rakugo* is immensely popular and growing. In highly institutionalized forms of discourse, like verbal art, it is relatively common to find pairs of short and long genres like *kodan* and *rakugo*. Western scholarly writing has the essay and the book; in western literature we find the epic and the ballad, the one-act play and the (regular?) play, the poem and the long poem, the short story and the novel. Many different relations can obtain between the members of these pairs. They may be separate but equal, one may be derived from the other, one may be "marked" with respect to the other (as long poem is to poem), they may be related as "major" to "minor" or as "greater" to "lesser." The pair whose relationship I propose to explore here is the last mentioned above, the short story and the novel. But before turning to this pair, I want to make explicit a few assumptions about genres which will inform the discussion to follow.

(1) There is at present no single consistent use of the term "genre." The most one can say is that it always refers to a subcategory of some larger category (or subcategory) of literary works. Thus the genre of drama is a subcategory of literature, the genre of comedy is a subcategory

of drama, the genre of farce is a subcategory of comedy, and so on. The fuzziness of the term arises not just from its being applied at different levels, but also from its being applied according to different criteria. Genre distinctions are based variously on subject matter (detective story, artist novel), narrative situation (confessional novel, dramatic monologue), surface linguistic form (sonnet, prose poem), effect sought in audience (tragedy, melodrama), mode of execution of text (drama) and so on.

(2) Genre is not solely a literary matter. The concept of genre applies to all verbal behavior, in all realms of discourse. Genre conventions are in play in any speech situation, and any discourse belongs to a genre, unless it is a discourse explicitly designed to flaunt the genre system. As Siegfried Schmidt observes, "It is one of the basic assumptions of communicative text theories (apart from the above mentioned assumption of the necessary social embeddings of texts) that texts in social communication always appear as manifestations of a socially recognizable text-type" (Schmidt 1978:48). Establishing typologies of text types is, as Schmidt stresses, an urgent priority. Within that project, it will be important to relate literary and non-literary genres, with a view to establishing comprehensive genre theories rather than the many local ones that obtain in literary criticism, folklore, anthropology and sociolinguistics. The term "genre" outside literature at present suffers from the same vagueness as within literature, and its boundaries with terms like speech event and speech situation are not clear. Candidates for non-literary genres are, for instance, the telephone conversation, lecture, interview, personal narrative, verbal duelling, therapeutic discourse.

(3) Genres are not essences. They are human institutions, historical through and through. The massive effort within literary criticism to maintain the lyric-epic-dramatic triad as ahistorical generic absolutes is seriously misdirected, though of great ideological interest. The myriad attempts to link the lyric-epic-dramatic triad with other phenomena, in paradigms of the type shown in table 1, are directed toward making these classical genre distinctions look natural rather than cultural, thus separating the sphere of art off from other spheres of discourse, and from social life in general.

We need to work out ways of describing the social mode of existence of genres. For instance, linguists customarily distinguish between a speaker's "use vocabulary" (forms the person both says and understands) and her or his "recognition vocabulary" (forms the person understands only), and it might be useful to distinguish likewise between use genres and recognition genres. In this society, literary genres belong to a large class of genres

Table 1

	Lyric	Epic	Dramatic
Phases of language development	Sensuous	Intuitive	Conceptual
Tense	Present	Past	Future
Person	First	Third	Second
Function of language	Expressive	Referential	Conative
Faculties of the soul	Feeling	Thinking	Volition
Functions of the nervous system	Emotive experience	Imaginative experience	Motoric experience
Worldviews	Psychologistic	Naturalistic	Idealistic
Stages of life	Youth	Maturity	Old age
Historical sequence	Subjective antithesis	Objective thesis	Synthesis
Aspects of the self	Soul	Body	Spirit[a]

[a] These are discussed in Hernadi (1972), especially pp. 31–35.

which are widespread as recognition genres, but highly specialized as use genres. Shifting to a related viewpoint, at a given historical moment we will have to distinguish among (a) productive genres, that is, those in which works are currently being composed without being anachronistic (*e.g.* now, the novel) (b) recognized genres, that is, those in which new works are not being composed, except as anachronistic revivals, but which most people know how to receive (*e.g.* now, animal fables) and (c) dead genres, that is, those that are only part of specialized, professional knowledge (*e.g.* now, the philosophical tale). I mean these suggestions just as examples of the kind of questions a social theory of genre might look at.

(4) Criterial features are not enough. Genre criticism has been heavily concerned with distinguishing genres from each other, with finding criterial or essential features by which a given work can unambiguously be identified as belonging to a particular genre. This system-oriented, structural approach needs to be complemented by a genre criticism that concerns itself not only with criterial features of genres, also but with non-essential and occasional ones, with characteristics that aren't relevant points of contrast with other genres, or with vaguer tendencies and trends not visible in all members of the genre, but present often enough to be noticed. Genres can be characterized not by an unambiguous discovery procedure for classifying texts, but by a cluster of characteristics and tendencies, only some of which may be present in a given text.

*   *   *

Not surprisingly discussions of the short story invariably call upon the
novel as a point of comparison, or rather of contrast. Brander Matthews'
classic *Philosophy of the Short Story (1901)* is typical in this respect:

> The difference between a Novel and a Novelet is one of length only:
> a Novelet is a brief Novel. But the difference between a Novel and a
> Short-story is a difference of kind. A true Short-story is something
> other and something more than a mere story which is short. A true
> Short-story differs from the Novel chiefly in its essential unity of
> impression. In a far more exact and precise use of the word, a Short-
> story has unity as a Novel cannot have it. . . .
>
> The novelist may take his time; he has abundant room to turn
> about. The writer of Short-stories must be concise, and compression,
> a vigorous compression, is essential. For him, more than for anyone
> else, the half is more than the whole. Again, the novelist may be
> commonplace, he may bend his best energies to the photographic
> reproduction of the actual; if he show us a cross-section of real life we
> are content; but the writer of Short-stories must have originality, and
> ingenuity. If to compression, originality, and ingenuity he add also a
> touch of fantasy, so much the better. (Summers 1963: 10–11)

Even in languages where the name of the genre makes no reference to
shortness (French *conte,* Spanish *cuento,* for instance), comparison with
the novel is the usual approach. For instance, Edelweis Serra in a recent
book on the Spanish American short story introduces his subject thus:

> El cuento es construcción y comunicación artística de una serie lim-
> itada de acontecimientos, experiencias o situaciones conforme a un
> orden correlative cerrado que crea su propia percepción como tota-
> lidad. El cuento es, pues, un limitado continuo frente al "ilimitado
> discontinuo" de la novela, segun Lukacs. . . . El cuento sería un
> orden de asociaciones y de correlaciones internas más cerradas, y la
> novela un orden ampliamente abierto; un orden de singularización y
> percepción sintética, el cuento; un orden de pluralización percibido
> mas analiticamente, la novela. (Serra 1978: 11–12)

> The short story is an artistic construction and communication of a
> limited sequence of events, experiences, or situations according to a
> closed correlative order which creates its own perception as a totality.
> The short story, then, is a limited continuity, in contrast with the
> "unlimited discontinuity" of the novel, according to Lukacs. . . . The

short story is a relatively closed order of internal associations and correlations, and the novel a wide open order; an order of estrangement and synthetic perception, the short story; an order of pluralization perceived more analytically, the novel. (translation mine)

Short story critics typically rely on comparisons with the novel as ways of fleshing out the "mere" fact of shortness, ways of talking about the short story as "something more than a story which is short." The problem with shortness, of course, arises from a sense that literary genres ought to be characterized by esthetic properties, and shortness seems altogether too quantitative, too material a feature to be given top billing. At the same time, for reasons I shall be exploring in a moment, it does seem inescapably the crucial fact. Contrasts with the more stably established novel open a way to associate this most pedestrian of properties with bonafide esthetic characteristics like compression, synthesis, "a touch of fantasy."

Frank O'Connor adopts the same contrastive tactic in his classic *The Lonely Voice*, though his comparison stresses different characteristics from Matthews and Serra:

> Always in the short story there is this sense of outlawed figures wandering about the fringes of society, superimposed sometimes on symbolic figures whom they caricature and echo—Christ, Socrates, Moses. . . .
>
> As a result there is in the short story at its most characteristic something we do not often find in the novel—an intense awareness of human loneliness. . . . The novel can still adhere to the classical concept of civilized society, of man as an animal who lives in a community, as in Jane Austen and Trollope it obviously does; but the short story remains by its very nature remote from the community— romantic, individualistic, and intransigent. (O'Connor 1962: 19, 21)

Often the lyric, the other conspicuous short genre, is brought in as a positive point of comparison. O'Connor has described the short story as "the nearest thing I know to lyric poetry" (Summers 1963: 100), and his words are echoed more recently by Rust Hills, who says "The successful contemporary short story will demonstrate a more harmonious relationship of all its aspects than will any other literary art form, excepting perhaps lyric poetry" (Hills 1977: 1). Ian Reid suggests a four-way comparison: "In its normally limited scope and subjective orientation [the short story] corresponds to the lyric poem as the novel does to the epic" (Reid 1977: 28).

The chief goal of the comparisons is obviously to distinguish and separate the short story from the novel, to establish the former as

> una estructura literaria de intrínseca validez, una criatura independiente dentro del area vasta de la narrativa, donde su deslinde categorial es praticable precisamente por su ser y existir autonomos frente a la novela. (Serra 1978: 14)

> a literary structure of intrinsic validity, an independent creature in the vast regions of narrative, where its categorical distinctiveness is possible precisely by virtue of its autonomous existence alongside the novel. (translation mine)

Characteristically in short story criticism, the short story is conceived as an autonomous genre, and the novel and lyric are brought into the picture simply as a rhetorical means for highlighting its particularities. Nothing about the novel is really needed to explain the short story.

Now structuralism has taught us that genres are never completely autonomous, but are always defined within the genre system with respect to each other. The statements relating the short story to novel and lyric are thus not gratuitous or simply rhetorical, though one understands why defenders of the short story might want to see them thus. Any attempt to describe a genre must make reference to other genres. But this does not mean relations between genres have to be symmetrical. The relation between the novel and the short story is a highly asymmetrical one, and it is this asymmetry that I would like to explore here. Their relation is not one of contrasting equivalents in a system (separate but equal), but a hierarchical one with the novel on top and the short story dependent. The dependency has both conceptual and historical aspects. The conceptual aspect is that shortness cannot be an intrinsic property of anything, but occurs only relative to something else. The historical aspect is that the novel is, and has been for some time, the more powerful and prestigious of the two genres. Hence, facts about the novel are necessary to explain facts about the short story, but the reverse is not so. The novel has through and through conditioned both the development of the short story and the critical treatment of the short story, but the reverse is not so. Between these paired genres, relations of long to short coincide with relations of unmarked to marked, of major to minor, of greater to lesser, even "mature" to "infant." There is nothing necessary or inevitable about such correspondences. Contrast for instance the relations between poem and long poem, where the longer genre is minor, and neither is stigmatized as lesser.

Let me give a small example of how this asymmetry comes to bear. The short story has a reputation as a training or practice genre, for both apprentice writers and apprentice readers. And it is in fact widely used in this way, in schools for example. Sociolinguistically, this use of the genre makes a lot of sense. The shorter a performance, as a rule, the less the participants have at stake in it, and the less is lost if it fails in any way. Relative to the novel, then the short story is the safer arena for the inevitable failures of apprenticeship. But only relative to the novel. That is, it is only because there are two prose fiction genres, one short and one long, that one of the two is singled out as the training ground, and it is because there is a hierarchical relation between the two that the novel can be viewed as the goal of the training. The same analysis applies to the traditional role of the short story as an experimental genre. It is only relative to the ("full-fledged") novel that the short story is seen as, and used as, the controlled lab for preliminary testing of devices before their release into the world at large. In sum, both the conception of and the practice of the short story are conditioned by its relation to the novel, as the smaller and lesser genre.

Now it is easy to see why thoughts of this dependency might be unwelcome to defenders of the ("modern") short story, seeking legitimacy for the genre. Yet, as the preoccupation with the novel in their writings suggests, such thoughts were inescapable, and tended to resolve themselves into some intriguing contradictions. Here is Boris Eikhenbaum in his now classic essay "O. Henry and the Theory of the Short Story" (1925):

> The novel and the short story are forms not only different in kind but also inherently at odds, and for that reason are never found being developed simultaneously and with equal intensity in any one literature. The novel is a syncretic form (whether its development be directly from collections of stories or complicated by the incorporation of manners-and-morals material); the story is a fundamental, elementary (which does not mean primitive) form. The novel derives from history, from travels; the story—from folklore, anecdote. The difference is one of essence, a difference in principle conditioned by the fundamental distinction between *big* and *small* form. Not only individual writers but also individual literatures cultivate either the novel or the short story. (Eikhenbaum 1968: 4)

Here at the same time as he tries to show that the story is more than a story which is short, Eikhenbaum seems to want to boil everything down to the question of length, even differences in history such as the traditional association of the novel with travels and the short story with folklore. "Bigness" and "smallness" become essences from which all other characteristics of both genres derive. The paradox is that bigness and smallness are precisely the features that cannot be conceived of as separate essences, for they are relative concepts. Smallness and bigness cannot be inherent properties of anything, they can only occur relative to something else. What are selected as essences distinguishing the novel and the short story and guaranteeing the autonomy of the two genres, are the very pair of relative terms that bind the two together. In Brander Matthews we see the same tendency. At the same time as "mere" shortness is downplayed, everything is explained in terms of relative length, including choice of subject matter. For instance:

> While the Novel cannot get on easily without love, the Short-story can. Since love seems to be almost the only thing which will give interest to a long story, the writer of Novels has to get love into his tales as best he may, even when the subject rebels and when he himself is too old to take any delight in the mating of John and Joan. But the Short-story, being brief, does not need a love-interest to hold its parts together, and the writer of Short-stories has thus a greater freedom. (Summers 1963: 11)

Here too, an "essential difference" between the two genres is posited on the relative feature of length. Moreover, notice that although Matthews starts out with a social explanation of length—that love is required to give interest to a long text—he then shifts to a purely formal explanation—the love interest is needed to hold the parts together.

The non-contradictory way to argue the integrity and self-containedness of the short story would be to describe it without taking cues from other genres. But clearly this would be even more misleading, if possible at all. The contradictions we do find in these classic discussions at least implicitly allude to the short story's dependence on the novel, though they vehemently deny it on the surface. Thanks to the work of these early apologists, their defensive stance can now be abandoned, and we can move on to recognize the dependent (rather than interdependent) relation between short story and novel. In a rather schematic way, I propose to raise eight points at which I think an understanding of the short story is increased by that recognition. The general suggestion is that some of the narrative structures, subject matters, narrative traditions, and critical attitudes characteristically associated with the short story are associated with it (a) because the short story has been tacitly seen as incomplete or fragmentary with respect to the totality and completeness of the novel, and (b) because the short story has often redeployed materials that were dissociated by the novel, often because they were devalued in literary or social terms. The historical hypothesis that arises is that as the novel consolidated itself in the 19th century, the short story tended to shift around into positions of "countergenre"[1] to the novel. The emergence of the "modern short story," usually located somewhere between 1935 and 1955, may be less the emergence of a new genre than the consolidation of a new relationship between genres.

The first four propositions I will examine concern the short story's "incompleteness" with respect to the novel:

Proposition 1. *The novel tells a life, the short story tells a fragment of a life.* One of the most consistently found narrative structures in the short story is the one called the "moment-of-truth." Moment of truth stories focus on a single point of crisis in the life of a central character, a crisis which provokes some basic realization that will change the character's life forever. A classic example is Joyce's "Araby," and indeed all the stories in *Dubliners.* Not a few critics regard the moment of truth as the canonic form of the modern short story. Writing on Melville, Robert Marler says:

> A fundamental element of the short story, then, is precisely this inner change. It may be an awakening, as in "The Beast in the Jungle," a momentary realization, as in "A Clean, Well-Lighted Place," or a change that goes unrecognized except by the discerning reader, as in Sarah Orne Jewett's "A White Heron," but a character moves, regardless of the minuteness of the displacement, from a state of relative ignorance to a state of relative knowledge. (Marler 1973: 429)

Now to some extent, the moment of truth stands as a model for the short story the way the life stands as a model for the novel. These are not normative models; there is no sense in which texts not conforming to them are automatically seen as unusual or deviant. At most we can talk about the novel/life correspondence and the short story/moment of truth correspondence as recognizable trends or typical forms. What I want to suggest is that there is more than an analogical relationship between these two sets of correspondences, that the identification of the short story form with moment of truth plot was to some degree prescribed by the prior association between the novel form and the life. The lurking associations are these: if the short story is not a "full-length" narrative it cannot narrate a full-length life; it can narrate a fragment or excerpt of a life. And if from that fragment one can deduce things about the whole life, then the more novel-like, the more complete, the story is. L. A. G. Strong voiced this attitude some 40 years ago, saying that the short story writer "may give us only the key-piece of a mosaic, around which, if sufficiently perceptive, we can see in shadowy outline the completed pattern" (Summers 1963: 42). This attitude, I would argue, was conditioned by what Ian Watt describes as a premise "implicit in the novel form in general: the premise, or primary convention, that the novel is a full and authentic report of human experience" (Rohrberger 1966: 125). Frank O'Connor regards the life as an all-out "essential form" for narrative, and at the same time assumes this form is not available to the short story:

> For the short-story writer there is no such thing as essential form. Because his frame of reference can never be the totality of a human life, he must be forever selecting the point at which he can approach it . . . In the standard composition that the individual life presents, the story-teller must always be looking for new compositions that enable him to suggest the totality of the old one.
>
> Accordingly, the story-teller differs from the novelist in this: he must be much more of a writer, much more of an artist—perhaps I should add, considering the examples I have chosen, more of a dramatist. (O'Connor 1962: 21–22)

Writers in both genres have played on the paired correspondences novel/life and short story/moment of truth. It was a overt opposition to the linear story-of-a-life novel that Virginia Woolf wrote *Mrs. Dalloway*, a novel-length exploration of a one-day fragment of a life, ending in a moment of truth. In "The Short Happy Life of Francis Macomber," Hemingway collapses the associations onto each other: Macomber's happy life, as opposed to his whole life, lasts only a few moments, and corresponds to his moment of truth. Short life, short story.

It must be kept clear that this relationship of whole to fragment is not a necessary one. To return to an earlier example, we do not see the poem as incomplete with respect to long poem. It is not logically necessary for a short genre to be seen as a dependency of, or a fragment of, or a baby brother of a corresponding larger genre. Nor is it an empirical necessity arising from inherent limitations on forms. The novel form is not "by its very nature" too big for the moment of truth structure; nor is the short story inherently too small to tell a whole life. It is neither a logical nor an empirical necessity, but rather a fact of literary history, that the short story has developed along lines in part determined by the novel. By novelistic standards, the moment of truth is an especially good fragment of a life to narrate because it projects itself by implication backward and forward across the whole life: "All my life I had been X until one day Y happened, and for the rest of my life I was Z." Thus, so the thinking goes, the fragmentary short story is nevertheless able to achieve some of the plenitude and totality of the novel.

These same assumptions underlie one of the more general commonplaces of short story criticism, namely that the short story relies on suggestion and implication while the novel uses explicit statement. For instance, H. E. Bates says:

> What Hemingway realized, and what it is important all short-story writers should realize, was that it is possible to convey a great many things on paper without stating them at all. To master the art of implication, of making one sentence say two or more different things, by conveying emotion and atmosphere without drawing up a tidy balance sheet of descriptions about them, is more than half the short-storywriter's business. (Bates 1941: 177)

In a similar vein, Frank O'Connor puts it, "Creating in the novel a sense of continuing life is the thing. We don't have that problem in the short story, here you merely suggest continuing life" (Summers 1963: 100). What is odd about such statements is not what they say about the short story, but what they say about the novel—that it does use "tidy balance sheets?" that it creates a sense of life by some means other than suggestion? Such statements seem to be efforts to cast a good light on the notion that the short story lacks internal space and achieves completeness only by referring beyond itself. In the process, they imply an almost ludicrous picture of the novel.

Proposition 2. *The short story deals with a single thing, the novel with many things.* This is a positive variant of the position outlined in 1. From this point of view, what is stressed in defining the genre is the word *single*, as in Poe's requirement of a "*single effect* to be wrought" (Poe 1967: 446), or Brander Matthews' dictum that "a short story deals with a single character, a single event, a single emotion, or the series of emotions called forth by a single situation" (Summers 1963: 10), or John Milton Berdan's definition of the genre as "a single dramatic episode, rendered credible" to which he adds, "the word 'single' in the definition has a very real place. It differentiates the 'tale' from the 'short story' as a form of literary art" (Berdan 1932: v).

Now this singleness argument does correspond to common short story practice. It is characteristic, for example, for short stories to be structured around single small-scale quests or socially identifiable single incidents like a party, an excursion, a funeral, a hanging, or some such pre-packaged fragment. And it is certainly commonplace for short stories to identify themselves by title as being about a single person—"The Prussian Officer," "The Adulterous Woman," "The Chemist's Wife," "Funes the Memorious," and so on. It is equally certainly a mistake to elevate this singleness to a criterial feature of the genre. For example, A. L. Bader has perceptively pointed out that it is common for short stories to juxtapose two parallel incidents, as happens, for instance, in Maupassant's "A Country Excursion," or Mansfield's "The Garden Party," though their titles suggest a single incident (Summers 1963: 43).

Once again, the point is that the stress in both short story theory and practice on singleness of impression, incident, and so on, is in part conditioned by the novel, against which the short story had to look for what was smaller and lesser. Berdan's observation that this singleness criterion does not apply to the tale is suggestive. The older tale was never a dependent countergenre to the novel. When it became so, it turned into the "modern short story."

Proposition 3. *The short story is a sample, the novel is the whole hog.* This proposition refers to the tendency for short stories to present themselves, usually through their titles, as samples or examples of some larger general category. This is another way in which the short story claims its relevance by referring outside itself to some more complete whole. One example is the day-in-the-life variety—"Christmas in Steamboat Junction," "Mr. Jones Goes to the Fair," "A Day in the Country," "In the Penal Colony"—where the point is not just the events themselves, but their supposed typicality. This is where the short story merges with the sketch (another genre whose name assumes incompleteness). Then there are the character types, like "A Country Doctor," "A Hunger Artist," "The Man of the Crowd," "The Man Who Grew Younger," "Jonas or The Artist at Work."[2] Then there are the emblems, stories given, perhaps ironically, as exempla of social or moral categories: "Grief," "Misfortune," "Politics," "Debts," "Wants."[3] Sometimes the generalization being illustrated is a type of story, as in "A Boring Story," "A Christmas Story," "The Immigrant Story," "Story of a Farmgirl,"[4] or Dylan Thomas's plain "A Story," whose everydayness he apologizes for in the opening paragraph: "If you can call it a story. There is no real beginning or end and there's very little in the middle. It is all about a day's outing, by charabanc, to Porthcawl, which, of course, the charabanc never reached, and it happened when I was so high and much nicer."

Even more common is the story titled by a quotation, whether a punch line, a cliché, or a proverb, which the story is understood to be illustrating. This is a favorite device of Flannery O'Connor, famous for "A Good Man is Hard to Find," "Good Country People," and "Everything that Rises Must Converge." But it is a common practice all over. Picking up Andrew Salkey's anthology of Caribbean short stories, for example, I find "Man, In England, You've Just Got to Love Animals," "A Free Country," "Any Lawful Impediment," "Birds of a Feather."[5] Here we see the short story harking back to two of its most conspicuous antecedents, first the exemplum, with the appended moral promoted to title, and second, the exemplum's countergenre, the joke with its punch line.

One small but revealing feature of short stories in this exemplary vein is that their characters are frequently given no proper name, or only a first name, like Bartleby the scrivener. This contrasts sharply with the novelistic tradition of characters with full proper names, especially in titles, where the individualized character him or herself is proclaimed as the interest of the book. The nameless trend in the short story is a generalizing one, and of course, biblical.

The exemplary or illustrative trend in the short story traces back not just to the medieval exemplum or the biblical parable, but to the use of the short narrative in eighteenth century periodicals like London's *The Spectator* and *The Rambler,* where it merges with the essay. In the eighteenth century, says H. S. Canby, "the novel developed freely. But the short story, by custom, remained a pendant to the essay, was restricted to the purposes of illustration. In this age, as never before or since, it was bound up to the service of didacticism. Its range was small. Its success was remarkable" (Canby 1913: 26). Outside fictional literature, illustration of course remains one of the main purposes for which narration is used, as in journalism and debate. This is one of the most conspicuous points of contact between imaginative literature and other kinds of discourse. Outside literature, the exemplary narrative is always a fragment of a larger discourse, never a complete whole. The various kinds of exemplary short stories likewise suggest their own incompleteness and, usually through titles, imply the larger context in which they are to be understood.

Proposition 4. *The novel is a whole text, the short story is not.* Here I refer to the very concrete fact that a novel constitutes a complete book (or books), while a short story never does. A short story is always printed as part of a larger whole, either a collection of short stories or a magazine, which is a collection of various kinds of texts. Except in schools, perhaps, individual short stories are usually read as part of a larger reading experience. Though this is not a determining factor, it is likely that the fact of not being an autonomous text reinforces the view of the short story as a part or fragment. In any case, if one is looking for an objective factor on which to hang the concepts of longness and shortness, I think it would be, at least in the present period, this fact of being or not being a complete book. This is certainly a more useful distinction than the traditional "able to be read in one sitting."

I turn now to another set of fairly generalized characteristics of the short story which, though not attached to the idea of the short story as incomplete, do relate to its status as minor and lesser genre with respect to the novel.

5. *Subject matter.* Just as it is used for formal experimentation, the short story is often the genre used to introduce new (and possibly stigmatized) subject matters into the literary arena. Bret Harte refers to this function, for example, in an 1899 retrospective on the origins of the American short story. Harte explains that he wrote "The Luck of Roaring Camp" because, as editor of *Overland Monthly,* he failed to find in all the materials submitted "anything of that wild and picturesque life which had impressed him, first as a truant schoolboy, and afterwards, as a youthful schoolmaster among the mining population" (Summers 1963: 8). For Harte the American short story signaled the end of the dominance of English models in American literature, the end of an era when "the literary man had little sympathy with the rough and half-civilized masses who were making his country's history: if he used them at all it was as a foil to bring into greater relief his hero of the unmistakable English pattern." In other parts of the world we similarly find the short story being used to introduce new regions or groups into an established national literature, or into an emerging national literature in the process of decolonization. In France, Maupassant through the short story breaks down taboos on matters of sexuality and class. In the establishment of a modern national literature in Ireland, the short story emerges as the central prose fiction genre, through which Joyce, O'Flaherty, O'Faolain, O'Connor, Moore, Lavin and so many others first document modern Irish life. Its role has been comparable in the emergence of the modern literature of the American South. In Canada, smalltown Ontario life was introduced, at an early stage of decolonization, in the comic stories of Stephen Leacock, and at a

later stage, in the more serious work of Alice Munro. In Latin America, it is through the short story that Horacio Quiroga introduces the marginalized society of the Argentine jungle frontier into literature; in Peru Jose María Arguedas first begins his exploration of modern indigenous life in the short story, before moving to the novel. It is in such regional (*i.e.* marginal with respect to some metropolis) writings that one sees most clearly the short story's relations to the sketch, a genre which it has now subsumed, and which was, as Ray West describes it, "a romantic means of catching the atmosphere of remote places" (Summers 1963: 28). On the other side, and perhaps moving toward the panoramic potential of the novel, it is also here on the regional periphery that the short story cycle has been most likely to make its appearance. Of the writers just mentioned, five wrote place-based short story cycles of the *Winesburg, Ohio* or *Dubliners* variety. (Joyce, *Dubliners;* Leacock, *Sunshine Sketches;* Munro, *Lives of Girls and Women;* Quiroga, *Los desterrados;* Arguedas, *El aylla.*) To some extent, such cycles do a kind of groundbreaking, establishing a basic literary identity for a region or group, laying out descriptive parameters character types, social and economic settings, principal points of conflict for an audience unfamiliar either with the region itself or with seeing that region in print. But the short story cycle sometimes is used to convey a particular social perspective too. Speaking of Sherwood Anderson's use of the cycle in *Winesburg, Ohio,* Ian Reid remarks:

> The tight continuous structure of a novel is deliberately avoided: Anderson said he wanted 'a new looseness' of form to suit the particular quality of his material. His people are lonely, restless, cranky. Social cohesion is absent in their mid-western town. Even momentary communication seldom occurs between any two of them. Winesburg is undergoing a human erosion caused by the winds of change blowing from the cities, by the destabilizing of moral codes, and by the intrinsic thinness of small-town life. The 'new looseness' of Winesburg Ohio can convey with precision and pathos the duality that results: a superficial appearance (and indeed the ideal possibility) of communal wholeness, and an underlying actual separateness. (Reid 1977: 47–8)

Reid's comments also suggest why the short story cycle rather than the novel might be chosen to portray, for example, the disorder of frontier society, or of traditional societies disintegrating in the face of modernization.

Obviously, whether a given subject matter is central or peripheral, established or new in a literature has a great deal to do with what is central and peripheral in the community outside its literature, a great deal to do, that is, with values, and with socioeconomic, political and cultural realities. In some cases at least, there seem to develop dialectical correspondences between minor or marginal genres and what are evaluated as minor or marginal subjects. So for example, we find the short story used especially often for portraying childhood experience (illustrated by such classics, as Joyce's "Araby," Cortázar's "End of the Game," Lawrence's "Rocking Horse Winner," and so many by Faulkner). Novels dealing with childhood experience seem relatively rare on the other hand, except for the specialized (marked) categories of the picaresque and the bildungsroman. Such a tendency might be explained purely in terms of length and interest—a child's perspective is too naive, too thin, too unrevealing to sustain "full-length" novel treatment. But isn't this really a way of saying that childhood experience is not considered normative or authoritative in the society, or that it is considered an incomplete basis for the supposed totalizing vision of the novel? Similarly, the short story has a tradition of dealing with rural or peasant life. This is a longstanding trend in Russia. Speaking of the *conte* in late 19th century France, Ian Reid observes,

> Not the least important tendency of those latter writers [Daudet, Flaubert, Maupassant], was their predilection for rural subjects and simple folk. Mostly it could be left to the novel to delineate those large-scale social patterns which were so amply extended in urban life; the short story seemed especially suitable for the portrayal of regional life, or of individuals who, though situated in a city, lived there as aliens. (Reid 1977: 24)

Reid's comment suggests an explanation based on some kind of natural or intrinsic literary possibilities of the various subject matters—rural life is small and thus appropriate to small genres. But of course it is essential to see such a view simply as an expression of the values held by the particular class who had proprietorship over the two genres, and for whom the novel was the privileged vehicle for dealing with the areas of experience they cared about most. When it comes time for a dominant class to bring what Frank O'Conner likes to call "submerged population groups" to the surface, the short story often comes into play. One might offer a similar explanation for the fact that in the age of empiricism, the short story seems to have been the special domain for the fantastic and the supernatural—topics marginalized and stigmatized by a novel consolidating itself around realism.

6. *Orality*. This is another consistent trend in the short story, ranging from the incorporation of oral-colloquial speech forms in the language of narration, (*e.g.* James' "The Beldonald Holbein" and others), through instances where an oral narrative is embedded in the story (*e.g.* Chekhov's "Gooseberries"), to instances where the whole text takes the form of represented speech, often first person narration in an oral setting (*e.g.* Poe's "The Tell-Tale Heart"). Oral style and formate are common not just in regional or "folk" trends in the short story, such as the Leskovian skaz, but also at the cosmopolitan end of the scale, in the work of Poe, Woolf, Kafka, Cortázar and Borges, for example. They are perfectly possible in the novel too, of course, as is amply demonstrated by Conrad and Faulkner, for example, or more recently by writers like João Guimarães Rosa (in his Brazilian masterpiece *The Devil to Pay in the Backlands*) or Robertson Davies *(The Deptford Trilogy)*. But orality is not a conspicuous or consistent tendency in the novel as it is in the short story. The conspicuous tradition in the novel has always been toward writing and bookishness. As is so often observed, the novel was born affirming its own writtenness, and many of the early specimens have an explicitly written framework—the manuscript of *Don Quixote,* the letters of *Pamela* and *Les Liaisons dangeureuses,* the (edited) memoirs of *Moll Flanders,* the inksplotched pages of *Tristram Shandy,* the mock latinities of *Tom Jones.* In a simultaneous celebration and interrogation of literacy and the written word, the early novel redeploys the authoritative voices of writing, of documents. (In the modern variant of this tradition, those voices are mocked and undermined—in Cortázar's *Hopscotch,* Nabokov's *Pale Fire,* the novels of Robbe-Grillet—but they are still at center stage.) The lesser authority of speech is redeployed in the "lesser" genre, supported by the literary antecedents of Chaucer, Boccaccio, the Arabian Nights. And supported, in many cases, by living (or dying) oral narrative traditions. The oral fairly tale, for instance, fed into the modern short story via the brothers Grimm. Bret Harte locates the roots of the (Anglo-)American short story in the oral tall tale and in the joke while American Jewish oral traditions, as well as speech patterns, also flourish in the genre. This is not to say that imitation of written forms is absent in the short story. It is as common there as orality. The travel journal appears, for example, in Poe's "Manuscript Found in a Bottle"; epistolary form in Cortazar's "Letter to a Young Lady in Paris"; the personal journal in many of James'

stories; scholarly discourse in Kafka's "Report to an Academy"; a new
Bible in John C17X McCrae's "Revelations 23:1—." Here the asymmetry
between novel and short story appears again. Oral form has not been particularly at home in the novel, while the written formats so typical of the
novel are likewise common in the short story.

The tradition of orality in the short story has special significance in
cultures where literacy is not the norm, or where the standard literary
language is that of an oppressor. The Mexican writer Juan Rulfo illustrates the first case. Of his single volume of short story masterpieces
(Rulfo 1967), many take the form of dramatized monologues and dialogues, such as the monologue of a father carrying his dying son to the
doctor, or the dialogue between a father and the son returning from a
futile attempt to get to the US. The second case, representation of oral
language in rejection of an oppressive literary standard, is exemplified by
the stories of such Black American writers as Toni Cade Bambara and
Sonia Sanchez (see Sanchez 1973), or Caribbean writers Samuel Selvon
and R. O. Robinson (see Salkey 1970).

In such contexts as these, the short story provides not just the "small"
place for experimentation, but also a genre where oral and nonstandard
speech, popular and regional culture, and marginal experience, have some
tradition of being at home, and the form best-suited to reproducing the
length of most oral speech events. Orality can be counted as one of the
important factors behind the flourishing of the short story in the modern
literatures of many Third World nations and peoples, where, not incidentally, it is taken much more seriously as an art form than it is elsewhere.

7. *Narrative traditions.* The novel and the short story are often associated
with different narrative traditions, as for instance in the statement by
Eikhenbaum quoted earlier, that the novel has its origins in history and
travel, the short story in anecdote and folklore. There is much truth in
such views. As suggested in the previous section, the novel does hark back
to history and document, while everywhere in the short story we see revivals and remains of oral, folk, and biblical narrative traditions, like the
fairy tale, the ghost story, parable, exemplum, fabliau, animal fable. Many
of these story types survive directly in oral culture, religious discourse,
and in literature for children. In mainstream literature, however, they
have by and large been absorbed by the short story, much as in the late
Middle Ages, the exemplum tended to absorb "all varieties of short narratives except the most indecent" (Canby 1913: 10). I have already mentioned a (no longer didactic) illustrative trend in the short story that
doubtless connects back to the exemplum. The parable we find in Borges

and Kafka, the fairy tale, degraded, in Maupassant or Juan Rulfo, the ghost story in Poe. Even more conspicuous, perhaps, is the animal fable, fully revived by Horacio Quiroga ("Anaconda"), played on by Julio Cortázar ("Axolotl," "Letter to a Young Lady in Paris"), vestigially present in the symbolic animals throughout the stories of García Márquez, or simply alluded to, by titles like James' "The Beast in the Jungle" or "The Death of the Lion." In the short story there are animals everywhere.

I mentioned earlier Virginia Woolf's incorporation of the moment-of-truth structure into the novel form. Her equally experimental short story collection, *The Haunted House and Other Short Stories* (published posthumously and in various stages of completion) gives us a near anthology of older narrative forms redeployed in a modern context: "Lappin and Lapinova" is an animal fable; "The Searchlight" an exemplum; "The Man Who Loved His Kind" a parable; "A Haunted House" a ghost story; "The Duchess and the Jeweller" a fairy tale. These alongside the newer forms like the slice of life ("The Mark on the Wall"), the moment of truth ("The Legacy") and an explicit commentary on the genre system, a short story titled "An Unwritten Novel."

Once again, the retention of older narrative traditions in the short story is only partly a question of length. Certainly it makes sense to talk about direct lines of descent from the older short (*i.e.* not-a-complete-book) genres down to the contemporary one, parallel to lines of descent from longer written antecedents down to the novel. But there are also indications that the old oral traditions are "relegated" to the short story, that because of their orality, their associations with folk culture, their didacticism and/or antirealism, the traditions were incompatible with the literary values of early bourgeois novelists and were left behind by the prestige genre, to reappear in the lesser one. In other words, it is not only a question of short forms evolving into other short forms. It is perfectly possible to write novels in the tradition of the animal fable (Richard Adams's *Watership Down*), the fairy tale (Tolkien's *Ring Trilogy*), the parable (Kafka's *Trial*) and the rest. But with the possible exception of the ghost story, such instances in the novel seem to have been isolated, recent, and highly marked.

8. *Craft versus art.* One of the most intriguing aspects of the short story's generic status is the widespread tendency for it to be viewed as a (skill-based) craft rather than a (creativity-based) art. This attitude has been particularly pronounced in the Anglo-American world, but it can be found everywhere. Anyone who has worked with the short story has had the unnerving experience of finding the library shelves groaning not with

short story theory, criticism and history, but with instruction manuals—
Short Stories for Fun and Profit, How to Write Stories that Will Sell and
so forth. Of what short story criticism there is, not a little turns out to be
the work of the major short story writers themselves—Poe, Chekhov,
O'Connor, O'Faolain (*cf*. Reid 1977: 2), and these too combine how-to
instruction with their critical analysis. No example could bring home
more clearly that basic ground rule of modern criticism: there is a thing
called serious criticism and a thing called serious art, and the two are
made only for each other.

The short story's status as craft rather than art is hugely overdeter-
mined of course. Its connections with folklore, with speech, humor, children's literature, with didacticism, the very notion of lack that goes with
shortness, all conspire to deny it the status of art. But what above all
creates the association with craft and skills is clearly the short story's ties
to journalism. In the realm of the commercial (as distinct from the literary)
magazine, the short story becomes anthema to the art-for-art's-sake values
that consolidated themselves in the modernist period. In fact, it became
exactly what those values are erected against. It is art commodified and
commercialized, art one tries to make a living at and (horrors!) possibly
even succeeds. Magazine stories are made to order, their tone, subject
matter, language, length controlled in advance by the other more powerful discourses in whose company they appear. They are entertainment.
The magazine context implies distracted reception in brief moments
between other activities. They are for a mass public—the whole point is
to achieve as massive a public as possible. This fact alone is decisive for
those who hold Mallarmé's view that "art is a mystery accessible only to
the very few." Magazine fiction is planned for obsolescence. Unlike books,
the text actually becomes garbage after a reading. There is no chance, not
any procedure for the mortality or immortality of a work to be determined on its merits. The whole point is to replace it with another, equivalent product in next week's or next month's issue. Everything pressures
for the development of techniques, formulae, production routines, assem-
bly lines, standard wages and prices.

One of the strangest responses to this commercialization of the short
story occurs in a book published in 1929 called *The Dance of the Machines*.
In the face of a good deal of patriotic boasting about the short story as the
American genre, the author, Edward J. O'Brien, condemns it as an instance
of the "mechanistic structures" increasingly taking over American life
and the American psyche. O'Brien juxtaposes the short story with two
other modern American phenomena, the machine and the army, concluding that the three "share so many qualities in common that they seem to

belong to the same strange family" (1929: 20), and advancing the view that "it is imperative for us to devise quickly all possible means of ensuring that we shall retain control of the machines and of ourselves rather than that the machine and mechanistic structures shall make us their slaves" (1929: 7).

The approach is certainly eccentric, but equally certainly, O'Brien is responding to historical realities. Indeed, his view of the short story is quite reminiscent of attitudes to television today. In the 1920s the short story was certainly the genre most conspicuously caught up in mass production, the genre where the artist had least autonomy or time for composition, the genre for which a technology had been elaborated to efficiently meet the demands of the market place, the one most tending toward standardization and a "lowest common denominator." In part the short story was the most conspicuous example of the supposed horrors of mass culture precisely because of its length, that is, because it was not a book, and appeared physically surrounded by the propaganda of consumerism. Probably the most terrifying thing was how easily, how comfortably and prosperously it sat there, traitor to a much beloved distinction between high and low art.

*   *   *

The eight points I have raised about the short story in this paper do not constitute yet another attempt to define that genre. They are not characteristics which, as Charles T. Scott puts it, "will unambiguously differentiate this class of discourses from some other" (Scott 1969: 131). Given the complexities of human institutions, the discovery of such characteristics will, I suspect, prove either impossible or quite uninteresting. The recognition that literary genres form a system rather than a roster of essences is an important one. At the same time, the linguistic model on which this recognition is based easily encourages one to oversimplify. There are few human institutions indeed for which morphophonemics is an adequate analogue. In the study of literary genres, oversimplification is likely in two chief directions. First, in relating genres to each other, the "phonemic" tendency is to see them as related to and differentiated from each other always in the same ways, and to search for a set of universal distinctive features of genre. Among other things, I have tried to suggest here that the novel and the short story are related to each other in ways that are fairly systematic, but at the same time specific to these two genres. Secondly, oversimplification is likely in the relating of literary genres to other systems of meaning and value in the society. Here, for instance, I have tried to suggest a few points at which the relation between novel and short story come into contact with other areas of the discourse system, and with values as to what kind of experience is normative or what kind of language authoritative. These are both directions which, I suggest, genre theory might fruitfully pursue.

NOTES

1. I take this from Guillén (1971: especially Chapter 5).

2. The first two of these stories are by Kafka, the third by Poe, the fourth by Jerome Charyn, the fifth by Camus.

3. Of these stories, the first two are by Chekhov, the others by Grace Paley.

4. Of the stories listed, the first is by Chekhov, the second by V. S. Naipaul, the third by Grace Paley, the fourth by Maupassant.

5. Salkey (1970). The stories are by Samuel Selvon, R. O. Robinson, Donald Hinds, and George Lamming, respectively.

REFERENCES

Bader, A. L. 1945. *The structure of the modern short story.* College English 7. Rpt. in: Summers 1963.

Bates, H. E. 1941. *The modern short story: a critical survey.* Boston: The Writer Inc.

Berdan, J. M., ed. 1932. *Fourteen stories from one plot.* New York: Oxford University Press.

Canby, H. A. 1913. *A study of the short story.* New York: Holt.

Eikhenbaum, B. 1968. *O. Henry and the Theory of the Short Story.* Trans. I. R. Titunik. Ann Arbor: University of Michigan.

Guillén, Claudio. 1971. *Literature as system.* Princeton: Princeton University Press.

Harte, Bret. 1899. The rise of the 'short story.' *Cornhill Magazine,* July 1899. Rpt. in: Summers 1963.

Hernadi, Paul. 1972. *Beyond genre: new directions in literary classification.* Ithaca: Cornell University Press.

Hills, Rust. 1977. *Writing in general and the short story in particular: an informal textbook.* Boston: Houghton Mifflin.

Hrdličkova, V. 1969. Japanese professional storytellers. *Genre* II(3): 179–210.

Marler, Robert. 1973. 'Bartleby the Scrivener' and the American short story. *Genre* VI(4): 428–47.

Matthews, Brander. 1901. *The philosophy of the short story.* Excerpted in: Summers 1963.

O'Brien, Edward J. 1929. *The dance of the machines.* New York: Macaulay.

O'Connor, Frank. 1962. *The lonely voice: a sketch of the short story.* Cleveland: The World Publishing Co.

O'Connor, Frank. 1963. "Interview with Anthony Whittier." In Malcolm Cowley, ed., *Writers at work: the Paris review interviews*. Rpt. in: Summers 1963.

Poe, Edgar Allan. 1967. "Review of Twice Told Tales." In David Galloway, ed., *Selected writings of Edgar Allan Poe*. Middlesex: Penguin.

Reid, Ian. 1977. *The short story*. Volume 37 in the series *The Critical Idiom*. London: Methuen.

Rohrberger, Mary. 1966. *Hawthorne and the modern short story: a study in genre*. The Hague: Mouton.

Rulfo, Juan. 1967. *The burning plain*. [*El llano en llamas.*] Trans. by George D. Schade. Austin: University of Texas Press.

Salkey, Andrew, ed. 1970. *Island voices: stories from the West Indies*. New York: Liveright.

Sanchez, Sonia. 1973. *We be word sorcerers*. New York: Bantam.

Schmidt, Siegfried J. 1978. "Some problems of communicative text theories." In Wolfgang U. Dressler, ed., *Current trends in textlinguistics*. Berlin: De Gruyter.

Scott, Charles T. 1969. On defining the riddle: the problem of a structural unit. *Genre* II(2): 129–42.

Serra, Edelweiss. 1978. *Tipología del cuento literario*. Madrid: Cupsa Editorial.

Summers, Hollis, ed. 1963. *Discussions of the short story*. Boston: D. C. Heath.

Watt, Ian. 1961. "Realism and the novel form." In Robert Scholes, ed., *Approaches to the novel*. Quoted in Rohrberger 1966.

West, Ray B. 1952. *The short story in America*. Excerpted in Summers 1963.

Woolfe, Virginia. 1972. *A haunted house and other short stories*. New York: Harcourt, Brace and World.

On Defining
Short Stories

ALLAN H. PASCO

COMPARED TO THE NOVEL, the short story has had remarkably little criticism devoted to it, and what theory exists reveals few definitive statements about its nature. For the last quarter century, critics have neglected generic questions and turned to the consideration of narration or *récit*. They hedge on definitions, origins, major traits, on just about everything having to do with the short story as a genre. I make this observation without censure, for one is doubtless wise to be circumspect with a genre of unequalled antiquity and adaptability. As Gullason, May, and many others have pointed out, it may be an "underrated art" but it remains remarkably hardy,[1] so much so that Mary Doyle Springer and Elizabeth Bowen have attempted to distinguish a "modern" and "artistic" short story of the last one hundred years from a more antiquated, inartistic predecessor.[2] The case is, however, difficult to make. Not only does one remember, with H. E. Bates, that "the stories of Salome, Ruth, Judith, and Susannah are all examples of an art that was already old, civilized, and highly developed some thousands of years before the vogue of *Pamela*,"[3] Clements and Gibaldi have argued convincingly that recent masterpieces continue in an age-old genre.[4] Indeed, without *parti pris* it is difficult to read certain Milesian tales or stories from the *Arabian Nights*, not to mention more recent masterpieces by such writers as Marguerite de Navarre, Chaucer, or Boccaccio, without being struck by the modernity of these creations from long ago. The subject matter may be different, the devices at variance, but no substantive trait or quality distinguishes them from the products of nineteenth- and twentieth-century practitioners. I do not say there is no difference. I argue rather that, similar to archetypes, which have certain key elements that are combined with other traits specific to a given epoch and are thus reconstituted, the short story genre has a central, identifiable set of characteristics which each age and each author deploys in different ways and with different variables. The result is generically recognizable, allowing for parallel and oppositional play, but specific to the author, age, and culture.

Just as claims for the recent origin of the short story are most difficult to defend, so the majority of us would agree that we cannot be decisive about any suggested birthplace or time. It surely finds its source in the earliest days of civilization. We all know that it is a human trait both to ask "Why?" and to tell stories in idle moments. We simply cannot explain why certain individuals choose to write them down, or why certain epochs have more such individuals than others. We only note that it began occurring rather early.

It might help if we could agree on a definition. Unfortunately, every time critics and theoreticians reach a modicum of agreement, some writer apparently takes it as a challenge and invents a contradiction to disrupt our comfortable meeting of minds. Certain poststructuralists have used the lack of really firm definitions, the absence of universally accepted conventions, the difficulty of firmly establishing an undeviating external reality, to justify denying importance to all but the reader. The texts, like other objectively verifiable truths, become mere pretexts of little ultimate importance. Genre, which has no physical existence, since it consists of a shared concept of a collective, thus nonindividualized reality, has fared even worse. A few recent reconsiderations may signal a change,[5] but for the most part, critics continue to view the matter of fictional genres with indifference. As Harry Steinhauer put it some years ago, "[T]here are tasks of greater substance to engage [members of the scholarly community] than the search for the phantom traits of the ideal novelle."[6] Perhaps it is time to suggest that this position may make interesting theory, but it represents an extreme that is too far removed from the actual mechanics of reading literature. When readers are actually reading, they quite properly act as though conventions, language, texts, civilization itself do exist, and they manage rather well to understand. To do so they achieve sufficient agreement to maintain communication within the surrounding contexts of composition and consumption.

E. D. Hirsch, Jr. has pointed to what is perhaps the most significant obstacle to defining genre. "Aristotle was wrong to suppose that human productions can be classified in a definitive way like biological species. . . . [A] true class requires a set of distinguishing features which are inclusive within the class and exclusive outside it; it requires a *differentia specifica*. That, according to Aristotle, is the key to definition and to essence. But, in fact, nobody has ever so defined literature or any important genre within it."[7] All of which is very persuasive. Nonetheless, several issues are raised by Hirsch's position. Most important, despite an all too indiscriminate admiration of science and the scientific, which pervades humanistic studies, biological typology does not benefit from a *differentia specifica*. The distinctive features are distinctive only in their plural congruence, when they function successfully to isolate—more or less and for the most part—a locus. As any good biologist knows, biological typology is rife with problems; every class has its own variation on the duckbilled platypus.

That said, I do suspect aesthetic genres are more problematic than biological species. In the latter case, only the definition is of human invention. The external referent may alter, but that alteration is at worst very slow. In aesthetics, however, both the classification and the objects under study come from the creative hearth of man and are subject to constant, sometimes revolutionary change. Moreover, since creativity, by definition, implies the devising of something new, no aesthetic definition can be anything but retrospective, and it must be revised and updated to accommodate innovations. The distinction between *novel* and *romance* on the basis of the presence of realistic or fantastic material is no longer helpful, for example, and current definitions of the novel need not, indeed should not, take subject matter into account. The hope of contriving a definition of short story which will remain useful until the end of time will be possible only when the short story dies as a genre. Although that has happened with the epic poem, it has not with the short story, and I shall be content to point to common ground. The indistinct, problematic outer edges of that area may be safely left for individual exploration.

Lexicographers are basically collectors. After gathering as many samples of usage as possible, and discarding the deviations, they compose a definition which comes as close to standard usage as possible. If the norm changes, adaptations or completely new formulations must be devised. Just as the reality referred to by linguistic signs is neither *ab ovo* nor *ad vitam aeternam,* so definitions must shift, change, adjust to reflect the reality circumscribed. Definitions are not God-carved and imposed from above. Rather, they reflect communal agreement. It may be regrettable that this accord is subject to change, has exceptions, and is seldom more than approximate, but it is a well understood and accepted fact of linguistics. It should not keep us from reaching that agreement necessary for almost any human and all social activity. Such accord is certainly a *sine qua non* of reading. On remembering Heinrich Wölfflin's magnificent effort, one might draw comfort from the realization that even topological failures may be helpful in understanding art. Though Wölfflin failed in his intention to define all art, he went far toward delineating "classical" and "baroque," the historical categories that had been largely exhausted by his time and could thus be looked at retrospectively.[8]

No generic definition of science or literature can hope to do more than draw attention to the dominant aspects of the system which will inevitably include elements to be found elsewhere. As Tynjanov explains with particular reference to literature, "Since a system is not an equal interaction of all elements but places a group of elements in the foreground—the 'dominant'—and thus involves the deformation of the remaining elements, a work enters into literature and takes on its own literary function through this dominant. Thus we correlate poems with the verse category, not with the prose category, not on the basis of all their characteristics, but only of some of them."[9]

The problems that cause difficulty in arriving at definitions of human creations should not cause us to join Léon Roudiez in concluding, "[T]he concept of genre is not as useful as it was in the past."[10] Acceptable definitions are even more needed these days, since most, though not all, of the generically controversial works (I think in particular of creations by Godard and Sollers) were *meant* to disrupt categories. For critics to deny the existence of the genre, novel, for example, deprives a Sollers of the opportunity to attack bourgeois society by undermining one of its conceptual categories. Surely, part of the enjoyment of works which fall on the edge of or between well established generic boundaries comes from their problematic nature as genre.

There comes a time when human cleverness, on the one hand, and stubborn ineptitude, on the other, must be reckoned with. It may be impossible to define a genre, but readers do it all the time, and they use their definitions as guides. That such readers are consequently led astray on occasion does not impede their behavior in the slightest. A reader may not know a lesson of the ancients and of modern psychology: that we see only what we are prepared for; we understand only what is within our ken. Nonetheless—however unconsciously—readers look for what they know. History is replete with the disasters caused by those who expectations did not correspond with their experience and who nonetheless clung to their misconceptions. As just one example we might remember the bizarre readings that several centuries of readers, who did not know the story of Job, accorded to Boccaccio's tenth tale of the tenth day about Griselda.[11] Perhaps such misdeeds are unimportant. Perhaps. I would rather conclude that there may be wisdom in laying groundwork which aids perception and understanding. Not only does it lead to communication, thus to civilization rather than the jungle, in art it can lead to the enjoyment of great beauty.

The work of defining a genre succeeds when the definition corresponds to general practice and understanding, when it includes the samples generally included, and excludes those normally left out, when its categories do not erroneously focus on elements which cause misapprehensions. No one element will ever serve as a discretionary touchstone. One hopes that the various traits together will provide a means of discrimination. The fact that both insects and snakes are cold-blooded, for example, does not prevent us from using "cold-blooded" in definitions of both. There will be problem cases which present intentional or unintentional difficulties, but until such exceptions become commonplace, they should be appreciated for the significance raised by their very deviations. They should not be allowed to negate existing definitions and certainly not the possibility of arriving at an accord.

If, then, one is justified in pulling short stories from the vast sea of narrations, the following definition might be advanced: a short story is a *short, literary prose fiction.* At first glance such a formulation seems uncontroversial but, at second remove, one realizes that every one of the definition's four key words covers a library of controversy. The usefulness of the formulation depends on what it truly means and on whether it serves to bring the short story into focus, at least retrospectively, while helping us as well to consider the subsets that are created by particular authors, movements, or periods.

The concept of "fiction" has challenged our best minds and elicited volumes of commentary, perhaps justifying a certain wary caution in dealing with it. For the purposes of discrimination, I pay particular attention to its linguistic referent. Though fiction may be propositionally true, it "deals in untrue specificities, untrue facts," as Thomas J. Roberts would have it,[12] and it explicitly or implicitly warns the readers of this state of affairs. Consequently, the primary creation of fiction—be it pattern, plot, or world—cannot be verified externally. The whole point of the writings of scientists, sociologists, and historians is that they can be verified and double-checked; however well-organized and abstract they may be, they are open to the control of objective validation, both in totality and in detail. Of course, current or historical events may be present in fiction without changing its primary thrust of creating an unverifiable complex in a reader's mind. Likewise, the occurrence of a lie or two, for example in Rousseau's *Les Confessions* (1781, 1788), does not fiction make, for

Rousseau clearly intended his work to present the general, rather than specific, truth of his character. Conversely, Jesus' parable of the prodigal son exists primarily in that focused image created by the words of the parable. There will, of course, be extremely problematic instances. One famous example, though in the realm of the novel, is the *Lettres de la religieuse portugaise* (1669). "Sontelles authentiques?" asks Philippe van Tieghem. "Il semble qu'on n'en puisse pas douter" (Are they authentic? It seems that we cannot doubt it).[13] In fact, of course, many scholars have doubted their authenticity. Are they indeed actual love letters from the nun Maria Alcoforade, or do we owe them to the literary skill of someone like Guilleragues? They seem just too well done, their haunting lyricism too unflawed for nonfiction. But, in truth, we do not know. Furthermore, the potential problem of illusion in conflict with reality does not seriously afflict the short story. This genre, most of us would agree, includes factual history only incidentally; it is fiction. While it is calumnious to doubt the virtuous Marguerite de Navarre's insistence on the truth of her stories, their artistry (in line with what I shall suggest further on) has raised them above mere reality. They are short stories.

The term *fiction* does, however, cover a difficulty of considerable magnitude. Most considerations of the short story insist upon the *story,* for the causally and chronologically constructed narration is generally viewed as central. I have argued at some length elsewhere that Balzac, in story and novel, subordinated narration to description, that he was interested in painting the portrait of an age and a civilization, rather than telling the events in the life of a Gobseck or a Père Goriot. Fiction's tendency toward the dominance of image is anything but rare after the early nineteenth century. It appears in an emphasis on what Joseph Frank has called "spatial form," what I have called "image structure," what others call tone, or mood, or focus, or theme (as in Frank O'Connor's "loneliness").[14] Whoever thinks that the events leading up to the moment when the Prussians leave the mad woman to die alone in the snowy woods are the main thrust of Maupassant's "La Folle" (1882) has missed the point and been drawn to the negligible plot rather than to the central focus on man's brutish pride and his resultant inability to communicate. Likewise for "Menuet" (1883), the touching portrait of two delicate remnants of former days, and for dozens of other tales by Maupassant. For these and an increasing number of stories in the twentieth century, plot—whether Todorov's single change in state or Prince's three or more conjoined events[15]—has the importance that it has in Robbe-Grillet's "La Plage" (1962), where three children walk along a beach leaving imprints in the sand which, the reader understands, will shortly be effaced by the timeless sea's tide. Of course, for many short stories, plot dominates. I could cite hundreds of examples, from the discovery and punishment of the adulterous monks of the thirty-second tale in the *Cent Nouvelles Nouvelles* (1462) to the progressive revelation of the hero's past as he falls from the Empire State Building to become "une méduse rouge sur l'asphalte de la cinquième avenue" (a red medusa on the asphalt on Fifth Avenue) in Boris Vian's "Le Rappel" (1962). *Fiction* may cover stories that are predominantly narrative or description.

Some have wanted to reserve the term *short story* for rather specific subject matter. Murray Sachs feels, for example, that for the "educated" *conte* "has a strong flavor of the unreal or the supernatural. . . . [T]he word *nouvelle* is sometimes confined because of etymology to narratives which have the character of real events (or 'news'), and is felt to be inapplicable to stories of the fantastic or the improbable."[16] Alfred G. Engstrom would disagree with Sachs. For him, "supernatural narrations (fairy tales, legends of demons, saints, gods and the like) and the tales of outright wizardry" are generally to be excluded from the *conte,* thus from the short story.[17] This distinction is, of course, similar to the old separation between the novel and the romance. While I might interject that *nouvelle* seems to be used primarily as a generic term to cover such subcategories as *conte,* tale, anecdote, and so on, and that *conte* maintains a strong association with its oral roots, I think all such discussions miss the point.[18] Ian Reid is right to be disturbed by the distinction, however much he accepts it. As Reid recognizes, "*Exempla* about tediously saintly figures, snippets of legend about marvels and eerie occurrences: such things differ quite patently from those tales that are imaginatively cohesive even when fantastic and elliptical, or from tales that explore a mental and moral dimension by evoking the preternatural, as in Hawthorne's 'Young Goodman Brown' with its symbols of devilry and witchcraft."[19] The key is not whether or not a myth, legend, or mythological story is recounted, it is whether it is done artistically.

Artistry constitutes a given of any definition of aesthetic genres. It needs be neither intended nor understood—to take into account Northrop Frye's compelling argument that Thucydides' *History of the Peloponnesian War* (424?—404? B.C.) could now be appropriately taken, not as history, but as art. Of course, "artistry," as a generic touchstone leaves much to be desired, for one thinks of the poor or failed art that graces certain popular magazines. Still, even such regrettable exemplars show a desire to touch readers aesthetically. One might then include certain stories published in, say, *Sunshine Magazine,* though one would doubtless exclude most tales catalogued in the Stith Thompson index. Few would deny that Perrault's

"Le Petit Poucet" (1697), Flaubert's "La Légende de saint Julien l'Hospi-talier" (1877), Anatole France's "Le Jongleur de Notre-Dame" (1892) are excellent short stories. The short story is open to any topic, any material. Whether one admits a particular work—say, one of the legends in Jacobus de Voragine's *Legenda aurea* (1255–56)—to the short story genre is open to discussion, but the deciding factor is usually not the presence or absence of a saint or supernatural events, but rather the artistry in the creation of a reality whose existence depends primarily upon the text in question. It must, in short, be an artistic fiction.

When I earlier suggested that a short story is a "short, *literary* prose fiction," I meant only that the creation must be artistically fashioned, with the apparent intention of making something beautiful. How one deter-mines the existence of such an intention is, of course, debatable, especially in specific instances. For our purposes, however, this is less important than establishing that there must be artistry for the short story to exist. While the problem is not often posed in these terms, short story criticism makes it clear that the story's implicit aesthetic goal is, though perhaps unstated, accepted. Certainly, the particular cast to the creation has been an important consideration for many interested in prescriptive theory. Ludwig Tieck emphasizes the importance of the narrative crux, that moment where things change, as does Ruth J. Kilchenmann, though she makes a bigger point of the plot rising to and falling from that crisis.[20] Others, like Ellery Sedgewick, stress the importance of the ending—"A story is like a horse race. It is the start and finish that count most"[21]—while for Chekhov neither beginning nor end really matters. Brander Matthews attempted to turn Edgar Allan Poe's less than precise com-ments into a rigid *Ars poetica,* and numerous writers and critics have held up O. Henry's trick endings as a model.[22] Some insist on highly developed character, others on a unique, unilinear plot, others on one device or another. I would rather say simply that the preferred devices and vehicles change through the ages without changing the short story from its primary thrust—whether real or merely perceived—of making an aesthetic unit.

Aesthetic canons change to some degree from individual to individual and to a large degree from age to age and culture to culture. The pre-Renaissance *Novillinos,* for example, were extremely short (one to two pages) and concentrated on the moment of revelation or resolution, on a wise judgment, a noble deed, a clever retort. When Boccaccio expanded the anecdote, exploiting a situation, elaborating on the circumstances leading to the resolution, the aesthetic value shifts from appreciation of vigorous effects to the skill in revealing the subtleties as they played one against the other. Had Gobineau written his expertly narrated short stories during the eighteenth century, when it was common in short and long fiction to string episodes onto a protagonist's perambulations, they would have been far more successful than they were in the mid-nineteenth century, when intensity and vividness were prized. Still, in all periods, though the values may change, though the concept of artistry may diverge, the effort to make art is easily discernible. Neglecting the specific aesthetic criteria of a specific age for the purposes of conceptualizing the genre as a whole does not, of course, prevent one from concentrating on a particular period and its values or, from another point of view, from doing a history of the genre where changing values and techniques are stressed. As René Wellek pointed out, relating an individual reality to a general value does not necessarily degrade the individual to a mere specimen of a general concept. It may in fact give significance to the individual, by providing a backdrop which adds depth of meaning to the example under consideration.[23]

To say that short stories are "prose" seems at first glance the least contentious claim possible. Of all the assumptions prevalent in anthologies and critical theory, this is surely the most common. Still, all one need do is bring attention to bear on the issue and one remembers fictional, indeed narrational, works of verse. (Verse is simply written language organized primarily by meter, which makes prose that written language where metrical rhythm exists only incidentally.) Do we really wish to exclude *fabliaux,* those marvelous verse-tales of the Middle Ages, from the short story? Of course, in an age that prides itself on its tolerance, it is difficult to approve of any exclusivity. Unlike the color line in a Birmingham bus depot, however, no harm comes from refusing *fabliaux* the status of short story. To the contrary, it does considerable good, for it emphasizes an essential but neglected characteristic. In the original versions (as opposed to prose translations), one understands how important the rhythm is to these medieval creations. Without it, they are much impoverished. The question is not whether the text contains a marked rhythm, for many fine novels and short stories do, but whether that rhythm constitutes a dominant element. As Victor Erlich explains in regard to the Russian Formalists, "[T]he differentia of verse [is] not in the mere presence of an element—in this case, a regular or semi-regular ordering of the sound-pattern—but in its status. In 'practical' language it was argued, in ordinary speech or in scientific discourse, rhythm is a secondary phenomenon—a physiological expedient or a by-product of syntax; in poetry it is a primary and 'self-valuable' quality."[24] As with the other issues I have discussed, there will be cases where judicious application of the touchstone remains difficult or impossible. I think of Dylan Thomas's "stories" or "fictions" or whatever, whose lush and rhythmical verbal palate "was not easily confined to literary categories and prescribed lengths," as was stated in an anonymous "Note" to *Adventures in the Skin Trade and Other Stories*.[25] Some might even wish to raise the issue of Edwin Arlington Robinson's poetry. For myself, though "Richard Cory" or "Miniver Cheevy" or "Old King Cole" would doubtless add luster of a certain sort to the short story, it would change the cast of the particular luminescence we all recognize. But the matter is open to disagreement. As said before, definitions in aesthetic matters are never definitive; they are guidelines *or* baffles that may at any point be abandoned by either readers or writers.

Which leaves the most difficult touchstone, "short." No one disputes the necessity of brevity to the short story, though there has been considerable discussion about the precise meaning of the trait. German critics retained the word *Novelle* for fictions of intermediate length and coined a new one for the very short: *Kurzgeschichte*. Should one instead follow E. M. Forster and separate short stories from novels at fifty thousand words,[26] it is easy to quibble with that figure, for it would include as short stories such works, generally considered novels, as *L'Immoraliste, L'Etranger,* and many others. While, as said before, inclusion or exclusion from a genre does not affect the quality of a work, it may encourage readers to read with inappropriate expectations. Arbitrariness is not in itself wrong. Even in the physical realm, at some point distinctions must be made. Everyone, for example, would agree that red is the color produced by rather long light waves (thirty-three thousand could be fitted into an inch); nonetheless, it is not easy to tell exactly where red becomes orange and orange yellow. The graduations are infinite, though perhaps not as numerous as in literature. Whatever categories be established, they should at least seem reasonable, and Forster's fifty thousand words is simply too long.

Perhaps because of the discomfiture caused by an arbitrary figure, be it eight thousand words or fifty thousand, most critics have felt more at home with Poe's claim that one should be able to read a short story at one sitting. The problem with the distinction is obvious, though William Saroyan is credited with pointing it out: some people can sit for longer periods than others.[27] There is a good deal to be said for Poe's criterion, however. Most importantly, it emphasizes the absolute impossibility of extreme arbitrariness, without denying the necessity of shortness, however it be defined. Brevity is affected by particular conditions, by individual idiosyncracies, and, as Paul Zumthor has said, by culture.[28] What is long for an American would be doubtless be very short for a Zulu. What seems short on an ocean cruise is impossibly long on a lunch break. As should be evident, however, I am not attempting to impose rigid rules. Excellent short stories of less than one thousand words exist (I think, for example, of Maupassant's "Le Lit" [1882]), as do those of over thirty thousand words (like Gautier's "La Jettatura" [1856]). Rather, I wish to take up the provocative suggestion that brevity imposes particular forms: "[C]'est que la brièveté n'est jamais aléatoire, mais qu'*elle constitue un modèle formalisant* (Brevity is never aleatory, but rather *it constitutes a formalizing model*).[29] I would not be quite so quick to categorize the way this formalizing function is actualized, but it seems to me that this insight, in combination with the other generic markers already discussed, goes far in allowing the definition I propose to be discrete.

Edgar Allan Poe's insistence on "one pre-established design" has been roundly condemned as having led to an abuse of formulas and formula writing. Nonetheless, the limitations of Poe's imitators do not impugn the wisdom of Poe's original intuition:

> A skilful literary artist has constructed a tale. If wise, he has not fashioned his thoughts to accommodate his incidents; but having conceived, with deliberate care, a certain unique or single *effect* to be wrought out, he then invents such incidents—he then combines such events as may best aid him in establishing this preconceived effect. If his very initial sentence tend not to the outbringing of this effect, then he has failed in his first step. In the whole composition there should be no word written, of which the tendency, direct or indirect, is not to the one pre-established design. . . . Undue brevity is just as exceptionable here as in the poem; but undue length is yet more to be avoided.[30]

Chekhov's famous dictum—that if one introduces a revolver or a shotgun in the early part of a story, it must go off before the end—similarly stresses the short story's need for economy. Because of its brevity, the short story remains as foreign to loosely motivated detail as it does to amplification. For precisely the same reasons that we become annoyed when even a good lecture goes beyond the allotted time, so readers begin to fidget when a "short" story begins to drag on, when one suspects that the main point is being dissipated or lost. Where many of the most telling effects of Proust's *A la recherche du temps perdu* come from the rediscovery only possible after having forgotten, readers of short stories have everything present. They may of course be inattentive but writers cannot count on it. Authors of short fiction especially must assume that their readers will pay attention and, most importantly, will remember what they read. If that is true, it would follow that readers will have less patience with repetition, which in one form or another is fundamental to most of the devices used to give form to all literature. I do not wish to suggest that there will be no repetition, only that it must be done with great discretion to avoid setting up the kinds of rhythm that turn prose into poetry, on the one hand, or, on the other, effects that seem overly obvious and thus heavy-handed or pedestrian.

For similar reasons, the short story is usually single- rather than multivalent. Both Dopplegänger and subplot do occur, though in nowhere near the frequency of longer fiction. There is indeed a marked tendency toward unity. Complexity comes more frequently from depth of implication than from obvious repetition or multiplicity. Even where doubling occurs, there is a particular simplicity about it which distinguishes it from the novel. Take for example, Maupassant's "Ce Cochon de Morin" (1882), where the humor depends on watching Morin's charges be dismissed only because his friend is more successful at *cochonnerie*. One's attention is constantly directed to the poetic injustice of it all, and the doubling is kept singular in effect. Maupassant's success with the short story, while his novels never quite measured up, can perhaps be attributed to his inability to handle the large number of strands involved in really fine novels. The manifest failure of *Bel Ami* (1885) comes not from the shallowness of the main character's characterization, it seems to me, but from the lack of total coherence. Each of the chapters makes a fine, occasionally a brilliant, short story, but the multiple effects which in a novel tie the chapters to the whole never quite succeed in glueing the segments of Maupassant's novel together. The work appears to be a sequence of beads strung on a reappearing name. The plurality which serves in the case of the novel to emphasize, nuance, or countervail runs the risk of appearing redundant and distracting, if not disruptive, in the short story.

Equally because of the need for brevity, the short story tends toward the general. Even when detail is rife, readers expect the vocabulary to bear more than its usual significance and are, I suspect, more prone than with the novel to universalize. Not only does every word carry a full weight of meaning, short stories also make frequent use of ellipsis. Readers expect to generalize, to read in depth and between the lines. With due regard for Robbe-Grillet's insistence on neutral creations that permit the reader to invent his own meaning, "La Plage" would not have anywhere near the power it has if the children were crossing a park to answer their mother's or nature's call. Instead, because of the sand and sea, we view the ephemeral children before a timeless—because cyclical—universe.

The epigrammatic *pointe* was long considered desirable, even essential, to the short story. At its worst, it consisted of the "surprise" ending, for example in Maupassant's "Le Mariage du lieutenant Laré" (1878), where the revelation has no real significance and does not encourage the reader to rethink what he has read. At its best, however, as in Villiers de l'Isle-Adam's "L'Enjeu" (1888) or Anatole France's "Le Procurateur de Judée" (1892), the conclusion throws a startling new light on the preceding fiction and accords profundity to what had seemed more limited. Despite the frequency of stories which draw to a conclusion where exclamation points seem appropriate, not all stories do. Just as Ronsard developed sonnets which manage successfully to turn around a center, rather than lead to an epigram, so many stories end when the portrait, or the tone, or the concept has been completed. As just one of many examples, one might think of Borges's "La Lotería en Babilonia" (1944), where the conclusion arrives when the potential of the permutations is evident.

For Zumthor, short texts are particularly oriented toward the present. He justifies his position by referring to the particular weight that language takes when the real time of the reading or performance is short. He goes on to consider another trait: "[L]a cohésion d'un texte de quelque longueur se perçoit progressivement, au fur et à mesure de la lecture: un moment survient où les indices en apparaissent, puis s'organisent dans l'imagination du lecteur en système idéal de règles de combinaison, hypothèse interprétative, confirmée ou infirmée par la suite. La cohésion du message bref est d'autre nature, au moins tendanciellement: elle est donnée d'emblée, empiriquement, sensoriellement, comme une certitude globale dont les conséquences éventuelles se déduisent au cours de la brève lecture ou de la brève audition" ([T]he cohesion of a text of some length is perceived progressively as the reading proceeds: a moment comes when the indications of this cohesiveness appear, then are organized in the reader's imagination as an ideal system of rules of combination, an interpretive hypothesis, confirmed or invalidated by what follows. The cohesion of a brief message is of another nature, at least tendentially: it is given at the beginning, empirically, sensorially, as a global certitude whose eventual consequences are deduced in the course of the brief reading or brief audition).[31] In short, brief works appear to overpower the narration; the sequence, whether chronological or causal, has less impact than the unit of perception or meaning that one grasps as a whole. In a sense, this is often true. The short story, in particular, has a noticable affinity for the epigrammatic, the formulistic, the epitome, the essential truth or idea or image which rises above time and negates whatever chronological progression the work possesses. Even in stories where change is of the essence, say, for example, "The Short Happy Life of Francis Macomber" (1936), one remembers Macomber's apotheosis as a "man" in confrontation with his wife as a failure, rather than the development leading up to the final scene. That, however, is not always the case. In a work like Maupassant's "Le Horla" (1887), it is the crescendo of fear rather than the fear itself which draws us, or, for one last example, in Camus's "La Pierre qui pousse" (1957), we center on d'Arrast as he progressively finds kingdom in exile.

I could continue discussing the ways brevity marks and indeed forms the short story without exhausting the subject. Authors' inventiveness seems unlimited. The point, however, is not an enumeration of the particular procedures and devices which might be listed under brachylogy, but to suggest the importance of that quality which distinguishes a short story from mere prose fiction. I would suggest that brevity constitutes the most significant trait of this particular genre. In large measure, it determines the devices used and the effects achieved. Certainly brevity constitutes the short story's greatest limitation. For a short story to succeed, the author must overcome the restraints of limited length and communicate not a segment, a tattered fragment, but a world.

In suggesting that one might view the short story as an artistically designed short prose fiction, I have been only secondarily interested in providing a definition. It is rather the defense of such a definition which might be helpful. The discussion of the constituent elements of a short story, while falling far short of a touchstone good in all cases and for all time, may help readers have productive rather than destructive expectations when they pick up a representative example. However impressed one might be by those who would avoid the problem of literary genres by denying them, it is indisputable that most readers are firmly conscious of genre and use their preconception to guide their reading. The more adequate that preconception, the more chance there is of an adequate reading which recognizes the true significance of the story, whether it be in line with or in revolt against that particular cluster of traits which I have treated here and which most of us, I suspect, recognize as a short story.

NOTES

1. See Charles E. May, "Introduction: A Survey of Short Story Criticism in America," in his *Short Story Theories* (Athens, Ohio, 1976), pp. 3–12; and Thomas A. Gullason, "The Short Story: An Underrated Art," in May, pp. 13–31.

2. Mary Doyle Springer, *Forms of the Modern Novella* (Chicago, 1976), p.

128   Allan H. Pasco

17; Elizabeth Bowen, "The Faber Book of Modern Short Stories," in May, pp. 152–58.

3. H. E. Bates, *The Modern Short Story: A Critical Survey* (Boston, 1972), p. 13.

4. See Robert J. Clements and Joseph Gibaldi, *Anatomy of the Novella: The European Tale Collection from Boccaccio and Chaucer to Cervantes* (New York, 1977); see also, e.g., Warren S. Walker, "From Raconteur to Writer: Oral Roots and Printed Leaves of Short Fiction," in *The Teller and the Tale: Aspects of the Short Story,* Proceedings, Comparative Literature Symposium, 23–25 Jan. 1980 (Lubbock, Tex., 1982), p. 14.

5. See, e.g., Gérard Genette, "Genres, 'types,' modes," *Poétique,* 32 (1977), 389–421; Jean-Marie Schaeffer, "Du texte au genre," *Poétique,* 53 (1983), 3–18; Heather Dubrow, *Genre* (London, 1982).

6. Harry Steinhauer, "Towards a Definition of the Novella," *Seminar,* 6 (1970), 174.

7. E. D. Hirsch, Jr., *The Aims of Interpretation* (Chicago, 1976), pp. 120–21.

8. See Heinrich Wölffin, *Principles of Art History: The Problem of the Development of Style in Later Art,* tr. from the 7th ed. (1929) by M. D. Hottinger (New York, n.d.).

9. Jurij Tynjanov, "On Literary Evolution" (1927), tr. C. A. Luplow, in *Readings in Russian Poetics: Formalist and Structuralist Views,* ed. Ladislav Matejka and Krystyna Pomorska (Cambridge, Mass., 1971), pp. 72–73.

10. Léon S. Roudiez, *French Fiction Today: A New Direction* (New Brunswick, N.J., 1972), p. 6.

11. See Enrico de'Negri, "The Legendary Style of the *Decameron,*" *Romanic Review,* 43 (1952), 166–89. The positive effects of reader focus according to generic understanding has been forcefully made by Dubrow, pp. 1–4, 8–44.

12. Thomas J. Roberts, *When Is Something Fiction?* (Carbondale, Ill., 1972), p. 11. See also, René Wellek and Austin Warren, *Theory of Literature* (New York, 1949), pp. 15–16, 221–22; Monroe C. Beardsley, *Aesthetics: Problems in the Philosophy of Criticism* (New York, 1958), pp. 419–37; and Michel Butor, *Répertoire* (Paris, 1960), pp. 7–8.

13. Philippe Van Tieghem, "Les Prosateurs du XVIIe siècle," in *Encyclopédie de la Pléiade,* ed. Raymond Queneau (Paris, 1958), III, 429.

14. See Joseph Frank, *The Widening Gyre: Crisis and Mastery in Modern Literature* (1963; rpt. Bloomington, Ind., 1968); Allan H. Pasco, "Descriptive Narration in Balzac's *Gobseck,*" *Virginia Quarterly Review,* 56 (1980), 99–108. For "tone" see Robert Pinget, "Pseudo-Principes d'esthétique," in *Nouveau roman: Hier, aujourd'hui,* ed. Jean Ricardou and Françoise van Rossum-Guyon (Paris, 1972), II, 311–24. For "mood," see Georg Lukács, *The Theory of the Novel* (Cambridge, Mass., 1971), pp. 51–52, or Eileen Baldeshwiler, "The Lyric Short Story: The Sketch of a History" (1969), in May, pp. 202–13. For "focus," see Mordecai Marcus, "What is an Initiation Story?" (1960), in May, pp. 189–201.

For "theme," see Frank O'Connor [Michael O'Donovan], *The Lonely Voice: A Study of the Short Story* (Cleveland, 1963).

15. See Tzvetan Todorov, "La Grammaire du récit," *Languages,* 12 (1968), 96; and Gerald Prince, *A Grammar of Stories* (The Hague, 1973), p. 31.

16. Murray Sachs, "Introduction," in *The French Short Story in the Nineteenth Century: A Critical Anthology,* ed. Murray Sachs (New York, 1969), p. 13.

17. Alfred G. Engstrom, "The Formal Short Story in France and Its Development Before 1850," *Studies in Philology,* 42 (1945), 631.

18. I have by no means exhausted the controversies surrounding "conte" and "nouvelle." One other position, which has had considerable mileage, might be mentioned: "Meanwhile [in the first half of the nineteenth century], the word *conte* was assuming a meaning that differentiated it from *nouvelle,* the former accepted as more concentrated, with one major episode, the latter more complex and consisting of several scenes" (Albert J. George, *Short Fiction in France 1800–1850* [Syracuse, N.Y., 1964], p. 234). The example of the *conte de fées* or fairy tale immediately points to the problems with such a distinction, for these tales are often remarkably complex.

19. Ian Reid, *The Short Story,* The Critical Idiom, no. 37 (London, 1977), pp. 8–9.

20. Reid, pp. 12–13.

21. Ellery Sedgewick, "The Telling of Tales," in *Novel and Story: A Book of Modern Readings,* ed. Ellery Sedgewick (Boston, 1939), p. 6; quoted in Bates, p. 17.

22. May, pp. 4–5.

23. See René Wellek, "Literary History," *Literary Scholarship: Its Aims and Methods,* ed. Norman Foerster, et al. (Chapel Hill, N.C., 1941), p. 124.

24. Victor Erlich, *Russian Formalism: History, Doctrine,* 3rd ed. (Paris, 1969), p. 213.

25. Anonymous editor, *Adventures in the Skin Trade and Other Stories,* by Dylan Thomas (New York, 1956), p. vii.

26. See E. M. Forster, *Aspects of the Novel,* (1927; rpt. New York, 1954), pp. 5–6.

27. Reid, p. 9.

28. See Paul Zumthor, "La Brièveté comme forme," in *Formation, codification et rayonnement d'un genre médiéval: la nouvelle,* Actes du Colloque International de Montréal, McGill University, 14–16 octobre 1982, ed. Michelangelo Picone, et al. (Montréal, 1983), p. 4.

29. I quote Zumthor—"Brièveté," p. 3—though, of course the idea that form is content and in their relationship the one is governed by the other is implicit in Aristotle. Nor is the thought that brevity may structure short stories new: see, e.g., Edward D. Sullivan, *Maupassant: The Short Stories* (London, 1962). Zumthor's contribution resides in his attempt to go beyond the "form equals content" truism and to show *how,* specifically, the quality of being short affects the form at

every level. See, also, Zumthor's *Essai de poétique médiéval* (Paris, 1972), pp. 339–404. I attempt to carry the analysis somewhat further.

30. Edgar Allan Poe, rev. of *Twice-Told Tales,* by Nathaniel Hawthorne, *Graham's Magazine,* 20 (1842), 298–300; rpt. in May, pp. 47–48.

31. Zumthor, p. 6.

The Nature
of Knowledge in
Short Fiction

CHARLES E. MAY

IN THE ANCIENT history of the human use of narrative as a mode of communication, the short story precedes the long story as the most natural means of narrative communication. Episodic expression in which *animal symbolicum* speaks as an individual precedes epic expression in which he speaks as a social animal. Primitive man's feeling of a solidarity of life was precisely that—a feeling—rather than a concept of the systematic pattern of social functioning. And these feelings of solidarity came to him in the midst of episodic encounters with the sacred, set apart from the profane reality of the everyday flow of life by his own individual emotional response to the experiences. These episodes in which the inner meaning of things was manifested, in which nature and the self were united in what for him was true reality, he attempted to stabilize for himself and communicate to others in stories that were short. Only later did man link these stories together and extrapolate from them a conceptual cosmology in accordance to which he guided his social life.

In his "panorama" of the English novel, Lionel Stevenson suggests the usual distinction between the two basic forms of fictional narrative by describing them this way: "One is the brief narrative that can be recounted on a single occasion. Thence emerged the fairy tale, the folk ballad, and eventually what is now called the short story. The other form is longer and more complex, requiring a series of sessions for its delivery. From it descended the saga, the epic, and finally the novel."[1] Stevenson expresses the prevailing critical bias that the long story is, by its very length, "more complex" than the short story and therefore more deserving of critical attention. Even those critics who recognize this view as a biased one still seem bound by it. In the first paragraph of their influential study of narrative, Robert Scholes and Robert Kellogg announce that their purpose is "to put the novel in its place," seeing it as only "one of a number of narrative possibilities." And Northrop Frye, in his often-anthologized essay on prose fiction in *Anatomy of Criticism,* notes the embarrassment of the literary historian who identifies fiction with the novel when he is forced to acknowledge the length of time the world managed to get along without the form.[2] However, in their concern with the wide variety of narrative forms that existed before the novel, neither of these studies mention, except as an aside, that form of prose fiction which originated in the most primal narrative impulse and which has developed with sophistication and vigor alongside the novel—the short story.

This attitude toward the short story, an attitude that hardly makes the form worth mentioning in the rarefied atmosphere of current "serious" criticism about "serious" literature, is not new in Anglo-American literary studies; it is, in fact, as old as criticism of the form itself. In 1901, in the first full-length study of the short story, Brander Matthews noted the "strange neglect" of the form in histories of prose fiction.[3] But for all his efforts to justify Poe's suggestive comments about the form made sixty years earlier and thus to establish the "art of the short-story," Matthews only succeeded in solidifying critical reaction against short fiction. Instead of Matthews' opinion—that the short story is a unique art form differing from the novel in substantive ways—it is the opinion of an anonymous reviewer in the London *Academy* which has remained: "The short story is a smaller, simpler, easier, and less important form of the novel."[4]

My own position about the two basic fictional forms is aligned with that of Russian Formalist critic B. M. Éjxenbaum, who says that the novel and the short story are not only different in kind, but also "inherently at odds." Genetically, the novel is a syncretic form, says Éjxenbaum, either developed from collections of stories or complicated by the incorporation of "manners and morals" material. The short story, on the other hand, is a "fundamental, elementary (which does not mean primitive) form." The difference between the two is one of essence, "a difference in principle conditioned by the fundamental distinction between big and small forms."[5] My assumption is that when we discuss the differences between long fiction and short fiction, we must discuss basic differences in the ontology and epistemology of the two forms. The short story is short precisely because of the kind of experience or reality embodied in it. And the kind of experience we find in the short story reflects a mode of knowing which differs essentially from the mode of knowing we find in the novel. My thesis is that long fiction, by its very length, demands both a subject matter and a set of artistic conventions that primarily derive from and in turn establish the primacy of "experience" conceptually created and considered; whereas short fiction, by its very length, demands both a subject matter and a set of artistic conventions that derive from and establish the primacy of "an experience" directly and emotionally created and encountered.

If the novel creates the illusion of reality by presenting a literal authenticity to the material facts of the external world, as Ian Watt suggests, the short story attempts to be authentic to the immaterial reality of the inner world of the self in its relation to eternal rather than temporal reality. If the novel's quest for extensional reality takes place in the social world and the material of its analyses are manners as the indication of one's soul, as Lionel Trilling says, the field of research for the short story is the primitive, antisocial world of the unconscious, and the material of its analysis are not manners, but dreams. The results of this distinction are that whereas the novel is primarily a social and public form, the short story is mythic and spiritual. While the novel is primarily structured on a conceptual and philosophic framework, the short story is intuitive and lyrical. The novel exists to reaffirm the world of "everyday" reality; the short story exists to "defamiliarize" the everyday. Storytelling does not spring from one's confrontation with the everyday world, but rather from one's encounter with the sacred (in which true reality is revealed in all its plenitude) or with the absurd (in which true reality is revealed in all its vacuity).

In his pre-Marxist attempt to develop a general dialectic of literary genres based on aesthetic categories and literary forms, Georg Lukács makes some brief comments that support this view. The lyrical nature of the short story is explained by Lukács by the fact that short stories deal with fragments of life. For whenever a fragment is lifted out of the totality of life, this very delimitation stamps the work with its origin in the author's will. Such a lifting of a fragment implies a "form-giving, structuring, delimiting act." However, in the short story, "the narrative form which pinpoints the strangeness and ambiguity of life, such lyricism must entirely *conceal itself* behind the hard outlines of the event." For Lukács, the short story is the most purely artistic form; it expresses the "ultimate meaning of all artistic creation as *mood*." The short story sees "absurdity in all its undisguised and unadorned nakedness, and the exorcising power of this view, without fear or hope, gives it the consecration of form; meaninglessness *as meaninglessness* becomes form; it becomes eternal because it is affirmed, transcended and redeemed by form."[6]

Lukács' suggestions here are important ones because they underlie an essential reason for the short story's neglect by serious critics of fiction. William Abrahams, *O. Henry Prize Story* editor, hinted at the reason in a public statement in 1970 by suggesting that there seems something unhealthy about the short story, something built into the form itself that is limiting. In the same year, Bernard Bergonzi echoed this view in the appendix to his *The Situation of the Novel*. The form of the short story, argues Bergonzi, "tends to filter down experience to the prime elements of defeat and alienation." Without justifying how the form of the story compels this view, Bergonzi suggests that the short story is limited "both in the range of literary experience it offers and its capacity to deepen our understanding of the world, or of one another."[7] Such a view, widely but tacitly held, is of course based on unstated assumptions about *how* one understands the world and other people and *what* one takes to be the reality of that world. It implies concomitant assumptions about epistemological, and therefore generic, distinctions between fictions that are long and fictions that are short.

My purpose here is to try to make clear a basic duality in modes of knowledge of the world and people in it manifested generically in the short story and in the novel. I make no apology in this study of the "story which is short" for not dealing extensively with the "story which is long." Critics and theorists of the novel, after all, have spent little or no time on the short story. If I argue strongly for the superiority of that mode of knowledge which finds its most adequate form in short fiction, I do so not merely to make up for previous neglect of the short story, but also to "lay bare" the biased and unexamined assumptions that have led Western literary critics and theorists to see the novel as the only mode of fiction worthy of consideration.

I begin with some assumptions about the nature of the novel generally accepted in contemporary criticism. In his influential study of the rise of the novel, Ian Watt notes that at its very beginning, the novel shows its allegiance to the theories of knowledge posed by Locke and Hume. According to Watt, the novel is distinguished from other genres by the attention that it pays to individual characterization and to detailed presentation of the environment. These two characteristics are based on the eighteenth-century empiricist view that one's character or identity is a result of interaction with his environment through duration. José Ortega y Gasset underlines the same realistic characteristic of the novel in his discussion of the shift from mythic to novelistic narrative. "The myth is always the starting point of all poetry," says Ortega, "including the realistic, except that in the latter we accompany the myth in its descent." Erich

Heller pushes this suggestion of the movement of long fiction from mythic mystery to rational understanding even further. Noting that the so-called "realistic" subject matter of Stendhal, Balzac, and Flaubert was not new, but rather that their epistemological assumptions were, Heller says that what is characteristic of the realistic novelists is their "passion for understanding, the drive for rational appropriation, the driving force toward the expropriation of the mystery. How tedious would be Balzac's descriptions if they were not alive with the zeal for absolute possession of the things described."[8]

However, the Locke-Hume view of reality is obviously not the only epistemological theory applicable to fiction, although one would think that many champions of the novel had never heard of Kant. Nor is the primary characteristic of all fiction that it exhibit the passion for the "expropriation of the mystery," although one would think that novel theorists had never heard of Ernst Cassirer or William James.

In his chapter on "The Perception of Reality" in *The Principles of Psychology*, William James opposes the Locke-Hume view with a phenomenological approach to reality. For James, there are many sub-universes of reality, each of which is real as long as it is "attended to." James urges, "*Whatever excites and stimulates our interest is real*," whether it be the world of the senses, the world of ideal relation, the world of madness, or the world of the supernatural. Each of these worlds is *sui generis*, says James, and reality resides within each one after its own fashion. "Every object we think of gets at last referred to one world or another of this or of some other list."[9]

Many philosophers since Kant and many psychologists since James have examined our notions of reality as they are determined by categories of expectation. Ernest Cassirer has developed theories of a bimodal approach to reality in which the everyday, practical world of experience and perception is opposed to the more primal world of mythic perception. More recently, psychologists such as Jerome Bruner and Arthur Deikman and philosophers such as Alfred Schutz have suggested that what we take for granted as everyday reality is only one construct or category of reality among many others. Thus the form of reality which is the basis of the novel and which accounts for its being valued as the only important fictional form is seen to be more problematical and arbitrary than hitherto believed.

As both Ortega and Lukács have noted, the world of the novel is the fallen world and marks the descent of the mythic. What Heller describes as the "passion for understanding, the drive for rational appropriation" is what creates the familiar world of everyday reality. According to Jerome

Bruner, what makes the world familiar is a process of model building in which we learn relations between objects and events that we encounter and therefore learn appropriate categories or structures of those objects and events. "On the basis of certain defining or critical attributes in the input, what are usually called cues, although they should be called clues, there is a selective placing of the input in one category of identity rather than another."[10]

The actual construction of the everyday world which the novel takes as its subject matter has been described by phenomenologist Alfred Schutz in such a way that helps us understand the difference between this world and the world the short story focuses on. Drawing from James's "The Perception of Reality," Schutz attempts to examine the "unexamined," that is, to describe the world that is taken for granted in everyday life, a world in which we suspend all doubts about this very world's reality. For James's "sub-universes of reality," Schutz substitutes the term "finite provinces of meaning," and moves James's phenomenology closer to that of Husserl's: "the orders of reality do not become constituted through the ontological structure of their Objects, but rather through the meaning of our experience." The finite character of the various provinces of meaning, says Schutz, rests upon the character of the unity of their own peculiar lived experience, that is, their cognitive style. What is compatible or harmonious in one of these finite provinces is not compatible in another. Furthermore, there is no conversion formula that can reduce one province of meaning to another: "The transition from one province of meaning to another can only be accomplished by means of a 'leap' (in Kierkegaard's sense)." However, because in the everyday life world one brackets the doubt whether the world could be otherwise than as it appears, the leap is accompanied by a specific shock which "bursts the limits" of that which we take to be the only real.[11]

That aspect of Schutz's description of the life-world of everyday most relevant to an understanding of the difference between the nature of knowledge in the novel and the short story focuses on the problem of intersubjectivity. In the everyday world, we take such intersubjectivity with others for granted. We know that different objects must appear differently to others, but in the social attitude of everyday, we set these aside by means of pragmatically motivated idealizations. The first such idealization Schutz calls the "interchangeability of standpoints," which he describes this way: "If I were there, where he is now, then I would experience things in the same perspective, distance, and reach as he does. And, if he were here where I am now, he would experience things from the same perspective as I." The second idealization Schutz calls the "congruence of relevance systems." We accept as a given that variances which arise from different biographical situations are irrelevant to practical goals. "Thus, I and he, we, can act and understand each other as if we had experienced in an identical way, and explicated the Objects and their properties lying actually or potentially in our reach."[12] Both these two idealizations form what Schutz calls the "reciprocity of perspectives." In the social or natural attitude of the everyday life-world, we take for granted that the life-world accepted by me is also accepted by everyone.

Schutz describes our encounter with the other in the everyday life-world as a process of conceptualization whereby we apply categories or type ideas based on previous experience to people we meet. The novel, which takes the everyday life-world as its province, focuses on experience in the same conceptualized way. The short story, on the other hand, throws into doubt our idealizations of the "interchangeability of standpoints" and the "congruence of relevance systems." In the short story we are presented with characters in their essential aloneness, not in their taken-for-granted social world. Such an understanding of the two different realms of the short story and the novel helps to account for one of the best-known discussions of the subject matter of the short story: Frank O'Connor's intuitive analysis in *The Lonely Voice*. The novel, says O'Connor, can "adhere to the classical concept of civilized society, of man as an animal who lives in a community . . . ; but the short story remains by its very nature remote from the community—romantic, individualistic, and intransigent." This is why, O'Connor says, the short story always presents a sense of "outlawed figures wandering about the fringes of society . . . As a result there is in the short story at its most characteristic something we do not often find in the novel—an intense awareness of human loneliness."[13]

The short story breaks up the familiar life-world of the everyday, defamiliarizes our assumption that reality is simply the conceptual construct we take it to be, and throws into doubt that our propositional and categorical mode of perceiving can be applied to human beings as well as to objects. The short story, more than the novel, presents the world as I-Thou rather than I-It. As Martin Buber says, in the world of I-It, man looks at the world as that world in which he has to live and in which it is comfortable to live. "In this chronicle of solid benefits, the moments of the Thou appear as strange lyric and dramatic episodes, seductive and magical, but tearing us away to dangerous extremes, loosening the well-tied context, leaving more questions than satisfactions behind them, shattering security—in short, uncanny moments we can well dispense with."[14]

Our preference for the security of the everyday life-world and therefore our preference for the novel over the short story has been suggested by psychologist Arthur Deikman in his discussions of the "action" versus the "receptive" modes of experience and the automatization versus the deautomatization processes. By action and reception, Deikman does not mean activity versus passivity, but rather the distinction between a state of striving to achieve personal goals as contrasted to a state organized around intake of the environment. In the receptive mode, the percipient becomes one with the environment (the I-Thou) instead of isolating and manipulating the object (the I-It). The action mode, the mode of everyday reality, says Deikman, has developed for insuring survival. Our developmental preference for it has thus led us to assume that it is the only proper adult mode; we therefore think of the receptive mode as pathological or regressive. This bias for the active, everyday encounter with the external world and our consequent scorn for the receptive mode of a more mystic, taking-in quality reflects our bias for the I-It world of the everyday and the novel that embodies it rather than for the I-Thou world of the uncanny moment and the short story that takes this experience for its own. In another study, Deikman develops this bimodal view further by noting that everyday reality is governed by what he calls "automatization"—a hierarchically organized developmental process" which creates "hierarchically organized structures that ordinarily conserve energy for maximum efficiency in achieving the basic goals of the individual: biological survival and psychological survival as a personality." Opposed to this state of everyday, ordered reality, Deikman posits the experience of deautomatization, which serves to reinvest actions and percepts with "attention." The result of deautomatization is a "shift toward a perceptual and cognitive organization characterized as 'primitive,' that is, an organization preceding the analytic, abstract, intellectual mode typical of present-day adult thought."[15]

The mode of thought characteristic of the "receptive" and characterized by deautomatization is described by Ernst Cassirer as mythic thinking. It is that mode of thought which becomes predominant during the nineteenth century when the short story is developed, and it is that mode of thought which the Russian Formalists suggest characterize the essential artistic function and device. The nature of mythic thought within the framework of the sacred, the attempt by the Romantics to recapture this mode of thinking in a secularized way, and the development of a critical approach which unites this mode of thinking with the essential nature of art itself—all help us to understand why the short story has been called both the most primitive mode of communication as well as the most artistic.

The short story from its beginnings is primarily a literary mode which has remained closest to the primal narrative form that embodies and recapitulates mythic perception and thought as Ernst Cassirer and others have described it. Cassirer says that when one is under the spell of mythic thinking, it is as though the whole world were simply annihilated; the immediate content, whatever it be, that commands one's religious interest so completely fills his consciousness that nothing else can exist beside and apart from it. The characteristic of such an experience, says Cassirer, is not expansion, but an impulse toward concentration; "instead of extensive distribution, intensive compression. This focussing of all forces on a single point is the prerequisite for all mythical thinking and mythical formulation."[16]

The short story form manifests this impulse toward compression and demands this intense focussing for the totality of the narrative experience primarily because it takes for its essential subject the mysterious and dreamlike manifestation of what Cassirer calls the "momentary deity." The production of the deity, the first phase of the development of theological concepts, does not involve investing them with mythico-religious images. Rather, says Cassirer, "it is something purely instantaneous, a fleeting, emerging, and vanishing mental content. . . . Every impression that man receives, every wish that stirs in him, every hope that lures him, every danger that threatens him can affect him thus religiously."[17]

This experience of the mythic has been described by Mircea Eliade as the encounter with the sacred. Any aspect of experience, no matter how commonplace, can become sacred provided that it falls within the mythical-religious perspective. As Eliade says, in the realm of the sacred, we are concerned with the paradox of the hierophany: "By manifesting the sacred, any object becomes *something else,* yet it continues to remain itself, for it continues to participate in its surrounding cosmic milieu."[18] Primitive man, says Eliade, desires to live in the sacred as much as possible, for to him it is equivalent to true reality as opposed to the illusion of everyday experience. If we can accept this kind of momentary experience (the break-up of the ordinary profane world by the experience of the sacred) as the primary source of religion, we can also see it as the primary source of that most primal of all art forms—the story that is short.

Because short fiction is so bound up with the experience of the sacred and mythic perception, it is no accident that the short story as we know it today got its most important impetus as an art form from the Romantic effort in the early years of the nineteenth century to regain through art what had been lost in religion. As M. H. Abrams has noted, the "characteristic concepts and patterns of Romantic philosophy and literature are a displaced and reconstituted theology, or else a secularized form of devotional experience."[19] This secularization of inherited theological ways of thinking is an attempt on the part of the Romantics to regain what many anthropologists have called "the sacred origin of storytelling." The effort can be most clearly seen in the "Preface to the Lyrical Ballads" and *The Biographia Literaria.*

Wordsworth and Coleridge announce that their purpose is an experiment with the two genres of lyric and ballad, or tale. The task was to choose ballad material, that is, "situations from common life," and then throw over these situations a certain "coloring of the imagination" which would present these ordinary things to the mind in an unusual way. The imagination or feeling makes the action important by means of this very coloring of the imagination, thus making a common, often overlooked, situation manifest. Coleridge's job was to deal with the supernatural events of ballad, but instead of simply attempting to create a sensation in the reader, as Wordsworth had scornfully described the work of the German Romantics, Coleridge was to try to create an emotion in the reader that would accompany such events "as if" they were real. In other words, Coleridge was to take pure feeling states, those moments when man has felt himself, "by whatever delusion," to be under the influence of the supernatural, and objectify them, "so as to transfer from our inward nature a human interest and a semblance of truth sufficient to procure for these shadows of imagination that willing suspension of disbelief for the moment which constitutes poetic faith." Wordsworth's task was similar; only the materials were different. He was to deal with everyday situations and events, and by means of the imagination give them such an "unfamiliar" look as to "excite a feeling analogous to the supernatural, by awakening the mind's attention from the lethargy of custom, and directing it to the loveliness and the wonders of the world before us."

Twenty years after *The Lyrical Ballads,* Shelley takes up the same argument for "familiarizing the unfamiliar" and "defamiliarizing the familiar." In his "Defence of Poetry," Shelley insists that the objects of reason and imagination are distinct, that whereas the object of the former is thought, the object of the latter is eternal form. It is the task of the artist to "perceive the synthesis between before unapprehended things . . . to perceive an order and rhythm and form that man doesn't usually see . . . to perpetuate this perception of order and meaning." Art, says Shelley, "lifts the veil from the hidden beauty of the world and makes familiar objects be as if they were not familiar."

The mode of literary criticism which has made these assumptions most important is that of the Russian Formalists in the early part of the twentieth century. Although the idea is expressed in various works of the

Formalists, it is perhaps most crystalized in Victor Shklovsky's essay "Art as Technique." Shklovsky says that the technique of the artist is to make objects "unfamiliar." The Formalists see such defamiliarization or distortion of everyday reality as the very stuff of art itself. As Shklovsky emphatically declares, *"Art is a way of experiencing the artfulness of an object, the object is not important."*[20] The modern structuralist approach to literature derives from the Formalist notion via the writings of Jan Mukarovsky of the so-called Prague School. Although he prefers the word "structure" to the Russian "form," Mukarovsky agrees that the basic trait of the art work is deformation followed by organization. The first disrupts our usual indifference by "making strange" and heightening our awareness, but it must be organized by the second to achieve the total structure. However, it is Morse Peckham's study, seemingly independent from the Formalist-Structuralist approaches, that pushes the defamiliarization notion to the ultimate extreme and best helps us understand the significance of the short story's dependence on this mode.

Peckham draws upon modern studies of perception to give the lie to the view that art represents "man's rage for order." Every human being brings to any situation in life an orientation which has been created from previous situations, a category that works because it filters out data not relevant to the orientation. However, says Peckham, since an "orientation does not prepare an individual to deal with a *particular* situation but only with a *category,* or kind, or class of situation, much of the suppressed data may very well be relevant." However, as a result of a continual reinforcement of the everyday category of consciousness and the efficiency of its use, the perceiver continues to suppress data to maintain his ordered experience. Thus, says Peckham, "there arises the paradox of human behavior: the very drive to order which qualifies man to deal successfully with his environment disqualifies him when it is to his interest to correct his orientation. To use an old expression, the drive to order is also a drive to get stuck in the mud."[21]

The question of the short story form's being "true" or "false" to reality and the corollary question of whether the short story is a natural form or a highly conventional one requires a reevaluation of what we mean when we use the terms "reality" and "natural." If one assumes that reality is only what one experiences everyday as one's well-controlled, ordered, and comfortable self, then the short story is neither realistic nor natural. If, however, one feels that immanent in the everyday exists some other reality that somehow evades him, if one's view is religious in the most basic sense, then the short story is more "realistic" than the novel can possibly be. From this point of view, the short story is closer to the nature of reality as we experience it in those moments when we are made aware of the inauthenticity of everyday life, those moments when we sense the inadequacy of our categories of conceptual reality.

The reality the short story presents us with is the reality of those subuniverses of the supernatural and the fable which exist within the so-called "real" world of sense perception and conceptual abstraction. It presents moments in which we become aware of anxiety, loneliness, dread, concern, and thus find the safe, secure and systematic life we usually lead disrupted and momentarily destroyed. The short story is the most adequate form to confront us with reality as we perceive it in our most profound moments.

NOTES

1. *The English Novel: A Panorama* (Boston: Houghton Mifflin, 1960), p. 3.

2. *The Nature of Narrative* (New York: Oxford University Press, 1966), p. 3; *Anatomy of Criticism* (Princeton: Princeton University Press, 1957), p. 303.

3. *The Philosophy of the Short-Story* (New York: Longmans, Green and Co., 1901), p. 13.

4. Reprinted in *What is the Short Story,* rev. ed., eds. Eugene Current-Garcia and Walton R. Patrick (New York: Scott, Foresman and Co., 1974), p. 50.

5. *O. Henry and the Theory of the Short Story,* trans. I. R. Titunk (Ann Arbor: University of Michigan Press, 1968), p. 4.

6. *The Theory of the Novel,* trans. Anna Bostock (Cambridge, Mass.: The MIT Press, 1971), pp. 51–52.

7. Abrahams' statement is quoted in "Short Stories: Their Past, Present and Future," *Publisher's Weekly,* 198 (Dec. 14, 1970), 12–15. Bernard Bergonzi, *The Situation of the Novel* (London: Macmillan and Co., Ltd., 1970), pp. 215–16.

8. Ian Watt, *The Rise of the Novel* (Berkeley: University of California Press, 1957), pp. 9–34; Jose Ortega y Gasset, *Meditations on Quixote,* trans. Evelyn Rugg and Diego Marin (New York: W. W. Norton & Co., Inc., 1961), p. 144; Erich Heller, "The Realistic Fallacy," in *Documents of Modern Literary Realism,* ed. George J. Becker (Princeton: Princeton University Press, 1963), p. 596.

9. *The Principles of Psychology* (New York: Dover Publications, 1950) II, 293–95.

10. "On Perceptual Readiness," *The Psychological Review,* 64 (1957), 123–52, rpt. in *Readings in Perception,* eds. David C. Beardslee and Michael Wertheimer (Princeton: D. Van Nostrand Co., Inc., 1958), pp. 687–88.

11. *The Structures of the Life World,* trans. Richard M. Zaner and H. Tristam Engelhardt, Jr. (Evanston, Illinois: Northwestern University Press, 1973), pp. 23–24.

12. Ibid., p. 60.

13. *The Lonely Voice* (Cleveland: World Publishing Co., 1963) pp. 19–21.

14. *I and Thou,* 2nd. ed. (New York: Charles Scribner's Sons, 1958), p. 34.

15. "Bimodal Consciousness," *Archives of General Psychiatry,* 25 (Dec. 1971), 481–89; "Deautomatization and the Mystic Experience," *Psychiatry,* 29 (1966), 324–38; rpt. in *The Nature of Human Consciousness,* ed. Robert Ornstein (New York: Viking Press, 1973), pp. 67–86 & pp. 216–33.

16. *Language and Myth,* trans. Susanne K. Langer (New York: Dover Publications, Inc., 1946), p. 32.

17. Ibid., p. 18.

18. *The Sacred and the Profane,* trans. Willard R Trask (New York: Harper & Row, Publishers, 1961), p. 12.

19. *Natural Supernaturalism* (New York: W. W. Norton & Co., Inc., 1971), p. 65.

20. "Art as Technique," *Russian Formalist Criticism: Four essays,* trans. and eds. Lee T. Lemon and Marion J. Reis (Lincoln: University of Nebraska Press, 1965), p. 12.

21. *Man's Rage for Chaos: Biology, Behavior, and the Arts* (Philadelphia: Chilton Books, 1965), p. xi.

PART FOUR
Historical Considerations

Notes on
the Novella

GRAHAM GOOD

ATTEMPTS TO DEFINE short fictional forms and distinguish them from the novel are often in danger of tautology. The emphasis on qualities like economy, concentration, or unity can seem to boil down to the idea that short fictions are different from novels because they are, well, shorter. This in turn may imply that prose fiction is a continuous, homogeneous fabric which can be cut and tailored to any length. Categories based purely on length are bound to be arbitrary; there is no magic number of words which constitutes the minimum for a novel or the maximum for a short story, and there are always borderline cases. So the tendency is to give up the business of formal genre definition for short fiction as hopeless or fruitless, and to deal with individual texts as parts of the author's whole *oeuvre,* within a general perspective on fiction dominated by the novel. Fiction is thus thought of as "the novel" plus assorted hangers-on of lesser proportions: the colon in NOVEL: A FORUM ON FICTION implies as much.

Short fiction is thus bedevilled for theorists by its *adjacency* to the longer form. Other genres can be *opposed* to each other more easily by basic plot-form (comedy *versus* tragedy) or medium of presentation (drama *versus* novel), where novel and short fiction are always in some awkward way *next* to each other, overlapping and interpenetrating. Nevertheless, there has been a number of efforts at disentangling the two, and what follows is an historical and comparative review of some of them, centering on the term "novella" and its complex semantic-historical relations with the novel.

I

Short fiction terminology is extremely varied and often inconsistent. The word "novella" is gradually gaining acceptance in English among publishers, writers, and latterly critics, to denote a fictional prose narrative of "medium" length. This usage is supplementing rather than supplanting "short story," which has been firmly established since the turn of the century. The older terms "tale" and simply "story" were still employed by writers like James and Conrad to refer to any narrative shorter than a novel, from about five to a hundred or more pages. But this usage was eroded in the late nineteenth century by the magazine term "short story," which, with its connotations of abruptness and curtailment, tended to confine itself to the lower end of this range—short story manuals still preach an ascetic brevity, attained by diligent cutting and paring away the fat, until the art comes to seem one of pure omission. For a while such erosiveness left the medium-length narrative in a terminological limbo, where it became a "short novel," a "long story," or even a "long short story" (I omit the vile diminutive, "novelette"). These terms are troublesome because they contain a qualification: like "long poem," they set themselves against an assumed expectation of a different length.

The comparison with Continental terminology is complex but instructive. The Italian word "novella" is first established in the early Renaissance to describe short narratives of the type collected by Boccaccio in the *Decameron*. In Spain the word was adopted as "novela," but gradually moved from stories of short to middle length to cover the full-length novel as well. It has never lost its original sense, however: Spaniards use "novela" to describe *Don Quijote* as a whole, in addition to the inserted tales it contains, besides of course the *Novelas Ejemplares*. The term "romance" mainly applies to epic and ballad material. In France "nouvelle" was a recognized term in the Renaissance; the novelty value of Boccaccio's genre was reaffirmed and redoubled in the collection *Les Cent Nouvelles Nouvelles*. By the eighteenth century "conte" had taken over in a variety of compounds like "conte oriental," "conte philosophique," or "conte moral." The term was still used by Balzac and Flaubert, and "nouvelle" was not clearly re-established until the later nineteenth century. Bourget helped to give currency to the word as a description of medium-length stories, and James borrowed it informally to speak of his longer tales. Maupassant used both "conte" and "nouvelle" to distinguish between his shorter and longer narratives. Gide called all of his fictions "récits," except for *Les Faux-Monnayeurs,* which alone received the designation "roman." In Germany the term "Novelle" achieved a much more decisive

dominance over the field of short fiction, being only marginally tres-
passed on by "Erzählung" (tale) and "Kurzgeschichte" (short story); the
latter is a relatively recent borrowing from Anglo-American usage.

Gerald Gillespie's essay "Novella, Nouvelle, Novelle, Short Novel? A
Review of Terms"[1] provides a neat tabulation:

English	(hi)story	tale		novel
Spanish	historia	cuento	novela	novela
Italian	storia	racconto	novella	romanzo
French	histoire	conte	nouvelle	roman
German	Geschichte	Erzhlung	Novelle	Roman

The most striking implication of this diagram[2] for our present purposes is
the fate of the word "romance" in the different languages. In Spain the
word was never of great importance, but in Italy, France, and Germany it
survived the transitions of the long narrative from verse to prose and
from chivalric to modern, domestic and social subject-matter. Thus in
German "Roman" may cover anything from Wolfram's *Parzifal* to Mann's
Buddenbrooks. In all three languages the "novel" term ("novella," "nouvelle," "Novelle") was reserved for short fiction, while the "romance"
term ("romanzo," "roman," "Roman") applied exclusively to longer fiction. In Germany, where "Novelle" was most successful in ousting rival
designations, a particularly sharp distinction of length and content was
made between the "Novelle" and the "Roman." In England, however, the
contrast of "Novel" and "Romance" was made purely by content between
narratives of equivalent length. As Tieck remarked reprovingly in 1829,
"We now know pretty well what we mean by 'Roman;' but the Englishman has for a long time been calling all of his 'Romane' 'Novellen.'"[3]
The romance/novel distinction between full-length prose narratives has
preoccupied much of the theory of fiction in England from Clara Reeve
onwards, often to the neglect of the shorter forms. In Germany, though,
the terminology focussed attention on the generic differences between
long and short fiction, and thus encouraged the development of a body of
theory about the novella which is largely absent in English.

Gillespie ends his essay by recommending the adoption of "novella"
into English to fill the gap between "short story" and "novel," even
though he acknowledges that the Continental "novella" terms overlap to
a considerable extent with what we know as the "short story." His suggested usage is followed by Mary Doyle Springer in her recent book
Forms of the Modern Novella (University of Chicago Press, 1975). She
takes the novella as a narrative of middle length (roughly 15,000 to

50,000 words) between the short story and the novel. From this point her
argument is not so much historical (she minimizes the links with the
Renaissance novella) or comparative (she mentions German novella
theory without discussion), as rhetorical, in the Chicago tradition. However, she does not offer an overall definition of the genre, but rather a
classification of sub-genres or rhetorical types: for her, "the task of defining the novella through its formal functions thus clearly arises because I
think it has no other way of being defined" (p. 15). Certain formal types,
she argues, are appropriate to the middle length; they would be under-
developed and unconvincing in the short story and over-extended and
tedious in the novel. The first of these types is the apologue, a narrative
whose main aim is to enforce a statement or thesis; and where character,
plot, and dialogue are less important than symbolic settings and authorial
commentary. A sub-category is the "example apologue," which exposes a
particular condition or way of life. Solzhenitsyn's *One Day in the Life of
Ivan Denisovich* makes the statement, "It is like this to be imprisoned in
a Soviet labor camp." Other types are the novella satire (such as *Animal
Farm*), which tends to be more tightly plotted than its episodic novel-
length counterpart; the "degenerative tragedy" (such as *Death in Venice*),
where a character gradually succumbs to a pre-determined fate; and serious
plots of character and learning. But beyond the initial criterion of length
there is still no global conception of the genre which holds the sub-genres
together.

A conception of this type is offered in Judith Leibowitz's *Narrative
Purpose in the Novella* (Mouton, 1974): "Whereas the short story limits
material and the novel extends it, the novella does both in such a way that
a special kind of narrative structure results, one which produces a generically distinct effect: the double effect of intensity and expansion" (p. 16).
This result is frequently achieved through repetitive structure: after the
first revelation or recognition the novella redevelops or re-examines the
situation, thus producing a greater thematic intensity.

Leibowitz, Springer, and Gillespie all situate the novella midway between the short story and the novel;[4] this has the advantages of roughly
reflecting current usage, and corresponding to the French triad "conte,"
"nouvelle," "roman." But here I propose to use "novella" to cover both
the short and the medium lengths. This has some justifications. (1) In the
Renaissance the term encompassed both the very brief stories in the
Decameron and the middle-length *Novelas Ejemplares* of Cervantes. (2)
In post-1800 German practice "Novelle" includes texts of under five and
well over a hundred pages. (3) The nineteenth-century English terms
"tale" and "story" covered both lengths. (4) "Short story" is a mainly

twentieth-century phrase for a particular type of magazine fiction; it has been applied to earlier and foreign fictions to which it is not always appropriate, though naturally it has a place within the family of terms I want to cover with "novella." (5) Short and medium lengths have enough in common in form, content and history to justify opposing them conjointly to the novel in the German manner, and employing a two-part model (novella/novel) in preference to a three-part one (short story/novella/novel).

II

Boccaccio's *Decameron* is the natural starting point for an historical approach to the prose novella. The hundred stories in the collection are told by agreement among a group of ten refugees from the plague in Florence. This contract for mutual entertainment to help pass the time is reminiscent of Chaucer's *Canterbury Tales:* in both cases a sense of group cohesion is maintained by the comments and disputes provoked by the individual stories. However, Chaucer's narratives are in verse, and are a mixture of *fabliaux* and romances; Boccaccio's are in prose, and though both ribald and edifying stories are included, the subject matter is largely middle-class, domestic and contemporary. The *Decameron* takes up elements of the medieval verse genres of the *fabliau* and the romance, and fashions them into a new genre, the prose novella. This form is distinguished from the folk-tale by its modernity of content, and though it remains strongly oral in character, the new context is of polite, cultivated conversation. The Boccaccian novella is also shorter than the *fabliau* or the romance; it consists of material which would have been merely an incident or episode in the older forms. These incidents are handled with great economy: usually dispensing with digression and description, the tales focus on neatness of plot, particularly on the unexpected "twist" whereby a situation or line of development is abruptly reversed. Though qualities of nobility and fidelity are sometimes shown, the primacy of plot more often calls for cunning and quick-wittedness on the part of the characters as they try to outsmart each other.

Cervantes' *Novelas Ejemplares* are longer and more elaborate and digressive than the stories in the *Decameron*. They are not set in a common framework, and are more varied in type. For example "Rinconete and Cortadillo" is a loosely linked series of episodes in which two poor youths are introduced into the life of a community of thieves. Interest centers on the milieu and life-style of the thieves, including their slang, rather than on the plot, and this provides an important alternative model for the novella. On the other hand, "The Jealous Extremaduran" has a classic Boccaccian plot: a rich old husband's endeavors to keep his young wife in total seclusion are foiled by a persistent and ingenious lover. But the tale is much more fully developed than anything in the *Decameron;* it contains long descriptions of the layout and defenses of the house, and also incorporates the text of a song performed by the seducer and a set speech at the end in which the husband displays an unexpected and perhaps uncharacteristic generosity to those who have deceived him.

Besides being the second major figure in the history of the novella, Cervantes is of course the first in the history of the novel. And the two achievements are related: *Don Quijote* itself has various inserted shorter narratives, and the *Novelas* may well include material Cervantes decided not to use in the novel. Viktor Shklovsky's analysis of "How *Don Quijote* Is Made"[5] asserts that the hero's primary function is not as a character of intrinsic interest, but as a unifying device for the diverse compositional units the author wanted to employ: the set speech, the poem, the proverb, and the novella. To begin with, Shklovsky says, Cervantes presented Don Quijote as a fool; yet he came to need him as a thread on which to hang examples of eloquence on such topics as "The Golden Age," or "Arms and Letters." Only in the middle of the novel did Cervantes begin to use the folly/wisdom contradiction artistically. Similarly, Sancho serves to accumulate text; embodying a type of wisdom which contrasts with the Don's classical rhetoric: the proverbial. The novellas are linked to the main text by various devices. The "discovered manuscript" of "Il curioso impertinente" is read aloud to the company at the inn where Don Quijote attacks the wineskins, an incident which interrupts the story shortly before its conclusion. Figures in the main action may disrupt sub-plot episodes; sub-plot characters may be integrated later into the main action. People are linked by texts, and texts by people: Dorothea and Cardenio both attract Don Quijote's attention by their songs; Cardenio tells his story to the knight, and then both listen to hers.

Shklovsky's analysis of how *Don Quijote* is stitched together out of smaller textual units carries some interesting implications about the historical relationship of the novel to the novella. In the chapter of his *Theory of Prose* just prior to the one on Cervantes, Shklovsky observes, "The collection of novellas preceded the modern novel: this statement does not imply the existence of a causal link, but rather establishes a chronological fact."[6] In this perspective, the tales-plus-framework structure of *Don Quijote* represents that of the *Decameron,* say, brought to a higher level of integration, and the novel genre itself is defined by its digestive capacities. Shklovsky goes on to analyze the different ways in which collections of tales are framed: the stories may delay the resolution of the frame situation, as in *The Thousand and One Nights,* or may be occasioned by a group agreement, as in Chaucer and Boccaccio, or linked together by the appearance of the same hero in each episode—this method leads to picaresque episodic narratives like *Lazarillo de Tormes* and *Gil Blas.* The conclusion drawn is that, "In general one can say that the framing device as well as the linking device have helped incorporate more and more external material into the novel."[7]

This formalist account of the rise, or rather coalescence, of the novel out of the novella-collection offers a parallel to the Marxist perspective put forward by Georg Lukács in his essay "Solzhenitsyn: *One Day in the Life of Ivan Denisovich.*" His historical thesis is that "the novella frequently appears either as a precursor to a conquest of reality by the great epic and dramatic forms, or as a rearguard, a termination at the end of a period."[8] On this view, the Renaissance novella anticipates the development of the social-realistic novel which reached its height in the nineteenth century. Only this major form, Lukács says, could encompass bourgeois society in an epic totality, but the minor form of the novella paves the way:

> From this viewpoint, Boccaccio and the Italian novella appear as forerunners of the modern bourgeois novel. They depict the world in an era in which the bourgeois forms of life were advancing victoriously, and were increasingly beginning to destroy the medieval forms in the most diverse areas of life, and to replace these with their own forms. In this world, however, there could not yet be a totality of objects, nor could there be a totality of human relations and behavior as interpreted by bourgeois society.[9]

The individualism and self-interest, the cunning and deceit which so often triumph in the separate incidents of the *Decameron* tales, develop into the picaresque novel and eventually into the social novel, or else, in *Don Quijote,* combine dialectically with the now decadent and inefficacious ideals of chivalric romance. The formal integration of the novella into the novel, so well described by Shklovsky, is made dependent by Lukács on the integration of bourgeois society.

Neither process, however, is fully complete until the nineteenth century. The novella continued to survive after the Renaissance largely within the new, capacious, syncretic genre of the novel, along with poems, speeches, dialogues, proverbs, parodies, letters, and digressive essays. The integration achieved by Cervantes was a fairly loose one, and it remained

so for his successors. Characters in the leisurely-paced novels of the seventeenth and eighteenth centuries are usually very willing to sit down and
hear and discuss a tale, which it seems a little ill-mannered to call an
interpolation. Fielding enlivens *Joseph Andrews* with "The History of
Leonora, or the Unfortunate Jilt," and *Tom Jones* with the Man of the
Hill's story. Prévost's *Manon Lescaut,* often published separately, was
originally a tale told as part of the *Memoirs of a Man of Quality.* Goethe's
novels abound in inserted novellas, and the Gothic novel was especially
prolific in subsidiary narratives; Maturin's *Melmoth the Wanderer* is a
complex tissue of tales within tales, united mainly by the successive appearances of the sinister hero. Only in the first part of the nineteenth
century, when the novel has fully "digested" novella material into a less
episodic and heterogeneous textual fabric, does the novella emerge into a
new phase of autonomy and distinction from the novel.

III

The development of the novella in the nineteenth century in the various national literatures of the West differs as much as that of the novel, if
not more. It is in Germany that the genre is revived and recognized earliest, practiced most widely, and defined most exhaustively. The way is
paved by Goethe: his *Unterhaltungen deutscher Ausgewanderten* of 1795
clearly takes the *Decameron* as its classical model. Again, the framing
situation is an escape from adverse social conditions: a group of fugitives
from the upheavals caused by the French Revolution agree to pass the
time of their retreat by telling each other stories. The first major theoretical formulation of the genre is also made with direct reference to the
Decameron, by Friedrich Schlegel in his *Nachricht von den poetischen
Werken des Johannes Boccaccio* of 1801. This is his definition:

> A novella is an anecdote, a hitherto unknown story, told as one would
> tell it in company, a story which must be capable of arousing interest
> in and of itself alone, without regard to any connection with the
> nations, the times, the progress of humanity, or even the relation to
> culture itself.[10]

These three features, the novelty of the plot, the oral character of the narrative situation, and the independence of the story from social and historical factors, become perennial, though not uncontested, themes in German
Novellentheorie. Goethe echoed the first point in his famous rhetorical
question to Eckermann in 1827: "Was ist eine Novelle anders als eine sich

ereignete, unerhörte Begebenheit?"[11] ("What is a novella other than an unheard-of event that has actually taken place?") This definition sets the novella in an intermediate zone of probability between fantasy or romance on one side, and the realistic novel on the other.

From this starting point, German novella theory developed a stock of generic indicators which, beyond the criterion of length, pointed up the distinction between the novel and the novella. Boccaccio remains an important model: the so-called *Falkentheorie* of Paul Heyse, which asserts the need for a single unifying symbol in a novella, is based on the falcon in the Ninth Tale of the Fifth Day. The other most important idea is Tieck's *Wendepunkt* or turning-point, where the story "unexpectedly takes a quite different direction, and develops consequences which are nevertheless natural and entirely in keeping with character and circumstances."[12] These terms are still commonly met with in criticism of the German novella, and are useful as long as they are not made definitive of the genre.

On a less technical and more philosophical level, the debate about the nature of the novella was renewed in the years around 1930 over the question of whether the genre is fundamentally tragic or conversational. Bernhard Bruch's "Novelle und Tragödie" contends that the post-1800 novella is only very distantly related to the Renaissance form. Rather, it becomes the bourgeois *Ersatzform* of true tragedy: "If tragedy is in essence an heroic form, the novella is entirely a bourgeois-sentimental one (*eine bürgerlich-empfindsame*)."[13] The greatness of tragedy was to show that some situations in real life are actually and irredeemably tragic. The novella lacks this objectivity: the fatalism is of the narrator's mood, and the stricken character's fate is private and exceptional. This is because the novella's formal function is to recall something that *once happened* to a man, whereas the tragic hero has to ask "What shall I do?" and make an ethical choice in the present. Instead of this heroic assertion of will and responsibility, the novella character tends to show an inner spiritual passivity. Both tragedy and novella are closed forms, with internal distance created by the stage frame and the narrative frame (present by implication even when formally absent) respectively; but where tragedy immediately presents an ethical choice in the present, the novella subjectively mediates through the personality of the narrator the story of a fated life already essentially past.

Adolf von Grolman's "The Strict Novella-Form and the Problem of its Breakup"[14] responds by re-emphasizing the social nature of the novella, which he defines as a reply to the question, "What's new?" This dialogic exchange can only happen in a culture where conversation is a civilized

art. The novella is a social form which gathers together a group of audi-
tors, and in that way is directed against solitude; but the corollary is that it
often tells the story of a solitary or outcast individual or group. Thus the
novella affirms the inclusive group identity of the listeners by the very act
of presenting the fate of the excluded: the normal and the abnormal recip-
rocally define each other.

Hermann Pongs, however, rejects this social emphasis in his essay on
"Possibilities of the Tragic in the Novella,"[15] and also makes an even
stronger distinction than Bruch between the Renaissance and Romantic
forms of the novella. Pongs asserts that Kleist transforms the old, socia-
ble, Romance-language novella by dissolving the conversational context
and freeing the genre to show the confrontation of the separated individual with Fate. The ironic distance from events created in the Mediterran-
ean novella by the narrator's being in company is strongly contrasted to
the "life-depths" of the German novella.

The German Novelle, however, despite the unparalleled amount of
theoretical and critical attention it has received is not a unique genre. The
"canon" of recognized classics which runs from Goethe's "Novelle" to
Mann's *Death in Venice* and beyond, could be matched without difficulty
in the other national literatures, even if the texts are differently classified
in their own cultures. There is no intrinsic reason why the theory of the
novella developed in Germany should not be applicable to novellas from
other countries, and we can sometimes find its key ideas echoed by writers elsewhere. For example, Frank O'Connor writes:

> The novel can still adhere to the classical concept of civilized society,
> of man as an animal who lives in a community, as in Jane Austen and
> Trollope it obviously does; but the short story remains by its very
> nature remote from the community—romantic, individualist, and
> intransigent.[16]

O'Connor argues that this individualism is not channeled through a single
hero, as in the novel, but through a "submerged population group" such
as "Gogol's officials, Turgenev's serfs, Maupassant's prostitutes, Chekhov's doctors and teachers, Sherwood Anderson's provincials, always
dreaming of escape."[17] Where the novel concerns individuals within
society, the short story treats groups which are outside it, or at any rate
outside the normal social experience to be expected of the reader. The
formal differences between the two genres stem from this. The novel,
O'Connor says, is based on chronological structure, whereas

The short story represents a struggle with Time—the novelist's Time; it is an attempt to reach some point of vantage from which the past and future are equally visible. The crisis of the short story *is* the short story and not as in a novel the mere logical inescapable result of what has preceded it. One might go further and say that in the story what precedes the crisis becomes a consequence of the crisis—*this* being what actually happened, *that* must necessarily be what preceded it.[18]

O'Connor's definition of the short story (which includes the novella in my terms) is the revelation through a crisis of the essence of a way of life removed from the mainstream of society. Independently, O'Connor arrives at the perennial theme of German *Novellentheorie:* the novella's field is the periphery of its society, the novel's is its center.

The association of the novella with tragic drama is made in Howard Nemerov's essay "Composition and Fate in the Short Novel." Stressing the fatefulness of organization and detail in several examples, he defines the genre "not as a compromise between novel and short story, but as something like the ideal and primary form, suggestively allied in simplicity and even in length with the tragedies of antiquity, and dealing in effect with equivalent materials."[19] But despite these isolated echoes, there has been little systematic attempt to apply German novella theory to short fiction in other literatures.

IV

Lukács' thesis about the novella's history may suggest an explanation for the genre's popularity in Germany. His view that the novella flowers before and after the novel may well be considered along with Eichenbaum's similar, though form-derived, thesis:

> The novel and short story are forms not only different in kind but also inherently at odds, and for that reason are never found being developed simultaneously and with equal intensity in any one literature. . . . Not only individual writers but also individual cultures cultivate either the novel or the short story.[20]

If we apply this to the situation in Germany, we find that the novella does indeed flourish principally after the great achievements of the *Goethezeit* in poetry, drama and the novel. Between 1830 and 1900 Germany failed to develop a social novel comparable in scope and artistry to that of England and France. The forces of industrialism, bourgeois democracy, and national unity which set the conditions for the social novel were retarded in Germany, where the more individual-centered and episodic form of the *Bildungsroman* remained the dominant novel type. Theodor Fontane was the only German social novelist of real stature before Thomas Mann made his debut with *Buddenbrooks* in 1900. In Lukács' terms, the political disunity and provincialism of Germany meant that its culture was unable to totalize itself in the major form of the novel, and so the novella, with its affinity to the atypical and regional rather than the central and national, became the best-adapted fictional form.

In the United States, similarly, the preconditions of the social novel were not fully present until late in the nineteenth century, with urbanization and the pacification and settlement of the West. Instead, the adventure novel, the historical novel and, above all, the "tale" were the most appropriate literary vehicles. Poe's aesthetic of intensity and unity of effect sets the pattern for the development of short fiction in America. In England the situation is almost opposite: the social novel dominates the mid-century, and short fiction tends to be dependent on other prose forms: the "tale" illustrates or blends into the "sketch" or the "scene," as in the early work of Dickens or George Eliot.[21] But the Lukács/Eichenbaum thesis seems to fail with regard to the cases of Russian and French fiction. In Russia the novellas of Pushkin or Leskov might be counted as precursors of the social novel, but they were rapidly followed by the work of Gogol, Turgenev, Tolstoy, and Dostoyevsky, all of whom wrote both novels and novellas of the highest quality. In France during the 1830's the fluorishing of the novella created by Merimée, Balzac, and Gautier coincides with the rise of the social novel of Stendhal and Balzac.[22] *La Comédie Humaine* contains many excellent novellas as well as novels, and Flaubert's *Trois Contes* can rank artistically with his achievements in the novel. It is wrong to state, as Lukács and Eichenbaum do, that the two forms cannot coexist. In the nineteenth century the novella may be completely overshadowed by the social novel (England), may flourish in its absence or as a prelude to it (America, Germany), or may coexist with it (France, Russia): the socially "peripheral" form of the novella can retain its generic characteristics and artistic vitality with or without the socially "central" form of the novel.

Although the Romantic revival and transformation of the novella, which opened up the possibilities of local color, atmosphere, mystery, and tragic or metaphysical implication, laid down the essential scope of the genre for the whole succeeding period, it is possible to discern a new impetus and new modifications from about 1880 onwards. In England during the last two decades of the nineteenth century the monopoly of the three-volume novel as the standard fictional form was effectively broken. New magazines appeared which preferred complete short stories to serials, and many new opportunities were opened up to writers of short fiction. Henry James rejoiced in chances to work in the form he called the "shapely *nouvelle*," Conrad began to produce his novellas of the sea and distant parts of the world, and Kipling's *Plain Tales from the Hills* (1888) created a new succinctness of form and crisp, teasing colloquialism of style. *The Yellow Book* and *The Savoy* provided an outlet for more pessimistic or naturalistic stories, particularly on *risqué* subjects like casual sex or suicide. Some specialized forms of short fiction were also pioneered at this time: Arthur Conan Doyle found a mass public for the detective story with his Sherlock Holmes series, as Wells did for the science fiction story.[23]

In France the novella was brought to a new, post-Flaubertian level of sophistication and artistry by Maupassant. His stories often combine brief but vivid evocations of a given milieu with a highly-shaped plot, frequently concerned with trickery in affairs of money, status, and sex. The "novelty" of many of these swindles and revenges is reminiscent of Boccaccio and the oldest strain in the history of the novella. The interplay of gullible innocence and cynical experience is shaped by Maupassant into a bitterly "worldly" vision of human selfishness and hypocrisy characteristic of his typical *roué* narrator, although there are post-romantic sensitivities to natural beauty and some moments of poignancy and despairing tenderness.

In Russia during the same period Chekhov was practicing a new form of the novella, one which has a minimal plot. Depending more on atmosphere and suggestion than on incident, it consists of a delicate interweaving of states of consciousness with particular scenes or relatively trivial events. The characters tend to have a gentle, even ineffectual, sensibility, and the instinctual drives and low cunning which motivate many of Maupassant's ingenious plots are largely absent. The subtlety of this kind of impressionistic fiction makes it less compatible with an oral narrative frame: the slightness of the plot provides little occasion for a live recounting. Conrad Aiken defines this type of story well in relation to two of its best practitioners:

> Miss Mansfield has followed Chekhov in choosing to regard . . . the short story "form" not as the means to the telling of a tale, and not always or wholly as the means for the "lighting" of a single human character, but rather as the means for the presentation of a "quintessence," a summation of a human life or group of lives in the single significant "scene" or situation or episode.[24]

This form derives not from the highly-plotted Boccaccian tradition which influences Maupassant, but from the nineteenth-century "scene" or "sketch" or "feuilleton." This genre had earlier nourished the social novel through the apprentice writings of several major writers, such as Dickens (*Sketches by Boz*), George Eliot (*Scenes from Clerical Life*), and Turgenev (*Sketches from a Hunter's Album*), but the key to the Chekhovian development of this form is the interposition of a less worldly, more sensitive and impressionable consciousness through which the scenes are viewed.

The range of the modern novella can be defined by these two poles: at one end the almost eventless record of the feelings and impressions of a passive and easily moved sensibility, and at the other the neatly and strongly plotted account of coarser motivations, combining trickery in the characters with sleight of hand in the narrative strategy. This second type is generally the subject of short story writing manuals, and emphasizes brevity and suspense. But between these extremes of introversion and extroversion there is a wide range of mixtures: a high degree of psychological complexity and atmospheric sensitivity is compatible with narrative suspense and surprise, as in the best novellas of Henry James or Lawrence.

V

The following points attempt to collate and summarize the principal ideas and perspectives we have surveyed, in order to indicate a cluster of features and possibilities central to the novella.

(1) In many formal respects, prose fiction of any length has a common repertory of features. Any device (e.g. a central symbol), technique (e.g. a narrative frame), point of view (e.g. first- or third-person narration), or content (e.g. ordinary or extraordinary) that is found in the novella *can* also be found in some novels. Historically as well as terminologically, the novella and the novel are intricately related, especially in their common defiance of traditional genres. Nevertheless, certain potentialities and characteristics tend to inhere in the shorter length, and certain others in the longer.

(2) Historically, the Renaissance novella precedes the novel, which itself develops out of collections of novellas: the separate stories become a sequence of episodes with recurring characters, and the frame merges with the picture. The novella is revived as an autonomous form during the Romantic period, and in the nineteenth century the novel and the novella are cultivated separately or together in different countries and in

the work of different authors. The late nineteenth century bequeaths to the twentieth several new categories of novella: the short story, the detective story, the science fiction story, the revived tale of trickery, and the impressionistic mood-piece.

(3) The novella has an element of novelty, either in plot, or in setting, or in both. Unlike the traditional stories of epic and romance whose outcome is already well known, the novella's story has not normally been heard before. The novel also contains "new" characters and modern settings, but they become familiar through the novel's extended and detailed method. Novelty of plot often consists of cheating or trickery to deceive the unwary for personal profit or gratification or revenge; and as the characters surprise each other, so the narrator surprises his listeners. Novelty of setting implies a distance between the social or geographical experience of the audience, and the experience, way of life, or sub-culture described in the novella. The novelty, though often "out of the ordinary," still lies within the realm of the possible. Even if the events are inexplicable in rational terms (as in the ghost story, for example) they are presented as actually having taken place in the real world in the knowable, retrievable, or witnessed past; this is not generally true of the fantasy, the folk tale, or the fairy tale. When the science fiction novella suspends the laws of space, time, or causality, substantiation is generally attempted.

(4) The novella is the written imitation of a live "telling," and has retained stronger oral characteristics than the novel. These may be implicit in tone and style, or may be explicitly incorporated into a "frame" setting, such as the dinner table after a meal, a long journey, or an enforced respite from some other activity, where stories are told to pass the time. From Boccaccio onwards, these settings tend to presuppose a cultural level where urbane conversation is normal, in contrast to the fairy tale, where the implied audience is naïve or credulous (e.g. children or rustics).

(5) The frame (implicit or explicit) creates an inner distance within the novella between the security and hindsight of the teller and the danger and doubt of the characters. The narrative situation is more central to the author's society than are the events narrated. The social stability of the frame may contrast with the solitude or outcast-status of the character or group in the story.

(6) The framed or socially mediated nature of the novella makes it more receptive than the novel to communal wisdom, practical guidance, or explicit reflections on the human condition (though of course these are present in many novels). The listener may learn how to avoid being duped, for example, or how human nature is defined by limit-cases of endurance or weakness or some other quality.

(7) The formal principle of the novella is intensity; of the novel, extensity. In regard to character, the appropriate method is dramatic or symbolic revelation rather than gradual development. In plot, the novella lacks the long chains of consequences, the cumulative interactions of self and other and world, which characterize the novel; instead it often focusses on simple natural or preternatural exigencies: apparitions, cataclysms like great storms or earthquakes, and individual declines and deaths. The novella is too short to build up evidence for a social-secular theory of causation, and hence is often fatalistic in implication.

(8) Like tragedy, the novella may deal with extreme cases, but its mediated retrospective form gives their outcomes a weight of inevitability qualitatively different from tragedy. In the novella the action usually ends before the telling begins. This means that the novella hero's story has a foregone conclusion: his suffering is distanced, where the tragic hero's is immediately present. In tragedy, the hero has the live audience; in the novella it is the narrator. In this presence, the tragic hero makes a decisive choice which brings on his death; the novella more often shows the gradual deterioration of a character into social isolation or death as if under a curse against which he cannot assert his will.

(9) The novella's oral quality, its assumption of a copresent teller and hearer in personal communication, contrasts with the novel's literary (written, printed) quality. The novel is a book; it is voluminous, volume-sized, where the novella has to be grouped with others to make up a book. Its length is related to the attention span of a live audience in a single sitting. Dramas are acted for spectators, novels are written for readers, but novellas are told to hearers. In drama, character and spectator are copresent, but the author is absent, in the novella, narrator and listener are fictively copresent, but the character is absent (even if he is the narrator's earlier self); in the novel, writer and reader are both in private, in isolation from each other. The novella is the social transmission (the telling in company) of extra-social content (the distant or excluded); the novel is the non-social transmission (through solitary writing and reading) of predominantly social content. The alternative tradition of the novel, the self-conscious and epistemologically playful fiction exemplified by Cervantes or Sterne or Joyce, which privileges the book as world, is equally dependent on the non-oral character of the novel. The novel is obsessed either with its own self-sufficient fictiveness or with its documentary truth to life. It sets itself to contain the world, or be self-contained, or both (Joyce's Ulysses). The novel is *literal* with the full ambiguity of that word: true, yet consisting only of letters. This epistemological opposition hardly affects the novella: aiming to convince us that something

extraordinary has happened, it depends on the direct personal credibility of the narrator, and on his powers of recollection and persuasion. It is not a textual matter, but one of trust.

(10) The novel is experienced as an open-ended process in the psychological present. The novella is a closed form whose end is latent in its beginning: there is usually some initial indication *that* the end is known, and this enhances the narrative art of holding in suspense *what* it is. The novella's opening projects a story whose past completeness strengthens the living presentness of its telling. The disturbing quality of the event or scene is balanced by the reassurance of its distance, its recollection in tranquillity. Following Gide's usage, Ramon Fernandez distinguishes "roman" and "récit" thus: "The novel represents events happening in time, in terms of those events' conditions of appearance and development. The 'récit' presents events that have happened, and whose reproduction is ordered by the narrator in accordance with the rules of exposition and persuasion."[25] "Le récit *fait connaître* et non point *naître* les événements."[26]

NOTES

1. *Neophilogus*, 51 (1967). I owe much to this article, and to Edith Kern, "The Romance of Novel/Novelle" in *The Disciplines of Criticism*, ed. Peter Demetz, Thomas Greene, and Lowery Nelson, Jr. (New Haven: Yale University Press, 1968), pp. 511–31; and Werner Krauss, "Novela, Novella—Roman" in *Novelle* ed. Josef Kunz (Darmstadt: Wissenchaftliche Buchgesellchaft, 1968), pp. 222–38. Kunz's anthology of German novella theory is thorough and extremely useful, though some of the pieces are abridged. The standard English-language work in this field is E. K. Bennett and H. M. Waidson, *A History of the German Novelle* (Cambridge: Cambridge University Press, 1961. John Ellis, *Narration in the German Novelle: Theory and Interpretation* (Cambridge: Cambridge University Press, 1974), eloquently attacks German orthodoxies about the "Novelle" and analyzes some standard German examples of the genre in the light of mainly Anglo-American theory of narration, treating them as "fiction" not radically distinct from the novel: roughly the opposite of what I attempt here.

2. Ann Shukman of Oxford University has supplied me with a Russian line as follows: istoriya, rasskaz, provest', roman. There is a Russian word "novella," but it means specifically a short story with emphasis on plot or action.

3. Kunz, p. 52.

4. Joseph Gibaldi, "The Renaissance Theory of the Novella,": *Canadian Review of Comparative Literature*, 2 (Fall 1975), 201–27, recommends that the term *novella* be reserved for the Renaissance form, which he views as sharply distinct from the modern.

5. "Wie Don Quijote gemacht ist," in *Theorie der Prosa,* trans. Gisela Drohla (Frankfurt: Fischer, 1966), pp. 89–130.

6. "La construction de la nouvelle et du roman," in *Théorie de la littérature,* trans. and ed. Tzvetan Todorov (Paris: Seuil, 1965), p. 189.

7. Shklovsky, p. 196.

8. Georg Lukács, *Solzhenitsyn,* trans. W. D. Graf (London: Merlin Press, 1970), p. 7. For earlier distinctions of the novella from the novel, see *Soul and Form,* trans. Anna Bostock (London: Merlin Press, 1974), p. 73; and *The Theory of the Novel,* trans. Anna Bostock (London: Merlin Press, 1971), pp. 50–51.

9. Lukács, *Solzhenitsyn,* p. 7.

10. Kunz, p. 41.

11. Kunz, p. 34.

12. Kunz, p. 53.

13. Kunz, p. 124.

14. Kunz, p. 154–66.

15. Kunz, pp. 174–82.

16. Frank O'Connor, *The Lonely Voice: A Study of the Short Story* (Cleveland: World Publishing Co., 1963), p. 21.

17. O'Connor, p. 18.

18. O'Connor, p. 105.

19. Howard Nemerov, *Poetry and Fiction: Essays* (New Brunswick, New Jersey Rutgers University Press, 1963), p. 245.

20. Boris Eichenbaum, "O. Henry and the Theory of the Short Story," in L. Matejka and K. Pomorosky, eds., *Readings in Russian Poetics* (Cambridge, Mass.: M.I.T. Press, 1971), p. 231.

21. See Wendell Harris, "English Short Fiction in the Nineteenth Century," *Studies in Short Fiction,* 6 (Fall, 1968), 1–93.

22. See Alfred Engstrom, "The Formal Short Story in France and its Development before 1850," *Studies in Philology,* 42 (1945), 627–39.

23. See Wendell Harris, *op cit.*

24. Conrad Aiken, *A Reviewer's A B C* (London: W. H. Allen, 1961), p. 291.

25. Ramon Fernandez, "La Méthode de Balzac: le récit et l'esthétique du roman," in *Messages* (Paris: Gallimard, 1926), p. 60.

26. Fernandez, p. 61.

From Tale
to Short Story

THE EMERGENCE OF
A NEW GENRE IN THE 1850'S

ROBERT F. MARLER

A WAVE OF TALES flooded American magazines during the expansive years of the 1850's. As art, all but a few of these works deserve the oblivion that time has bestowed, but because of them the period from 1850 to the beginning of the Civil War has been discredited and generally ignored in the history of American short fiction. As a result, the early evolution of the American short story from the magazine tale has been overlooked. In this essay, I propose as a broad hypothesis that the decay of the immensely popular tale fostered the development of the short story as a new genre. If as a total body the fiction has but little aesthetic appeal, that mediocrity prompted a substantial reaction in the decade's literary criticism and among writers of short fiction. Until mid-century, Irving, Poe, and Hawthorne dominated the field, but by 1850 Poe was dead and Irving and Hawthorne had all but abandoned the writing of tales. Melville's short works were condemned to their long obscurity, and not until Henry James was a notable tradition of American short fiction again established. A gap in literary history such as this should have inspired a reevaluation long ago. Yet in 1923 Fred Lewis Pattee fixed what has remained the usual verdict when he complained that the short story all but "ceased to be distinctive" and "seemed to disappear as a reputable literary form."[1] Since then scholars have skimmed the decade's short fiction, occasionally using the material for social and cultural history; but the historical changes that were revolutionizing the short forms have escaped notice.

In retrospect, the major theoretical differences between tale and short story are fairly well known, although, unlike novel and prose romance, the short forms have not attracted much critical enquiry. Northrop Frye's distinctions, which are based on characterization, establish poles around which the fictions cluster in actual practice. The tale, according to Frye, is analogous to the prose romance, and the short story is analogous to the novel. In the tale there are no "'real people'"; characters, as "stylized figures which expand into psychological archetypes," account for the "subjective intensity" not found in the novel or short story and for the tendency toward allegory. "Idealized by revery," such characters are derived from the heroic mold and remain inscrutable and isolated from representations of actual society. The short story, by contrast, deals with characters who have "personality" and wear "their *personae* or social masks"; accordingly, the author requires a stable society, and his fictive world tends to be an imitation of the actual world of men.[2] Unlike the figures of romance, characters in the short story have an inner consciousness. The tale may itself illustrate directly a state of mind or a psychological condition. In the short story, however, such states, dynamic and developing, remain internal and determine motivation and conduct; they are communicated to the reader through inference or through a narrator's penetration of the mind and his report of what is there. Writing of Poe's characters, W. H. Auden said, "Personages who are the embodiment of . . . [unitary] states cannot, of course, change or vary in intensity either through changes in themselves or their environment."[3] Auden, in fact, criticizes Poe's characters for not being human beings subject to the laws of nature, for not being, that is, realistic. Though he may have preferred that Poe had written short stories, he is right about Poe's characters; they belong to the tale and would be destroyed by common reality. They cannot change, nor can Irving's or Hawthorne's, though in tales like "My Kinsman, Major Molineux" and "Roger Malvin's Burial," Hawthorne begins to point toward the short story.

During the fifties, short fiction was preeminently periodical material. If we discount the poor specimens in the newspapers or the tales in the few remaining gift annuals, then the major outlet for writers—serious authors or hacks—was the magazines. Most of the leading general magazines carried four or five tales in each issue; and, with the number of periodicals increasing and the circulation expanding, at least until the Depression of 1857,[4] the supply to meet the demand was enormous. The legacies of Irving, Poe, and Hawthorne are found there, where the comparatively balanced effects of Irving's sentimentalism, Poe's sensationalism, and Hawthorne's moralism were so heavily emphasized, distorted, and unconsciously parodied that the decay of the tale is unmistakable. The most visible symbol of decadence and commercialism was Robert Bonner's highly successful fiction factory, the *New York Ledger*,[5] though tales only somewhat less exploitative than the *Ledger's* are everywhere and in astonishing quantity. Works by such vendors as "Ned Buntline," E. D. E. N. Southworth, Sylvanus Cobb, Jr., Caroline Chesebro', Timothy Shay Arthur, and the young Horatio Alger, Jr., typify the times. Random titles from leading magazines suggest the tenor of marketable products: "A Gift From Heaven," "An Old Maid's First Love," "Frank Ward's Second Love," "Kissing With a Moustache," "Two Scenes in the Life of a City Belle," "Passages for a Sentimentalist," "The Rival Heroes; Or, the Privateersman's Reward. A Tale of Revolutionary Times," "Nat. Puckett, the Indian-Hater," and "Hannibal: A Nigger." These and others like them cluster about the polar definition of the tale. They constitute a datum of conventional practice in commonplace short fiction, and a quick summary of their obvious characteristics, derived from a sample of more than a thousand magazine tales, demonstrates why critics were rebelling against the standardization of taste and the decline of art.

Characters are romance figures or stereotypes illustrating popular values and ideals. They have no interior life beyond what the invariably omniscient narrator asserts they have. Their virtue or sinfulness accords with notions of Protestant piety; their powers of action, motives, and appearance follow popular specifications. They tend to be overtly allegorical, illustrating by their routine names, stereotyped dress, and extreme conduct the simplified outline of an idea or belief. Their problems and conflicts are simple, restricted to clear-cut resolutions. The fictive world is usually remote in time and place; but if the locale is labelled a part of the nineteenth-century world, the setting is nonetheless exaggerated, with topical allusions and specific details serving as tenuous ties to real life. In the sentimental and moralistic tales, in fact, such details often formed a veneer of surface realism intended to convince the reader of the "truth" of the fiction's explicit message. In general, cities are sinks of sin; the country is a pastoral ideal though regularly threatened by evil. Negroes, Indians, Jews, and most foreigners are inferior; Mormons and Catholics are satanic. Meaning is explicit and, as a reflection of what ought to be, depends on poetic justice and happy endings for confirmation. The reader's pleasure, therefore, rises from his recognition of the triumph of a simple, ideal order along with the confirmation of his middle-class values. Authors, lavishing didactic passages on theme, avoid not only ambiguity, complexity, and richness but also problems that might discourage a casual reader. Profundity is rare; the optimistic ideal is hardened doctrine derived from popular beliefs about Christianity and American democracy. Plots are designed to "prove" the moral, regardless of violations of a work's basic premises. The inflated "literary" style, which relies on circumlocutions, formal diction, and the blandly humorous burlesque that develops when the subject is low, insinuates that the flattered reader is intelligent and sophisticated.

It is no wonder that Hawthorne condemned in "Feathertop," his last tale, the empty figures of romance that peopled the world of fiction. Melville's response to market conditions and the writer's lot is a cry of real pain: "Dollars damn me. . . . What I feel most moved to write, that is banned,—it will not pay." The complaint of genteel poet and tale teller Richard Henry Stoddard is an echo: "How can you help the trash you write—for pay?"[6] But the reaction was broader and deeper than the complaints of Hawthorne, Melville, and Stoddard. A survey of contemporary criticism and commentary pertaining to short fiction[7] shows the dissatisfaction with the conventional tale and reveals opinion that was congenial to the development of the short story. This is not to say that the short forms were, like the romance and novel, recognized as independent genres: the terms "tale," "story," "short story," and "sketch" were interchangeable. However, despite the absence of conscious classification, critical separation of the two genres was in process. If we can demonstrate that fact, we shall be prepared to delineate the evolutionary course of short fiction; we can account for differences between such works as Melville's short story "Bartleby, the Scrivener" and his tale "The Bell-Tower"; and we may recover as historically significant such pre-Civil War tales and short stories as Harriet Prescott Spofford's "Circumstance," "In a Cellar," and "Yet's Christmas Box," Rose Terry Cooke's "Ann Potter's Lesson" and "Eben Jackson," Howells's "A Dream," and Rebecca Harding Davis's "Life in the Iron Mills."

The primary targets of attacks in the magazines were sentimentalism and didactic moralism. It was probably Charles Godfrey Leland who, as editor of a faltering *Graham's,* angrily asserted that "nearly all the most unmistakable *trash*—downright, decided illiterate *stuff* which no schoolboy could mistake for anything else—which we receive, is of the kind which the writers choose to regard as pathetic and sentimental, and which is quite as invariably characterless and drawling."[8] Critics, of course, recognized the legitimate use of sentiment. "Sentiment, as an element of literature, is the intellectual embodiment of feeling; it is thought imbued with a coloring and an atmosphere derived from emotion. . . ."[9] That definition is typical; but, cautioned the critic, sentiment, when allied with "a feeble and impressible mind," "a capricious fancy," or "a selfish disposition," is unreliable; sentimentalism is the dangerous result. Sentimentalism was not simply emotion in excess of what the situation warranted, unless by situation we specify some abstract standard from our personal experience or real life. Characters and their situations deserved every bit of the emotion the readers bestowed on them. But the point is that writers exaggerated situations and attenuated and simplified characters for the sake of emotion. Sentimentalism exalted ideals that Americans subscribed to, although they obviously lived according to a more practical set of values. Hence, the more realistic the characters, the more apparent the hypocrisy. Sentimentalism was, in fact, optimistic during the fifties; for despite the misery and suffering it thrived on, it was associated with a simplistic world view that assured happiness in this life or the next. Moreover, if a mother or child died in the course of several double-columned pages of fine print, the sacrifice, however painful for the dying, worked in the interest of the living, who learned the value of one or another ideal (charity, forgiveness, innocence, honesty, etc.). When employed to make hardships bearable, sentimentalism became a force for conservatism because it supported the status quo; but it also was an agent for tepid reform because it exaggerated for condemnation the period's social ills, such as poverty, disease, crime, child labor, alcoholism, selfish capitalism, and domestic difficulties. As propaganda, its emotionalism, anti-intellectualism, and conventional appeal to women had become epidemic.

It was making critics ill. Americans, it was often said, are a practical people who require fiction "to answer to our want as human beings, of mixed earth and spirit. . . . We cannot suffer the mortal to shake off his cares of earth, his crown of thorns, and deliver himself to a land of dream and vapour. . . ."[10] Many critics and reviewers complained that the sentimental world of fiction was dishonest when writers urged that it was identical to the world of fact.[11] Sentimentalists concentrating on soft, dream-like fancies instead of everyday life[12] forced characters, as even *Godey's Lady's Book* noticed, to confront issues in tales that never occur in the real world.[13] Leland, demanding real life in fiction, blamed sentimental tales on lazy writers who fed the market "puling pathos, sentimental transcendentalism, vague reverie and the whole tribe of trash."[14] Another critic charged the crimes to German imports, and thus repeated a standard rebuke.[15] And Henry Clapp, Jr., the Bohemian editor of the avant-garde New York *Saturday Press* and staunch advocate of Walt Whitman, maintained a weekly barrage against sentimentality, puffing, and mindless authors such as Sigourney, Southworth, and Cobb.[16] By 1860, Henry Giles obliged to blast anything remotely attributable to sentimentality. "Sentimentalism is either a disease of the moral nature, or a perversion of imag-

ination; either the illusive confounded with the actual, or fancy taken in
preference to fact; either an emotional self-deception or a pretentious un-
realism."[17]

The excesses of didacticism that religiosity and moralism supported
were another major liability for short fiction. "Next to the Bible," a
commentator wrote in a familiar thesis, "the reading of fiction is probably
the most important of all reading to the young,—the most important for
good and evil."[18] To assure the triumph of righteousness in a world of absolute and unambiguous good and evil, many ostensibly realistic works
were designed so that the characters fulfilled the necessity of evil's defeat,
but in doing so they appeared jarringly inconsistent or they implied
meanings that contradicted the explicitly stated moral intent. Because the
contradiction between the real and the ideal was obvious, works of fiction
frequently separated into two parts, sacrificing unity to doctrine. Authors
included lengthy preachments and explanations in expository passages,
typically in long introductions and dénouements. The exhortation in discursive prose battled with the fictive illusion, and again the result was a
bipartite structure that the public accepted on ethical grounds but that
critics increasingly deplored on aesthetic grounds. "The tale and the argument kill each other."[19]

In 1851, Henry T. Tuckerman praised Hawthorne's tales for the undercurrent of significance that Poe, in his reviews of *Twice-Told Tales,* had
admired in Hawthorne's sketches and essays and in "The Minister's Black
Veil." Hawthorne, said Tuckerman, "shadows forth,—hints,—makes signs
. . . ;—in a word, addresses us as nature does—that is, unostentatiously,
and with a significance not to be realized without reverent silence and
gentle feeling."[20] Here, as a response to didacticism, was a theme that
others would echo. If positive morality was to be a rule, it should, said a
critic, be apparent in a work's entire development, not "written out in a
few pithy words on the last page."[21] The ability to suggest, to evoke,
without resorting to explanations was increasingly praised. Tacked-on
moral tags became a sign of mediocrity, even if "the brilliancy of style is
on them like the sun."[22] Or, as another reviewer said, "a story should
speak the idea the writer has in view, without the necessity for elaborate
introduction and explanation."[23] And in a brief reference to Melville,
probably by Rufus W. Griswold, the critic objects to lecturing narrators; it
is a fault when the writer appears before the reader "in his own person,"
for he has no more right to do it than a dramatist has the right to step before the footlights.[24] A work of fiction, however, was expected to have
some meaning other than the point of its plots or descriptions. Irving's
tales, for example, were judged defective because they do not "lead to

some definite end"; they rely too heavily on an "illustrative talent," on decorations that "delight us into a forgetfulness of the purpose or want of purpose of the whole. . . ."[25] "The great nuisance of American literature," said Leland, "its incubus, is—not story writing—but stories which are nothing else."[26]

By rejecting didacticism and also the moral allegory associated with it and by encouraging authors to embody an undercurrent of significance, the critics were forwarding two principles that Poe had advocated. Both principles are, of course, applicable to either tale or short story. However, Poe's concept of the "single effect," as modified by critics, has a bearing on the short story's history. The publication in 1850 and 1856 of the Griswold edition of Poe's collected works,[27] along with Poe's notoriety, elicited commentary that kept Poe's tales before the public and his critical principles before the other critics and reviewers who could apply them. Furthermore, "The Poetic Principle," which, like Poe's reviews of *Twice-Told Tales,* includes the doctrine of brevity and the concept of "the totality of effect or impression," was posthumously published twice in 1850, for the first time in August in the *Home Journal* and then in October in *Sartain's Union Magazine,* thus giving additional exposure to Poe's ideas. Later, in opposing the serial publication of fiction, *Sartain's* said that "an acute critic [Poe?] has remarked that a short story, which can be finished at a sitting, is best fitted to rivet the reader's attention; and that novels are of imperfect interest, inasmuch as they are perused at different times, and, therefore, with different states of mind, by the same individual."[28] Tuckerman wrote that the brevity of the tale "is a wise economy of resources, and often secures permanent renown by distinctness of impression unattained in efforts of great range."[29] And *Graham's* noted that Hawthorne's tales "convey that unity of impression which indicates a firm hold on one strong conception."[30]

On the magazine circuit, the idea of the single effect developed along two primary lines. It was often transformed into a token for unity and thus tied to plot, in which case the plot's climax became the point of release for "the shock," "the explosion," "the dominant impression," "the unity of impression," or, perforce, "the single effect." As a result the single effect was incorporated into the formula for conventional plotting. But plot, or story as it was called, was rarely considered a very important element in fiction: "Plain storytelling . . . is entirely beyond, or rather beneath, his [Hawthorne's] capacity." Critics depreciated plot because "the most paltry tale-maker for magazines or newspapers can easily excel . . . in the mechanical portion of . . . art."[31] Consequently, the single effect as merely a synonym for the climax lost force as a principle for short fiction. Along the second line of development, however, the single effect came to be associated with the undercurrent of significance; it meant the dominant impression made on the reader, and the point became particularly important to the short story.

William Peden observes that "the short story, brief, elliptical, and unwinking, tends to ask questions rather than to suggest answers, to show rather than attempt to solve."[32] This quality of the modern story is largely the result of the single-effect principle and the growth of realism. Endowed now with minds, the chief characters in short stories are therefore subject to the inner complexities that experience imposes. They undergo internal changes as they are affected by the choices they make and by what happens to them. Such changes typically appear as the movement from a relative state of ignorance to a relative state of knowledge, and the movement occurs even when a character ironically rejects or ignores the knowledge. The ironic vision in the twentieth century is responsible for fairly radical modifications; but as a characteristic of the nineteenth-century short story this change has been regularly remarked in stories of James, Howells, and Edith Wharton. Furthermore, the change frequently instills a sense of mystery, a mystery in keeping with what remained vital in the romantic spirit. That is, the short story's brevity and its representation of the experiential world, which discouraged the inclusion of the supernatural and of symbols that are not first functional within the fictive world's natural order, conspire to force meaning beneath the surface where, by the nature of its indistinctness, it gives the impression of being inexplicable. The fiction dramatizes the mystery; and, free of unnecessary explanations, that mystery is what the reader intuits or feels, though typically it remains unstated and unsolved. It is, finally, that "shock of recognition" that constitutes the single effect; and the effect differs from the tale's effect according to the illusion of actuality that the short story provides; for even during the transitional years of the fifties the "elliptical" short story tended "to show rather than attempt to solve."[33]

To summarize: commentary in leading publications attacked the excesses of sentimentalism, deplored the distortions of moralism and didacticism, and depreciated the importance of plot. Critics, while simultaneously retaining the single-effect concept and the necessity of implied significance, were encouraging the modification of the conventional tale. If they also advocated a realistic world of fiction, then they had, more or less unintentionally, established basic conditions suitable for the development of the new genre.

Advocates of a realistic fictive world are not difficult to find; their comments, however, seldom depended upon sustained argument or an expressed philosophical foundation. Nor is there much evidence to suggest that a self-conscious movement existed. Yet realism and the writers called "Realists" were active enough to provoke controversy. Critics and reviewers accepted realism in fiction as the convincing and plausible representation of natural men, even if eccentric, in their usual surroundings. Because the concepts were derived from the older vraisemblance or verisimilitude after the extraordinary or supernatural subjects were stripped away, there was little restriction placed on the unusual so long as it was possible. "The first element of tale writing," said Alice B. Neal Haven, "indeed, of any description, is naturalness; forgetting this, the charm is destroyed, be the language ever so well chosen, or the thoughts daintily expressed." "Stereotyped incident" and "hackneyed plots are as much out of favor with the public as unnatural language"; "the plot and incident" should be "arranged with a thought to the ordinary sequence of events . . . ."[34] Even Hawthorne was condemned for his "fog of mystery" that destroyed the real world.[35] Editor Leland emphatically directed those who would write for him to stop imitating the romances of the old days. Walter Scott is obsolete; the author who would write "absolutely, perfectly, and vividly true to daguerreotype-like studies of life" is bold indeed.[36] Although America has more original subjects for fiction than any other country, he said, writers "go on rhyming and romancing away in the same old rigmarole vein, as though old custom, if not the law of the land, enjoined it on them to be as pretty and as affected, and ornamental as possible."[37] In 1854, three years before he became editor of *The Atlantic,* James Russell Lowell wrote to C. F. Briggs, editor of *Putnam's,* that "the truth to everyday . . . is essential in stories of life and the world,"[38] and before he left the editor's chair in 1861, Lowell included a sizeable volume of short fiction marked by realistic characters and colloquial dialect.

Verisimilitude (Poe's "earnestness")[39] was traditionally a term used to commend an author for making the extraordinary or marvelous convincing by direct references to actual life. In the fifties verisimilitude, like vraisemblance its synonym among reviewers, was deemed Poe's highest achievement. As the subjects for fiction were increasingly taken from everyday life, however, the techniques that had always been associated with verisimilitude further encouraged the illusion of real life. A laudatory article on Thackeray in the *Southern Quarterly Review* indicates that realism was early in the decade favorably recognized. "All we contend for is that the capability of representing the words and actions of men so naturally as to make us, in spite of ourselves, look on them as real rather than fictitious characters, is a power which is confined to writers of very great merit. . . ."[40] Similarly, Parke Godwin observed of Thackeray that it is "this remarkable realism which gives his books their aspect of an actual transcript of the life of society."[41] *Putnam's* said bluntly that the success of English fiction depends on its "actuality," which "is the very genius and spirit of modern English fiction. . . . The democratic principle has ordered romance to descend from thrones and evacuate the palace."[42] The influence of realism occasioned controversy, and the debate is readily demonstrated in the matter of French literature. For example, *The Democratic Review,* in a characteristic article praising Balzac's realism in his descriptions of French life and manners, elevated the Frenchman above Bulwer and Thackeray.[43] Despite their immoralities, George Sand, Flaubert, and Stendhal, among others, were acclaimed.[44] The opposition is represented by the conservative *North American Review.* Commenting on Champfleury's *Le Réalisme,* the *Review* said that "Realism," as a mode relying on the close observation of actual life, was meant for young writers who made up an absurd "School." These authors are "extraordinary writing engines," literary Bohemians who believe that their "epoch" is "condemning them to a species of photography in literature which they are pleased to style 'observation.'"[45] That the vocabulary and the ideas that it represents were current long before the eighteen-eighties is clear evidence of realism's mid-century growth.

Hawthorne recognized the change. In his preface to the 1851 edition of *Twice-Told Tales,* he writes of his tales in much the same way he wrote of the prose romance in "The Custom House" and in the prefaces to *The House of the Seven Gables* and *The Blithedale Romance.* The short form is analogous to the longer. But the tales, he said, lack the solidity of nature and have sentiment instead of passion: "even in what purport to be pictures of actual life, we have allegory, not so warmly dressed in its habiliments of flesh and blood as to be taken into the reader's mind without a shiver."[46] The tone is lightly ironic and apologetic as the famous man underrates the dated work of earlier years. It was in part, perhaps, an indulgence for effect,[47] but there can be no doubt that it was also Hawthorne's own recognition that the times, tastes, and fiction were changing. If hacks and scribbling women had debased romance, the trend in short fiction was toward what Perry Miller called the era's "Victorian realism."[48]

Melville's fictive essay "Hawthorne and His Mosses"[49] and his tales and stories reveal that, like Hawthorne, he also was aware of the changing tastes and that he sought a way of dealing with popular demand while retaining his integrity as a serious artist. Melville's "techniques of disguise," as William Charvat called them,[50] refer to Melville's creation of a surface for his fiction that would have popular appeal that would conceal the important meanings beneath the surface. The familiar concept is implicit in Melville's enthusiastic review of Hawthorne's tales. He believed that Hawthorne had mastered, like Shakespeare, the art of telling the truth; that is, Hawthorne concealed the darkest mysteries from "the superficial skimmer of pages." To Melville, the actual world is a façade, even a lie. The fictive world is an artifice that leads to Truth, though, paradoxically, the writer must begin with the materials of real life to penetrate to the core of meaning. Hence, actuality is fundamental to the art of fiction. It is now apparent that Melville's theory of fiction, what we know of it directly, and what Edgar Dryden has uncovered on the basis of the review of Hawthorne,[51] could readily accommodate the short story with its illusion of actuality and its undercurrent of mystery. We should recognize, then, that the importance of implied significance is continuous among Poe, Hawthorne, and Melville. Moreover, it is time to lighten the traditional emphasis on Poe's reviews of *Twice-Told Tales* and acknowledge that, with Hawthorne's tales as a constant, the critical commentary of the three masters of short fiction describe a smooth transition from the tale to the short story.

Circumstances moved Melville to write both tales and short stories. Before "Bartleby" in 1853, he had tried to win the public with his surface of romance; but the failure of *Pierre* (1852), which is understandable given the critics' growing respect for realism, is evidence that Melville's idea of the prose romance with its large doses of philosophy, exhortation, and elaborate rhetoric was hardly suitable for large sales. Depressed by *Pierre's* rejection and burdened by financial troubles, he agreed to write for the middle-class *Putnam's Monthly*. But the decadence of magazine tales and critics' disillusionment with all the trash would have discouraged Melville, who knew well the magazine marketplace, from trying that type of thing. Besides, his modification, even parody, of the tall-tale formula in "The Town-Ho's Story" (Chapter 54 of *Moby-Dick*), which had satisfied *Harper's New Monthly* as an advertisement for *Moby-Dick,* shows his ability to use the popular Southwestern humor for his own purposes. Indeed, the tall tale, having received the East's stamp of approval, was a force for realism because the colloquial teller (as opposed to the narrator in the frame) was often convincing as a personality and because many such narratives relinquished their humor for the serious treatment of human foibles.[52] By comparison to Poe's and Hawthorne's usual tales, "The Town-Ho's Story" cleaves to actuality despite the violence and adventure. "Bartleby, the Scrivener" is a fully developed short story. Firmly embedded in a social context but simultaneously a reflection of the attorney-narrator's mind, the narrative is the attorney's history rather than a tale about Bartleby.

The narrator moves from a state of relative ignorance to one of awareness marked, paradoxically, by intense perplexity. Bartleby, however, is static. He appears as a romantic stranger because he is alien to the attorney's limited experience in the world of Wall Street; therefore, the attorney represents him as mysterious and strange because that is the way he sees him. Throughout the story, the narrator remains convincing as a human being with a consciousness afflicted by perfectly human complexities. Because what the scrivener has meant to the attorney cannot be abstracted and analyzed, however, the mystery remains as a rich undercurrent.

At the opposite pole stands "the Bell-Tower," which is obviously a tale. Bannadonna, the Promethean mechanician, is overtly symbolic, unencumbered by the restrictions of natural law. Remote in time and place, the Italian Renaissance setting is evoked in a poetic style, and the allegory, at once psychological and social with oblique references to American materialism and original sin, is provocative but submerged. Yet even here one feels the tug of actuality as the omniscient narrator, seemingly compelled to test the grand ideals, relinquishes by degrees his initial detachment and becomes a man of the fifties, himself a focal point, as if Melville would not sustain his fictive illusion. With his other short works, Melville stands at a crossroads in the history of American short fiction. The diptychs, notably "The Paradise of Bachelors and The Tartarus of Maids," emphasize allegory and are stiffened by heavy thematic interests. In "The Lightning-Rod Man" and "The Happy Failure" the moral intention seems to dominate. In retrospect it appears that Melville, searching for forms capable of popular appeal and implied portent, mixed genres. The difficulty critics have found in judging the value of these pieces may be partly explained by the deficiencies of the works as either tale or short story: a thorough assimilation required the length of "Benito Cereno." However, the remainder of the fictions achieve their effects from the illusion of actuality. That illusion, except in "Benito Cereno," relies primarily on the credibility of the first-person narrators who, as Warner Berthoff has shown, are most vivid when they are "most occupied with the presentation of actual facts."[53] Short stories like "I and My Chimney," "The Apple-Tree Table," and even "Cock-A-Doodle-Doo!" with its satiric parody of routine tales and their simplistic dualisms and easy answers, represent the narrators' experiences and natural attitudes. In them hitherto unquestioned beliefs are abruptly overturned.

Overall, the composite fictional worlds of the three leading authors demonstrate a broad shift from Poe's overt romance and verisimilitude to Hawthorne's neutral ground of actual and imaginary and thence to Melville's mimetic portrayals and reliance on facts for the profound probing of everyday reality. The generalization is too neat, of course. There are exceptions and plenty of room for disagreement about particulars. Still, the shift, as a historical movement, is abundantly demonstrated in the critical commentary I have been exploring and in the fiction of the three major authors. It appears also in the works of less well-known writers, although the extent of the whole shift can only be suggested here. Urban fiction was increasing. Though the city remained a picture of sin and evil, such authors of tales as Fitz-James O'Brien and Fitz-Hugh Ludlow, as they dramatized the nightmare, relied on urban local color for verisimilitude. Influenced by Poe, O'Brien, a good judge of the fiction market, exchanged Poe's "earnestness" for the detailed specifics of New York City. For the sake of sales he carefully specified time, place, and topical events.

Equally important were the growing popularity of regionalist fiction in general and New England local color in particular. This early development of a larger movement culminated before the Civil War in the fine, but too often ignored local-color short stories of Rose Terry Cooke, the best of which are "Ann Potter's Lesson" and "Eben Jackson." Harriet Prescott Spofford, capable like most of the period's professionals of producing extravagant tales, also showed her mastery of mimetic representation in "Knitting Sale-Socks" and "Yet's Christmas Box." In fact, Editor Lowell cultivated the trend in the *Atlantic,* and the magazine stands in symbolic contrast to Bonner's *Ledger.* It was also Lowell who recognized the tentative realism of Rebecca Harding Davis's "Life in the Iron Mills," a depressing but overwritten attack on industrialism. And finally it is worth noting that the young W. D. Howells published one of his first short stories just at the outbreak of the War. Entitled "A Dream," the story is an excellent example of how far the transformation of the tale had progressed; for Howells, in attacking the falsity of a dream-like sentimental view of life, indicates that conventional, romantic optimism leads to despair.[54]

In one tale published in 1856, a hopeful young authoress is told emphatically that "tales are a perfect drag."[55] Here in accidentally modern idiom sounds the keynote of the era. When the tale's decadence had become the object of satire, then we may assume that knowledge of the genre's decline was widespread through the marketplace. Change was inevitable; and, if I am correct in my thesis that the short story as an independent genre emerged during the eighteen-fifties, then we are, as Northrop Frye said, in a better position to examine works according to conventions the authors selected.[56] If a critic as perceptive as W. H. Auden can judge Poe's romance figures as a "negative characteristic"[57] in all his tales, then it is understandable if unfortunate that a half century of Melville criticism has failed to come to terms with Melville's tales, short stories, and mixtures of the two and has failed to establish his role in the history of our short fiction.

NOTES

1. Fred Lewis Pattee, *The Development of the American Short Story* (New York, 1923), p. 145. Ray B. West, Jr., provides a more balanced view in his *The Short Story in America, 1900–1950* (Chicago, 1952), pp. 1–25.

2. *Anatomy of Criticism* (Princeton, 1957), pp. 304–306, 308.

3. "Introduction," *Edgar Allan Poe: Selected Prose, Poetry, and Eureka,* ed. W. H. Auden (New York, 1950), p. vi.

4. Frank Luther Mott, *A History of American Magazines: Volume II: 1850–1865* (Cambridge, Mass., 1938), pp. 4, 9–11.

5. See Mary Noel, *Villains Galore: The Heyday of the Popular Story Weekly* (New York, 1954), pp. 69–85.

6. "Feathertop: A Moralized Legend," *International Monthly Magazine,* V (1852), 185. Melville's complaint is in a letter to Hawthorne, 1(?) June 1851, in *The Letters of Herman Melville,* eds. Merrell R. Davis and William H. Gilman (New Haven, 1960), p. 128. Stoddard's remark is in his "To Sundry Critics," *International Monthly Magazine,* V (1852), 319.

7. The survey is based on approximately two hundred items of critical commentary appearing in twenty-seven representative magazines published in the major cultural centers of the Eastern United States for the years 1850–1861 inclusive.

8. "Editor's Easy Talk," *Graham's Magazine,* LII (1858), 276. Charles Godfrey Leland, as editor, probably wrote the article.

9. "Laurence Sterne," *North American Review,* LXXXI (1855), 386–87.

10. "Sentimental Prose Fiction," *Southern Quarterly Review,* XVII (1850), 360.

11. Ignatius (pseud.), "Matter of Fact and Matter of Fiction," *Harper's New Monthly Magazine,* XV (1857), 658–61.

12. See Fitz-James O'Brien, "Our Young Authors—Mitchell," *Putnam's Monthly Magazine,* I (1853), 74–78.

13. (Sarah Josepha Hale?), "Editor's Table," *Godey's Lady's Book,* LIV (1857), 370. For a typical attack on feminine fiction, see "Parlor Periodicals," *United States Magazine and Democratic Review,* XXX (1852), 13–16.

14. "To Readers and Correspondents," *Graham's Magazine,* I (1857), 468.

15. "Goethe and the Satanic Philosophy," *United States Magazine,* I (1854), 119–120.

16. See, for examples, "Character Versus Sentiment in Art," *Saturday Press,* III (June 23, 1860), and "Gilding," III (Sept. 29, 1860). The pages of the *Press* in the microfilm that I used, supplied by the Pennsylvania Historical Society, are not numbered.

17. "Sentimentalism," *Harper's New Monthly Magazine,* XXI (1860), 204.

18. "Miss Yonge's Novels," *North American Review,* LXXX, (1855), 441–442.

19. "Critical Notices," notice of *Alban, A Tale, Southern Quarterly Review,* XXI (1852), 241.

20. "Nathaniel Hawthorne," *Southern Literary Messenger,* XVII (1851), 344. This article which deserves further attention, was obviously influenced by Poe's review of *Twice-Told Tales;* it is significant because it affirms the integrity of the tale as art and because Tuckerman was a critic of some stature.

21. "A Chapter on Novels," *North American Review,* LXXXIII (1856), 348–349.

22. Lord Lovell (pseud.), rev. of the tale "Elkanah Brewsters Temptation," by Charles Nordhoff, *Saturday Press,* II (Nov. 26, 1859).

23. "Chit-Chat," *Graham's Magazine,* XLVIII (1856), 546.

24. (Rufus W. Griswold?), "Authors and Books," *International Miscellany,* I (1850), 472.

25. William Landor (Horace Binney Wallace?), "Washington Irving, His Works, Genius, and Character," *Sartain's Union Magazine,* VII (1850), 288. Irving was still popular during the fifties, but his reputation was fading with the Knickerbocker school. The attack on Irving's short fiction in this article, objective by the decade's standards, indicates that no idol was immune.

26. "To Readers and Correspondents," *Graham's Magazine,* LII (1858), 184.

27. *The Works of Edgar Allan Poe* (New York: Redfield, 1850–56).

28. Champion Bissell, "Serials and Continuations," *Sartain's Union Magazine,* VIII, (1851), 273.

29. Tuckerman, p. 347.

30. "Review of New Books," *Graham's Magazine,* XL (1852), 443.

31. "Hawthorne," *North American Review,* LXXVI (1853), 228–231.

32. *The American Short Story: Front Line in the National Defense of Literature* (Boston, 1964), p. 9.

33. Austin Wright, in his *The American Short Story in the Twenties* (Chicago, 1961), pp. 159–160, develops the concept of the single effect in terms of form: form he defines "as the principle that unites and organizes the story." The primary principle is "unified *action* so treated as to possess some particular emotional power." The "emotion or effect" "inheres in the action."

34. "American Female Authorship," *Godey's Lady's Book,* XLIV (1852), 145–148.

35. "Nathaniel Hawthorne," *To-Day, A Boston Literary Journal,* II (1852), 177.

36. "To Readers and Correspondents," *Graham's Magazine,* LIII (1858), 87–88.

37. "To Readers and Correspondents," *Graham's Magazine,* LI, (1857), 82.

38. Quoted in Pattee, pp. 154–155.

39. See "Tale-Writing—Nathaniel Hawthorne," *Complete Works of Edgar Allan Poe,* ed. James A. Harrison (New York, 1902), XIII, 148.

40. "The Genius and Writings of Thackeray," *Southern Quarterly Review,* IXX (1851), 87–88.

41. "Thackeray's Newcomes," *Putnam's Monthly Magazine,* VI (1855), 284.

42. "Villette and Ruth," rev. of Charlotte Brontë's *Villette* and Elizabeth Gaskell's *Ruth, Putnam's Monthly Magazine,* I (1853), 536.

43. "Henri [sic] de Balzac," *United States Magazine and Democratic Review,* XXXII (1853), 325–329.

44. "French Literature," *United States Magazine and Democratic Review,* XLII (1858), 388–393.

45. "Contemporary French Literature," *North American Review,* LXXXVI (1858), 232.

46. *The Complete Works of Nathaniel Hawthorne,* ed. George Parsons Lathrop (Boston, 1882), I, 14–16. These remarks from the Preface were given further currency when they were also published as "What Hawthorne Says of Himself, and his 'Twice-Told Tales,'" *Literary World,* VIII (1851), 210–211.

47. Randall Stewart, *Nathaniel Hawthorne: A Biography* (New Haven, 1948), p. 115.

48. Miller's point is that English novels were sweeping America: but, despite the popularity of this "Victorian realism," American authors continued to write romances. "Romance and the Novel," *Nature's Nation* (Cambridge, Mass., 1967), p. 258. Authors of short fiction, because they were more sensitive to popular demand, turned readily to "Victorian realism."

49. *Literary World,* VII (1850), 125–27, 145–47.

50. "Melville," in *The Profession of Authorship in America, 1800–1870: The Papers of William Charvat,* ed. Matthew J. Bruccoli (Columbus, Ohio 1968), pp. 239, 257–258.

51. Edgar Dryden, *Melville's Thematics of Form: The Great Art of Telling the Truth* (Baltimore, 1968). See especially pp. 20–29, upon which my remarks are based.

52. See Warner Berthoff's discussion of the tall tale and Melville's use of it under the more inclusive term of "the told story" in *The Example of Melville* (Princeton, 1962), pp. 133–138. Among the readable examples of tall tales turned serious, see John of York (William C. Tobey), "Ben Wilson's Last Jug Race," *Spirit of the Times,* May 24, 1851, p. 157; "Tom Wade and the Grizzly Bear," *Spirit of the Times,* June 14, 1851, pp. 194–195; "A Duel Without Seconds: A Daguerreotype from the State House of Arkansas," *American Whig Review,* XI (1850), 418–422; Philemon Perch (Richard Malcolm Johnston), "Five Chapters of a History," *Porter's Spirit of the Times,* Dec. 19, 26, 1857, pp. 241–242, 258–260. In each of these short stories, a character undergoes an experience that has profoundly moved him, and the absence of humor indicates the depth of the emotional response. In "Tom Wade and the Grizzly Bear," the effect depends more upon the fear and psychological deterioration of a secondary character than upon the conventional bear fight.

53. Berthoff, p. 123.

54. Rose Terry Cooke, "Eben Jackson," *Atlantic Monthly*, I (1858), 524–536; "Ann Potter's Lesson," *Atlantic Monthly*, II (1858), 419–428; Harriet Prescott Spofford, "Knitting Sale-Socks," *Atlantic Monthly*, VII (1861), 138–151; "Yet's Christmas Box," *Harper's New Monthly Magazine*, XX (1860), 644–659; Rebecca Harding Davis, "Life in the Iron Mills," *Atlantic Monthly*, VII (1861), 430–451; William Dean Howells, "A Dream," *Knickerbocker; or New York Monthly Magazine*, LVIII (1861), 146–150.

55. Alice B. Neal Haven, "Flora Farleigh's Manuscript, An Attack of Authorship and How It Was Cured," *Godey's Lady's Book*, LIII (1856), 430. See also Rose Terry Cooke's parody of feminine fiction in "Miss Muffet and the Spider," *Harper's New Monthly Magazine*, XX (1860), 764–771; and Fitz-James O'Brien's satire of female scribbling and mass-produced literature in "Sister Anne," *Harper's New Monthly Magazine*, XXII (1855), 91–96.

56. Frye, p. 305.

57. "Introduction," *Edgar Allan Poe*, p. vi.

Vision and Form

THE ENGLISH NOVEL AND THE
EMERGENCE OF THE SHORT STORY

WENDELL V. HARRIS

IT IS A DIFFICULT TASK to attempt to assess the nature and power of unconscious assumptions or implicit definitions of an earlier period. When
such assumptions are not in themselves startling, the attempt runs the
danger of seeming to labor mightily to bring forth a mouse. But, having
acknowledged the dangers, I state my argument: that the province of fiction, as recognized by serious writers from Fielding to Hardy, was defined
essentially as the presentation of life in latitudinal or longitudinal completeness, very often both; that this paralleled the characteristic intellectual concern with the fabric of society during the middle years of the
eighteenth century and during the greater part of the Victorian period;
and that these mutually reinforcing views of the province of intellectually
respectable fiction and of the nature of worthwhile intellectual endeavor
go far to explain the generally insignificant place of shorter fiction in
England until late in the nineteenth century. The genre awaited the coming of the appropriate vision.

Fielding preeminently and, in significant degrees, the other important
mid-eighteenth-century novelists were, like Pope and Dr. Johnson, sur-
veyors of a broad human panorama. Their novels constitute their own
"essays on man," in several volumes. "Let observation, with extensive
view/Survey mankind from China to Peru" could well be the poetic motto
of the time—and the same impulse dominates the novel in mid-century.
This is damped down in the latter years of the eighteenth century and the

early part of the nineteenth—though the two most significant novelists during what would otherwise have been a barren fifty years for the novel, Austen and Scott, represent it in their own ways—but reasserts itself in the great new generation of novelists in the 1840s and 1850s. After Fielding, the model of contemporary historical writing governed the novel; during the latter two-thirds of the nineteenth century that model, reinforced by the kind of organic all-encompassing consciousness best represented by Carlyle, suggested what should be the characteristic excellences of the novel. The two major dimensions of historical narrative—the longitudinal tracing of sequence and the latitudinal or comprehensive survey of interrelationships within a briefer period—set the legitimate tasks for fiction. The occasional call for shorter, more compact novels after the French manner[1] could hardly be heeded until this implicit expectation lost its force.

As Ian Watt, citing parallel views from E. M. Forster, Oswald Spengler, and Northrop Frye, points out, the novel reflects an appreciation of time as "the shaping force of man's individual and collective history."[2] Leo Braudy has argued that the word "history" in the title of the masterwork of the first English author who seriously considered the nature of fiction—*The History of Tom Jones*—has yet to be given its due weight by critics[3]; more critical attention might profitably be diverted from Fielding's description of the novel as a comic epic in prose to his preoccupation with history. Now of course the word "history" had come into rather general usage as a descriptive term distinguishing the more realistic fiction from the fairy-tale world of the romance: thus Mary Manley contrasted "Little Histories" (essentially realistic novella) with "Romances" in a preface of 1705 and Samuel Croxall describes novels (really *novella*) as "Imitations of History" in the preface to his 1720 collection. Defoe described *Roxana* (1724) as a "History" because it had a foundation in "Truth of Fact," contrasting it with the mere "Story."[4] But Fielding applies the word to his novels in a more precise manner. Leo Braudy's study of the new developments in the narrative form of Hume's *History of England*, Gibbon's *The Decline and Fall of the Roman Empire*, and Fielding's four novels builds on what he describes as a skeletal similarity: "all three writers use a prose narrative to treat problems of the individual in society, problems of the human character in history."[5]

In *Joseph Andrews* and *Tom Jones*, Fielding certainly occupies himself with the writing of history sufficiently to make us aware that the relation between history and fiction is of signal importance to him. To write history is to draw the manners of the species man and thus illustrate both the

variety of human character and the constancy with which certain dominant characteristics shape individuals through history. "The Lawyer is not
only alive, but hath been so these 4,000 Years."[6] Fielding is redefining the
reality which should be the subject of history—it is not the public sequence of events but the continuous panorama of human nature. The adventures of Tom Jones reveal the variety and interrelationship of the
multiform possibilities of human character; therefore, those adventures
constitute not merely his "life" but a *history*. Further, both the sequence
of those adventures and the intricate reticulation of society which inter-
connects a variety of human types are important in Fielding's novels;
Fielding had his own claim on a twentieth-century motto, "Only connect."
The sequential and comprehensive model he offered was enormously influential. Variety of character and situation, the close interweaving of incident, and the chronicling of a substantial stretch of time came to be
categorical expectations. This is implicit, for example, in the preface to
the first English translation of the *Sorrows of Werter* (1779) which explains that "those who expect a Novel will be disappointed in this work,
which contains few characters and few events"[7]; it is explicit in Smollett's
1753 definition of the novel as "a large diffused picture, comprehending
the characters of life, disposed in different groupes, and exhibited in various attitudes, for the purposes of a uniform plan . . . to which every individual figure is subservient."[8]

The rise of the novel coincided with the rise of a more self-critical, self-
conscious style of history-writing as well as with the rise of the middle
class. The genre grew, flourished, and prospered through the nineteenth
century when the historical consciousness was so great that it has been
said, not altogether facetiously, that the nineteenth century discovered
history. The century certainly gave itself to the tracing of chains of causes
and effects, and of the subtle interweaving of relations throughout society
and across time. In the process, the great prophet-essayists of the century
were led from region to region of intellectual speculation in their attempt
to encompass the meaning of history and of society.

Carlyle not only had the greatest influence on other writers of any of
the nineteenth-century English sages, but among them he offers the most
complete paradigm of the course of the intellectual striving to connect all
things. The effort led Carlyle from German romanticism to the struggle
to assimilate the rigorously organized logic of German idealism and thence,
by way of a monumental tour of the French revolution, to the condition of
England and on through time and across frontiers in quest of the indubi-
table leader. But through it all he remained certain that "Wondrous truly
are the bonds that unite us one and all; whether by the soft binding of

Love or the Iron chaining of Necessity." The well-known passage from
his first great work continues:

> Wert thou, my little Brotherkin, suddenly covered up with the
> largest imaginable Glass bell . . . thou art no longer a circulating
> venous-arterial Heart, that taking and giving circulated through all
> Space and all Time: there has a hole fallen out in the immeasurable,
> universal World-tissue, which must be darned up again!
>
> I say, there is not a red Indian, hunting by Lake Winnipeg, can
> quarrel with his squaw, but the whole world must smart for it: will
> not the price of beaver rise?[9]

That sense of organic interrelationship, which speaks, on the one hand,
in the grand metaphor of the roaring loom of time and, on the other, in
the homely but terrible incident of the Irish widow, runs through almost
the whole of the Victorian prose writers. Ruskin, Arnold, Morris, even
Mill, found themselves constantly expanding the temporal and intellectual contexts in which basic social questions should be considered; each
conducted his own survey of the great network of human interaction seeking to discover the point of leverage from which the interlinked structure
of society could be altered.

The novelists conducted similar surveys of the great nexus in their fictive histories. The worlds of the great Victorian novels depend on the
shaping of each individual by the interaction between the pressures of the
socioeconomic world and the choices made by the individual. *Vanity Fair*
implies not only the variety and venality of the world but its bustling interconnections in space and time; the vast web of human endeavors which
makes up *Bleak House*—some evil, some saintly, some grotesque, a few
insane—represents only the most spectacular example of Dickens' concern to show the rippling effect of each human action intersecting with
others. *Middlemarch,* which, we remember, George Eliot described as
showing "the gradual action of ordinary causes,"[10] sweeps across the great
center of English social structure. Though Hardy's novels seldom exhibit
so crowded a stage as those of the earlier authors, the actions of his characters extend through time and across the lives of others in designedly
unexpected ways. Indeed, much of what may seem forced coincidence or
unnecessary development of subplots in Hardy is after all the result of his
difficulties in fulfilling—with a reduced cast of characters and restricted
social horizon—what had come to be regarded as the mission of the
novel: to see and illustrate the interconnectedness of things.

Though the action of time upon the individual, of class upon class, of

man upon man, is the driving force in the great nineteenth-century novels, so universal and pervasive is this conception that it passes almost
without comment by novelists or critics. The emergence of a number of
differing novelistic modes was recognized, usually in contrasting pairs—
the novel of character and the novel of situation, the realistic and the
idealistic novel, the historical novel and the novel of contemporary life—
but all these developed within the bounds of the undeclared necessary
condition: the novel must chronicle the changes wrought by time and the
vast interconnectedness of human actions.

Walter Bagehot, not quite a sage and certainly of a different temper of
mind from Carlyle and those he most influenced, nevertheless illustrates
with a unique explicitness the effect on the novel of the age's preoccupation with time and the great web of society. The only worthwhile novels
for him belong to the class he calls "ubiquitous," which "aims at describing the whole of human life in all its spheres, in all its aspects, with all its
varied interests, aims, and objects. It searches through the whole life of
man; his practical pursuits, his speculative attempts, his romantic youth,
and his domestic age. It gives an entire picture of these. . . ."[11] Further,
in discussing what he called the "penal code" of the novel—"the appor-
tionment of reward and punishment to the good and evil personages
therein delineated"—he advances his own interpretation of the nature of
the world and its proper delineation in fiction. Providence, he says, appears
to work "by scheme of averages. Most people who ought to succeed, do
succeed; most who do fail, ought to fail. But there is no exact adjustment
of 'mark' to merit. . . . 'on the whole,' 'speaking generally,' 'looking at
life as a whole,' are the words in which we must describe the providential
adjustment of visible good and evil to visible goodness and badness. And
when we look more closely, we see that these general results are the consequences of certain principles which work unseen, and which are effec-
tual in the main, though thwarted here and there."[12] It is apparent that
the adequate representation of such a world in a novel requires that time
be allowed for slow causes to operate, that a variety of characters and situations be included, and that action and reaction be broadly traced.

Elsewhere, Bagehot applies this joint view of the nature of the world
and of the novel more directly to the structure of the novel. The novelist,
he says, "must enter into each [character] individually, and he must bind
them all together. He must be in each and over all . . . [and] imbue his
tale with the feelings of the secret relation between the characters which
suggest the reasons why their destinies are interwoven, and which determine the limits of their mutual influence on each other's career."[13]

It is true that the economic advantages which publishers and circulating libraries exploited in the three-volume novel, the lack of periodical outlets for short fiction, and the more immediate recognition possible to the novelist all militated against the earlier development of the true short story in England. But in nineteenth century England a great portion of what Lionel Stevenson has happily called the "agglomerative impulse" which led writers to the longer forms of fiction[14] would seem to have derived from a view of the purpose of fictional narrative very similar to Bagehot's.

Thus, during the long period from Fielding and Richardson to the emergence of Kipling, Stevenson, and the myriad short story writers of the 1890s, the entire province of fiction was seen as largely identical with that of the novel of the time. The old Romance soon went out of fashion—despite Clara Reeve's 1785 defense, the taste for the wonderful being satisfied for a time by the Goths: Walpole, Beckford, Lewis, and Radcliffe. Short fiction could be anecdotal—it was obviously well adapted to the humorous contretemps, but the only other alternatives likely to suggest themselves were miniatures either of the Gothic romance or the novel. The first led to the tale, tending, as Northrop Frye has suggested, not only to stylization but to the "nihilistic and untamable": to ghost stories, wild adventures, hair-breadth escapes.[15] The second tended simply to disaster. That short fiction which tried to follow the novel in holding ordinary life up to the light lacked space to follow either the extensive or longitudinal models provided by the novel—it was unable to create world enough and time. Unfortunately, the closer the tale approached the novel, the further it was forced to move from the essentially ahistorical, sonnet-like, and highly focused vision which is characteristic of the true short story. That is why the bulk of the short fiction of writers like Dickens, Trollope, or Hardy seems so uninspired—it tried to translate a vision for which the short fiction piece simply could not be appropriate. So long as they clung to the central nineteenth-century view of the proper scope for fiction, shorter fiction was almost bound to go awry in the hands of even the best novelists. Dickens could employ short fiction in the interest of a humorous yet sentimental moral vision; Thackeray could employ it for satire; Trollope could touch up personal experiences into pleasant anecdotes which immediately slight the importance of the incidents they set forth. Hardy, more ambitious, tried to translate the historically structured narrative of the novel into the briefer form by looking before and after, tracing in unsatisfyingly bare outline how complex relationships came to be.

We may define the true short story impressionistically through certain qualities: it should be crisp, taut, lean, focused, unified. We may define it technically by enumerating those devices for getting under way, shifting scenes, and concluding, for implying, suggesting, symbolizing, and summing up, which produce those qualities we expect, and which fill the great majority of the books on the short story which, row on row, make up the dreary PN 3375 area of the stacks. But we also have a categorical expectation of which we are likely to be no more explicitly aware than were Victorian novel readers: the essence of the short story is to isolate, to portray the individual person, or moment, or scene in isolation—detached from the great continuum—at once social and historical, which it had been the business of the English novel, and the great concern of nineteenth-century essayists, to insist upon.

Frank O'Connor is expressing this when he finds that the short story looks for its central characters to the lonely or defiant, those outside conventional society. "The novel can still adhere to the classical concept of a civilized society, of man as an animal who lives in a community . . . but the short story remains by its very nature remote from the community— romantic, individualistic, and intransigent."[16] The short story is indeed the natural vehicle for presentation of the outsider, but also for the moment whose intensity makes it seem outside the ordinary stream of time, or the scene whose significance is outside our ordinary range of experience. Corollaries follow. Whereas in the novel the significance of events is defined only over time, in the short story the significance is, implicitly or explicitly, immediate. Where in the novel each character or event is understood only as part of a far-reaching web (the warp of that web being the flow of time, the weft the social structure), the short story illuminates only a small portion of the web (though it may imply the nature of the rest). Where the novel frequently exhibits a structure of symbols, the story may well become one.

Such qualities began to appeal to a variety of kinds of writers in England at the end of the nineteenth century. To begin with, Kipling's India offered a whole world of outsiders; the *Civil and Military Gazette* afforded only brief space for their treatment; the historical convention was shed and the English short story arrived. The immediately subsequent writers of the *Yellow Book* school, like Dowson, Crackanthorpe, D'Arcy, and Harland, had the advantage of having read Kipling and of knowing what the French were accomplishing in the short story, but they must also have been attracted to the genre by a Paterian disinclination to take a cosmic or even expansive or longitudinal view of the world. The famous conclusion to *The Renaissance* is, in fact, not at all discordant with main streams of Victorian thought in emphasizing that not only human life but the entire visible universe is but a vast organic whole made up of elements constantly recombining. But where the major essayists and novelists had been fascinated by the vision of an organic structure of human endeavor which distributes and redistributes the effect of every human action, Pater's vision was of course a chillier one which emphasized every man's isolation. To those for whom Pater spoke, the wider the view one took, the less comfortable. The magic of the great Victorian prophets had come to seem mere verbal legerdemain. The everyday world revealed itself to be no better for the declamations of the Victorian idealists, and the cities and countryside were unquestionably much the worse for the practical result of economic utilitarianism. The strong common sense of the Benthams, Mills, and Harrisons had won a victory, but lost the green and pleasant land.

Many writers of the 1880s and 1890s turned therefore with relief to the isolable, the detachable. The incompatibility of their views with that which supported the great nineteenth-century tradition of the novel is manifested in their inability to master the longer form. But they were clear that quite another sort of vision had value, that the expression of that vision was the task of the short story, and that the legitimacy of that aim and that form was still largely unrecognized. As Lena Milman wrote in an essay on Henry James published in the *Yellow Book* in 1895: "It is not yet ours to realise how the most exquisite in life are just those passing emotions, those elusive impressions which it behoves the artist to go seeking, over them so cunningly to cast his net of words or colour as to preserve that emotion, that impression, for the delight of mankind forever. We are too apt to regard the short story as the cartoon for a possible novel, whereas any elaboration of it is as thankless a process as the development of a fresco from an easel painting. The treatment, the pigment, the medium, the palette are other from the very beginning."[17]

Writers like Arthur Morrison, Henry Nevinson, George Gissing, and Edwin Pugh discovered the short story to be appropriate to the isolating vision in yet another way. They were less interested in showing how the English lower class intermingled with and in part resulted from the larger structure of society than in trying accurately to depict the life it lived. Or, to take a third example, H. G. Wells' delight in probing scientific and pseudoscientific possibilities led him to desire a form which, when necessary, would lift his characters out of time and society almost as completely as his time machine.

If the readers' expectation of prose fiction had been adequately summed up by those purposes commonly advanced and defended by authors and critics from the 1740s to the 1880s—to amuse, instruct, and extend the readers' sympathies—short fiction could have fulfilled them quite as well as the full-length novel. But in addition to these stated expectations, there was the implicit assumption that fiction should portray an extensive panorama, the various parts of which were cunningly interconnected. Because the sudden illumination of the isolated individual, moment, or scene did not suggest itself as a significant intellectual goal, there was no suitable task for short fiction to undertake. Thus only, perhaps, can one account for an entire century during which thousands of pieces of short fiction were written, but hardly a single short story as we have recognized that form since it began to emerge in the 1880s and 1890s. Before that, to write serious fiction in England was to write a species of history, to integrate; only at the end of the nineteenth century did fiction begin to reflect reality perceived as a congeries of fragments. New, generally tighter kinds of novels could and did participate in the new vision, but its preeminent vehicle was the short story. A new mode of intellectual assimilation had found its literary correlative.

NOTES

1. For instance, see the anonymous "The Art of Story-Telling," *Fraser's,* 53 (January 1856), 722–32. Cited by Richard Stang, *The Theory of the Novel in England, 1850–1870* (New York, 1959), p. 115.

2. *The Rise of the Novel* (Berkeley and Los Angeles, 1957), p. 22.

3. *Narrative Form in History and Fiction* (Princeton, 1970).

4. One is indebted to Joan Williams for bringing together in *Novel and Romance, 1700–1800* (New York, Barnes and Noble, 1970) one hundred and one statements on the eighteenth-century novel. Manley's preface to *The Secret History of Queen Zarah* will be found on pages 33–39; Samuel Croxall's preface on pages 71–72; Defoe's preface to *Roxana* on pages 80–81.

5. *Narrative Form in History and Fiction,* p. 5.

6. *Joseph Andrews,* ed. Martin Battestin (Middletown, Conn., 1967), Bk. III, Ch. 1.

7. Williams, p. 308.

8. Dedication to *The Adventures of Ferdinand Count Fathom* (London, 1971 [Oxford English Novels]), p. 2.

9. *Sartor Resartus,* Vol. I, *Collected Works,* Sterling ed. (Boston, 1885), pp. 185–86.

10. *The George Eliot Letters,* ed. Gordon S. Haight (New Haven, 1955), V, 168.

11. "The Waverly Novels," Vol. II, *The Collected Works* (Cambridge, Mass., 1965), p. 46.

12. *Walter Bagehot's Works,* II, 60.

13. "A Novel or Two," *National Review* (October 1855), cited in Stang, p. 126.

14. "The Short Story in Embryo," *English Literature in Transition,* 15:4 (1972), 261–68.

15. *Anatomy of Criticism* (Princeton, 1957), p. 305.

16. *The Lonely Voice* (Cleveland, 1963), p. 21.

17. "A Few Notes on Mr. Jones," *Yellow Book,* 7 (October 1895), p. 72.

PART FIVE
The Modern Short Story

The Short Story

ANTON CHEKHOV

To A. N. Pleshcheyev
Moscow. Sept. 30, 1889.

THE SHORT STORY, like the stage, has its conventions. My instinct tells me that at the end of a novel or a story, I must artfully concentrate for the reader an impression of the entire work, and therefore must casually mention something about those whom I have already presented. Perhaps I am in error.

To A. S. Souvorin
Moscow. April 1, 1890.

You abuse me for objectivity, calling it indifference to good and evil, lack of ideals and ideas, and so on. You would have me, when I describe horse-thieves, say: "Stealing horses is an evil." But that has been known for ages without my saying so. Let the jury judge them; it's my job simply to show what sort of people they are. I write: you are dealing with horse-thieves, so let me tell you that they are not beggars but well-fed people, that they are people of a special cult, and that horse-stealing is not simply theft but a passion. Of course it would be pleasant to combine art with a sermon, but for me personally it is extremely difficult and almost impossible, owing to the conditions of technique. You see, to depict horse-thieves in seven hundred lines I must all the time speak and think in their tone and feel in their spirit, otherwise, if I introduce subjectivity, the image becomes blurred and the story will not be as compact as all short stories ought to be. When I write, I reckon entirely upon the reader to add for himself the subjective elements that are lacking in the story.

To Alex. P. Chekhov
Moscow. April, 1883.

You underscore trifles in your writings, and yet you are not a subjective writer by nature; it is an acquired trait in you. To give up this acquired subjectivity is as easy as to take a drink. One needs only to be more honest, to throw oneself overboard everywhere, not to obtrude oneself into the hero of one's own novel, to renounce oneself for at least a half hour. You have a story in which a young wedded couple kiss all through dinner, grieve without cause, weep oceans of tears. Not a single sensible word; nothing but *sentimentality.* And you did not write for the reader. You wrote because *you* like that sort of chatter. But suppose you were to describe the dinner, how they ate, what they ate, what the cook was like, how insipid your hero is, how content with his lazy happiness, how insipid your heroine is, how funny is her love for this napkin-bound, sated, overfed goose,—we all like to see happy, contented people, that is true,—but to describe them, what *they* said and how many times they kissed is not enough—you need something else: to free yourself from the personal expression that a placid honey-happiness produces upon everybody. . . . Subjectivity is a terrible thing. It is bad in this alone, that it reveals the author's hands and feet. I'll bet that all priests' daughters and clerks' wives who read your works are in love with you, and if you were a German you would get free beer in all the Bierhalle where the German women serve. If it were not for this subjectivity you would be the best of artists.

To Alex. P. Chekhov
Babkin. May 10, 1886.

In my opinion a true description of Nature should be very brief and have a character of relevance. Commonplaces such as, "the setting sun bathing in the waves of the darkening sea, poured its purple gold, etc.,"— "the swallows flying over the surface of the water twittered merrily,"— such commonplaces one ought to abandon. In descriptions of Nature one ought to seize upon the little particulars, grouping them in such a way that, in reading, when you shut your eyes, you get a picture.

For instance, you will get the full effect of a moonlight night if you write that on the mill-dam a little glowing star-point flashed from the neck of a broken bottle, and the round, black shadow of a dog, or a wolf, emerged and ran, etc. Nature becomes animated if you are not squeamish about employing comparisons of her phenomena with ordinary human activities, etc.

In the sphere of psychology, details are also the thing. God preserve us from commonplaces. Best of all is it to avoid depicting the hero's state of mind; you ought to try to make it clear from the hero's actions. It is not necessary to portray many characters. The centre of gravity should be in two persons: him and her. . . .

I write this to you as a reader having a definite taste. Also, in order that you, when writing, may not feel alone. To be alone in work is a hard thing. Better poor criticism than none at all. Is it not so?

To E. M. Sh——
Melikhovo. Nov. 17, 1895.

I read your story with great pleasure. Your hand is acquiring firmness, and your style is improving. I like the whole story, except the ending, which appears to me to lack force. . . . But this is a matter of taste and not so important. If one is to talk about flaws one should not confine oneself to details. You have a defect and a very serious one. In my opinion it is this: you do not polish your things, and hence they seem frequently to be florid and overloaded. Your works lack the compactness that makes short things alive. There is skill in your stories; there is talent, literary sense, but very slight art. You put your characters together in the right way, but not plastically. You are either too lazy or you do not wish to slough off at one stroke all that is useless. To make a face from marble means to remove from the slab everything that is not the face. Do I make myself clear? Do you understand ? There are two or three awkward expressions which I underlined.

To I. L. Shcheglov
Moscow. Jan. 22, 1888.

Oh you of little faith,—you are interested to know what flaws I found in your "Mignon." Before I point them out I warn you that they have a technical rather than a critico-literary interest. Only a writer can appreciate them, but a reader not at all. Here they are. . . . I think that you, an author scrupulous and untrusting, afraid that your characters will not stand out clearly enough, are too much given to thoroughly detailed description. The result is an overwrought "motleyness" of effect that impairs the general impression.

In order to show how powerfully music can affect one at times, but distrustful of the reader's ability to understand you readily, you zealously set forth the psychology of your Feodrik; the psychology is successful, but then the interval between two such moments as "amari, morire" and the pistol-shot, is dragged out unduly, and the reader, before he reaches the

suicide-scene, has had time to recover from the pain of "amari, morire."
But you must give the reader no chance to recover: he must always be
kept in suspense. These remarks would not apply if "Mignon" were a
novel. Long, detailed works have their own peculiar aims, which require a
most careful execution regardless of the total impression. But in short
stories it is better to say not enough than to say too much, because,—
because—I don't know why! At all events, remember that your failings are
considered flaws only by myself, (altogether unimportant, flaws) and I am
very often mistaken. Perhaps you are right and not I. . . . It happens
that I have been mistaken quite often, and I have held other opinions than
those I have just expressed. On occasion my criticism has proved worthless.

Chekhov and the
Modern Short Story

CHARLES E. MAY

ANTON CHEKHOV'S short stories were first welcomed in England and America just after the turn of the century as examples of late nineteenth-century realism, but since they did not embody the social commitment or political convictions of the realistic novel, they were termed "realistic" primarily because they seemed to focus on fragments of everyday reality. Consequently, they were characterized as "sketches," "slices of life," "cross-sections of Russian life," and were often said to be lacking every element which constitutes a really good short story. However, at the same time, other critics saw that Chekhov's ability to dispense with a striking incident, his impressionism, and his freedom from the literary conventions of the highly plotted and formalized story marked the beginnings of a new or "modern" kind of short fiction that combined the specific detail of realism with the poetic lyricism of romanticism.[1]

The primary characteristics of this new hybrid form are: character as mood rather than as either symbolic projection or realistic depiction; story as minimal lyricized sketch rather than as elaborately plotted tale; atmosphere as an ambiguous mixture of both external details and psychic projections; and a basic impressionistic apprehension of reality itself as a function of perspectival point of view. The ultimate result of these characteristics is the modernist and postmodernist focus on reality itself as a fictional construct and the contemporary trend to make fictional assumptions and techniques both the subject matter and theme of the novel and the short story.

CHARACTER AS MOOD

The most basic problem in understanding the Chekhovian shift to the "modern" short story involves a new definition of the notion of "story" itself, which, in turn, involves not only a new understanding of the kind of "experience" to be embodied in story but a new conception of character as well. Primarily this shift to the modern is marked by a transition from the romantic focus on a projective fiction, in which characters are functions in an essentially code-bound parabolic or ironic structure, to an apparently realistic episode in which plot is subordinate to "as-if-real" character. However, it should be noted that Chekhov's fictional figures are not realistic in the way that characters in the novel usually are. The short story is too short to allow for character to be created by the kind of dense detail and social interaction through duration typical of the novel.

Conrad Aiken was perhaps the first critic to recognize the secret of Chekhov's creation of character. Noting that Chekhov's stories offer an unparalleled "range of states of consciousness," Aiken says that whereas Poe manipulates plot and James manipulates thought, Chekhov "manipulates feeling or mood." If, says, Aiken, we find his characters have a strange way of evaporating, "it is because our view of them was never permitted for a moment to be external—we saw them only as infinitely fine and truthful sequences of mood."[2] This apprehension of character as mood is closely related to D. S. Mirsky's understanding of the Chekhovian style, which he described as "bathed in a perfect and uniform haze," and the Chekhovian narrative method, which Mirsky says "allows nothing to 'happen,' but only smoothly and imperceptibly to 'become'."[3]

Such a notion of character as mood and story as a hazy "eventless" becoming is characteristic of the modern artistic understanding of story. It is like Conrad's conception in *Heart of Darkness,* for to his story-teller Marlowe, "the meaning of an episode was not inside like a kernel but outside, enveloping the tale which brought it out only as a glow brings out a haze." More recently, Eudora Welty has suggested that the first thing we notice about the short story is "that we can't really see the solid outlines of it—it seems bathed in something of its own. It is wrapped in an atmosphere."[4] Once we see that the short story, by its very shortness, cannot deal with the denseness of detail and the duration of time typical of the novel, but rather focuses on a revelatory break-up of the rhythm of everyday reality, we can see how the form, striving to accommodate "realism" at the end of the nineteenth century, focused on an experience under the influence of a particular mood and therefore depended more on tone than on plot as a principle of unity.

In fact, "an experience" phenomenologically encountered, rather than "experience" discursively understood, is the primary focus of the modern short story, and, as John Dewey makes clear, "an experience" is recognized as such precisely because it has a unity, "a single *quality* that pervades the entire experience in spite of the variation of its constituent parts."[5] Rather than plot, what unifies the modern short story is an atmosphere, a certain tone of significance. The problem is to determine the source of this significance. On the one hand, it may be the episode itself, which, to use Henry James's phrase, seems to have a "latent value" that the artist tries to unveil.[6] It is this point of view that governs James Joyce's notion of the epiphany—"a sudden spiritual manifestation, whether in the vulgarity of speech or of gesture or in a memorable phase of the mind itself."[7]

On the other hand, it may be the subjectivity of the teller, his perception that what seems trivial and everyday has, from his point of view, significance and meaning. There is no way to distinguish between these two views of the source of the so-called "modern" short story, for it is by the teller's very choice of seemingly trivial details and his organization of them into a unified pattern that lyricizes the story and makes it seem natural and realistic even as it resonates with meaning. As Georg Lukács has suggested, lyricism in the short story is pure selection which hides itself behind the hard outlines of the event; it is "the most purely artistic form; it expresses the ultimate meaning of all artistic creation as *mood*."[8]

Although Chekhov's conception of the short story as a lyrically charged fragment in which characters are less fully rounded realistic figures than they are embodiments of mood has influenced all twentieth-century practitioners of the form, his most immediate impact has been on the three writers of the early twenties who have received the most critical attention for fully developing the so-called "modern" short story—James Joyce, Katherine Mansfield, and Sherwood Anderson. And because of the widespread influence of the stories of these three writers, Chekhov has thus had an effect on the works of such major twentieth-century short story writers as Katherine Anne Porter, Franz Kafka, Bernard Malamud, Ernest Hemingway, and Raymond Carver.

THE MINIMAL STORY

The most obvious similarity between the stories of Chekhov and those of Joyce, Anderson, and Mansfield is their minimal dependence on the traditional notion of plot and their focus instead on a single situation in which everyday reality is broken up by a crisis. Typical of Chekhov's minimalist stories is the often-anthologized "Misery," in which the rhythm of the old-cab driver's everyday reality is suggested by his two different fares, a rhythm Iona himself tries to break up with the news that his son is dead. The story would indeed be only a sketch if Iona did not tell his story to his uncomprehending little mare at the end. For what the story communicates is the comic and pathetic sense of the incommunicable nature of grief itself. Iona "thirsts for speech," wants to talk of the death of his son "properly, very carefully."[9] He is caught by the primal desire to tell a story of the break-up of his everyday reality that will express the irony he senses and that, by being deliberate and detailed, will both express his grief and control it. In this sense, "Misery" is a lament—not an emotional wailing, but rather a controlled objectification of grief and its incommunicable nature by the presentation of deliberate details.

The story therefore illustrates one of the primary contributions Chekhov makes to the modern short story; that is, the expression of a complex inner state by presenting selected concrete details rather than by presenting either a parabolic form or by depicting the mind of the character. Significant reality for Chekhov is inner rather than outer reality, but the problem he tried to solve is how to create an illusion of inner reality by focusing on external details only. The answer for Chekhov, and thus for the modern short story generally, is to find an event that, if expressed "properly," that is, by the judicious choice of relevant details, will embody the complexity of the inner state. T. S. Eliot later termed such a technique an "objective correlative"—a detailed event, description, or characterization that served as a sort of objectification or formula for the emotion sought for. Modern short story writers after Chekhov made the objective correlative the central device in their development of the form.

Like Chekhov, whom she greatly admired, Katherine Mansfield was often accused of writing sketches instead of stories because her works did not manifest the plotted action of nineteenth-century short fiction. The best known Mansfield story similar in technique and theme to "Misery" is "The Fly." The external action of the story is extremely slight. The unnamed "boss" is visited by a retired friend whose casual mention of the boss's dead son makes him aware of his inability to grieve. The story ends with the boss idly dropping ink on a fly until it dies, whereupon he flings it away. Like "Misery," the story is about the nature of grief; also like Chekhov's story, "The Fly" maintains a strictly objective point of view, allowing the details of the story to communicate the latent significance of the boss's emotional state.

However, Mansfield differs from her mentor, Chekhov, by placing more dependence on the symbolism of the fly itself, regardless of whether one perceives the creature as a symbol of the death of the boss's grief, his own manipulated son, or the trivia of life that distracts us from feeling. Moreover, instead of focusing on the inarticulate nature of grief that goes deeper than words, "The Fly" seems to emphasize the transitory nature of grief—that regardless of how much the boss would like to hold on to his grief for his son, he finds it increasingly difficult to maintain such feelings. Such an inevitable loss of grief does not necessarily suggest that the boss's feelings for his son are negligible; rather it suggests a subtle aspect of grief—that it either flows naturally or else it must be self-consciously and artificially sought after. The subtle way that Mansfield communicates the complexity of the boss's emotional situation by the seemingly irrelevant conversation between the boss and his old acquaintance and by his apparently idle toying with the fly is typical of the Chekhovian device of allowing objective detail to communicate complex states of feeling.

Chekhov's "Aniuta" also depends on a rhythm of reality being momentarily broken up by a significant event, only to fall back once again. The story opens with the medical student walking to and fro cramming for his anatomy examination, repeating his lessons over and over as he tries to learn them by heart, while Aniuta silently does her embroidery to earn money to buy him tea and tobacco. The fact that she has known five others before him who left her when they finished their studies indicates that the story depicts a repetitive event just as his sounding out his lines is repetitive. When the young medical student tries to learn the order of ribs by drawing them on Aniuta's naked flesh, we have an ironic image of the typical Chekhov device of manifesting the internal as external. After she is used for the sake of "science," she is then used for the sake of "art" when the artist borrows her for his painting of Psyche.

The fact that the story ends as it began with the student walking back and forth repeating his lessons seems to reaffirm the usual charge against Chekhov—that "nothing really happens" here. But what has happened is that by the means of two objectifications it is revealed that Aniuta is used both body and soul. The doctor tries to "sound" Aniuta's body, just as the artist tries to capture her soul, but neither is able to reveal her; only Chekhov can "sound" her by his presentation of this significant episode. We know nothing about Aniuta in any realistic detail, nor do we know the workings of her mind, but we know everything we need to know about her to understand her static situation.

Many of the stories of twentieth-century writers after Chekhov depend on this same use of objective detail and significant situation to reveal subtle moral and emotional situations. For example, in Joyce's "Clay," it is not through introspection that we know Maria, but rather by the seemingly simple details and events of the story itself. However, Joyce goes beyond

Chekhov's use of simple detail to reveal a subtle emotional state by making all of his apparently "realistic" references to Maria ironic revelations of her manipulated and lonely situation. Joyce, like Mansfield, also depends more on the use of a central symbol than Chekhov does, in this case, the clay itself, which is an objective correlative not only of Maria's malleable nature, but of the decay of her possibilities. Similarly, Joyce's "Eveline" depends solely on homey details such as dusty curtains, the photo of a priest, and the sound of an organ-grinder's song to objectify Eveline's entrapment by the paralysis of the past.

One of the most reticent of Chekhov's stories, a story so pure and clean that it presages the lucid limitations of Ernest Hemingway, is "The Lady with a Lapdog"—a paradigm for the story of the illicit affair. It is never clear in the story whether Gurov truly loves Anna Sergeevna or whether it is only the romantic fantasy that he wishes to maintain. What makes the story so subtle and complex is that Chekhov presents the romance in such a limited and objective way that we realize that there is no way to determine whether it is love or romance, for there is no way to distinguish between them. Although Gurov feels that he has a life open and seen, full of relative truth and falsehood like everyone else, he knows he has another life running its course in secret, a true life, and the false only was open to others. "All personal life," he feels, "rested on secrecy."[10]

However, there is no way to determine which is the real life and which is the false. At the end of the story, Gurov and Anna wonder how they can free themselves from their intolerable bondage, but only Chekhov and the reader are aware that there is no way to free themselves, for the real bondage is not the manifest one, but the latent bondage all human beings have to the dilemma of never knowing which is the true self and which is the false one. Although it seems to the couple that they would soon find the solution and a new and splendid life would begin, at the same time it is clear to them that they had a long way to go and that the most complicated part of it was only just beginning. Indeed, what seems so simple is indeed complicated. This device of presenting a seemingly simple external situation in such a way as to suggest emotional complexities beneath it is typical of the best of Hemingway's short stories.

Hemingway's debt to Chekhov lies in the radical limitation of authorial comment and the complete dependence on situation, a situation often so limited, with so much of what we usually expect in narrative left out, that all we have is dialogue and description. "Hills Like White Elephants" is perhaps the best example of Hemingway's use of the Chekhov device of allowing the bare situation to express a complex emotional dilemma. Beneath the surface level of "Hills Like White Elephants," a story made up mostly of silences, lies a complex emotional conflict between what the man thinks is "reasonable" and what the girl wants emotionally. The key to the silences of the story is the seemingly irrelevant detail announced at the beginning that the train will arrive in forty minutes. If delivered dramatically, the actual dialogue of the story would actually take only about fifteen minutes. Consequently, the story contains approximately twenty-five minutes of silence, a silence more telling in many ways than the dialogue itself. Moreover, the exposition of the story—that is, what the couple's life is like, what the girl wants, and what the man wants—is communicated by simple details, such as the man looking at their bags which have labels from all the hotels where they had spent nights and the girl looking at the dry hills and the fertile hills on the two sides of the valley. The bare situation and the seemingly trivial dialogue reveal a complex moral and emotional problem about the girl's proposed abortion which cannot be talked about directly.

Hemingway's focus on radically realistic events and his minimal description of such events seem obviously influenced by Chekhov. In his famous iceberg analogy, Hemingway echoes the typical Chekhovian idea about limiting his stories: "If a writer of prose knows enough about what he is writing about he may omit things that he knows and the reader, if the writer is writing truly enough, will have a feeling of those things as strongly as though the writer had stated them. The dignity of movement of an ice-berg is due to only one-eighth of it being above water."[11] Hemingway's seemingly inconclusive stories such as "Hills Like White Elephants" and his highly detailed stories such as "Big, Two-Hearted River" are Chekovian in their use of concrete details to reflect complex states of mind. What critics have referred to as Hemingway's "objective magic" and his creation of stories that seem like "nightmares at noonday" derive from Chekhov's use of the objective correlative, his objective style, and his love of irony and understatement.

BETWEEN DREAM AND REALITY

Such Chekhov stories as "Sleepy" and "The Bishop" make use of another significant modern short story technique: focusing on reality as an ambiguous mixture of the psychic and the external. "Sleepy" marks a sort of realistic half-way point between the symbolic use of the hypnogogic state by Poe and its being pushed to surrealistic extremes by Kafka. Chekhov presents a basically realistic situation of the young Varka being literally caught in a hypnogogic state between desirable sleep and undesirable reality. The two realms blend indistinguishably in her mind until the hallucination takes over completely and she strangles the baby so she can sleep as "soundly as the dead." Although the irony of the ending is obvious, it is the hypnotic rhythm of the events and the hallucinatory images that blend dream and reality which makes the story a significant treatment of the short story device of dissolving the rhythm of everyday reality into the purely psychic.

The two modern short story writers who have pushed this technique to extremes are Katherine Anne Porter and Franz Kafka—Porter by using illness and the approach of death to create dream-like realms of psychic reality and Kafka by making use of crisis situations to transform everyday states into nightmarish and surrealistic experiences. In "Pale Horse, Pale Rider," Miranda is caught up in a dual world of dream and delirium made up both of the real world of war and death and the fantasy world of her illness and her love for the young man Adam. Porter takes Chekhov's use of the hallucinatory state and pushes it to ritualistic extremes to embody Miranda's death wish. Similarly, Kafka's "The Judgement" begins in a realistic way, until as a result of a crisis confrontation between father and son, it turns into hallucinatory unreality which dramatizes suppressed emotional forces finally bursting forth. What makes this movement from phenomenal reality into the hallucination of dream so different from the early nineteenth-century use of the motif is that the dream-like reality is presented as "realistically" and as concretely as external reality itself.

With "The Bishop," Chekhov blurs the lines between fantasy and reality for a more serious thematic purpose than in the relatively simple "Sleepy." For here he links it with a theme that forms the center of one of his most frequently discussed works, "A Dreary Story," a theme which also preoccupies the stories of Porter and Kafka, as well as the stories of many other modern short story writers later on—the conflict between the presentational self and the problematical "real" self; the result is a lack of genuine communication and sympathy between the central character and others. The Bishop feels that the whole time he has been a Bishop, "not one person had spoken to him genuinely, simply, as to a human being. . . . he still felt that he had missed what was most important, something of which he had dimly dreamed in the past." (I, 46–47). Caught in the rhythm of his professional reality, the Bishop searches for his real self in reverie and hallucinatory memory. In this story, Chekhov moves closer to the kind of grotesque distortion of nightmare reality characteristic of Kafka. From the Bishop's sense of confusion, it is only a relatively small step to Kafka's country doctor, who in "great perplexity" is caught between external reality and psychic nightmare.

Katherine Anne Porter, in "The Jilting of Granny Weatherall," intensifies the hallucinatory effect of illness and impending death that we see in "The Bishop" by centering her story on Granny on her deathbed, hovering between hallucination and memory and trying to justify her past presentational self. Both the crucial past event of Granny's life and her present situation are so blended together that it is difficult for the reader to separate them. Like "The Bishop," the story mingles past and present, but Porter exceeds Chekhov's use of the technique by presenting seemingly disconnected and irrelevant details of Granny's physical and psychic experience in such a fragmented way that the reader must tie the various details together in order to understand the overall pattern of Granny's failure and the cause of her final jilting.

The best known story of Franz Kafka which presents the theme of the presentational self within a framework of nightmarish situation and detail is of course "Metamorphosis." Here Kafka pushes the hallucinatory device of Chekhov to its utmost extreme by forcing Gregor Samsa to face his real self in a metaphor that must be taken as reality. The drastic step Kafka takes is to make the transformation of the psychic into the physical the precipitating premise which the entire story follows. The only suspension of disbelief required in the story is that the reader accept the premise that Gregor Samsa awakes one morning from uneasy dreams to find himself transformed into a giant dung beetle. Once one accepts this event, the rest of the story is quite prosaic and realistic. The transformation of Gregor indicates the objectification of an inner state; the basic tension in the story that makes the reader not sure whether to laugh or to cry is between the horrifying yet absurd content and the matter-of-fact realistic style.

IMPRESSIONISM AND ART AS REALITY

In Chekhov's "A Dreary Story," Professor Stepanovitch, like the Bishop, searches for his real self in the face of his impending death. Also like the Bishop, he desires to be loved not for his fame or label, but as an ordinary man. In the climactic moment of realization, similar to that epiphanic moment of Gabriel in Joyce's "The Dead," the professor, striving to know himself, comes to the realization that there is no common bond to connect all his thoughts, feelings, and ideas. "Every feeling and every thought exists apart in me; and in all my criticisms of science, the theatre, literature, my pupils, and in all the pictures my imagination draws, even the most skillful analyst could not find what is called a general idea, or the god of a living man. And if there is not that, then there is nothing" (I, 529). Although this lack of a general idea is often cited as the professor's ultimate negative characteristic as a man, as well as reflective of Chekhov's own most negative characteristic as an artist, such a critical judgment reveals a failure to understand Chekhov's modern point of view and indeed the modern short story. The professor's lack of a general idea ironically is the basis for his one means of salvation, the acceptance of the relativistic and impressionistic view via art which his young ward Katia objectifies. But as Katia tells him, he has no instinct or feeling for art, and his philosophizing about it only reveals he does not understand it.

Chekhov's adoption of such a relativistic and impressionistic point of view is what makes him both a master of the short story and an innovator of its modernity. As Nadine Gordimer has said about short story writers: "theirs is the art of the only thing one can be sure of—the present moment. . . . A discrete moment of truth is aimed at—not *the* moment of truth, because the short story doesn't deal in cumulatives."[12] Peter Stowell has made a strong case for understanding Chekhov's modernism as a result of his impressionistic point of view. The ambiguous and tenuous nature of experience perceived by the impressionist, says Stowell,

> drives the author to render perceptually blurred bewilderment, rather than either the subject or the object. What is rendered is the mood, sense, feel, and atmosphere that exists between perceiver and perceived, subject and object. Literary impressionists discovered a new way to depict a new way of seeing and knowing. Literary impressionists discovered modernism."[13]

More recently, Suzanne C. Ferguson has attempted to show that the so-called modern short story is not a discrete genre at all, but rather a manifestation of impressionism. As Ferguson points out, "when all we have in the world is our own experience of it, all received knowledge becomes suspect, and the very nature of knowledge becomes problematic" and we must "confront the possibility that we cannot know anything for certain, that the processes we follow in search for truth may yield only fictions."[14]

Although indeed Ferguson's suggestion may reflect the negative side of the modernist temperament, there is also a positive aspect to such relativism which has been explored by such so-called postmodernist writers as Jorge Borges, John Barth, Robert Coover, and others; that is, that if reality is a fictional construct and the writer wishes to focus on the nature of reality, then he has little choice but to focus on the nature of art and fiction-making itself. If reality is a fiction, an artistic construct, then art perhaps provides the only means to experience reality. Both sides of this modernist predisposition can be seen in such Chekhov stories as, on the one hand,

"The House with an Attic" and on the other hand, "Easter Eve" and "The Student."

For Chekhov, art as a means to experience true reality is a complex religious, aesthetic, and sympathetic process. Like the professor in "A Dreary Story," the artist in "The House with an Attic" is too bound by "general ideas," too wedded to philosophizing and rhetoric to truly enter into the human realm of art and participate in its mysterious unity. He says a man should feel superior even to what is beyond his understanding; otherwise he is not a man but a mouse afraid of everything. "Phenomena I don't understand," he tells the young Genia, "I face boldly, and am not overwhelmed by them. I am above them" (I, 545). Unlike Olga in "The Grasshopper" who only knows the external trappings of art, Genia, nicknamed "Misuc," genuinely wishes the artist to initiate her into the domain of the "Eternal and the Beautiful." But it is a realm that the artist knows only through rhetoric.

The central scene in the story is the artist's confrontation with Genia's older sister, Lida, who scorns him for not portraying the privations of the peasants. While she insists that the highest and holiest thing for a civilized being to do is to serve his neighbors, he says the highest vocation of man is spiritual activity—"the perpetual search for truth and the meaning of life." Becoming carried away with his own rhetoric, he insists: "When science and art are real, they aim not at temporary, private ends, but at eternal and universal—they seek for truth and the meaning of life, they seek for God, for the soul" (I, 552). While both Lida and the artist are individually right in their emphases on serving the other and searching for the eternal, neither actually genuinely embodies these ideals, any more than the artist and the doctor embody them in "Aniuta." Their failure is reflected by contrast with Genia whom they both misuse and manipulate for their own ends.

For Chekhov, the only way that the eternal can be achieved is aesthetically through a unification with the human. It is best embodied in his two most mystic stories which deal with the nature of art: "Easter Eve" and "The Student." Both stories focus on the tension between disorder and harmony, between separation resulting from everyday reality and unity achieved by means of story and song. In an in-between time between death and resurrection, in an in-between place on the ferry between darkness and chaos, Ieronim tells his story of Brother Nikolai and his extraordinary gift of writing hymns of praise. Chekhov comes as close here as anywhere in his letters and notes to describing his own aesthetic. As Ieronim says, canticles are quite a different thing from writing histories or sermons; moreover, it is not enough to know well the life of the saint or the con-

ventions that govern the writing of canticles. What matters, he says, is the
beauty and sweetness of it.

> Everything must be harmonious, brief and complete. There must be
> in every line softness, graciousness and tenderness; not one word
> should be harsh or rough or unsuitable. It must be written so that the
> worshipper may rejoice at heart and weep, while his mind is stirred
> and he is thrown into a tremor. (I, 464)

In contrast to the silence of the dark river and the remembered beauty
of Nikolai's songs is the chaos and restlessness of the celebration the narrator enters, where everyone is too caught up in the "childishly irrespon-
sible joy, seeking a pretext to break out and vent itself in some movement,
even in senseless jostling and shoving" to listen to the songs of Nikolai.
The narrator looks for the dead brother but does not regret not seeing
him. "God knows, perhaps if I had seen him I should have lost the picture
my imagination paints for me now" (I, 468). Indeed, it is the creation of
Nikolai in the narrator's imagination that justifies Ieronim's story, just as
it is Nikolai's songs that sustain Ieronim. For the key to the eternal for
Chekhov is the art work which serves to unify human experience; thus
Ieronim sees the face of his brother in the face of everyone.

"The Student" begins with a sense of disorder and lack of harmony.
However, it is once again song or story that serves to heal a fractured
sense of reality. After the student tells the story of the Last Supper and
Peter's denial of Christ, which itself takes up about one third of this very
short story, he says he imagines Peter weeping, "The garden was deathly
still and very dark, and in the silence there came the sound of muffled
sobbing." And with this final imaginative projection, the power of the
story affects the two listeners. The student says the fact that they are affected must mean that what happened to Peter has some relation to them,
to the present, to the desolate village, to himself, and to all people. The
widow wept not because of the way he told the tale, but "because her
whole being was deeply affected by what happened in Peter's soul."

Although it may not be the manner of the student's oral telling which
affects the two women, it is indeed the story itself. For, although the story
does not reveal what is passing through Peter's soul, it compels the reader/
listener to sympathetically identify with Peter in his complex moment of
realization. Indeed the revelation of character by means of story presentation of a crucial moment in which the reader must then imaginatively
participate is the key to Chekhov's much discussed "objectivity" and yet
"sympathetic" presentation. The student thus feels joy at the sense of an

unbroken chain running from the past to the present. He feels that "truth and beauty" which had guided life there in the garden had continued without interruption: "always they were the most important influences working on human life and everything on the earth . . . and life suddenly seemed to him enchanting, ravishing, marvelous and full of deep meaning."[15] As in "Easter Eve," here we see the only means by which Chekhov feels that the eternal can be achieved, through the aesthetic experience and sense of unity that story and song create.

Both Sherwood Anderson and James Joyce similarly focus on the significance of the aesthetic experience as being the means both for a religious participation with the "eternal" and a sympathetic participation with the other. For example, Joyce's "The Sisters" focuses on story and art as a religious/aesthetic experience which dominates the collection *The Dubliners,* and Anderson's "Death in The Woods" centers around "story as the only means to know the other. "The Sisters," like both "Easter Eve" and "The Student," emphasizes the religious-like nature of the aesthetic experience which the old priest has communicated to the young boy while he was alive and which he embodies to him now in his death. "Death in the Woods" is particularly like "The Student" in its emphasis on how only story itself can reveal the mysterious nature of human communion.

Like Chekhov, both Anderson and Joyce focus on the central themes of isolation and the need for human sympathy and the moral failure of inaction which dominate the modernist movement in the early twentieth century; both abjure highly plotted stories in favor of seemingly static episodes and "slices" of reality; both depend on unity of feeling to create a sense of "storyness"; and both establish a sense of the seemingly casual out of what is deliberately patterned, creating significance out of the trivial by judicious selection of detail and meaningful ordering of the parts. The result is an objective-ironic style which has characterized the modern short story up to the present day. It is a style that, even as it seems realistic on its surface, in fact emphasizes the radical difference between the routine of everyday reality and the incisive nature of story itself as the only means to know true reality. Contemporary short story writers push this Chekhovian realization to even more aesthetic extremes.

THE CONTEMPORARY SHORT STORY

The contemporary short story writer most influenced by the Chekhovian objective/ironic style is Bernard Malamud, and the Chekhov story that seems most similar to Malamud's stories is "Rothschild's Fiddle," not only because the central conflict involves a Jew, but because of its pathetic/ comic ironic tone. Iakov Ivanov's business as a coffinmaker is bad in his village because people die so seldom. His unjustified hatred for the Jewish flautist Rothschild who plays even the merriest tunes sadly, and his feeling of financial loss and ruin align Iakov with all those figures that Malamud's Manischevitz identifies in "The Jewbird" when he says to his wife, "A wonderful thing, Fanny. Believe me, there are Jews everywhere." Chekhov's attempt to capture the sense of Yiddish folktale in "Rothschild's Fiddle" makes the story closer to a parable than most of his other best known stories.

Iakov feels distressed when his wife dies, for he knows that he has never spoken a kind word to her and has shouted at her for his losses. That Iakov has always been concerned with profit and loss rather than his family is also revealed when his wife asks him if he remembers when they had a baby and it died. He cannot remember and tells her she is dreaming. Iakov's epiphanic realization comes after his wife's death when he goes to the riverbank and remembers the child his wife had mentioned. But Chekhov's irony is more complex here than the simple sentimentality that such a realization might have elicited. Even as Iakov becomes lost in the pleasure of the pastoral scene, he wonders why he has never come here before and thinks of ways he could have made money at the riverbank. He laments once again his losses and thinks that if people did not act from envy and anger, as he has with his wife and Rothschild, they could get great "profit" from one another.

When he becomes ill and knows that he is dying, Iakov thinks that one good thing about it is that he will not have to eat and pay taxes. Thus he thinks life is a loss while death is a gain, for since we lie in the grave so long, we may realize immense profits. As he is dying, only Rothschild is there to pity him, and thus Iakov leaves Rothschild his fiddle. As Rothschild later tries to play the tune Iakov played, the result is so sad that everyone who hears it weeps. The new song so delights the town that the merchants and government officials vie with each other to get Rothschild to play for them. Thus, at the end, a profit is realized from Iakov's death.

"Rothschild's Fiddle" is an ironic parable-like story about the common Chekhov theme of loss and the lack of human communion which Malamud typically makes his own. Malamud's short stories are often closer to the oral tradition of parable than they are to the realistic fiction of social reality. However, although one can discern traces of the Yiddish tale in Malamud, one also realizes that his short stories reflect the tight symbolic structure and ironic and distanced point of view that we have come to associate with the short story since Chekhov. Malamud's stories move inevitably toward a conclusion in which complex moral dilemmas are not so much resolved as they are frozen in a symbolic final epiphany or ironic gesture. His characters are always caught in what might be called the demand for sympathy and responsibility. But the moral/aesthetic configuration of his stories is such that the reader is not permitted the luxury of an easy moral judgment.

The fact that Jews, that is, those who are alienated and suffering, are everywhere, which seems so obvious in "Rothschild's Fiddle," is of course a common theme in such Malamud stories as "The Mourners" in which the landlord Gruber, after trying to evict the unwanted and self-centered Kessler, finally pulls a sheet over himself and kneels to the floor to become a mourner with the old man. It is the central dilemma in "The Loan" in which Kobotsky arrives to ask for a loan from his old friend, Lieb the baker. When Lieb's wife Bessie, who has her own history of woes to recite, will not allow the loan, the two old friends can only embrace and part forever as the stench of the corpse-like burned bread lingers in their nostrils. Like "Rothschild's Fiddle," these stories present one sufferer who can understand the suffering of another. The bitter-sweet conclusions of most of Malamud's tales are typical of his Chekhovian refusal to give in to either sentimentality or condescension.

However, perhaps the contemporary short story writer who is closest to Chekhov is Raymond Carver. In Carver's collection of stories, *What We Talk About When We Talk About Love,* language is used so sparingly and the plots are so minimal that the stories seem pallidly drained patterns with no flesh and life in them. The stories are so short and lean that they seem to have plot only as we reconstruct them in our memory. Whatever theme they may have is embodied in the bare outlines of the event and in the spare dialogue of characters who are so overcome by event and so lacking in language that the theme is unsayable. Characters often have no names or only first names and are so briefly described that they seem to have no physical presence at all; certainly they have no distinct identity but rather seem to be shadowy presences trapped in their own inarticulateness.

The charge lodged against Carver is the same one once lodged against Chekhov, that his fiction is dehumanized and therefore cold and unfeeling. In a typical Carver story, "Why Don't You Dance," plot is minimal; event is mysterious; character is negligible. A man puts all his furniture out in his front yard and runs an extension cord out so that things work just as they did when they were inside. A young couple stop by, look at the furniture, try out the bed, have a drink, and the girl dances with the owner. The conversation is functional, devoted primarily toward making purchases in a perfectly banal, garage-sale way. At the conclusion, the young wife tells someone about the event. "She kept talking. She told everyone. There was more to it, and she was trying to get it talked out. After a time, she quit trying." The problem of the story is that the event cannot be talked out; it is completely objectified in the spare description of the event itself. Although there is no exposition in the story, we know that a marriage is over, that the secret life of the house has been externalized on the front lawn, that the owner has made a desperate metaphor of his marriage, that the hopeful young couple play out a mock scenario of that marriage which presages their own, and that the event itself is a parody of events not told, but kept hidden, like the seven-eighths of the iceberg that Hemingway said could be left beneath the surface of prose if the writer knew his subject well enough.

THE WILL TO STYLE

From its beginnings as a separately recognized literary form, the short story has always been more closely associated with lyric poetry than with its overgrown narrative neighbor, the novel. Regardless of whether short fiction has clung to the legendary tale form of its early ancestry, as in Hawthorne, or whether it has moved toward the presentation of the single event, as in Chekhov, the form has always been a "much in little" proposition which conceals more than it reveals and leaves much unsaid. However, there are two basic means by which the short story has pursued its movement away from the linearity of prose toward the spatiality of poetry—either by using the metaphoric and plurasignative language of the poem or by radically limiting its selection of the presented event.

The result has been two completely different textures in short fiction— the former characterized by such writers as Eudora Welty in the forties and fifties and Bernard Malamud in the sixties and seventies whose styles are thick with metaphor and myth, and the latter characterized by such writers as Hemingway in the twenties and thirties and Raymond Carver in the seventies and eighties whose styles are thin to the point of disappearing. This second style, which could be said to have been started by Chekhov, became reaffirmed as the primary mode of the "literary" or "artistic" short story (as opposed to the still-popular tale form) in the twenties by Mansfield, Anderson, and Joyce; and it was later combined with the metaphoric mode by such writers as Faulkner, Katherine Anne Porter, Flannery O'Connor, and others to create a modern short story which still maintains some of the characteristics of the old romance form even as it seems to be a radically realistic depiction of a single crucial episode.

The charge often made against the Chekhovian story—that it is dehumanized and therefore cold and unfeeling—has been made about the short story as a form since Hawthorne was criticized for his "bloodless" parables. However, such a charge ignores the nature of art that has characterized Western culture since the early nineteenth century and which Ortega y Gasset so clearly delineated in *The Dehumanization of Art*. In their nostalgia for the bourgeois security of nineteenth-century realism, critics of the short story forget that the royal road to art, as Ortega delineates is, "the will to style." And to stylize "means to deform reality, to derealize: style involves dehumanization." Given this definition of art, it is easy to see that the short story as a form has always embodied "the will to style."[16] The short story writer realizes that the artist must not confuse reality with idea, that he must inevitably turn his back on alleged reality and, as Ortega insists, "take the ideas for what they are—mere subjective patterns—and make them live as such, lean and angular, but pure and transparent."

The lyricism of the Chekhovian short story lies in this will to style in which reality is derealized and ideas live solely as ideas. Thus Chekhov's stories are more "poetic," that is, more "artistic" than we usually expect fiction to be; they help define the difference between the loose and baggy monstrous novel and the taut, gemlike short story. One final implication of Chekhov's focus on the "will to style" is the inevitable self-consciousness of fiction as fiction. If the term "modernism" suggests, as most critics seem to agree, a reaction against nineteenth-century bourgeois realism, which, a la Chekhov, Joyce, Anderson, and others, manifested itself as a frustration of conventional expectations about the cause-and-effect nature of plot and the "as-if-real" nature of character; then postmodernism pushes this movement even further so that contemporary fiction is less and less about objective reality and more and more about its own creative processes.

The primary effect of this mode of thought on contemporary fiction is that the story has a tendency to loosen its illusion of reality to explore the reality of its illusion. Rather than presenting itself "as if" it were real—a mimetic mirroring of external reality—postmodernist fiction makes its own artistic conventions and devices the subject of the story as well as its theme. The underlying assumption is that the forms of art are explainable by the laws of art; literary language is not a proxy for something else, but rather an object of study itself. The short story as a genre has always been more apt to lay bare its fictionality than the novel, which has traditionally tried to cover it up. Fictional self-consciousness in the short story does not allow the reader to maintain the comfortable cover-up assumption that what is depicted is real; instead the reader is made uncomfortably aware that the only reality is the process of depiction itself—the fiction-making process, the language act.

Although Anton Chekhov could not have anticipated the far-reaching implications of his experimentation with the short story as a seemingly realistic, yet highly stylized, form in the work of John Barth, Donald Barthelme, Robert Coover, and Raymond Carver, it is clear that the contemporary short story, for all of its much complained-of "unreadability," owes a significant debt to the much-criticized "storyless" stories of Chekhov. For it is with Chekhov that the short story was liberated from its adherence to the parabolic exemplum and fiction generally was liberated from the tedium of the realistic novel. With Chekhov, the short story took on a new respectability and began to be seen as the most appropriate narrative form to reflect the modern temperament. There can be no understanding of the short story as a genre without an understanding of Chekhov's contribution to the form. Conrad Aiken's assessment of him in 1921 has yet to be challenged: "Possibly the greatest writer of the short story who has ever lived."[17]

NOTES

1. Early reviews of Chekhov can be found in *Chekhov: The Critical Heritage,* ed. Victor Emeljanow (London: Routledge and Kegan Paul, 1981). See the twelfth essay in this volume by John Tulloch, "Chekhov Abroad: Western Criticism."

2. Conrad Aiken, "Anton Chekhov," 1921; reprinted in *Collected Criticism* (New York: Oxford University Press, 1968), pp. 148–53.

3. D. S. Mirsky, "Chekhov and the English," 1927; reprinted in *Russian Literature and Modern English Fiction,* ed. Donald Davie (University of Chicago Press, 1965), pp. 203–213.

4. Eudora Welty, "The Reading and Writing of Short Stories," 1949; reprinted in *Short Story Theories,* ed. Charles E. May (Athens: Ohio University Press, 1976), pp. 159–77.

5. John Dewey, *Art of Experience* (New York: G. P. Putnam's Sons, 1934), p. 37.

6. Quoted by Gorham Munson, "The Recapture of the Storyable," *The University Review* 10 (Autumn 1943): 37–44.

7. *Stephen Hero,* ed. Theodore Spencer (New York: New Directions, 1944), p. 51.

8. Georg Lukács, *The Theory of the Novel,* trans. Anna Bostock (Cambridge, Mass.: MIT Press, 1971), p. 51.

9. *The Image of Chekhov,* trans. Robert Payne (New York: Alfred A. Knopf, 1976), p. 104. In this edition "Misery" ("Toska") is translated as "Heartache."

10. *Select Tales of Tchehov,* trans. Constance Garnett (London: Chatto and Windus, 1961), I, 16. Further citations from this edition are identified by page and volume in parenthesis in the text.

11. *Death in the Afternoon* (New York: Charles Scribner's Sons, 1931), p. 192.

12. Nadine Gordimer, "The Flash of Fireflies," in *Short Story Theories,* p. 178.

13. Peter Stowell, *Literary Impressionism: James and Chekhov* (Athens: University of Georgia Press, 1980), p. 243.

14. Suzanne C. Ferguson, "Defining the Short Story: Impressionism and Form," *Modern Fiction Studies* 28 (Spring 1982): 13–14.

15. *The Image of Chekhov,* pp. 222–23.

16. *The Dehumanization of Art and Other Writings on Art and Culture* (Garden City, New York: Doubleday Anchor Books, 1956), p. 23.

17. *Collected Criticism,* p. 149.

Defining the Short Story

IMPRESSIONISM AND FORM

SUZANNE C. FERGUSON

THAT THERE IS no large and distinguished corpus of short story theory because the short story does not exist as a discrete and independent genre is a hypothesis—repugnant to many, of course—that ought to be taken seriously on occasion, if only to contemplate the perspective the hypothesis provides. "Intuition" or even "experience" may tell us that the "short story" exists, but defining it has proven surprisingly resistant to critical effort. A 1976 anthology, Charles May's *Short Story Theories*,[1] demonstrates the problematic situation. Short stories are defined in terms of unity (Poe, Brander Matthews, and others), techniques of plot compression (A. L. Bader, Norman Friedman, L. A. G. Strong), change or revelation of character (Theodore Stroud), subject (Frank O'Connor), tone (Gordimer), "lyricism" (Moravia), but there is no single characteristic or cluster of characteristics that the critics agree absolutely distinguishes the short story from other fictions. Thomas Gullason begins by lambasting Poe's formulas for "unity of effect" as "destructive," but ends up praising the short story for its "compact impact," which comes from "distillation" and "telescoping."[2] Norman Friedman's valiant effort to discover "What Makes a Short Story Short?" leaves the distinct impression that it is a short story because it is—well—a *short* story.[3]

A structuralist conception of fiction[4] tends to confirm the suspicion that there may be no rational way to distinguish "short story" from other narratives in the same mimetic mode: *all* stories, short and long, have certain required properties of narrativity—characters, place, events, a "beginning, middle, and an end," and coherence among the parts. All stories can be reduced to minimal statements of the required elements or expanded by the inclusion of optional developments in the narrative chain, as long as they maintain a discoverable coherence in their interrelationships. Like the sentence, the story has "slots" where various elements may be inserted; beyond a basic minimum of noun phrase plus verb phrase or existent plus event (character plus action), both the sentence and the story may be almost infinitely expanded. *Tristram Shandy* and *Ulysses* suggest an extreme range of options for the extrapolation of simple narrative sequences into long and complex ones. Similar expansion could be applied to any story, from "The Town Mouse and the Country Mouse" to "Indian Camp"; but of course the "best" short stories give us a sense of the inevitability of each sentence and persuade us that they are as complete as possible, that any addition or deletion would destroy their aesthetic wholeness. Whereas the omission of an entire sentence from Aesop's "The Town Mouse and the Country Mouse" would likely jeopardize its narrative coherence, we might add several without destroying its elegant symmetry or its moral. Indeed, its basic structure is the foundation of a number of nineteenth-century novels. We might remove one or more sentences from "The Fall of the House of Usher" or even (sacrilege!) "Araby"—providing we chose carefully—or add a few—providing we imitated carefully—without altering its theme or quality for most readers.

What accounts, then, for the persistent notion that the "modern" short story is a new genre, something different from the tale and sketch that preceded it? In fact, the modern short story shows all the same shifts in sensibility and technique that affected the novel and the long story (or nouvelle) around the end of the nineteenth century, but these changes "look" different in the short story precisely because it is physically short. The main formal characteristics of the modern novel and the modern short story are the same: (1) limitation and foregrounding of point of view, (2) emphasis on presentation of sensation and inner experience, (3) the deletion or transformation of several elements of the traditional plot, (4) increasing reliance on metaphor and metonymy in the presentation of events and existents, (5) rejection of chronological time ordering, (6) formal and stylistic economy, and (7) the foregrounding of style. All these elements are associated with the literary movement called impressionism, or, more specifically in fiction, the tradition of Flaubert. I will argue that, just as impressionism dominates the mainstream of the novel in the late nineteenth and early twentieth centuries, so it does that of the short story. But the short story, because it has fewer "optional" narrative elements in its structural "slots," manifests its formal allegiances to impressionism even more obviously than does the novel and, consequently, seems more radically different from earlier short fiction than the impressionist novel seems different from the realistic novel that preceded it.

Let me take the characteristics in the order listed above, briefly illustrating each one. The limiting of point of view to that of a character or characters in the narrative and the emphasis on the presentation of sensation and inner experience are inextricably related. The same impulses that turned nineteenth-century philosophy away from positivism and toward phenomenology turned writers to the representation of experience *as* experienced by individuals. The importance of this philosophical shift in the interpretation of reality cannot be over-estimated in an attempt to understand what happened to writers' representations of reality. Imitation of how things "feel" or "seem" to the characters became the preferred subject of fiction rather than the imitation of "how things are" in the "real" world. Where the characters' attitudes and responses had always been a part of a more comprehensive view of the world, the subjectivity of "reality" now became the prevailing mode of understanding, and the exploration of subjectivity became the elusive "object" of fictional imitation.

In the impressionist short story, even more than in the impressionist novel, the author conceals himself, presenting the entire narrative from a point of view within the story, that of the characters' subjective experience of events, their "impressions," by using either first-person narrative or the Jamesian "method of the central intelligence." This emphasis on subjectivity inevitably affects the typical themes of modern fiction: alienation, isolation, solipsism, the quest for identity and integration. The characters, the experiencing subjects, are seen as isolated from other experiencing subjects, with only rare moments of communion or shared experience possible to them. Frank O'Connor's contention that the modern short story deals with outsiders, lonely individuals cut off from society, is true,[5] but that theme is equally typical of modern novels.

The preoccupation of impressionist authors with epistemological themes is another outgrowth of subjectivism, for when all we have in the world is our own experience of it, all received knowledge becomes suspect, and the very nature of knowledge becomes problematic. This uncertainty affects the concept of plot: the Aristotelian intertwining of knowledge with action is unraveled; protagonists become passive observers; the "absence" which impels the plot is absence of knowledge of some truth that could go beyond the merely personal to achieve a general validity. It is often the reader, rather than the character, who must directly confront the possibility that we cannot know anything for certain, that the processes we follow in search of truth may yield only fictions.[6]

Like the limiting of point of view and the theme of alienation, the quest for knowledge about reality is common to impressionist novels as well as short stories. In longer works of the earlier twentieth century, however; these features are usually less prominent than in shorter works because of the long works' elaborating of plot and character, their density of specification, and the like. Comparison of *Ulysses* with "The Dead" and of "The Dead" with "An Encounter" or "The Sisters" will clarify this contention. The theme of quest for reliable, transpersonal knowledge about the world is present in all three "genres"—novel, nouvelle, story—but there are complementary or ancillary themes in the longer works, along with multiplication of episodes in the plot, proliferation of detail in descriptions, and, in *Ulysses,* the diversification of styles in the texture of the work. Although all these factors actually do manifest the theme of the quest to define reality, the reader tends to be less aware of the theme as such and more engrossed in the richness of the longer works' texture. The compactness and focus of the short stories makes the theme more readily apparent.

It is in the realm of plot that the modern short story is most different from earlier short fiction and in which it appears to be most different from the novel. The deemphasis of physical action in impressionist fiction (or the disjunction of physical action from thought and feeling), which leaves adjustments of thought or feeling as the true "events" of the plot, makes the articulation of plot in many cases obscure. A related problem is the increasing expectation of the writers that their readers will have internalized the elements of traditional plots so thoroughly that the writers can presume readers will supply missing elements. The deletion of expected elements of the plot—from any "slot" in the story—is the hallmark of the late nineteenth- and early twentieth-century short story. There are two basic methods of deletion: that in which elements are simply omitted, which results in what I call "elliptical" plots, and that in which unexpected, dissonant existents or events are substituted for the omitted elements, which yields "metaphoric" plots.

Elliptical plots may omit the exposition and never get back to it (as in "Cat in the Rain" or "Hills Like White Elephants"); or pass over what would ordinarily be "dramatized" or extensively reported parts of the middle, episodes that develop the plot conflict (Kipling stories such as "Love O' Women" and "Mrs. Bathurst," or Faulkner's "A Rose for Emily"); or leave out closure (Chekhov's "On the Road" and many others). Impressionist novels more rarely begin *in medias res* without going back to fill in the beginning at some later point in the narrative, and they almost never omit important stages of the middle, because one of the basic principles of the novel is to develop and elaborate. Elements left out at their "normal" chronological point in the narrative sequence turn up elsewhere (as in *The Good Soldier*).

To understand the notion of "elliptical" plots, it is helpful to look at some actual stories and propose for them "hypothetical" plots that might form the "natural" or "deep structure" bases of the narratives (By hypothetical plot I mean something more specifically formulable than the bare-bones structuralist "fabula": a counter-story, with a beginning, middle, and end, that tells "what happened" in chronological order.) In "Clay" a hypothetical plot is the story of Maria's life from the time when she had a "home" with Alphy and Joe's family, through the breakup of the family and her making a new "home" in the laundry, to the time of the actual story, at the end of which she (perhaps unconsciously) acknowledges her desolation, her "homelessness." The reader must to some extent construct this hypothetical plot in order for the actual story to seem meaningful. The act of constructing a hypothetical plot is what we ask students to perform when we ask them, "Who is Maria?"; "What is her relation to Alphy and Joe?"; "Why does she live at the laundry?"; "How do we know she won't get married?"; and the like.[7]

The actual plot of "Clay" deletes expository material and neglects to provide episodes showing Maria's desire for a home and family to which she could belong. The past when she had a sort of home is referred to in only a few phrases, and the bleakness of her life in the laundry is seen only obliquely in Maria's deliberately optimistic view of herself in the role of "peacemaker" to the unruly laundresses. This actual plot consists of three episodes, two of them developing tension and the third climatic. Maria prepares for the All Hallows party, hoping to reconcile Joe and Alphy and thus restore the conditions of a past in which she was relatively happy; she travels to the party, buying a piece of cake as an "offering" and losing it en route because of the distraction of a man flirting with her; after causing some distress at the party because of her concern at losing the cake, she is rejected (tricked) by an unthinking neighbor girl and consoled by the appreciation of her wishful song. The parts of the hypothetical plot that are omitted are represented metonymically by the episodes Joyce has written. Maria's experience at the party is representative of her life, or so we interpret the story.

In "Eveline," the darling of structuralist analysts, a hypothetical plot might be said to begin with Eveline's loss of her mother's love (through death), to run through her opportunity to find a new love with Frank, and to end with her acknowledgment that she cannot throw off the bonds of habit that link her, without love, to her father and her home. Here the actual plot begins after Eveline has been offered the chance to escape but before she rejects it. Both "Clay" and "Eveline" begin almost at the crisis of the traditional, "hypothetical" plot. Eveline is on the brink of an action that would change her life; Maria has her plan to reconcile the brothers. Eveline cannot act; Maria is deflected. For Eveline there is tumult, inevitable (though untold) recognition; for Maria there is a simple retreat. Only the reader recognizes that Maria means little to Joe's family, that her future is not to reconcile and reunite the family but to move on alone into death.

In both stories, the exposition and earlier stages of conflict are alluded to in the protagonists' memories, but only the climaxes are dramatized. Although aesthetic closure is achieved in "Eveline" in the concluding images of the inundating sea, and in "Clay" in Maria's rendition of "I Dreamt that I Dwelt in Marble Halls" and Joe's reaction to it, the themes keep on unraveling into the futureless future beyond the end of the stories. The sense of a double plot in all such stories is strong; we recognize a story that has not been fully told lying behind the one that *is* told. Reading the stories, we become detectives, piecing together the main elements of the hypothetical plots in order to rationalize the actual plots.

In addition to stories in which parts of the plot are omitted, there are stories in which the elements of the hypothetical plot are represented at the surface level by sets of images or events—often trivial and unrelated to each other—that are analogous to and substitutes for events in the hypothetical plot; that is, they stand in relation to the theme of the story as the chain of events does in a normal plot, and the chain of events is left implicit. These I call "metaphoric" plots. "Ivy Day in the Committee Room" and "The Gambler, the Nun, and the Radio" are extreme examples. The surface events of these stories are disconnected and of little apparent significance, but they suggest a deep level at which themes of profound human import are developed.

The theme of "Ivy Day" is the debasement of Parnell's ideals in the behavior of his nominal followers. The conversation in the Committee Room exemplifies the dishonor while it implicitly evokes the image of Parnell and his struggle to give the Irish political freedom, an image the reader must remember independently of what is told in the actual story. Seen in retrospect, each separate, fragmentary episode is a small betrayal. As we read the story, however, we gather up seemingly random threads: the rejection of the old by the young, the chicaneries and temporizing of the political hacks, the disreputable activities of the clergy. A sort of climax is achieved in the plan to welcome Edward VII—opposite to Parnell, the "uncrowned king"—to Ireland on an official visit, although he represents not only English domination but womanizing, the pretext on which Parnell—the faithful lover of another man's wife—was brought down. The episodes of the plot are not only metaphoric in this case but ironic: the day that is meant to honor Parnell dishonors his memory. Joe Hynes's poem, banal but sincere, is the best a sorry lot can do to retrieve past heroism, and the popping corks of stout bottles complete the humans' feeble salute.

In Hemingway's story, the figures of the gambler and the nun are protagonists of auxiliary elliptical narratives within the actual plot, and they and the radio are vehicles of metaphors whose tenor is the theme of a general quest for the "opium of the people." Mr. Frazer, who plays the radio and contemplates the gambler and the nun, is in some obscure way the protagonist of another story of which we know too few details even to hypothesize a plot, as well as of the actual story, whose ironies bring him to a conclusion about the meaninglessness of experience and the nature of the opiums of the people.

Without our sense of how traditional plots work, these stories would simply be accounts of "what happened"; they seem to lack the obligatory coherence of existent and event of ordinary narrative. The disorder is of course intentional, and it imitates the surface disorder of the world in which we seek coherence. Combining our intuitive knowledge of "storiness" with a symbolic reading of the actual events and characters, we find the narrative element in the works and perceive them as short stories rather than random accounts of unrelated characters and happenings. A long impressionist fiction that would depend so heavily upon the reader's intensive interpretation of symbolic incidents and figures for the basis of its narrative sequence seems unworkable, and I am unable to name one. Metaphoric episodes or subplots are relatively common, however: the French architect episode in *Absalom, Absalom!*, the excursion to "M———" in *The Good Soldier*, and the owl-eyed man scenes of *The Great Gatsby* suggest themselves. The stylistic vagaries of *Ulysses* function similarly, although like other, later novels, *Ulysses* has already gone beyond the boundaries of impressionism in so many ways that one should probably not include it here. Instead of asking the reader to measure a subjective view against a traditional, "realistic" view, postimpressionist fiction denies the existence of the latter altogether.

Elliptical and metaphoric plots affirm Joseph Frank's conception of a spatially rather than a temporally organized form in modern fiction. In focussing on the crisis of a hypothetical narrative, or in representing that narrative only in figures or analogues, such plots devaluate temporal sequence and the chain of cause and effect. The deemphasis of the orderly unfolding of an action through time is closely related to the emergence of "epiphany" as an ordering device. The notion of single "moments" of experience as determiners of the quality of a whole life appears to be mystical in origin, and in secular literature it goes back at least to Wordsworth, but is has become characteristic of modern fiction both as an item of belief and a structural principle. In the modern novel, we move from epiphany to epiphany, or in Woolf's image, along a series of small revelations, "matches struck unexpectedly in the dark."[8] In the short story, we frequently see only one such privileged moment, which takes the place of the traditional "turning point," the climax of the plot. Not much actual dramatized time passes, although in the memory and fantasy of the characters large reaches of "time" may be covered. The narrator of "A Rose for Emily" tells his story after Emily's funeral, and his "epiphany" takes place when someone picks an iron-grey hair from her pillow, but the "story" covers many years in the life of Miss Emily Grierson, not just or not even most importantly the moment of her death. The actual plot unfolds the story of the town's discovery; but the more interesting story is the hypothetical plot the reader must puzzle out and restore to its "natural" chronology in order to understand the actual story. Time is as malleable here as in *The Sound and the Fury* or *Absalom, Absalom!*, but we are not so much concerned with its operations. Nevertheless, we must make a conscious effort to restore chronology in order to understand Miss Emily's story. In the foregrounding of time and in the temporal displacements between the hypothetical and actual plots, "A Rose for Emily" is an extreme case of the deviousness of many modern stories, which overtly seem to disdain temporal order but covertly remind us how time-bound we are.

The use of setting in impressionist fiction is also different from that in earlier fiction. Insofar as impressionism is an extension of realism in its sensational, experiential aspect, settings are established through the use of detail to give verisimilitude. That these details are chosen as much or more to reflect the mood of the characters perceiving them as to convey a location for the action and the characters' social standing marks a significant difference between realism and impressionism. Drawing upon the romantic (even Gothic) tradition, impressionist settings are frequently used metaphorically to substitute for representation of action or analysis. The fragmentary description of the house, street, and alleys that form the beginning of "Araby" has to convey more than just the location of the events; it must stand in place of hypothetical episodes in which the boy's character would be developed in the context of his family and his larger social environment; it must convey his class, his situation, his innocence, his predilection for romance: in short, his sensibility and his *need* to engage in some meaningful action. These initial paragraphs, though they record no specific events, substitute for the exposition of a traditional plot.

In the modern novel, setting is used for similar purposes, but in most novels it supplements rather than replaces other kinds of character and plot development. Although it is often difficult, even for purposes of analysis, to separate "setting" from some aspects of "characterization,"[9] it is probably true that setting is a more significant factor in the modern story than in the nouvelle and novel in terms of proportion of discourse space allotted to it.

Techniques of limiting point of view, constructing elliptical or metaphoric plots, using representative details for setting and character development go hand in hand with the impressionists' attention to stylistic economy and the foregrounding of style. In transforming the plot by deletion and substitution, writers also made their language more economical: dense with meaning as it is in poetry. From Flaubert forward, impressionist fiction foregrounds style in the emphasis on rhythmic prose, exact diction, and a high reliance on figures, particularly simile and metaphor. The author may disappear as commentator on the action, but he calls attention to himself through the special "signature" of his style.

Stylistic foregrounding has both negative and positive effects: although Hemingway's and Faulkner's highly mannered styles may grow tedious, even self-parodic, in their novels, in the stories they are a force for cohesiveness, imparting a special coloration or atmosphere that binds the often disparate events and characters together. Though Joyce said he wrote *Dubliners* in a style of "scrupulous meanness," few readers would agree; the beauty of Joyce's style, applied to the squalor of the subject, gives these stories their classic quality. By and large—except for Lawrence—the great short story writers have reputations as outstanding stylists, and much of the praise for their style, in terms of its "jewelling" or "polish," arises from a sense of the care lavished in the search for *le mot juste* by writers from Poe to Kipling, Joyce, Mansfield, Hemingway, Faulkner, Porter, Welty, both O'Connors, O'Faolain, Bowen, Updike. The attribution of "lyricism" to the story also comes in large measure from the attention to style, the deliberation that is so apparent in manipulating diction, figuration, and syntactic and phonemic patterning to achieve precise tonal effects.

Even the association of the short story with certain national traditions—French, Russian, Irish, and American—can be seen to be linked with its impressionist elements rather than a particular national "gift." Turgenev and Chekhov, among the Russians, display in particular the foregrounding of setting, the reduction of physical action, and the elevation of mood changes to the status of plots; a recent book, in fact, treats Chekhov with James as an impressionist.[10] Among the French, Maupassant is preeminent in the short story; his techniques of compression and suggestion come directly from Flaubert, not from a tradition of the short story. Though Crane and James are the first Americans properly to be called impressionist writers, Poe and Hawthorne foreshadow impressionist techniques in the focus on inner states, the substitution of setting for action, and the use of fallible, ambivalent narrators in first-person (Poe) and third-person (Hawthorne) in both long and short fiction. George Moore follows Turgenev, Joyce follows Moore and Flaubert, in changing the mainstream of Irish short fiction from anecdote to impression.

What has made the modern short story seem distinct from the novel, in addition to the different distribution and proportion of narrative elements, is finally a matter of prestige. Given the emphasis on its status as a work of art and the insistence by many turn-of-the-century writers on stylistic elegance (a sure sign of "high" art!), the story began to be read more intensively. The deletion of traditional plot elements also demanded a more attentive reading, one in which the reader is conscious of narrative technique and style as keys to meaning. As the story became more obviously artful, its artistry was the more remarked in criticism. James and Wells thought in terms of a "golden age" or "millenium" of the short story, and writers began to establish reputations solely on the basis of their short fiction.

The idea that a "true" short story grew out of some older, amateurish form of the early nineteenth century is not borne out by the evidence. Although earlier there is a finer line between "popular" and highbrow stories, and though much nineteenth-century short fiction belongs to the specialized subgenres more characteristic of popular than serious fiction, the mainstream short story of the nineteenth century is as likely to deal with the same concerns as the novel of its time as the modern story and the modern novel are apt to deal with modern concerns. Brevity, however, is not well suited to the vision of Victorian fiction, in which men and women move through a complex society, posing goals and working toward them with greater or less success. One can imagine a short story about Dorothea Brooke or Willoughby, but not a very impressive one. Thus, though coherent and competently written, few Victorian short stories are of much interest to the modern reader.

In bringing to a close this sketch of the relations between impressionist conceptions and techniques and the forms of early modern fiction, I would like to focus on a point implicit in much of the rest of my argument. Comparison of nineteenth-century short and long fictions with their modern counterparts reveals one final way in which short stories seem different from longer ones in their formal identities. The less we are occupied with verisimilitude, with physical action, with extended characterization, the more obvious it is that the element which binds the whole *into* a whole is what readers perceive as a governing *theme* and often express as "the author's intention": in old-fashioned stories, the "moral." This "semantic" aspect of the story we abstract from its lexical aspect— the events, existents, and authorial commentary—as we see that organized in the syntactic aspect—plot, temporal ordering. Theme is what readers constitute as they study the significance and relationships of the various elements and locate the "storiness" emerging from the often obscure system the author provides. In realistic literature, the interplay of character and action in the plot is the primary vector of theme. In the modern, impressionist short story, in which plot is frequently suppressed, in which characterization is often achieved by having the characters perceive something or somebody "other" rather than acting or being themselves described by an implied author, in which setting may displace event, and in which the very sentence structures or figurative language may imply relationships not otherwise expressed, the readers' ability to recognize a theme is paramount to their acceptance of the work as belonging to the genre, "story." Oddly, this kind of narrative, whose most typical epistemology assumes the privacy of truth in individual experience, becomes the genre in which the readers' abstraction of theme—the statement of an interpretation—is a major factor in their differentiating it from other kinds of narrative. The moral is no longer an easily abstractable truism verified by an implied author, but a complex and hardly won proposition whose validity remains conditional and implicit, unconfirmed by the authorial voice, giving the story both "unity of effect" and a certain vagueness or mystery.

In attempting to show that the "modern short story" is a manifestation of impressionism rather than a discrete genre, I have cited many of the same characteristics that others have observed in arguing that the short story *is* a genre. That the short story *seems* very different from the novel in its plot, in the proportions of action to setting and character, or in the prominence of theme over vicarious experience, I concede, yet the context of impressionism seems to me a more comprehensive vantage point from which to interpret these differences than that of genre.

Any perspective, of genre or mode, is only a starting point in the interpretation and assimilation of a literary work. The complex adjustments in reading process we make in going from "The Town Mouse and the Country Mouse," Grimms' fairy tales, or "Wandering Willie's Tale" to "The Jolly Corner" or "The Gambler, the Nun, and the Radio" are considerable: greater, I would argue, than those we make in going from *The Good Soldier* or *To the Lighthouse* to "Soldier's Home" or "Ivy Day in the Committee Room." (Those who argue from a generic perspective would likely agree.) Nevertheless, our knowledge of Aesop or a fairy tale or Scott's tale—or any of the stories we heard as children or read in adolescence, no matter how crude or cheap—provides us with the basic knowledge of the fictional codes that we need to begin reading sophisticated modern short stories and their longer relatives. The question "What is a short story?" or even "What is an impressionist short story?" is probably not as important a question in the long run as other, specific questions we might ask about the relations of long and short stories, popular and highbrow stories, hypothetical and actual plots, or stories and reality. The object of such criticism is not, finally, to find generic or modal boxes to put stories into, but to open the boxes and let stories out for more illuminating scrutiny.

NOTES

1. Charles E. May, ed. *Short Story Theories* (Athens: Ohio University Press, 1976).

2. Thomas Gullason, "The Short Story: An Underrated Art," in May, pp. 20–21, 30.

3. Norman Friedman, "What Makes A Short Story Short?" in May, pp. 131–46.

4. Beginning with V. K. Propp in *Morphology of the Folktale* (1928) and reaffirmed in later structuralist critics such as Claude Bremond and A. J. Greimas in *Communications,* 8 (1966), 60–76 and 28–59; Roland Barthes, "An Introduction to the Structural Analysis of Narrative," trans. by Lionel Duisit in *NLH,* 6 (1975), 237–72; Seymour Chatman, *Story and Discourse* (Ithaca, NY: Cornell University Press, 1978), pp. 43–48.

5. Frank O'Connor, from *The Lonely Voice* (1963), in May, p. 86–89.

6. The fictionality of all (subjective) truth becomes an obsession in postmodern writing; it is a given in the work of Borges, Robbe-Grillet, Pynchon, and others, rather than an intuition against which the characters struggle, as in impressionistic fiction.

7. These are types of questions it would be pointless to ask about the characters in Borges or Barthelme, or even in such a relatively conservative postmodern story as Pynchon's "Entropy," for these characters *have* no "other" existence; the tie with a "real" world, in which we might imagine the characters as acting and suffering, is broken.

8. Virginia Woolf, *To the Lighthouse* (New York: Harcourt Brace & World, 1955), p. 240.

9. Chatman, pp. 138–45.

10. Peter Stowell, *Literary Impressionism, James and Chekhov* (Athens: University of Georgia Press, 1980).

The Lyric Short Story

THE SKETCH OF A HISTORY

EILEEN BALDESHWILER

WHEN THE HISTORY of the modern short story is written, it will have to take into account two related developments, tracing the course of the larger mass of narratives that, for purposes of clarification we could term "epical," and the smaller group which, to accentuate differences, we might call "lyrical." The larger group of narratives is marked by external action developed "syllogistically" through characters fabricated mainly to forward plot, culminating in a decisive ending that sometimes affords a universal insight, and expressed in the serviceably inconspicuous language of prose realism. The other segment of stories concentrates on internal changes, moods, and feelings, utilizing a variety of structural patterns depending on the shape of the emotion itself, relies for the most part on the open ending, and is expressed in the condensed, evocative, often figured language of the poem. In present day literary theory, the term "lyric" refers of course not so much to structure as to subject and tone, and it is mainly to these aspects of the brief narrative that the adjective is meant to call attention in the phrase "lyrical" story. Obviously, the distinction between prose narrative and verse remains absolute: the "lyrical" story, like any other, includes the essentials of storytelling—persons with some degree of verisimilitude engaged in a unified action in time—and the medium remains prose. Looking at the "lyrical" narrative historically, one sees that some writers, a minority, devoted themselves exclusively to this form, while others were able to utilize the "epical" mode as well. Still, there exists a definite line of development within the "lyrical" vein, explicitly so titled as early as 1921 by Conrad Aiken, in a review of *Bliss and Other Stories*. The purpose of the present essay is to sketch the outline of this history by indicating briefly the writers that we need to examine and by suggesting something of their special contributions.

It seems clear that it is in the loosely structured, yet unified, sketches of Turgenev's *A Sportsman's Notebook,* with their subtle discrimination of shades of emotion, their famous "shimmering" tone and lovingly detached attention to the physical details of natural objects and scenes that the lyrical story first emerges as a distinctive form. Episodic in construction, few of the pieces revolve around a conventional plot; rather, more often than not, the author gently leads us through an interlude of time depicted by means of minute, impressionistic touches—not without occasional motifs or semi-symbolic figures—in such a way that the senses are alerted and the feelings softened and made reflective. At first glance, one thinks of Turgenev as working on a canvas crowded with characters, yet the more insistent impression is of a few distinct personages, each of whom is complete within his own aura, his own emotional tone and setting. Through the tactful managing of aesthetic distance and the use of a narrator-observer perfectly attuned to the nuances of nature and human feeling, Turgenev carefully controls and subtly shades tone. Although he works within the limits of naturalism, Turgenev exhibits a supreme power of cloaking all in a dream-like incandescence, of casting the gently melancholy light of his own vision uniformly over natural objects and human events.

Despite his respect and admiration for Turgenev, Chekhov, the next practitioner of the lyric story, works in a different vein, devoting almost his entire attention to reporting small, emotionally laden situations from the point of view of two or three characters. Forsaking the trappings of conventional plot as did Turgenev, Chekhov concentrates his attention on severely limited occasions, diffusing over them a humorous or melancholy light and reporting them with the absolute fidelity of naturalistic art. At times, however, these self-imposed limitations are transcended and Chekhov's story achieves a larger, freer, more musical dimension. Representative of the pieces that rise to the level of truly poetic utterance are "The Schoolmistress," "Easter Eve," "The Bishop," "Gusev," and "The Lady with the Dog," although these are foreshadowed by such earlier sketches as "The Student" and "The Pipe."

The "musicality" of Chekhov's major stories is exactly described by D. S. Mirsky's comment that while the author's prose is not "melodious," the architectonics of his stories is akin to that of a musical composition. "At once fluid and precise," the narratives are built on "very complicated curves . . . calculated with the utmost precision." The structure of a Chekhov story, then, is "a series of points marking out with precision the lines discerned by him in the tangled web of consciousness." According to Mirsky, Chekhov

> excels in the art of tracing the first stages of an emotional process, in indicating those first symptoms of a deviation when to the general eye, and to the conscious eye of the subject in question, the nascent curve still seems to coincide with a straight line. An infinitesimal touch, which at first hardly arrests the reader's attention, gives a hint at the direction the story is going to take. It is then repeated as a leit-motif, and at each repetition the true equation of the curve becomes more important, and it ends by shooting away in a direction very different from that of the original straight line.

Thus in "The Lady with the Dog" the straight line is the hero's attitude towards his vacation affair with the young wife, an intrigue that he regards as passing and even trivial, while the "curve" is created in the growth of his overwhelming and all-pervasive love for her. (Mirsky adds that in many of Chekhov's stories these lines are complicated by "a rich and mellow atmosphere" arising from the abundance of emotionally significant detail. The effect, then, is poetical, even lyrical, and, as in lyric, it is not plot development that arouses interest. On the contrary, the reader experiences "infection" by the poet's mood. To Mirsky, Chekhov's stories are, in short, "lyrical monoliths": the episodes are themselves deeply conditioned by the whole and without significance apart from it.)

There is a sense in which all of Chekhov's work is symbolical, but in some stories symbols perform central structural functions. The symbols of "The Lady with the Dog" are perhaps least well defined, but certain large metaphors—mostly related to place—are important vehicles of extended meaning. Thus the sea, the hotel room, the provincial concert hall, the house behind the barbed fence, the Yalta resort, all signify states of mind (freedom, imprisonment, vulgarity, longing) and suggest meaning beyond mere physical fact. In "The Schoolmistress," symbols are more precise and more limited in effect. Objects like the teacher's faded photograph of her mother, which has a direct relation to the girl's hallucinatory vision of the woman in the railway carriage, both unify the story and underline the tragic theme of contrast between what is and what might have been as they recapitulate the past and insert it violently into the present. The difficult, painful journey by cart to the town is itself conventionally symbolic of the entrance into one's tragic destiny, here elaborated by the romantic encounter at the crossroads, the accident at the pond, and the "descent into hell" at the village tavern.

It is traditional "natural" symbols that dominate "Easter Eve," one of the most appealing of all Chekhov's narratives. Here, the symbolism of the Christian Resurrection surrounds Ieronim's account of the death of his fellow monk and the earthly end of a perfect love of charity. Ferrying his passengers across the river to the monastery for the Paschal service, Ieronim questions the meaning of suffering, loneliness, and pain even as he and his companion view with ecstasy the scene of the great Easter fire on the far side of the stream. Thus it is as much through the plethora of suggestion surrounding such traditional symbols as a river passage, the Resurrection, light and darkness, as by means of action or characterization that Chekhov dramatizes profound human emotions. In "Gusev," possibly an atypical Chekhov work, the subject is the death at sea of a simple Russian soldier returning to his village after a campaign in the East. The story gains its flavor by certain devices used to characterize the soldier, for example, a foil in the person of the "intellectual" Pavel, and to suggest the quality of his inner life, particularly the delirious dreams of Gusev's return to the snowbound village, with its terrifying motif of the bull's head without eyes, and the account of the meaningless fight with Chinese men, counterpointed by the exquisite scene of the boatmen with the canaries. As the dying Pavel bitterly chattered, "Gusev was looking at the little window and was not listening. A boat was swaying on the transparent, soft, turquoise water all bathed in hot, dazzling sunshine. In it there were naked Chinamen holding up cages with canaries and calling out: 'It sings, It sings!'" The rapid alternation of scenes in the sick bay with dream sequences and idyllic interludes such as the scenes glimpsed through the porthole, with accompanying shifts of tone, becomes a major structural device and creates an extremely vivid, surrealistic effect.

When Chekhov, like Turgenev, raises tone to the level of a major device, we see an important step away from the conventional tale of reported action (the "epical" story) toward a condition approaching that of the lyric poem. Besides freeing the short story from the limitations of conventional plot, Turgenev and Chekhov consciously exploited language itself to express more sharply states of feeling and subtle changes in emotion. With these authors, the locus of narrative art has moved from external action to internal states of mind, and the plot line will hereafter consist, in this mode, of tracing complex emotions to a closing cadence utterly unlike the reasoned resolution of the conventional cause-and-effect narrative. It is here that we observe the birth of the "open" story. Besides the use of the emotional curve, other new patterns of story organization are beginning to emerge, such as the alternation of scenes and moods for

a "surrealistic" effect, the circling around a central dilemma or set of feelings, the record of a moment of intense feeling or perception which contains its own significant form.

The English disciples of Turgenev and Chekhov, especially A. E. Coppard and Katherine Mansfield, exploited some of these innovations in
their own way. In Coppard, outward action is again strictly subordinated
to inner feelings, for all is directed to portraying the intense moment (as
in "Dusky Ruth") or in tracing its secret sources ("The Field of Mustard")
or showing the growth of personhood through deep emotional involve-
ment ("Fishmonger's Fiddle"), or the profound though fitful emergence
of individual identity ("The Hurly Burly"). Coppard, moreover, can use
language with some of the "piety," delicacy, and precision of the English
metaphysicals, as Ford Madox Ford has pointed out. In addition, an important source of his poetic effects is his carefully controlled use of setting. The closing section of "The Field of Mustard" affords a fair sampling
of the blend of these factors in Coppard's narratives as we see strong infu-
sion of feeling, delicate use of verbal devices including rhythm, continuity
of mood among character, setting and theme, and metaphoric use of natural detail. As the unhappy women huddle together along the path of their
way home from an afternoon's faggot-gathering in the autumn wood and
when each has revealed her former love for the romantic rake Rufus
Blackthorn, Rose expresses her envy for Dinah, who has at least the joy of
her children.

> "Ain't you got a fire of your own indoors?" grumbled Dinah.
>
> "Yes."
>
> "Well, why don't you set by it then!" Dinah's faggot caught the
> briars of a hedge that overhung, and she tilted round with a mild
> oath. A covey of partridges feeding beyond scurried away with ruck-
> ling cries. One foolish bird dashed into the telegraph wires and
> dropped dead.
>
> "They're good children, Dinah, yours are. And they make you a
> valentine, and give you a ribbon on your birthday, I expect?"
>
> "They're naught but a racket from cockcrow till the old man
> snores—and then its worse."
>
> "Oh, but the creatures, Dinah!"
>
> "You—you got your quiet trim house, and only your man to look
> after, a kind man, and you'll set with him in the evenings and play
> your dominoes or your draughts, and he'll look at you—the nice
> man—over the board, and stroke your hand now and again."
>
> The wind hustled the two women close together, and as they

stumbled under their burdens Dinah Lock stretched out a hand and touched the other woman's arm. "I like you, Rose, I wish you was a man."

Rose did not reply. Again they were quiet, voiceless, and thus in fading light they came to their homes. But how windy, dispossessed, and ravaged roved the darkening world! Clouds were borne frantically across the heavens, as if in a rout of battle, and the lovely earth seemed to sigh in grief at some calamity all unknown to men.

Less sure in the development of her own voice, Katherine Mansfield, like Coppard, sometimes achieves the exact balance between realistic detail and delicate suggestiveness that the lyric story demands. Occasionally, as in "The Escape," Miss Mansfield is extremely successful in her use of the epiphany to reflect and resolve emotional complexities. One or two of the earliest pieces show the author's experiments in the pastel mood-piece, for example, "Spring Pictures" and "The Wind Blows." A more sustained lyricism occurs in the mature, two-part story composed of "The Prelude" and "At the Bay." A number of readers have approached "The Prelude" as a novelistic excursus, while others see it as a naturalistic portrayal of a moment of family life and again others take it as representing the culminating appearance of the child Kezia, the autobiographical cipher for the Miss Mansfield herself. If, however, one places Linda Burnell at the center of the narrative—where she quite properly belongs—the story immediately appears as a delicate tracing of the ebb and flow of the woman's emotional life at a crucial period in her development. This life, though presented within a densely realistic context, is most effectively revealed through several powerful symbols: the dream sequences, birds, and especially the aloe tree. Growing on a grassy mound in the drive before the Burnells' house in the country, the tree occupies a focal point as well in the revelation of Linda's consciousness. The gnarled, ancient, seldom-blooming aloe, with its sharp-edged leaves and its roots clutching the earth like claws, is an effective "objective correlative" for the woman with her tangled emotional life of love and hatred, sensitivity and cruelty, fertility and sterility.

In a scene near the close of the story, the tree provides an effective culminating image for the feelings and themes the narrative has developed. As solitary as the ancient tree, Linda Burnell is obsessed by desires of fright and escape. As she and her mother leave the cribbage-playing couple in the drawing room for a moonlight walk in the cool park, this episode takes place:

"I have been looking at the aloe," said Mrs. Fairfield. "I believe it is going to flower this year. Look at the top there. Are those buds, or is it only an effect of light?"

As they stood on the steps, the high grassy bank on which the aloe rested rose up like a wave, and the aloe seemed to ride upon it like a ship with the oars lifted. Bright moonlight hung upon the lifted oars like water, and on the green wave glittered the dew.

"Do you feel it, too," said Linda . . . "Don't you feel that it is coming towards us?"

She dreamed that she was caught up out of the cold water into the ship with the lifted oars and the budding mast. Now the oars fell striking quickly, quickly. They rowed far away over the top of the garden trees, the paddocks and the dark bush beyond. Ah, she heard herself cry: "Faster! Faster!" to those who were rowing.

Thus, in an interior monologue built around mingled images of imprisonment and flight, love and hatred, Katherine Mansfield reveals the deeply complex emotional life of the protagonist, while surrounding it with a profusion of sensuous detail and minor episodes. Elizabeth Bowen has suggested that when Miss Mansfield's "other side—the high-strung susceptibility, the almost hallucinatory floatingness" unites with her "factual firmness," a unique blend of narrative qualities results. It is this occasionally successful and even eloquent combination that is Miss Mansfield's "signature" among story writers in the lyric vein.

To call D. H. Lawrence a poetic writer is, in the mouths of many, to do no more than call attention to the overpowering sensuality and passion of some of his most characteristic work or to glance at the vein of natural mysticism that occasionally gleams there. Yet when in his shorter pieces Lawrence permits structure itself to be guided by the shape of feeling he can—despite the limitations of his language—achieve a directly lyrical effect. Although overburdened with thematic considerations, a story like "The Blind Man" illustrates in part this achievement. Other pieces, like "The Christening," provide clearer examples of Lawrence's capacity to portray a group in the throes of intense and contradictory feelings while deriving the narrative's structure from the very ebb and flow of emotion.

Virginia Woolf, likewise, moves the locus of narrative from autonomous external action to interior life. Aside from their interest as illustrative of a rather well thought out epistemology and its accompanying morality, Mrs. Woolf's delicately wrought *Monday or Tuesday* pieces exemplify the use of all the arts of language at the service of narrative whose sole concern is to represent the curve of feeling. The title sketch itself, with its exquisite,

forever elusive motif of the heron in flight and its suggestion of the ultimate linking of inner and outer space, shows essentially poetic gifts at
work. "A Summing Up" and "The String Quartet," delicately sensuous
revelations of the self to itself, each with its climactic epiphany, offer excellent illustrations of Mrs. Woolf's handling of lyric narrative, although
the much-anthologized "Kew Gardens" also reveals her essential talents.
In "Kew Gardens" Mrs. Woolf depicts, with precise sensory detail and in a
strictly sustained tone of what might be called reflective torpor, the passing of a July afternoon when the garden is at the height of its beauty.
Groups of people drift along, fragmentary conversations occur, hinting
larger tragedies and comedies, a snail inches its way along a leaf. The
rhythm is languorous, the pace slow but pervaded by a current of excitement, and the whole pulsates with teeming life, an effect achieved of the
piling up of sound, smell, and color images. The opening and closing sections are classic—

> From the oval-shaped flower-bed there rose perhaps a hundred
> stalks spreading into heart-shaped or tongue-shaped leaves half-way
> up and unfurling at the tip red or blue or yellow petals marked with
> spots of colour raised upon the surface; and from the red, blue, or yel-
> low gloom of the throat emerged a straight bar, rough with gold dust
> and slightly clubbed at the end. The petals were voluminous enough
> to be stirred by the summer breeze, and when they moved, the red,
> blue and yellow lights passed one over the other, staining an inch of
> the brown earth beneath with a spot of the most intricate colour. The
> light fell either upon the smooth, grey back of a pebble, or, the shell
> of a snail with its brown, circular veins, or falling into a raindrop, it
> expanded with such intensity of red, blue and yellow the thin walls of
> water that one expected them to burst and disappear . . . Then the
> breeze stirred rather more briskly overhead and the colour was flashed
> into air above, into the eyes of the men and women who walk in Kew
> Gardens in July.

. . . .

> Thus one couple after another with much the same irregular and
> aimless movement passed the flower-bed and were enveloped in layer
> after layer of green blue vapour, in which at first their bodies had
> substance and a dash of colour, but later both substance and colour
> dissolved in the green-blue atmosphere. How hot it was! So hot that
> even the thrush chose to hop, like a mechanical bird, in the shadow of
> the flowers, with long pauses between one movement and the next;
> instead of rambling vaguely the white butterflies danced one above
> another, making with their white shifting flakes the outline of a shat-

tered column above the tallest flowers . . . Yellow and black, pink
and snow white, shapes of all these colours, men, women, and children . . . wavered and sought shade beneath the trees. . . . but
their voices went wavering from them as if they were flames lolling
from the thick waxen bodies of candles . . . Wordless voices, breaking the silence suddenly. . . . But there was no silence; all the time
the motor omnibuses were turning their wheels and changing their
gear; like a vast nest of Chinese boxes all of wrought steel turning
ceaselessly one within another the city murmured; on top of which
the voices cried aloud and the petals of myriads of flowers flashed
their colours into the air.

Virtually abandoning external action, choosing as a subject shifts of
emotion more subtle and more private than those depicted by Turgenev
or Lawrence, tracing with the diction and rhythms of the poet the "fall of
the atoms on the mind," Mrs. Woolf definitively abandoned the conventional short story to choose new subjects, new themes, new structures, and
new language. Like that of Turgenev, her work marks an almost total
break between old and new. Later writers in the lyric vein, especially the
Americans, may—with the exception of Sherwood Anderson—be viewed
as elaborators rather than discoverers in this mode.

Everyone knows the egregious failures of *Winesburg, Ohio,* but not
everyone sufficiently credits its successes. For cutting the story free once
for all from the tale, the moral fable, the romantic reverie, the journalistic
jeu, Anderson places us all in his debt, but he follows the best practitioners of the lyric story in his fusing of the skills of the naturalistic writer
with those of the poet. I have written elsewhere of his circular, hovering,
"Chinese box" structure, of the fragmentation of chronological sequence,
the repetitive, incantatory rhythmic effects, the ritualized dialogue, the
use of natural symbols, the insistence that all other narrative elements
must be subordinated to the shape and growth of the emerging emotion.
"Sophistication" and "Hands," from the *Winesburg* volume, provide respectively a less and a more disciplined example of his characteristic
achievement, although "Death in the Woods" represents his art at its
highest point.

A very different voice is that of Conrad Aiken, the only one of the lyrical short story writers who is also an accomplished poet and thus a kind of
test case. While stories like "The Dark City" and—in a different way—
"Strange Moonlight" demonstrate Aiken's mastery of sensuous detail, his
ability to create structure from interwoven motifs (see the moonlight-
gold-goldfinch-medal-peachtree cluster) and his variation of delicately
shifting tones and straightforward chronological structure for the sake of

a culminating emotion, still his fondness for the allegorical, the hallucinatory, and the lush inhibit Aiken's success with the pure lyrical narrative.

Far more relentless in curbing a tendency to romanticism is Katherine Anne Porter. The success of stories like "The Circus" rests on Miss Porter's ability to achieve maximum effect with a minimum of materials through a careful control of mood, impeccable selection of detail, and the sparest possible external action, which is in turn always responsible to the movement of inner feeling. "The Grave" is both a more profound and a more unified instance of short story art as it moves freely backward and forward in time, quietly utilizing natural symbolism and an excellent example of the epiphanic ending. Miss Porter works through indirection and omission, shunning the fulsome, the over-elaborated and the strained. At best, her work achieves the severity of structure and purity of language that mark for instance the great sonnets of our language, although her precedents are entirely within the narrative tradition. Her ability to seize a nexus of complex feeling and to capture its nuances in precise but evocative language is rivalled only by that of her contemporary and admirer, Eudora Welty.

Doubtless there are lyrical elements in Miss Welty's "Death of a Traveling Salesman," "A Worn Path," "Livvie," and "Powerhouse," stories marked by a broad range of suggestion, careful management of tone, the use of metaphor as a major structural device, and the abandonment of conventional plot sequence for the sake of the presentation of a developing emotion or pattern of feeling. The same traits appear in purer form in "A Curtain of Green" and "A Memory," the latter reminiscent in its different way of Anderson's treatment of adolescent emotion recollected in adult tranquillity. Although Miss Welty is a master of the suggestively concrete detail, she moves further away from naturalism than either Anderson or Katherine Anne Porter. Perhaps what is different in her is a greater detachment, a higher degree of negative capability, than either of the other writers possesses. Her tone is alert, yet retrospective, and she is probing springs of feeling that lie at the exact border between the silent, unconscious life of memory and desire and the daylight dream of order. Imagery and symbol (the Edenic complex in "A Curtain of Green," the picture-frame metaphor in "A Memory") are totally responsive to and consumed by passion; they not only assist expression, they are themselves "expressive." In many ways, Miss Welty's language is as delicate as Virginia Woolf's though it has nothing in it of the precious or the diffuse. One of her characteristic interests is the reconciliation of opposites, and the structural pattern of her stories sometimes arises from a dialectical movement from pole to pole of feeling or attitude.

Finally, in a discussion of the American lyrical short story, one would want to mention the work of a young writer of varied talents, John Updike. At a far reach from the expansive Olinger stories is the kind of achievement hinted at in "Sunday Teasing" (*The Same Door*) and brought much closer to fruition in the title story of *The Music School,* as well as in "Harv is Plowing Now" and "Leaves," from the same volume. In the latter story the reader is struck equally by the variety and disparity of the materials and by the faultlessness of their integration, a union created far below—or above—the level of story-line, theme, or motif. "Leaves" may best be described as a sophisticated quest story in the modern manner; at the same time it is an intense probing of the perennial question of moral guilt and of man's movement in and out of purely natural processes, and it is overlain with a profound sense of beauty, reflected or "expressed" in its own art. The manner is ostensibly descriptive and essayistic; details of action are presented in hints and indirections and kept carefully subordinated to an estimate of their effect and meaning. The issue of How to be gradually modulates to the question of What to say, thus the reflexive references to the writing of the story: "And what are these pages but leaves? Why do I produce them but to thrust, by some subjective photosynthesis, my guilt into Nature, where there is no guilt?" Updike's method of construction is to present isolated blocks of description that are yet joined by a continuity of persistent inquiry in the narrative voice. In "Leaves," the author also creates a unifying motif in the grape leaves, with their analogue in Whitman's "Leaves of Grass," to which Mr. Updike refers in the unexpectedly dramatic close of the story.

Here, then, is a sketch of the form an extended account of the development of the lyric story might take, tracing, as it will have to do, a strong line from the inception of this mode with Turgenev, through Chekhov and his English disciples, to Sherwood Anderson and such contemporaries as Eudora Welty and John Updike. Certainly, other writers will need to be taken into consideration, and the work of the authors examined here must be more fully and more carefully assessed. But even to look at the history of the short story from the point of view suggested will tend to make clear that there is, alongside the flow of the realistic, conventional, "epical" narrative that constitutes the mainstream, a parallel development of a mode which can be perfectly distinguished by its characteristic subjects, structures, tone, and language. No complete account of the growth of the serious story can afford to neglect this phase of literary history.

PART SIX

Authors on Aspects of
the Short Story

Some Aspects of
the Short Story

JULIO CORTÁZAR
Translated by Aden W. Hayes

ALMOST ALL THE stories I have written belong to the genre known as
"fantastic" for lack of a better term, and they are opposed to that false
realism which consists of believing that everything can be described and
explained as it was accepted by the scientific and philosophical optimism
of the eighteenth century; that is, within a world directed more or less
harmoniously by a system of laws, principles, cause-and-effect relations,
defined psychologies, and well-mapped geographies. In my case, the suspicion of another order, more secret and less communicable, and the rich
discovery of Alfred Jarry, for whom the true study of reality lay not in its
laws, but in the exceptions to those laws, have been some of the orienting
principles of my personal search for a literature beyond all ingenuous realism. I am certain that there exist certain constants, certain values which
hold for all short stories, fantastic or realistic, dramatic or humorous. And
I think that perhaps it is possible to show here those invariable elements
which give a good short story its peculiar atmosphere and make it a work
of art.

A discussion of the short story should interest us especially, since
almost all the Spanish-speaking countries of America give the story great
importance, which it has never had in other Latin countries like France or
Spain. As is natural among younger literatures, in our countries spon-
taneous creation almost always precedes critical examination, and that is
as it should be. No one can claim that short stories should be written only
after learning their rules. In the first place, there are no such rules; at
most one can speak of points of view, of certain constants which give a

structure to this genre which is hard to pigeonhole. In the second place, the short-story writers themselves don't have to be theoreticians and critics, and it is natural that the latter enter the scene only when there exists a body of literature which permits inquiry and clarification of its development and its qualities. In America, in Cuba, just as in Mexico or Chile or Argentina, a great number of short-story writers worked from the beginning of this century on, without knowing each other, discovering each other almost posthumously. But someday definitive anthologies will be made, as they are in Anglo-Saxon countries, for example, and we will all know just how far we've come. For the moment, I will speak of the short story in the abstract, as a literary genre.

A short story, in the final analysis, moves in that projection of man where life and the written expression of life engage in a fraternal battle, and the result of that battle is the story itself, a live synthesis as well as a synthesis of life, something like the shimmering water in a glass, the fleeting within the permanent.

Only images can transmit that secret alchemy which explains the profound resonance which a great story has within us, which in turn explains why there are so few truly great stories. To understand the peculiar character of the short story, it must be compared to the novel, a much more popular genre about which there are many options and ideas. It has been pointed out, for instance, that the novel develops on paper, and therefore in the time taken to read it, with no limits other than the exhaustion of the artistic material. For its part, the short story begins with the notion of limits—in the first place, of physical limits, so that in France, when a story exceeds twenty pages, it is called a nouvelle, something between the short story and the proper novel. In this sense, the novel and the short story can be compared analogically with the film and the photograph, since the film is, essentially, an "open order" like the novel, while a successful photo presupposes a circumscribed limitation, imposed in part by the reduced field which the camera captures and also by the way in which the photographer uses that limitation esthetically. I don't know if you have heard a professional photographer talk about his art; I have always been surprised by the fact that, in many cases, they talk much as a short-story writer might. Photographers like Cartier-Bresson or Brassai define their art as an apparent paradox: that of cutting off a fragment of reality, giving it certain limits, but in such a way that this segment acts like an explosion which fully opens a much more ample reality, like a dynamic vision which spiritually transcends the space reached by the camera. While in films, as in the novel, a more ample and multifaceted reality is captured through the development of partial and accumulative elements, which do not exclude, of course, a synthesis which will give a climax to the work. A high quality photograph or story proceeds inversely; that is, the photographer or the story writer finds himself obliged to choose and delimit an image or an event which must be meaningful, which is meaningful not only in itself, but rather is capable of acting on the viewer or the reader as a kind of opening, an impetus which projects the intelligence and the sensibility toward something which goes well beyond the visual or literary anecdote contained in the photograph or the story. An Argentine writer who is a boxing fan told me that in the struggle between an emotive text and its reader, the novel always wins on points, while the story must win by a knockout. This is true in the sense that the novel progressively accumulates effects upon the reader while a good short story is incisive, biting, giving no quarter from the first sentence. Don't take this too literally, because a good short-story writer is a very clever boxer, and many of his early blows can seem harmless when really they are undermining his adversary's most solid resistance. Take whatever great story you like and analyze its first page. I would be surprised it you found any gratuitous, merely decorative elements. The short-story writer knows he can't proceed cumulatively, that time is not his ally. His only solution is to work deeply, vertically, heading up or down in literary space. This, which seems like a metaphor, nevertheless expresses the essential aspects of the method. The story's time and space must be condemned entities, submitted to a high spiritual and formal pressure to bring about that opening I spoke of. Ask yourself why a certain story is bad. It is not bad because of the subject, because in literature there are no good or bad subjects, there is only a good or bad treatment of the subject. Nor is it bad because the characters are uninteresting, since even a stone is interesting when a Henry James or a Franz Kafka deals with it.

We said that the short-story writer works with material which we term meaningful. The story's significant element seems to reside mainly *in its subject,* in the act of choosing a real or imaginary happening which has that mysterious property of illuminating something beyond itself, to the extent that a common domestic occurrence, such as we have in so many admirable stories of a Katherine Mansfield or of a Sherwood Anderson, is converted into an implacable summary of a certain human condition or the burning symbol of a social or historical order. A story is meaningful when it ruptures its own limits with that explosion of spiritual energy which suddenly illuminates something far beyond that small and sometimes sordid anecdote which is being told. I think, for instance, of the themes of the majority of the admirable stories of Anton Chekhov. What is there in them which is not sadly ordinary, mediocre, often conformist or uselessly rebellious? What is told in these stories is almost like what we, as children, shared with our elders in boring gatherings; we heard our grandparents or our aunts tell the little insignificant family tales of frustrated ambitions, of local dramas, of living-room anguish, of a piano, of tea and cakes. But nevertheless, the stories of Katherine Mansfield, of Chekhov are significant; something explodes in them while we read them, and it offers us a kind of break in daily routine which goes well beyond the anecdote described. You will have realized by now that the mysterious significance does not lie only in the subject of the story, because really, the majority of the bad stories which we have all read contain episodes like those treated by the authors we've mentioned. The idea of significance is worthless if we do not relate it to the ideas of intensity and tension, which refer to the technique used to develop the subject. And this is where the sharp distinction is made between the good and the bad short-story writer.

A story writer is a man who, surrounded by the din and clamor of the world, and bound, to a greater or lesser degree, to the historical reality which holds him, suddenly chooses a certain subject and makes a story out of it, and this choosing of a subject is not so simple. Sometimes the story writer elects his subject and other times he feels as if it were imposed on him irresistibly; it forces him to write it. In my case, the great majority of my stories were written outside my will, above or below my conscious reasoning, as if I were no more than a medium through which an alien force passed and took shape. But this, which can depend on the individual temperament, does not change the essential fact, that in a certain moment, there is a subject, be it invented, chosen voluntarily, or strangely imposed from a plane where nothing is definable.

It seems to me that the subject from which a good story will emerge is always exceptional, but I don't mean by this that a subject must be extraordinary, uncommon, mysterious, or singular. On the contrary, it can be about a perfectly trivial and everyday occurrence. It is exceptional in that it is like a magnet: a good subject attracts an entire system of connected stories, it solidifies in the author, and later in the reader, many notions, glimpses, sentiments, and even ideas which virtually were floating in his memory or his sensibility. A good subject is like a good sun, a star with a planetary system around it of which, many times, we were unaware until the story writer, an astronomer of words, revealed it to us. Or rather, to be more modest and more up to date at the same time, a good subject has something of the atomic about it, a nucleus around which the electrons whirl; and, when all is said and done, isn't this a proposal of life, a dynamic which urges us to get outside ourselves and enter a more complex and more beautiful system of relations? Many times I have asked myself: What is the essential quality of certain unforgettable stories? At the same time we read them we read many others, which can even be by the same authors. And yet the years pass, and we live, and forget everything else, but those little, insignificant stories, those grains of sand in the immense sea of literature are still there, throbbing, pulsating inside us. Isn't it true that everyone has his own collection of stories? I have mine, and I can give you some names. I have Poe's "William Wilson," Maupassant's "Ball of Tallow," Truman Capote's "A Christmas Memory," Jorge Luis Borges's "Tlön, Uqbar, Orbis Tertius," Juan Carlos Onetti's "A Dream Come True," Tolstoy's "Death of Ivan Ilyitch," Hemingway's "Fifty Grand," Isak Dinesen's "The Dreamers," and I could go on and on. You will have noticed that not all these stories are a must for every anthology. Why do they remain in my memory? Think of the stories you haven't been able to forget and you will see that they have the same characteristic. They bring together a reality which is infinitely more vast than that of the simple anecdote, and that is why they have influenced us with a power which we would not suspect from the modesty of the apparent content and the brevity of their texts. And that man who, in a given moment, chooses a subject and turns it into a story will be a great writer if his selection contains, sometimes without his conscious knowledge of it, that fabulous opening from the small to the large, from the individual and circumscribed to the very essence of the human condition.

Nevertheless, we must clear up this notion of meaningful subjects. The same subject can be profoundly significant for one writer and insipid for another; the same subject will resound loudly, awaken enormous interest in one reader, and will leave another indifferent. In sum, we can say that there are no subjects which are absolutely insignificant. There is a mysterious and complex alliance between a certain writer and a certain subject in a given moment, just as there can be the same alliance later between certain stories and certain readers. This seems the right time to mention something which often happens to me and to my friends who are writers. Frequently in the course of a conversation someone will recount an amusing or moving or strange episode and then, addressing himself to the story writer present, will say: "There you have a great subject for a story; it's yours, I'll give it to you." I've been given heaps, tons of subjects in this way, and I've always answered kindly, "Thank you very much," and I've never written a story with any one of them. But once a friend was distractedly telling me about the adventures of one of her maids in Paris. As I listened to her story, I felt it could become a story. For her, those episodes were no more than curious anecdotes; for me they suddenly took on a meaning which went far beyond their simple and common content.

That is why, every time I am asked "How can you distinguish between an insignificant subject, no matter how interesting and emotional it might be, and another, significant one?" I have replied that the writer is the first to feel that undefinable but captivating effect of certain subjects, and that is precisely why he is a writer. Just as for Marcel Proust, the taste of a madeleine dipped in tea would open an immense fan of memories which were apparently forgotten, so the writer reacts to certain subjects in the same way in which, later on, the reader will react to his story. All this is predetermined by the sensation, by the irresistible fascination that the subject creates in its creator.

The story writer stands before his subject, before that embryo which already is life, but which has not yet taken on its final form. For him that subject makes sense, it has meaning. But if everything could be reduced to that, it would mean very little. Now, as the last state of the process, like an implacable judge, awaits the reader, the final link in the creative process, determining the success or failure of the cycle. And it is now that the story must become a bridge, it must become a passage, it must give a start which projects its initial meaning, already discovered by the author, to this recipient who is more passive, less aware, and often indifferent, the reader. Unskilled story writers mistakenly imagine that simply writing smoothly and flatly about a subject which has impressed them will impress the reader, too. They show the same kind of ingenuousness as someone who thinks his child is beautiful, and takes it for granted that everyone else finds him beautiful as well. With time and with his failures the story writer who is capable of overcoming that first, rather simpleminded phase learns that in literature, good intentions are not enough. He discovers that to recreate in the reader that fervent emotion which prompted him to write the story, he must possess the craft of a writer, and that craft consists, among other things, of creating that climate of every great story which forces us to keep reading, which captures our attention, and which isolates the reader from everything around him so that later, after he has finished the story, he can go back and link it to his own situation in a new, enriched way, a deeper or more beautiful way. And the writer can momentarily kidnap the reader only with a style based on intensity and tension, a style in which the formal and expressive elements totally adapt themselves to the essence of the subject. They give it a penetrating and original visual and auditory form; they make it unique, unforgettable; they fix it forever in its time, in its place, and in its most primordial sense. What I call intensity in a story consists of the elimination of all intermediary ideas or situations, of all the filler and transitional material that the novel permits and even demands. Probably none of you has forgotten "The

Cask of Amontillado" by Edgar Allan Poe. The extraordinary aspect of this story is the sweeping omission of all description of the ambience. By the third or fourth sentence we are already in the heart of the action, witnessing the inexorable fulfillment of revenge. Hemingway's "The Killers" is another example of the intensity obtained by the elimination of everything which does not bear directly upon the action. But let us think now of the stories of Joseph Conrad, D. H. Lawrence, Kafka. In them, each in its own way, the intensity is of another type, which I prefer to call tension. It is an intensity wrought because the author brings us slowly to what is related. Even while we are still far from learning what will occur in the story, we cannot escape the story's atmosphere. In the case of "The Cask of Amontillado" and "The Killers," the events, stripped of all introduction, engulf us and snare us. By contrast, in a gradual and rich story by Henry James, "The Lesson of the Master," for example, one feels immediately that the facts themselves are of little importance, that all that matters is in the forces that unleash them, in the subtle web which announces them and accompanies them. But both the intensity of action and the internal tension of the story are products of what I before called the craft of the writer, and it is here that we approach the end of this little tour of the short story.

In my country and now in Cuba, I have read stories by a great variety of authors, young and old, from the city and from the countryside, drawn to literature for esthetic reasons and by social pressures of the moment, radically committed and uncommitted. Well then, even if it sounds self-evident, in Argentina as well as here, the good stories are being written by those who know their craft, in the sense that I have used the term. An example from Argentina can make this more clear. In many of our central and northern provinces there exists a long tradition of oral tales which the gauchos told in the evenings around a campfire and which fathers still tell to their children. When a regionalist writer gets hold of these tales, the surprising majority are turned into very bad short stories. What has happened? The tales themselves are good, they translate and synthesize the experience, the sense of humor, and the fatalism of the men of the countryside. Some even reach tragic or poetic dimensions. When you hear them from the mouth of an old native of the region, while sipping glasses of maté, you feel something like an abolition of time, and you think that the Greek bards told the deeds of Achilles in the same way, to the wonderment of shepherds and travelers. But then, just when a Homer should appear, one who would make an *Iliad* or an *Odyssey* of that collection of oral traditions, in my country a gentleman turns up who thinks that the culture of the cities is a sign of decadence, according to whom the story writers we all love are esthetes who write for the sole delight of the leisure classes; and that gentleman believes that to write a story, you have only to record the traditional tale, conserving as much as possible of the spoken tone, the rustic turns of phrases, the faulty grammar, the stuff called local color. I don't know if that method of writing popular stories is cultivated in Cuba. I hope not, because in my country it has produced only indigestible volumes which interest neither the men of the countryside, who prefer to continue listening to stories between drinks, nor the readers from the city.

On the other hand, and again I refer to Argentina, we have had writers like Roberto J. Payró, Ricardo Güiraldes, Horacio Quiroga, and Benito Lynch, who, often beginning with very traditional subjects they heard from the mouths of the old settlers like a Don Segundo Sombra, have known how to develop this material and turn it into works of art. But Quiroga, Güiraldes, and Lynch knew the writer's craft well. They accepted only meaningful and enriching subjects, just as Homer must have tossed out many magical and bellicose episodes in order to use only those which have come down to us because of their enormous mythic force, their resounding mental archetypes, or "psychic hormones," as Ortega y Gasset called myths. Quiroga, Güiraldes, and Lynch were writers of universal dimensions without local or ethnic or populist prejudices; that is why, after carefully choosing the subjects of their tales, they forced all their ferment, all their deep or towering projection into a literary form, the only one capable of transmitting their values to the reader. They wrote tensely; they showed intensely. There is no other way for a story to work to hit the bull's-eye of the reader and stick in his memory.

The example I have cited could be of interest to Cuba. Obviously, the revolution offers infinite possibilities to the story writer: the city, the countryside, the struggle, work, different psychological types, conflicts of ideology and character; and all this exacerbated by your visible desire to express yourselves, to communicate yourselves as you never have been permitted to do before. But how is all this to be translated into great stories, into stories which reach the reader with force and power? Here I would like to apply concretely what I have already said on a more abstract level. Enthusiasm and goodwill by themselves are not enough, just as the craft of the writer alone is not enough to write stories which establish literarily (that is, in the collective admiration, in the memory of a people) the greatness of this revolution in progress. Here, more than anywhere else, a total fusion of the two forces is required, that of the man totally committed to his national and world reality and that of the writer clearly sure of his craft. In this there can be no mistake. No matter how experienced, no matter how good a story writer is, if he hasn't a deep affection or if his stories are not born of a profound sense of life, his work won't get beyond a simple esthetic exercise. But the opposite would be even worse because the fervor, the will to transmit a message are worth nothing if the stylistic and expressive instruments, which make communication possible, are missing. We are now at a crucial point in the problem. I believe, and I say this after having carefully weighed all the elements concerned, that to write for a revolution does not mean, as many think, that we must write about the revolution itself. In the revolutionary writer a freely chosen individual and collective commitment is joined to the cultural freedom conferred by the mastery of his craft. If that responsible and lucid writer decides to write fantastic literature, or psychological literature, or return-to-the-past literature, his act is still an act within the revolution, even though his stories do not concern themselves with the individual and collective practices which the revolution adopts. Contrary to the criteria of many people who confuse literature with pedagogy, literature with teaching, literature with ideological indoctrination, a revolutionary writer has every right to address a reader who is much more complex, much more spiritually demanding than that reader imagined by inexperienced writers and critics who are convinced that their personal world is the only world that exists, that the concerns of the moment are the only valid concerns. Let us repeat Hamlet's admirable statement to Horatio, applying it to all that surrounds us in Cuba: "There are more things in heaven and earth . . . than are dreamt of in your philosophy." A writer's work is not foreign to the revolution just because it may not be accessible to everyone. On the contrary, this demonstrates that there is a great body of potential readers who in a certain sense are much more divorced than the writer from the goals of the revolution, from those goals of culture, of freedom, of fulfillment of life which the Cubans have set up to the admiration of everyone who cares for Cuba and understands it. The higher the aims of the writers dedicated to this, the higher the ultimate goals of their nation. Watch out for the facile demagogy of those who demand a literature accessible to everyone! Many do so only because of their evident incapacity to understand more ambitious works. They loudly demand subjects of the people without suspecting that often the reader, no matter how unsophisticated he is, will distinguish instinctively between a poorly written popular story and a more difficult and complex story which will force him to leave, for a moment, his circumscribed little world and will show him something else, no matter what it is, but something different. Stories about popular subjects will be good if, like any other story, they are guided by the demanding and difficult internal mechanics stated earlier. Years ago I saw proof of this in Argentina among a group of men from the countryside which a few of us writers visited. Someone read a story based on an episode of our war of independence, written with deliberate simplicity to put it, as the writer said, "at the level of the country people." The story was heard politely, but it was easy to see that it hadn't struck home. Then one of us read "The Monkey's Paw," the deservedly famous story of W. W. Jacobs. The interest, the emotion, the surprise, and finally the enthusiasm, were extraordinary. I remember that we spent the rest of the night talking about witchcraft, sorcerers, and diabolical revenge. And I'm sure that Jacobs's story is still alive in the memories of those illiterate gauchos, while the supposedly popular story, written with them in mind, with its vocabulary, its obvious content, and its patriotic causes, must be as forgotten as the writer who made it. I have seen the emotion of unsophisticated people provoked by a presentation of *Hamlet,* a difficult and subtle work if ever there was one, which is still the subject of learned studies and infinite controversies. It is true that those people cannot understand many of the matters which excite the specialists in Elizabethan theater. But what does that matter? Only their emotion matters, their wonderment and their excitement over the tragedy of the young Prince of Denmark. All of which proves that Shakespeare truly wrote for the common man, in the sense that his subject was deeply significant to everyone, on different levels, yes, but available to some extent to everyone. And the theatrical treatment of that subject had the intensity which belongs to great writers, thanks to which even the most rigid barriers fall and men accept each other and fraternize on a level which transcends culture. Naturally, it would be ingenuous to believe that every great work can be understood and admired by untutored people; this is not the case, nor can it be. But the admiration provoked by Greek or Shakespearean tragedies, the passionate interest which is aroused by many difficult stories and novels, should make those partisans of the evil known as "popular art" suspect that their idea of "the people" is biased, unjust, and, in the last analysis, dangerous. You do the people no favors if you offer them a literature which they can assimilate without effort, passively, like those who go to the cinema to see cowboy movies. The people must be educated, that is the first step, a pedagogical and not a literary task. It has been a gratifying experience for me to see how, in Cuba, the writers I most admire participate in the revolution, giving the best of themselves, without sacrificing any of their possibilities on the altar of a supposedly popular art which will be of no use to anyone. One day Cuba will reckon with a group of stories and novels which will have transposed today's revolutionary saga to the esthetic plane, to the timeless dimension of art. But these works will not have been written because of duty or obligation or on order. Their subjects will appear when the time is right, when the writer feels he must mold them into stories or novels or plays or poems. These subjects will contain an authentic, profound message because they will not have been chosen out of a need to teach or to proselytize, but rather because of an irresistible force upon the author; and he, using all the resources of his art and technique, sacrificing nothing to anyone, will transmit his work to the reader in the way all fundamental things are transmitted: from blood to blood, from hand to hand, from person to person.

The Faber Book of
Modern Short Stories

ELIZABETH BOWEN

THE SHORT STORY is a young art: as we now know it, it is the child of this century. Poetic tautness and clarity are so essential to it that it may be said to stand at the edge of prose; in its use of action it is nearer to drama than to the novel. The cinema, itself busy with a technique, is of the same generation: in the last thirty years the two arts have been accelerating together. They have affinities—neither is sponsored by a tradition; both are, accordingly, free; both, still, are self-conscious, show a self-imposed discipline and regard for form; both have, to work on, immense matter— the disoriented romanticism of the age. The new literature, whether written or visual, is an affair of reflexes, of immediate susceptibility, of associations not examined by reason: it does not attempt a synthesis. Narrative of any length involves continuity, sometimes a forced continuity: it is here that the novel too often becomes invalid. But action, which must in the novel be complex and motivated, in the short story regains heroic simplicity.

An art having behind it little tradition is at once impetuous and halting, and is very affectable. Its practitioners are still tentative, watching each other: some positive and original mind is wanted to renew impetus, or to direct it. The short story as an art has come into being through a disposition to see life in a certain way. But the writer himself may stay unaware of this new disposition if he has not already seen it made evident elsewhere in art: only the rare writer does not look for a precedent. In England, the limitations of narrative prose with its *longueurs,* its conventions dangerous to truth, had appeared for a long time to be impassable: oblique narration, cutting (as in the cinema), the unlikely placing of emphasis, or symbolism (the telling use of the object both for its own sake and as an image) were unknown. The short story was once the condensed novel; it needed a complex subject and depended for merit on the skill with which condensation had been effected. The short stories of James and Hardy show, in their excellence, a sober virtuosity: they are *tours de force* by practised executants, side-issues from the crowded imagination. They show, *qua* the short story, no urgent aesthetic necessity; their matter does not dictate their form. Their shortness is not positive; it is nonextension. They are great architects' fancies, little buildings on an august plan. They have no emotion that is abrupt and special; they do not give mood or incident a significance outside the novelist's power to explore. Their very excellence made them a dead end: they did not invite imitation or advance in any way a development in the short story proper. That impetus that it needed, the English short story had to get from abroad. Rumour, the translation and easier circulation of foreign books, also a widening curiosity, brought Tchehov and Maupassant into the English view.

The influences of two foreign masters on an affectable new form have necessarily run counter to one another. Tchehov stands (or stands with us) for an emancipation of faculties, for a romantic distension of the form of the story to let in what might appear inchoate or nebulous. Maupassant stands for astringency, iron relevance. Tchehov opened up for the writer tracts of emotional landscape; he made subjectivity edit and rule experience and pull art, obliquely, its way. His work was a system of irritations beautified; he secreted over the grit inside his shell. His hero was the sub-man; he crystallized frustration, inertia, malaise, vacancy, futile aspiration, shy or sly pretentiousness. He dragged that involuntary sub-life of the spirit up into the impassive light of art. The suffering, too-intelligent and submissive bourgeois is typified in him; he came of that class which fosters its own annihilation, and which revolution cannot obliterate. He was, in art's sense, a political force in art, revolting against the aristocratic rejection of matter for manner's sake. He made his own manner, commanding it so completely as to suggest less discipline than it had—and this has, on the whole, made him a dangerous influence. He has been made to sponsor self-concern, license, fortuity.

Maupassant was the born popular writer, battered by Flaubert into austerity. His themes were simple: lust, cruelty, money and that sort of rose-pink fancy that has such a charnel underneath. He transcribed passions in the only terms possible—dispassionate understatement. There was an uninterrupted communication between his thought and his senses; his sort of erotic nearness to what he wrote of gave him a cautious language that never exceeds art. He saw life in a glare; life composed itself for him into pictures in primary colours, outlines in black chalk. His writing was energetic, ruthless, nervous and plain. Tchehov sustained with his subject a sensitive, sometimes painful, flirtation: Maupassant touched nothing of which he was not the prey. His hardness and capability made him that rare thing—the first-rate *unliterary* writer.

Till lately, Maupassant has repelled the bulk of the English, or has been read for reasons not connected with art. His work shows unhuman fire, like an animal's eye; his uncomplexity is not sympathetic. His finish appeared to have a touch of the shop about it, a faded smartness not yet fully 'period.' He had not been taught impersonality for nothing: the artist without tricks very seldom starts a school. Tchehov's cloudy detachment, charged with pity, has been more acceptable here; his deceptive looseness got him imitators. Tchehov started in England a new, a prose romanticism, romanticism of suburbs and provinces. He influenced at second-hand, through the work of Katherine Mansfield, a group of writers who did not know him directly, or only turned to him later. This group is now in turn exerting an influence, so that Tchehov may be indirectly copied by writers who do not read, or intend to read, him at all. It is arguable that, had Tchehov not been translated and first given his vogue by a few eclectics, a large body of English stories might have remained unwritten. He was a great incentive, but should not be a model. He has been devoutly and unconsciously parodied; we have suffered outpourings of minor dismay, or mediocre sentiment. From the dregs of his influence our most vital short story writers now seem to revolt.

This cult of Tchehov has had, however, its natural boundaries. The Irish Sea makes a bigger break in sentiment than the Atlantic, and Irish and American writers of the short story have—for all their differences in temper—strong common qualities. Extraverted coldness in art, objectivity, may be the fruit of a life that is, or has been lately, physically exciting or uncertain, life that is quick, rough or lived at high nervous tension, in which either sexual or political passion makes society unsafe. Precipitate feeling makes for hard form in art. The younger Irish writers have almost all carried arms; American civilization keeps the Americans, nervously, armed men: fact there overtops fantasy. There is a state of living in which events assault the imagination, stunning it: such a state of living enforces its own, a now no longer unique, literature. Amazement—involuntary and to a degree fathomed—is part of poetry. In the short story, semi-poetic, amazement is not only not fathomed but not stated; but has to be made evident. The writer must so strip fact of neutralizing elements as to return to it, and prolong for it, its first power: what was in life a half-second of apprehension must be perpetuated. The extraverted short story—

bare of analysis, sparse in emotional statement—is the formula for, never the transcript of, that amazement with which poetry deals. The particular must be given general significance. Narration is bound to be exact and impassive. This method, which was Maupassant's, is now in the hands of the Irish, the Americans, some of the younger English. Liam O'Flaherty, Hemingway have perfected it. It has dangers, which are now becoming apparent—style may be too much deflated, feeling is threatened with an oversimplification that makes it savage and dull.

Properly, this collection—which invites the reader to study the development of the short story in English since, roughly, 1910, to notice its variations and watch its trend—ought to include the work of Americans. The superiority, in general, of the American short story to the British has been too eagerly claimed on the far side of the Atlantic, but this is not enough to make the claim invalid. The American level of workmanship is higher; also, to-day, from the American pen our used language starts with new vitality. The American story writer has as his matter a hybrid psychology, city life at once slick and macabre and a wide continent not yet at all fully explored by art—and he has the habit of travel. The inclusion, here, of American short stories would heighten the standard of the collection and make for a wider view. But it would mean the exclusion, to make space, of a number of English stories equally vital and serious, if not so finished in their carrying-out. Moreover, the best American writing is as positively American as French writing is French: its imposing foreignness must raise all sorts of issues not relevant to the study of English work. The English short story—however much it may have owed, initially, to abroad—must advance always inside the national limitations. Irish short stories are included because the tie between the two countries, however irksome, has made some kind of affinity, however artificial. On the Irish side, indignation has been fruitful; the long, hopeless, romantic quarrel has bred literature. And in Ireland the English language is not yet stale.

Protection in art is only justified by a fairly strong claim for the home product. Such a claim the stories here will have to substantiate. To select them was not easy. In this country, within the past fifteen years, the non-commercial or free short story—that is to say, the story unsuitable, not meant to be suitable, for the popular, well-paying magazines, and free, therefore, not to conform with so-called popular taste—has found a wider opening: it has come to have an eclectic vogue. Production in this department has consequently increased. But, unhappily, the free story is being fostered with less discrimination than good faith. It is too generally taken that a story by *being* non-commercial may immediately pretend to art.

Emancipation from commercial conventions was excellent—but now a fresh set of conventions threatens to spring up and to prove as tyrannous, dangerous to living work. Too many free stories show, both in technique and subject, a desolating and nerveless similarity. The public gets slated by the free short story's promoters for not giving such stories a more grateful reception, or supporting the magazines in which they appear. But why should anyone tolerate lax, unconvincing or arty work—work whose idiom too often shows a touch of high-hat complacency? The commercial short story writer had his own, hard-learnt, competence: the new, non-commercial story, if it is to be important, should be able to make its way, any distance, on its intrinsic merits—it still has to be, in one sense or another, subsidized. Subsidy dishonours what ought to be, in the great sense, a popular art. At present, a very large number of free stories lack verisimilitude, are pompous, dissatisfying—they are not up to the mark. But what is the mark?

The mark is, the completeness, or spherical perfection, latent in any story that is projected rightly; a completeness to which any story having the germ of real life should be capable of expanding, but which too few reach—at an indefinable moment the writer's purpose slackens, or some adventitious emotion starts to deform the story. The first necessity for the short story, at the set out, is *necessariness.* The story, that is to say, must spring from an impression or perception pressing enough, acute enough, to have made the writer write. Execution must be voluntary and careful, but conception should have been involuntary, a vital fortuity. The sought-about-for subject gives the story a dead kernel, however skilfully words may have been applied: the language, being *voulu,* remains inorganic. Contrived, unspontaneous feeling makes for unquickened prose. The story should have the valid central emotion and inner spontaneity of the lyric; it should magnetize the imagination and give pleasure—of however disturbing, painful or complex a kind. The story should be as composed, in the plastic sense, and as visual as a picture. It must have tautness and clearness; it must contain no passage not æsthetically relevant to the whole. The *necessary* subject dictates its own relevance. However plain or lively or unpretentious be the manner of the story, the central emotion—emotion however remotely involved or hinted at—should be austere, major. The subject must have implicit dignity. If in the writer half-conscious awe of his own subject be lacking, the story becomes flooded with falseness, mawkishness, whimsicality or some ulterior spite. The plot, whether or not it be ingenious or remarkable, for however short a way it is to be pursued, ought to raise some issue, so that it may continue in the mind. The art of the short story permits a break at what in the novel would be the crux of the plot: the short story, free from the *longueurs* of the novel, is also exempt from the novel's conclusiveness—too often forced and false: it may thus more nearly than the novel approach æsthetic and moral truth. It can, while remaining rightly prosaic and circumstantial, give scene, action, event, character a poetic new actuality. It must have had, to the writer, moments of unfamiliarity, where it imposed itself.

The writer's imagination must operate in the world, whether factual or fantastic, that is most natural to it. The one nineteenth-century writer, in English, of the short story proper, Edgar Allan Poe, dealt almost wholly in fantasy: in England, in the same century, the much humbler F. Anstey, with a few little-known stories, followed. Since Poe's day, it has been the English rather than the Americans who have occupied the fantastic domain. Pure, objectified or projected fantasy (as opposed to private, escapist fantasy, or to *Bovaryisme*) stays, on the whole, with our older writers, or writers early in time, such as Richard Middleton, who died young by his own act. Rudyard Kipling and H. G. Wells, with some of their greatest stories, Walter de la Mare, E. M. Forster, Algernon Blackwood and M. R. James have each added to a terribly likely world, whose oddness has a super-rationality, which is waiting just at the edge of normal experience. Younger writers have, now and then, each projected his own ray into it. The fantasy story has often a literary beauty that is disarming; the one test one can apply is: does the *imagination* find this credible? Any crazy house against moonlight might, like the House of Usher, split right down to show the moon: there is assent at once, but no way to check up. Fancy has an authority reason cannot challenge. The pure fantasy writer works in a free zone: he has not to reconcile inner and outer images.

There is only one pure (or externalized) fantasy story in this book: the separate nature and problems of the fantasy story set it apart; also, the general trend of the short story has been, lately, towards inward, or, as it were, applied and functional fantasy, which does not depart from life but tempers it. Pure (as opposed to applied) fantasy has, it is true, reappeared in the apocalyptic writing of Dylan Thomas: the delirium or the dream. This may be another beginning. Up to now, however, and during most of the period this collection covers, writers have, rather, tended to explore and annotate different kinds of escape or of compensation. The retreat from fact that private fantasy offers has been as grateful in life as its variations are fascinating to art. Man has to live how he can: overlooked and dwarfed he makes himself his own theatre. Is the drama inside heroic or pathological? Outward acts have often an inside magnitude. The short story, within its shorter span than the novel's, with its freedom from forced complexity, its possible lucidness, is able, like the poetic drama, to measure man by his aspirations and dreads and place him alone on that stage which, inwardly, every man is conscious of occupying alone.

The Flash
of Fireflies

NADINE GORDIMER

WHY IS IT that while the death of the novel is good for post-mortem at
least once a year, the short story lives on unmolested? It cannot be
because—to borrow their own jargon—literary critics regard it as merely
a minor art form. Most of them, if pressed, would express the view that it
is a highly specialized and skilful form, closer to poetry, etc. But they
would have to be pressed; otherwise they wouldn't bother to discuss it at
all. When Chekhov crops up, it is as a playwright, and Katherine Mansfield is a period personality from the Lady Chatterley set. Yet no one suggests that we are practicing a dead art form. And, like a child suffering
from healthy neglect, the short story survives.

"To say that no one now much likes novels is to exaggerate very little.
The large public which used to find pleasure in prose fictions prefer movies, television, journalism, and books of 'fact,'" Gore Vidal wrote recently
(*Encounter,* December 1967). If the cinema and television have taken
over so much of the novel's territory, just as photography forced painting
into wastelands which may or may not be made to bloom, hasn't the short
story been overrun, too? This symposium is shoptalk and it would seem
unnecessary for us to go over the old definitions of where and how the
short story differs from the novel, but the answer to the question must lie
somewhere here. Both novel and story use the same material: human experience. Both have the same aim: to communicate it. Both use the same
medium: the written word. There is a general and recurrent dissatisfaction with the novel as a means of netting ultimate reality—another term
for the quality of human life—and inevitably there is even a tendency to
blame the tools: words have become hopelessly blunted by overuse, dinned

to death by admen, and, above all, debased by political creeds that have twisted and changed their meaning. Various ways out have been sought. In England, a return to classicism in technique and a turning to the exoticism of sexual aberration and physical and mental abnormality as an extension of human experience and therefore of subject matter; in Germany and America, a splendid abandon in making a virtue of the vice of the novel's inherent clumsiness by stuffing it not with nineteenth-century horsehair narrative but twentieth-century anecdotal-analytical plastic foam; in France, the "laboratory novel" struggling to get away from the anthropocentric curse of the form and the illusion of depth of the psychological novel, and landing up very much where Virginia Woolf was, years ago, staring at the mark on the wall. Burroughs has invented the reader-participation novel. For the diseased word, George Steiner has even suggested silence.

If the short story is alive while the novel is dead, the reason must lie in approach and method. The short story as a form and as *a kind of creative vision* must be better equipped to attempt the capture of ultimate reality at a time when (whichever way you choose to see it) we are drawing nearer to the mystery of life or are losing ourselves in a bellowing wilderness of mirrors, as the nature of that reality becomes more fully understood or more bewilderingly concealed by the discoveries of science and the proliferation of communication media outside the printed word.

Certainly the short story always has been more flexible and open to experiment than the novel. Short-story writers always have been subject at the same time to both a stricter technical discipline and a wider freedom than the novelist. Short-story writers have known—and solved by nature of their choice of form—what novelists seem to have discovered in despair only now: the strongest convention of the novel, prolonged coherence of tone, to which even the most experimental of novels must conform unless it is to fall apart, is false to the nature of whatever can be grasped of human reality. How shall I put it? Each of us has a thousand lives and a novel gives a character only one. *For the sake of the form.* The novelist may juggle about with chronology and throw narrative overboard; all the time his characters have the reader by the hand, there is a consistency of relationship throughout the experience that cannot and does not convey the quality of human life, where contact is more like the flash of fireflies, in and out, now here, now there, in darkness. Short-story writers see by the light of the flash; theirs is the art of the only thing one can be sure of—the present moment. Ideally, they have learned to do without explanation of what went before, and what happens beyond this point. How the characters will appear, think, behave, comprehend, tomorrow or at any other time in their lives, is irrelevant. A discrete moment of truth is aimed at—not *the* moment of truth, because the short story doesn't deal in cumulatives.

The problem of how best to take hold of ultimate reality, from the technical and stylistic point of view, is one that the short-story writer is accustomed to solving specifically in relation to an area—event, mental state, mood, appearance—which is heightenedly manifest in a single situation. Take fantasy for an example. Writers are becoming more and more aware of the waviness of the line that separates fantasy from the so-called rational in human perception. It is recognized that fantasy is no more than a shift in angle; to put it another way, the rational is simply another, the most obvious, kind of fantasy. Writers turn to the less obvious fantasy as a wider lens on ultimate reality. But this fantasy is something that changes, merges, emerges, disappears as a pattern does viewed through the bottom of a glass. It is true for the moment when one looks down through the glass; but the same vision does not transform everything one sees, consistently throughout one's whole consciousness. Fantasy in the hands of short-story writers is so much more successful than when in the hands of novelists because it is necessary for it to hold good only for the brief illumination of the situation it dominates. In the series of developing situations of the novel the sustainment of the tone of fantasy becomes a high-pitched ringing in the reader's ears. How many fantasy novels achieve what they set out to do: convey the shift and change, to and fro, beneath, above, and around the world of appearances? The short story recognizes that full comprehension of a particular kind in the reader, like full apprehension of a particular kind in the writer, is something of limited duration. The short story is a fragmented and restless form, a matter of hit or miss, and it is perhaps for this reason that it suits modern consciousness—which seems best expressed as flashes of fearful insight alternating with near-hypnotic states of indifference.

These are technical and stylistic considerations. Marxist criticism sees the survival of an art form in relation to social change. What about the socio-political implications of the short story's survival? George Lukács has said that the novel is a bourgeois art form whose enjoyment presupposes leisure and privacy. It implies the living room, the armchair, the table lamp; just as epic implies the illiterates round the tribal storyteller, and Shakespeare implies the two audiences—that of the people and that of the court—of a feudal age. From this point of view the novel marks the apogee of an exclusive, individualist culture; the nearest it ever got to a popular art form (in the sense of bringing people together in direct participation in an intellectually stimulating experience) was the nineteenth-century custom of reading novels aloud to the family. Here again it would seem that the short story shares the same disadvantages as the novel. It is an art form solitary in communication; yet another sign of the increasing loneliness and isolation of the individual in a competitive society. You cannot enjoy the experience of a short story unless you have certain minimum conditions of privacy in which to read it; and these conditions are those of middle-class life. But of course a short story, by reason of its length and its *completeness,* totally contained in the brief time you give to it, depends less than the novel upon the classic conditions of middle-class life, and perhaps corresponds to the breakup of that life which is taking place. In that case, although the story may outlive the novel, it may become obsolete when the period of disintegration is replaced by new social forms and the art forms that express them. One doesn't have to embrace the dreariness of conventional "social realism" in literature to grant this. That our age is threshing about desperately for a way out of individual human isolation, and that our present art forms are not adequate to it, it is obvious to see in all the tatty dressing-up games, from McLuhan's theories to pop art, in which we seek a substitute for them.

This symposium is also concerned with the short story as a means of earning a living. I'd like to say here that I have never understood why writers are always asked bluntly what they earn (as if we were children, whose pocket money must be flatteringly exclaimed over) while businessmen would never be expected to reveal the intimacies of tax return and bank balance. I'd like to think that this is because they know we're after something more than money; and it's *that* they're not old enough to know about. . . . Snobberies aside, writing stories is generally regarded as the most unlikely way of earning money, only just less hopeless than writing poetry. It goes without saying that publishers nurture their short-story writers mainly in the hope that they will write novels sooner or later. And yet I believe that writers of short stories (I'm not talking about popular hacks, of course) have more chance of working without compromise than novelists have. The novel that doesn't sell represents anything from one to five years' work—years that, economically speaking, then, the locusts have eaten. If a short story doesn't find a home (and sometimes one's more interesting stories must wait until the particular review or anthology, in which their quality is recognized, comes along), it does not represent the same loss in terms of working time. Other stories have been written within the same few months or the same year that enable the writer to go on eating. The novelist whose book sells poorly may have to turn to some other means of earning, during the next few years while he is writing (or would like to write) another novel—the journalism, teaching, etc., that takes him away from the only work he really cares to do. The short-story writer, with less capital tied up over a long period of time, as it were, has a better chance of keeping the integrity of assiduity to his own work. Also, once out of the best-seller class (and this would include a majority of serious novels, and virtually all experimental ones) a novel is dead, so far as sales are concerned, after a year. A short-story collection often represents stories that before book publication have earned money through individual publication in magazines, and which will continue to earn, long after publication and sale of the book, through individual publication in anthologies. I know that certain stories of mine are still earning money for me, fifteen years after they were written.

Although my novels have always sold better, initially, than my story collections, and now and then I have had unexpected windfalls from novels (mainly through translations), I think I can say that my short stories have provided my bread-and-butter earnings. (And this despite the fact that there are two of the highest-paying American magazines to whom my work is not offered, because I should not like to see it published in them.) Of course, part of the reason is that quite a large number of my stories have been published in *The New Yorker*. My living as a short-story writer has been earned almost entirely in America. In England, only *Encounter* and *London Magazine* regularly publish stories of quality, for which the payment is meager. Sporadically—apparently for prestige—one of the Sunday newspaper color magazines buys a story for a more realistic sum—say £80 or £90: about the level of an American literary review. No story-writer could write only what he pleased and continue to eat, in England. In my own country, South Africa, both the limited size of the publishing industry and the limited size and tastes of the reading public would make it impossible for any serious writer to live off local earnings. And yet—such is the resilience and obstinacy of short-story writers—almost all the interesting fiction written by local Africans (not *white* South Africans) has taken the form of short stories.

In literature, the short story has always been a small principality. If threatened, it seems to me still remarkably independent, gloriously eccentric, adventurous, and free. After all, in the last few years, Ingeborg Bachman wrote "Among Murderers and Madmen," Borges wrote "The Handwriting of God," and LeClézio wrote his "little madnesses," including "It Seems to Me the Boat Is Heading for the Island."

The Hallucinatory
Point

MAURICE SHADBOLT

A SYMPOSIUM always tempts foolish generalizations into the light; but at least the fool who generalizes has the consolation that he will not be alone.

I should like to be able to discuss the economic and literary health of the short story at length. But upon its economic health I am no authority. All I can say for myself is that I've always found it an economically unhealthy form; and I've never expected it to be other. Of the twenty-five odd stories and novellas I have published in three separate volumes over the past eight years, perhaps no more than two or three have found prior publication in magazines. It is years now since I tried a short story upon a magazine, in my own country or outside. Length may be part of the problem: most editors appear to like short stories short, and it is ten years since I wrote a story much under 10,000 words; some have been two or three times that length. So I write with book publication, and book publication only, in mind. And publishing stories in book form has, for me, been relatively effortless. I know the experience of most writers is the reverse. Evidently I have been fortunate with my publishers—who so far haven't got the profitable novel they have been hoping for either. So I don't feel I have the occasion for despair, or complaint. I have always found it relatively easy to subsidize the writing of my short stories through a variety of free-lance work—from travel-writing to book-reviewing. This means, of course, that a number of stories have gone unwritten, or gone dead on me; but possibly they deserved no life. To me only one thing matters in connection with the short story: publication. So long as I can publish, I have no cause for grievance. So long as I can publish, the short story exists as an effective form for me. So long as I publish, I can be read. And I have reason to believe I am read.

It might help if I explain how I see the short story. To state the obvious, the short story is craft before it is art. (My personal definition of the short story, incidentally, excludes the sketch; the sketch is craft alone, a form of journalism. Isaac Babel seems to me the only writer who has ever made the sketch something more.) What I am trying to stress is that a rewarding short story is inconceivable without some high degree of conscious or instinctive craftsmanship. Whereas a rewarding novel, indifferently written, is still indeed conceivable. This is not to boost the short story or belittle the novel; it is simply to help define both forms. The short story is demonstrably not a popular form, but I believe those of us who engage ourselves with it are asserting, in our different ways, the abiding importance of craft at a time when its importance needs asserting. We may not even be short-story writers primarily; we may also be novelists, poets, or essayists. In the novel, for example, we may be able to get away with doing some things badly, so long as other things are done well, and write something reasonably or even entirely successful. But in the short story everything must be done well, and every element balanced, if the story is to succeed on any terms at all. The short story is a craftsman's challenge to the writer, any writer, and may again—if successful—reward the reader in proportion to the extent of the challenge embraced. For the real challenge is—at least in my view of the short story, which may be idiosyncratic—no less than the endeavor to pull as much of life as a story can bear into the fewest possible pages: to produce, if possible, that hallucinatory point in which time past and time future seem to co-exist with time present, that hallucinatory point which to me defines the good or great short story; a point which, like a stone tossed in a pool, sends ripples widening across all that we see and know, and all that we have never really seen and known, at the very instant that it sinks out of sight itself. The ripples, perhaps, are what we see as art. The stone, with its point of impact, is craft—the craft which is properly out of sight at the end. In great part, then, the challenge of the short story is also the challenge of pure storytelling—not storytelling to some end, but storytelling primarily for the sake of the story. Anything else is secondary. That is why it is no use going to a particular short story in hope of ascertaining a writer's individual vision as one might go to a particular novel with some such quite legitimate expectation. A storywriter's vision may only be seen in the accumulation of his work, often more obviously in his bad or indifferent stories than in his good; and then only an implicit and perhaps ambiguous vision, full of shifting shades. If he is any kind of architect at all, the story-writer will build a house in which truth, in some variety, can take up residence; and he, as much as the reader, may in the end be surprised by the nature of his guest.

And that is why anthologies of short stories, whatever their kaleidoscopic delights, seem to me with few exceptions unsatisfying—the exceptions being those compiled by unashamedly individualist anthologists, without pretense at impartiality or range, who seek, as a hungry man seeks food, those stories which will sustain their own view of life. On the whole the short story would be better off without anthologies, but I don't doubt they will exist as long as publishers do. I might add that I've always been conscious of the limitations of any one of my stories seen in isolation (as happens in anthologies). Seen in isolation, a story seldom seems more than a performance; seen in context, in the context of other stories, it always has the possibility of being more. In writing stories I often feel closer to the painter than to the novelist: the painter who sets out to exhaust the possibilities of a theme, from diverse directions, before moving to another. Thus I seem to spend as much time in giving a book shape as I do on the writing of stories within the book. This is not generally true, I know; and I may be making a virtue of necessity. But it also may be that I'm impure as a storyteller in the sense that I'm dissatisfied with the short story as a thing in itself, an end in itself, or irritated by the limitations of that end. My last book, for example, was an experiment with the triptych form; it seemed to me a way of overcoming the limitations imposed by the nature of the short story. The perils of the form should be clear, and need no restating here: performing seals, doing the same tricks over and over, are more evident in the short story than in any other form of literature.

Yet, with all this said, or confessed, I remain convinced that the things the short story *can* do well are also things which can be done well in no other way; and that the short story, at its best, and as we know it in the twentieth century, is the purest and most penetrating of literary forms. At its best it usurps the territory of the lyric poem even as its precision, and the intensity of light it sheds, makes most novels appear the overblown monsters they are. What this adds up to is perhaps the belief that natural storytellers will continue to strive within the form even if publication prospects become more and more faint. If the short story continues to survive all considerable commercial pressures, there must be a reason; there has to be a reason. And the reason is, I suggest, that many writers know that they are able to give the best of themselves within the form. The modern short story is a writer's form; the modern novel is a reader's.

Thus the temptation away from the short story: the urgency of the need to communicate. And we are all familiar with the collections of glittering fragments (disguised as novels) which often result. "The saddest thing about the short story," said Frank O'Connor, "is the eagerness with which those who write it best try to escape from it. It is a lonely art, and they too are lonely." I am not sure I subscribe to O'Connor's romantic conclusion, but I can't help but agree when he adds: "They seem forever to be looking for company"—or readers, perhaps.

But I still can't, for the life of me, think of the short story as a sick or dying art. As a literary form, I don't think it has ever really begun to exist in most European literatures, anyway (the Irish and Maupassant excluded). It is primarily a child of the literary frontier—shaped and given flexibility and resonance in Russia to the east, America to the west. And that it has lost none of its urgency and bite on virgin terrain for literature has been demonstrated by South African, Australian; and New Zealand experience. Frank O'Connor suggested one good reason why. "The short story," he wrote, "is the art form that deals with the individual when there is no coherent society to absorb him: when he has to exist, as it were, by his own inner light. . . ." Or when (my Antipodean codicil) a coherent society has hardly begun to exist.

A sick or dying art? It is not evident to me, when I consider, say, Tillie Olsen's *Tell Me a Riddle;* or Patrick White's *The Burnt Ones.* Or, among a score of other authors, the work of James Purdy, J. F. Powers, Bernard Malamud, Flannery O'Connor, John Cheever. And possibly the much-abused Salinger has formally done more for the short story than anyone since Chekhov, in giving it a new sense of abundance (as well as once again demonstrating how grotesquely misnamed a form "the short story" is). If a sick or dying art saves its most mature fruit till last, then there could, of course, be something in the argument; but I lack the historical and critical knowledge to debate the issue. The only real test of art I know (and all such tests are finally subjective) is relevance—and resonance. On this test the short story still functions, more often than poetry, and on the whole less fitfully and more urgently than the novel. Again I must make clear that I exclude the short story as it has largely been known in England, where it has seldom outgrown its origin in the anecdote and the throwaway tale, and then often in the hands of outsiders, such exiled children of the literary frontier as Katherine Mansfield.

Our (Western) civilization is, with apparent reason, ceaselessly searching itself for symptoms of decay; and, in cultural life, actively embracing the slightest symptom. Maybe it is all up with painting as we have known it. Maybe it is all up with the novel. Maybe it is all up, naturally enough, with the short story too. In that case short-story writers who take craft seriously—as, in the nature of things, they must—can be seen as a furtive resistance movement, saying no to history, and tapping out tiny messages to the future, if there is one.

Of course I over-dramatize. But so long as we have a civilization (or civilizations) which values the personal voice as distinct from the collective creation—then presumably we shall need literature in some recognizable form or other; we shall need vehicles which allow one mind to engage with another, one imagination to engage with another, one vision to engage with another. Literature at the moment has several useful vehicles for the personal voice and vision in the poem, the novel, the essay, the printed play, the short story. It may be that there are other vehicles to come. And it could be that the essay, for example, will usurp much of the natural territory of the short story. What matters is not the survival of a particular literary form, what matters is not even literature itself; what matters is the personal voice and vision as it has been, and can be, conveyed. What matters, in fact, is the personality able to make some sense of the untidy business of being human. I find myself unable to contemplate the short story apart from larger issues. The short story, as we know it, is hardly a century old, a Johnny-come-lately of literature, and perhaps already a sighing Cinderella past the stroke of midnight; and as a product of a particular time, and largely of particular places, it may indeed have an inbuilt and speedy obsolescence. But all I am really saying, or trying to say, is that the short story has still not proved a useless or unworthy vehicle for the personal voice. What else is there to say?

On Writing

RAYMOND CARVER

BACK IN THE MID-1960s, I found I was having trouble concentrating my attention on long narrative fiction. For a time I experienced difficulty in trying to read it as well as in attempting to write it. My attention span had gone out on me; I no longer had the patience to try to write novels. It's an involved story, too tedious to talk about here. But I know it has much to do now with why I write poems and short stories. Get in, get out. Don't linger. Go on. It could be that I lost any great ambitions at about the same time, in my late twenties. If I did, I think it was good it happened. Ambition and a little luck are good things for a writer to have going for him. Too much ambition and bad luck, or no luck at all, can be killing. There has to be talent.

Some writers have a bunch of talent; I don't know any writers who are without it. But a unique and exact way of looking at things, and finding the right context for expressing that way of looking, that's something else. *The World According to Garp* is, of course, the marvelous world according to John Irving. There is another world according to Flannery O'Connor, and others according to William Faulkner and Ernest Hemingway. There are worlds according to Cheever, Updike, Singer, Stanley Elkin, Ann Beattie, Cynthia Ozick, Donald Barthelme, Mary Robison, William Kittredge, Barry Hannah, Ursula K. LeGuin. Every great or even every very good writer makes the world over according to his own specifications.

It's akin to style, what I'm talking about, but it isn't style alone. It is the writer's particular and unmistakable signature on everything he writes. It is his world and no other. This is one of the things that distinguishes one writer from another. Not talent. There's plenty of that around. But a writer who has some special way of looking at things and who gives artistic expression to that way of looking: that writer may be around for a time.

Isak Dinesen said that she wrote a little every day, without hope and without despair. Someday I'll put that on a three-by-five card and tape it to the wall beside my desk. I have some three-by-five cards on the wall now. "Fundamental accuracy of statement is the ONE sole morality of writing." Ezra Pound. It is not everything by ANY means, but if a writer has "fundamental accuracy of statement" going for him, he's at least on the right track.

I have a three-by-five up there with this fragment of a sentence from a story by Chekov: ". . . and suddenly everything became clear to him." I find these words filled with wonder and possibility. I love their simple clarity, and the hint of revelation that's implied. There is mystery, too. What has been unclear before? Why is it just now becoming clear? What's happened? Most of all—what now? There are consequences as a result of such sudden awakenings. I feel a sharp sense of relief—and anticipation.

I overheard the writer Geoffrey Wolff say "No cheap tricks" to a group of writing students. That should go on a three-by-five card. I'd amend it a little to "No tricks." Period. I hate tricks. At the first sign of a trick or a gimmick in a piece of fiction, a cheap trick or even an elaborate trick, I tend to look for cover. Tricks are ultimately boring, and I get bored easily, which may go along with my not having much of an attention span. But extremely clever chi-chi writing, or just plain tomfoolery writing, puts me to sleep. Writers don't need tricks or gimmicks or even necessarily need to be the smartest fellows on the block. At the risk of appearing foolish, a writer sometimes needs to be able to just stand and gape at this or that thing—a sunset or an old shoe—in absolute and simple amazement.

Some months back, in the *New York Times Book Review,* John Barth said that ten years ago most of the students in his fiction writing seminar were interested in "formal innovation," and this no longer seems to be the case. He's a little worried that writers are going to start writing mom and pop novels in the 1980s. He worries that experimentation may be on the way out, along with liberalism. I get a little nervous if I find myself within earshot of somber discussions about "formal innovation" in fiction writing. Too often "experimentation" is a license to be careless, silly or imitative in the writing. Even worse, a license to try to brutalize or alienate the reader. Too often such writing gives us no news of the world, or else describes a desert landscape and that's all—a few dunes and lizards here and there, but no people; a place uninhabited by anything recognizably human, a place of interest only to a few scientific specialists.

It should be noted that real experiment in fiction is original, hard-earned and cause for rejoicing. But someone else's way of looking at things—Barthelme's, for instance—should not be chased after by other writers. It won't work. There is only one Barthelme, and for another writer to try to appropriate Barthelme's peculiar sensibility or *mise en scene* under the rubric of innovation is for that writer to mess around with chaos and disaster and, worse, self-deception. The real experimenters have to Make It New, as Pound urged, and in the process have to find things out for themselves. But if writers haven't taken leave of their senses, they also want to stay in touch with us, they want to carry news from their world to ours.

It's possible, in a poem or a short story, to write about commonplace things and objects using commonplace but precise language, and to endow those things—a chair, a window curtain, a fork, a stone, a woman's earring—with immense, even startling power. It is possible to write a line of seemingly innocuous dialogue and have it send a chill along the reader's spine—the source of artistic delight, as Nabokov would have it. That's the kind of writing that most interests me. I hate sloppy or haphazard writing whether it flies under the banner of experimentation or else is just clumsily rendered realism. In Isaac Babel's wonderful short story, "Guy de Maupassant," the narrator has this to say about the writing of fiction: "No iron can pierce the heart with such force as a period put just at the right place." This too ought to go on a three-by-five.

Evan Connell said once that he knew he was finished with a short story when he found himself going through it and taking out commas and then going through the story again and putting commas back in the same places. I like that way of working on something. I respect that kind of care for what is being done. That's all we have, finally, the words, and they had better be the right ones, with the punctuation in the right places so that they can best say what they are meant to say. If the words are heavy with the writer's own unbridled emotions, or if they are imprecise and inaccurate for some other reason—if the words are in any way blurred—the reader's eyes will slide right over them and nothing will be achieved. The reader's own artistic sense will simply not be engaged. Henry James called this sort of hapless writing "weak specification."

I have friends who've told me they had to hurry a book because they needed the money, their editor or their wife was leaning on them or leaving them—something, some apology for the writing not being very good. "It would have been better if I'd taken the time." I was dumbfounded when I heard a novelist friend say this. I still am, if I think about it, which I don't. It's none of my business. But if the writing can't be made as good as it is within us to make it, then why do it? In the end, the satisfaction of having done our best, and the proof of that labor, is the one thing we can take into the grave. I wanted to say to my friend, for heaven's sake go do something else. There have to be easier and maybe more honest ways to try and earn a living. Or else just do it to the best of your abilities, your talents, and then don't justify or make excuses. Don't complain, don't explain.

In an essay called, simply enough, "Writing Short Stories," Flannery O'Connor talks about writing as an act of discovery. O'Connor says she most often did not know where she was going when she sat down to work on a short story. She says she doubts that many writers know where they are going when they begin something. She uses "Good Country People" as an example of how she put together a short story whose ending she could not even guess at until she was nearly there:

> When I started writing that story, I didn't know there was going to be a Ph.D. with a wooden leg in it. I merely found myself one morning writing a description of two women I knew something about, and before I realized it, I had equipped one of them with a daughter with a wooden leg. I brought in the Bible salesman, but I had no idea what I was going to do with him. I didn't know he was going to steal that wooden leg until ten or twelve lines before he did it, but when I found out that this was what was going to happen, I realized it was inevitable.

When I read this some years ago it came as a shock that she, or anyone for that matter, wrote stories in this fashion. I thought this was my uncomfortable secret, and I was a little uneasy with it. For sure I thought this way of working on a short story somehow revealed my own shortcomings. I remember being tremendously heartened by reading what she had to say on the subject.

I once sat down to write what turned out to be a pretty good story, though only the first sentence of the story had offered itself to me when I began it. For several days I'd been going around with this sentence in my head: "He was running the vacuum cleaner when the telephone rang." I knew a story was there and that it wanted telling. I felt it in my bones, that a story belonged with that beginning, if I could just have the time to write it. I found the time, an entire day—twelve, fifteen hours even—if I wanted to make use of it. I did, and I sat down in the morning and wrote the first sentence, and other sentences promptly began to attach themselves. I made the story just as I'd make a poem; one line and then the next, and the next. Pretty soon I could see a story, and I knew it was my story, the one I'd been wanting to write.

I like it when there is some feeling of threat or sense of menace in short stories. I think a little menace is fine to have in a story. For one thing, it's good for the circulation. There has to be tension, a sense that something is imminent, that certain things are in relentless motion, or else, most often, there simply won't be a story. What creates tension in a piece of fiction is partly the way the concrete words are linked together to make up the visible action of the story. But it's also the things that are left out, that are implied, the landscape just under the smooth (but sometimes broken and unsettled) surface of things.

V. S. Pritchett's definition of a short story is "something glimpsed from the corner of the eye, in passing." Notice the "glimpse" part of this. First the glimpse. Then the glimpse given life, turned into something that illuminates the moment and may, if we're lucky—that word again—have even further-ranging consequences and meaning. The short story writer's task is to invest the glimpse with all that is in his power. He'll bring his intelligence and literary skill to bear (his talent), his sense of proportion and sense of the fitness of things: of how things out there really are and how he sees those things—like no one else sees them. And this is done through the use of clear and specific language, language used so as to bring to life the details that will light up the story for the reader. For the details to be concrete and convey meaning, the language must be accurate and precisely given. The words can be so precise they may even sound flat, but they can still carry; if used right, they can hit all the notes.

PART SEVEN

Cognitive Approaches to Story

Story Comprehension

AN INTRODUCTION

TEUN A. VAN DIJK

THE INTEREST IN PSYCHOLOGY and AI for stories is part of a more embracing attention for processes underlying the production and the comprehension of discourse. For several reasons, stories are attractive material for experiments and computer simulations: they may have rather simple forms, they have identifiable 'schematic' structures, they are about human action, and will often feature many other properties which are interesting for models of discourse processing.

The attention for discourse in psychology is rather recent, at least in its actual widespread form: after occasional, but sometimes seminal, studies on discourse between the thirties and the early seventies, we now witness publication of a great number of books and papers on various aspects of discourse processing. In psychology, work on discourse is a natural extension of psycholinguistic research on the syntax and semantics of sentences as it was inspired *e.g.* by generative-transformation grammar. At approximately the same time as in linguistics itself, where the development of so-called 'text grammars' began to take shape in the early seventies, the psychologist started to devise models and carry out some experiments about more 'natural' units of language use and communication. In both disciplines, for instance, it appeared that the interpretation of sentences also depends on the interpretation of other sentences within the same discourse. And more in general, there was increasing curiosity for cognitive models of more complex semantic information processing. The historical background of this interest has been sketched in several of the papers of this issue. The prominent starting point in this history of discourse psychology has been the work of Bartlett, whose classical book,

Remembering (1932) paid extensive attention to the ways stories are understood, memorized and reproduced. In fact, Bartlett should not only be seen as the founder of an elementary theory for story comprehension and reproduction in experimental (cognitive) psychology, but also of a related theory in social psychology. With his method of 'serial reproduction' he tried to simulate in the laboratory how stories find their way in the social context (*A* tells *B,* who tells *C, . . . etc.*). Later, similar methods were used to study the spreading of rumors for instance (Allport and Postman 1947). Unfortunately, this social psychological branch of the original work of Bartlett has had much less renewed interest in actual research. After the long prevailing tradition of behaviorism, in which of course semantic information processing of this complex nature could hardly be accounted for (*e.g.* in terms of the Stimulus-Response (S-R) paradigm), renewed interest for meaning and conceptual information processing permitted a 'rediscovery' of the basically gestaltist ideas of Bartlett. Especially the notion of 'schema,' taken as an organizing principle of knowledge and experiences, was paid attention to and formulated in more explicit ways. Similarly, it was re-emphasized that memory is not simply 'reproductive' but 'reconstructive,' due to the intervening functions of such memory schemata: a language user will hardly reproduce (fragments of) a story, but add probable details (inferred from his knowledge schema), make permutations, give explanations of strange events, establish lacking coherence, familiarize what is strange, *etc.* And, what is important, not arbitrary meaning units of the story will become irretrievable ('forgotten') but especially those which do not belong to the 'gist' or 'upshot' of the story.

Most of these original findings have been confirmed in later, methodologically more adequate, theoretical models and experiments. Some of the features of these later theories of the seventies were already assessed in the precursor papers of the sixties (for a survey, *cf. e.g.* van Dijk and Kintsch 1977). I will not go into the details of these more general principles of discourse comprehension here, but will focus on the development and major ideas of story comprehension research in the seventies.

Above, I have been systematically referring to both work in cognitive psychology and artificial intelligence. Work on story processing comes from both areas, which, in fact, are now slowly beginning to merge into a larger 'cognitive science.' Although the methods of inquiry in these two branches of cognitive science are rather different (*e.g.* carrying out experiments vs. building and running computer programs, respectively), and although there is certainly also a difference in topics of interest, they share an important common attention for the processes of *understanding, e.g.* of language. The psychologist in that case will often be more interested in the precise cognitive processes, memory constraints, decoding strategies, storage capacity, retrieval conditions and contextual factors of understanding. The researcher in artificial intelligence, on the contrary, will try to satisfy the demands of a running, and hence algorithmically explicit, program which at the same time should preferably have some psychological plausibility. Thus, the precise forms of representation of semantic information, and hence of discourse, will be crucial in such programs, as well as the knowledge which is necessary to make understanding by the computer possible.

One of the earlier approaches to story comprehension in AI was made in Charniak's (1972) dissertation on children's stories. He there showed in detail the respectable amount of knowledge of the world which is necessary to understand a single sentence of a very simple children's story. He indicated that such knowledge, *e.g.* about a birthday party, must be organized, and predictively used during the understanding of a story about such a party, especially also in those cases where world-information was not explicitly expressed in the story.

Some years later these ideas were followed by a further elaboration of the model of organized representation of this kind of knowledge of the world which plays such an important role in understanding: Minsky at MIT (1975) introduced the notion of *frame*, Schank (1975) at Yale adopted the notion of *script* from Abelson (1973) which led to very fruitful collaboration (see above all Schank and Abelson 1977) in which also other important notions were (re-)introduced, such as plans, goals, themes, *etc.* At the same time the group working at the University of California at San Diego (Norman, Rumelhart and others) did similar work on the organization and use of knowledge in language understanding, using the classical term of *schema*. Although there are differences between these approaches and the notions they use, the main point is that they have a common aim: the effective representation of knowledge or beliefs in the memory of language users. Schank and others in this issue show how these basic ideas further developed to a rich, though of course not yet perfect, theory about the nature and the role of knowledge in discourse processing.

Characteristic of this approach is a representation of both stories and our knowledge of stereotypical episodes (scripts) in terms of *events* and *actions, e.g.* formulated in Schank's 'conceptual dependency' system. This system is an elaborated combination of ideas from Fillmore's well-known 'case grammar' and ideas from the theory of 'lexical decomposition' using language independent basic semantic concepts. For our purposes it is important that a story and its memory representation are taken as a connected sequence of action or event concepts. In order to be able to understand such a sequence, motivations, reasons and causes, intentions and purposes must be identified or inferred from our knowledge of human action in given contexts. And, as we saw above, if such activities are part of socially stereotypical episodes (going to the movies, giving a party or doing an exam) our knowledge of such episodes as it is organized in scripts will help to interpret and organize the information of the text.

Of course, these important ideas about the links between knowledge organization and language understanding are not without a number of issues which still must be treated and problems which must be solved, both about discourse structures and structures of knowledge as well as about the processes and strategies of the *use* of such knowledge. We will come back to some of these problems below.

At the same time the experimental psychologists also started their work on discourse and stories. The more prominent among them present their actual views in this issue. It was striking to see that, often independently, from several sides converging hypotheses were formulated and experimentally confirmed. At the University of Colorado at Boulder Kintsch published his first book of papers on the processing and representation of meaning, including new results on discourse understanding (Kintsch 1974), soon followed by several papers on story comprehension, sometimes written in collaboration with his assistants (and myself). At the same time Bower at Stanford had begun work on story processing (Bower 1974), thereby using the important concept of 'macrostructure,' while Thorndyke, in the same department, came up with one of the first experimental dissertations on story comprehensions (Thorndyke 1975) basing his study on the recent text-linguistic and text-psychological results on the structures and processing of discourse and stories.

Interesting for our discussion is the appearance in psychology of *story grammars*. Especially Rumelhart's (1975) influential paper on narrative schemata set the scene for much theoretical and experimental research on stories. He thereby referred to work of the anthropologist Colby (1973) and to the undisputed originator of structural analysis of stories, Propp (1968), whose work was translated from Russian thirty years after its first publication. We will come back to this tradition in narrative theory below. Among those using story grammars in their experiments we should also mention Jean Mandler, also from the La Jolla campus of the University of California at San Diego, who, together with Nancy Johnson, also in this issue, carried out experiments about the role of story schemata in adult's and children's comprehension of stories.

We will see below that we can now even distinguish two main streams of work on stories: those who work with story grammars, and those who prefer an AI-orientation based on the analysis of action sequences (plans, goals, motivations, scripts, problem solving, *etc.*). The debate between the two directions can be easily followed through the papers of this issue. I hope to show below that the controversy is not fundamental: both approaches are each other's necessary complements.

In a somewhat different perspective we should finally also mention the early dissertation of Bonnie Meyer (1975) who showed that recall for discourse is determined by hierarchical textual structures. Here too there existed a link with linguistic discourse analysis: she borrowed her theoretical tools from Grimes' interesting book on discourse structures, which was only published in 1975. Grimes himself came from the 'tagmemic' linguistics school of Kenneth Pike, in which early and extensive descriptive work was done on discourse structures in many languages (*cf. e.g.* Longacre 1977).

This small survey is far from complete, but is meant to give a first introduction into the major directions of research represented in this issue. It is difficult to say when and where and by whom it was all started: Barlett's work of fifty years ago was clearly an important historical starting point. Occasional later work on stories was not really followed through. Perhaps 1972 should be singled out as the year when several earlier ideas in the areas and directions mentioned got into 'books': we have mentioned Charniak's thesis; then, in the same year, the very influential book on Human Problem Solving by Newell and Simon was published, yielding an important AI-background for later thinking about plans, strategies and problem-solving in story comprehension; thirdly, Freedle and Carroll (1972) published a series of important papers about language comprehension and the acquisition of knowledge, which also contained first papers on discourse comprehension (*e.g.* by Crothers, Frederiksen and Freedle); finally, from my own perspective I might mention publication of my dissertation on text grammar, in which linguistic text grammars were related with story grammars, and where reference was made *e.g.* to Bartlett in order to motivate the introduction of macrostructures of stories, both in grammar and in cognitive models (van Dijk 1972). From that year on, many papers and books on discourse and stories and their processing appeared in linguistics and psychology, cross-fertilizing each other in a very fruitful way, giving rise to a now very broad and diverse framework of cognitive research.

THE STUDY OF NARRATIVE: A BRIEF SURVEY

A model of story comprehension should not only be based on a theory of understanding, but also on a theory of narrative, because the processing of a discourse also depends on the structures of that discourse. Narrative discourse is a specific type of discourse and may, in part, be defined in terms of the conventional categories, rules and other constraints which distinguish it from other discourse types. In a cognitive perspective this means that language users must be able to recognize a story when they hear/read one, to distinguish between a story and a non-story, and to produce a story. This means that they must (implicitly) know the categories, rules and constraints defining a narrative discourse, and be able to strategically use these in processes of production and comprehension. For meta-theoretical reasons not to be specified here we may therefore distinguish between an abstract theory of narrative structures on the one hand and a theory of narrative processing on the other. The first kind of theory will typically characterize the approach taken in literary theory and discourse studies, the latter may be found in cognitive psychology and AI. Clearly, the first theory is an abstraction from the second: empirically speaking the narrative categories and rules represent our knowledge of narrative, and narrative structures are part of our cognitive representation of a narrative discourse during production or comprehension. Heuristically, however, the first theory, *viz.* the so-called *narrative grammar,* may also be used as a partial and hypothetical model for the cognitive representation of narrative if the rules and categories are not only formal devices for structural descriptions but also have so-called psychological 'plausibility.' We will return to these psychological aspects of narrative processing below, and will now focus on the theory of narrative structures.

The theory of narrative has two major orientations, the first is typical for traditional literary studies, the second came from anthropology and was later also adopted in poetics. Traditional narrative studies were essentially 'theories' of the novel—although there are also specific studies of short-stories, fables and other types of narratives (genres). Traditional narrative theory, which basically is a contemporary version of Aristotle's ideas about epic as sketched in his *Poetics,* has been inspired by the views of Henry James, *e.g.* as expressed in the prefaces to his novels (see James

1934 for a collection). More specifically these ideas were later (re-)formulated by people like Lubbock (1965) and Forster (1927), who influenced much anglo-saxon work on narrative in the subsequent decades. This approach was rather informal and intuitive and focussed on those notions which seemed intuitively important aspects of the novel: the relation between fiction and reality, the organization of plots, the kind of characters, the parameters of time and place, the point of view of the narration (*viz.* the relations between author, narrator and represented characters), the use of symbols, and the style of the novel (see *e.g.* Stevick 1967 for a survey).

Although most certainly a number of the issues treated in this tradition were relevant for the theory of narrative, the approach was rather unsystematic. No sound definitions of concepts were given, no level distinctions in narrative texts were made and, due to the absence (at least originally) of a serious linguistics, no account of the relation between narrative structures and their verbal manifestations could be given. In other words: given a certain novel, the narrative concepts should be 'analyzed' from it in an intuitive way. Moreover, there were no over-all narrative structures in which the various concepts would find their place. In fact, there was no theory of the very notion of a narrative: that a novel was a narrative was taken for granted, and no systematic comparison with non-literary, everyday stories, was made.

In a similar vein, post-war German literary scholarship also featured some influential studies of which the results combined with the earlier anglo-saxon tradition: *viz.* Hamburger (1968), Lämmert (1967) and Stanzel (1964), which were the major works the students in literary scholarship were confronted with in their study of narrative. Besides the notions mentioned above, these books came with interesting, though methodologically inadequate for the reasons mentioned above, views about stylistic manifestations of the perspective of narration, the relations between author and reader, types of narrators (implicit, explicit, auctorial, *etc.*), the links between time and tense, temporal shortcuts in plots, the role of flashbacks and 'previews,' *etc.* Although in neighboring disciplines, such as philosophy and linguistics, methods and theories were developed which would have been able to make many of the more interesting notions more explicit (or show the irrelevance of others), this tradition is still very much alive in actual literary scholarship.

The second major direction of narrative studies in this century also was founded some fifty years ago, *viz,* by the Russian Formalists (see Erlich 1955, for an introduction). This group of literary scholars, linguists and anthropologists had a much more 'modern' approach, which in fact it had

in common with the early beginnings of structural linguistics. They focussed on the 'formal' analysis of (literary) discourse inspired also by construction principles of avant-garde art of that time—and introduced many
important narrative notions, e.g. about the thematic structure of stories,
the difference between the canonical structure of a narrative (the 'story'
or 'fable') and its possible literary transformations (the 'plot' or 'sujet').
The names associated with this work are e.g. Šklovskij, Éjxenbaum and
Tomaševskij.

Whereas most of this original work was already done at the same time
as the Russian Revolution, it only became known some fifty years later.
Thus Todorov's (1965) translation was one of the highlights of the rise of
structuralism in France. From our actual point of view, though, it was
mainly Propp's (1928/1968) book on *The Morphology of the Folktale*
which set the firm background for the later 'structural analysis of the narrative,' which also mainly developed in France at first (see e.g. *Communications,* 8 (1966) and the introduction by Barthes (1966)). Propp's work,
after its (first, rather defective) translation in 1958, was introduced in
France by the anthropologist Claude Lévi-Strauss whose work influenced
literary scholars very decisively in the beginning years of structuralism.
Both the work of Propp himself, and that of those in France who continued it (Barthes 1966; Todorov 1969; Bremond 1973; Greimas 1966;
and others), was also received positively by American anthropologists,
such as Dundes and Colby. Propp's analysis of the Russian folktale was
the first serious systematic analysis of 'simple' narrative structures: he distinguished a number of thematic invariants (which he calls 'functions')
and devised an elementary syntax for them ('Lack.' 'Arrival of the Hero,'
'Departure of the Hero,' 'Trial of the Hero,' *etc.*), although this syntax was
not very flexible. It should be noted—a point often overlooked by literary
theorists—that Propp's functions are not proper narrative categories, but
rather fixed 'themes' characterizing the specific content of simple narratives like folktales. Only sufficient abstraction from these functions allows
the establishment of more general narrative categories (*e.g.* 'initial state of
balance,' 'disruption' . . . 're-establishment of the state of balance') (see
especially Bremond 1973, for a critical and further development of the
Proppian tradition). Against this background both anthropologists and
literary theorists applied structural analysis to a great number of, mostly
simple, narratives, such as myths, James Bond stories, *etc.* (for a survey of
structuralist poetics, *cf.* Culler 1975).

In the meantime both structural and generative linguistics also became
pervasive in this area. Thus, structural semantics in France was applied by

Greimas (1966) in the account of Proppian narrative structures. For our discussion it is interesting to note that he uses a case grammar type of semantics, which involves a rather elaborate analysis of events and actions into predicates and various actor types, both at the level of sentences and of the text as a whole. At the same time he uses semantic lexical decomposition: he analyzes lexemes into more basic semantic primitives (semes). With these primitives he then characterizes the thematic structure of narratives (and of other texts for that matter). This allows reformulation of the Proppian functions in more elementary semantic terms, and more in general a link between narrative and other discourse structures, *viz.* the semantic ones. I mention this book briefly here because its French and style of writing is not easily accessible; yet, it contains several of the basic components which later will occur in more explicit theories of narrative.

Generative grammatical ideas were combined with the ideas of the structural analysis of narrative, but this mostly occurred outside of France (where the structural paradigm was solidly entrenched and Chomsky never really got widely accepted). Thus, early on, George Lakoff wrote a paper with a generative rule system for narratives, which he 'dared' to publish only several years later (Lakoff 1972). Important in this and in other works following (see *e.g.* Prince 1973) was the methodological advance which consisted of the more systematic formulation of narrative *categories,* of *formation rules* and of *transformation rules.* In other words, we now slowly approached a serious *explicit* theory of narrative, that is a syntax of such a theory.

Since generative grammar did not and could not describe discourse structures, however, there was of course only an adoption of its formal set-up, but not a real connection between the linguistic and the narrative grammars. In fact, there was no formal link between the (linguistic) discourse structures and the (intuitively chosen) narrative ones. This has led several researchers, including myself, to first work out some fragments of a (generative) grammar for abstract discourse structures: a *text grammar* (*cf. e.g.* van Dijk 1972, 1977a; Petöfi and Rieser 1973; Halliday and Hasan 1976; Dressler 1977; van Dijk and Petöfi 1977). According to the fashion of the period, my own text-grammar should be an account of the native speaker's competence to produce and understand any 'grammatical' discourse of the language. So, the grammar should enumerate all and only texts underlying the possible discourses of a language, together with their structural descriptions. The rather programmatic and not yet very substantial grammatical fragments pertained on the one hand to all kinds of coherence phenomena holding between propositions of texts (PRO-forms, articles, *etc.*) and on the other hand introduced so-called 'semantic deep structures' of the text-as-whole, *viz. macrostructures.* How such global semantic structures were linked to those of the actual sentences was a problem which could not yet be solved. Important for my argument here, though, is that the postulation of semantic macrostructures permitted a serious mapping of narrative structures in the text: narrative categories did not pertain to isolated sentences or propositions, but rather to whole stretches of a text, *viz.* those dominated by a macroproposition. Thus, a narrative system was set up and combined with the linguistic discourse structure via the semantic macrostructures. This mapping did not do more than apply a number of semantic insertion constraints. The narrative system was based on ideas from structural analysis on the one hand and new results in sociolinguistic studies of *natural narratives* (stories of personal experience) obtained by Labov and Waletsky (1967) on the other. They found that everyday stories about a serious topic ('Were you ever afraid to die?') would often consist of a canonical structure of categories like Setting, Complication, Resolution, Evaluation and Coda. This structure may of course undergo several transformations: certain categories will change place or be absent in some story. The story as a whole will in context also be preceded by a presentation category, to which one should also add Comment categories in the interaction context. It was shown that these categories were translatable into a generalized Proppian narrative syntax, so that basically this kind of elementary grammar could be taken as a rather general and faithful account of simple narratives. It was finally—though briefly—shown that the narrative system should not only be characterized in terms of global categories, but also in terms of the more local *action and event structure.* The latter structure was defined in terms of the philosophy and logic of action (*e.g.* of von Wright 1967; *cf.* van Dijk 1976, 1977a) but not explicitly linked to the connected propositional sequence underlying the discourse, which would have made the mapping between the narrative and the discourse complete. For further details, examples, background and references about this textgrammatical approach to narrative, see van Dijk (1972). For linguistic models of narrative, in general, see the survey of Gulich and Raible (1977).

I have taken the liberty to extend a little bit on my own contribution to the development of the theory of narrative, because it shows how various sources and ideas can fruitfully be combined and developed in a unified theoretical framework. It also will explain my further theoretical remarks to be made below. Interesting—for myself—is the fact that much of my theorizing in that period (around 1970), *e.g.* the formulation of the macrostructure ideas, was influenced by hunches and arguments of a cognitive nature, although I hardly knew about cognitive psychology at the time. Yet, I had by chance read a few crucial books, *viz.* Bartlett's, Neisser's (1967) introduction to cognitive psychology, and Miller *et al.*'s classic of 1960 about plans. In the form of their TOTE-units the latter provided me with some (though unintended) theoretical background psychology and (very) early AI for the notion of global structures and the role of plans in action, which again permitted combination of macrostructures and narrative structures. Several of the notions mentioned here were some years later also to appear in psychological and AI models of narrative, which shows a nice convergence of ideas about the matter (especially since most developments in the area were rather independent).

To close the circle of this brief survey of narrative studies and psychological work on narrative, I should, also from my perspective, mention my paper of 1975 (van Dijk 1979) in which I played amateur psychologist (with a group of literary students) by carrying out several semi-natural experiments (in the classroom) in which subjects had to recall (at various delays) and summarize the Dutch version of a Boccaccio story from the *Decameron.* One of the reasons for doing that rather primitive experiment was an empirical assessment for the notion of (semantic) macrostructure, which I had left alone since my thesis of 1972, due to a lack of appropriate theoretical or formal tools to get the link between macrostructures and microstructures explicit. The experiment clearly showed that those propositions which were theoretically the macrostructural ones in the story would be produced, especially after longer delays (three weeks and longer) and in summaries, with much higher probability. The macrostructures were obtained by a first, still rather informal, set of *macrorules.* Moreover, a narrative grammar was written, which would be the global narrative syntax for the global (macrostructural) content. Note that at the time I still spoke of 'macrostructures' both in case of the semantic ones and the narrative ones. In order to avoid confusion and to stress their distinct theoretical nature, the categorical structure of narrative has later been taken as a type of *superstructure,* to which I will turn below.

Striking for this combination of a systematic and a historical survey of both story comprehension and narrative studies is that roughly at the same time David Rumelhart must have been writing his paper on story schemata which also had a story grammar, whereas Schank and others were beginning work on episode/script representation and hence also on simple 'stories,' and Kintsch his experiments on meaning and comprehension of discourse, which eventually led to our further collaboration.

SOME ISSUES FROM NARRATIVE (META-)THEORY

In the survey given above we have seen where the more important ideas about narrative come from: Russian Formalism, French structuralism, combinations with TG-ideas and textgrammar, anthropology and sociolinguistics now being completed by independent further research—also on narrative structures proper—in psychology and AI. Before I proceed to a brief evaluation of these latter contributions, a summary of the major theoretical issues on narrative is necessary. My contention is that if a number of distinctions are not clearly made, our theoretical thinking on narrative and discourse (and their processing models) will get—or remain—muddled. In fact, my main problem with much of recent (and classical) research is that different kinds of categories, levels, rules, *etc.* have been mixed up, and on the other hand, that 'exclusivistic' approaches were taken in a certain direction which only represented certain fragments of narrative theory. What I will say here holds for an abstract, general theory of narrative. Both for particular theories of various narrative discourse types, and for cognitive and social models, further details and other kinds of notions will be necessary.

A first important distinction which should be made is that between *discourse* and *narrative,* or more precisely between the linguistic textual structures of the discourse and the narrative structures manifested by the discourse. Narrative structures are not characterized by a (linguistic) grammar of the discourse, but are to be accounted for by a separate system of rules. In fact, as we know from comics and movies, narrative structures need not be expressed in natural language at all. This means that the link between narrative structures and the actual discourse must go via the underlying semantic or conceptual structure of the discourse (*viz.* its 'text base'). A system of narrative rules (a 'grammar') would consist *e.g.* of formation rules, transformation rules, categories and—for certain specific narrative traditions—a 'lexicon' of typical narrative themes, *e.g.* Propp's functions.

Note that such 'independent' systems are not at all a bizarre invention of the theorist. Not only do language users have intuitions about them, but also we are sometimes trained at school to isolate and 'formalize' them. Thus, linked to morphonology and syntax we have well-known prosodic and metrical systems, which can be formulated independently and then applied to the specific sound system of a given language. Then, at the level of the global organization of content, we also have this kind of *superstructures,* as I call them, in argumentative discourse, in scientific papers, *etc.* Such structures are *global schematic forms,* defined by the respective syntactic components of their respective theories, consisting of a hierarchically organized sequence of categories. The 'content' of the discourse may be inserted into the open slots of the superstructural schema. The independent nature of formal discourse schemata is perhaps best known from the very existence of logic, with its formation and derivation rules: it is the abstraction of valid forms of argumentative discourse, consisting of various kinds of premises and a conclusion (see van Dijk 1980 for details about the link between superstructures and macrostructures). In other words, we should distinguish between the (general) *form* of a narrative and its (actual) *content,* which of course is an old insight made more salient in structuralism—which we will try to make explicit. Now, we will call a story any discourse which has a narrative structure. Hence, we distinguish between a *discourse type* (stories), its *narrative global form* (superstructure or schema), its *narrative global content* (macrostructures; which may be conventionalized as well, as in Propp's functions) and, of course, the actual linguistic expression of these in the form of a sequence of sentences: a discourse. The global content of a story, also called *plot,* should of course not be confused with the denotata of the story, *viz.* the sequence of events of some possible world: it is where the story is about, but about which we may also have other discourse types (*e.g.* a police protocol).

In order to see how narrative structures can at all be expressed by a natural language discourse, we should indicate how and where they are mapped on structures of the discourse. As we have already suggested above, this mapping takes place, first of all, at the macro-level: the superstructural schema is mapped on the (highest) macrostructural level of the story as a whole, *viz.* by assigning narrative categorial functions to macropropositions, *e.g.* as follows:

(1) M_1: It was a beautiful day =: Setting

Or conversely, given the narrative schema we may assign a macroproposition to one of the category slots. In other words, the narrative schema assigns a further functional/categorical organization to the sequence of macropropositions derived from the propositional text base of the discourse with the aid of macrorules (see van Dijk 1977b and, in more detail, van Dijk 1980 for definition and examples of application of these rules; see also van Dijk and Kintsch 1977; and Kintsch and van Dijk 1978).

As is usual for the links between syntax and semantics, the narrative categories have constraints on the global semantic content which they dominate. Thus, for instance, a Complication will require an 'interesting' event, often an event or action which interferes with the wishes or goals of a main protagonist, and a Resolution will dominate the (global) action of a person with the purpose to restore the original or new positive conditions.

Given these global constraints we may now make a next important theoretical distinction, *viz.* between an *action discourse* in general and a *story* (or narrative discourse) in particular. This means that stories are a particular kind of action discourse, but also that not all action discourses are stories. An action discourse is a discourse which is interpreted as a sequence of actions and their properties. Note, that this definition holds for the discourse, *not* for isolated sentences, which may well not be about action at all: *It was a beautiful day* . . . , *She was very pretty* . . . , *etc.* An action discourse will, however, mostly feature action sentences. An action discourse may be about any sequence of actions, under the only condition that the discourse itself is *coherent* (*cf.* van Dijk 1977a). This means, roughly speaking, that the respective propositions of the discourse, expressed by the sequence of sentences, are interpreted as a related set of *facts, e.g.* events and actions in some possible world. The relation will often be *conditional:* one fact will make another fact possible, probable or necessary (and conversely, be a possible, probable or necessary condition for it). Now, whereas the macrostructures, which represent the 'theme,' 'topic' or 'gist' of the discourse, define the *global* coherence, the local coherence is defined in terms of these connection conditions, and some further conditions about identity or contiguity of individuals, which need not be specified here.

From these general conditions of discourse coherence it follows that action discourses are coherent if they denote 'connected' action and event sequences. Since, however, discourses for various pragmatic and cognitive reasons need not be fully explicit, they will represent only part of the actions and the events of such a sequence. In order to establish formal coherence, thus, inference processes must take place which derive 'missing link' propositions from our knowledge (scripts, frames, episodic memory, *etc.*). In order to understand how action sequences are 'coherent,' *i.e.* meaningful, rational, *etc.*, we must draw upon our general knowledge about meaningful action and interaction. That is, we will bring to bear, in action discourse comprehension, our knowledge that actions have underlying motivational structures (wishes, desires, wants, preferences, *etc.*), decision structures and intentional structures, which include the formation of purposes (aims) representing the local and ultimate (indirect) goal(s) which is expected to be brought about as a consequence of an action. Similarly, we know that actions may have complex component structure, *e.g.* consist of preparations, attempts, auxiliary actions, and results (outcomes). Finally, we know that complex action sequences must be intended globally, so that macrostructures of action, *viz. plans,* play an important role, both in the formation and the execution and control of a complex sequence (see van Dijk 1976, 1977a, and 1980 for detail). In other words, action descriptions may involve all these defining components of actions and action sequences. This kind of knowledge about human action is very general: it accounts both for the general structures of action and for conditions on 'meaningful' action, involving rationality, cooperation, goal-directedness, and motivations. In a sense there is a trade-off of these conditions with the very conditions on the coherence of action discourse: if we do not 'understand' an action sequence we will also fail to (fully) understand its description, because we will ignore the motivations (reasons, *etc.*), goals, and internal order of the described action sequence.

Much of the work which has been carried out, *e.g.* in AI, on 'stories' actually is about action discourses more in general. It goes without saying, therefore, that the structures of such discourses, but also their processing and representation, is predominantly characterized in terms of the action structures briefly mentioned above. The models proposed, indeed, are a regular part of the semantics for action discourse, because they specify the normal or stereotypical as well as the bio-physical and cognitive aspects of the denotata of such a discourse. In other words, we are able to interpret each proposition of an action discourse in relation to other propositions of that discourse *via* the denoted action structures.

However, this is not the whole 'story,' because, as we suggested above, not each action discourse is a story in the strict sense (we sometimes loosely use the term 'story' in order to denote other discourse types, even lectures or announcements, or various kinds of other action description discourse, such as 'news stories' or 'protocols'). In other words, we will take as a story only those action discourses which in addition have a specific *narrative structure* as has been sketched above. Intuitively, 'stories' which do not have such a narrative structure will be considered as lacking a 'point.' People will ask *why* we tell this, or 'what happened.' Thus, if I describe in detail how I came home from my office, I have given an action discourse which may be used in a police protocol—but I have not told a story in the case that nothing particular, interesting, disturbing, funny, or unexpected, *viz.* nothing 'narratable' happened. The intuitive notions used here are the possible semantic constraints on the narrative category

of the Complication. In other words, we expect a real story to be about
events and actions which interfere with normal or expected courses of
events or actions, *e.g.* such that goals cannot be reached. Similarly, a 'real'
story will contain a description of actions which took place 'next': how a
person reacted to these events or actions, *e.g.* re-established the conditions for reaching a goal. We here find the narrative category of Resolution. We see that on the one hand the structure of action, and on the other
hand the pragmatic conditions of informativeness and psychological needs
for 'fun' or 'thrill' (suspense, unusualness, *etc.*) combine to rather fixed
general categories of stories. These categories and their rules of syntax
and semantics have become conventional in our culture, such that language users would notice when a story is ill-formed in many cases.

We have seen that the global narrative schema does not directly organize the sequence of propositions of a story, but its macrostructures. In
other words, the additional structures of a story, as they are postulated in a
story grammar do not pertain to specific descriptions of action sequences,
but to sequences of macropropositions derived from them. From this it
follows, rather trivially, that if action discourses are taken a narrative
schema does not play a role in processing or memory representations. On
the other hand, *if* such narrative structures are present, and if these involve structures which are additional to the structure of the action description itself, they *should* have an influence in story comprehension. This in
fact has been demonstrated in many experiments. If there would not be an
effect of narrative structures, we would probably have to revise *not* (only)
our theory of narrative, but also our whole information processing paradigm, which assumes that organizing structures facilitate comprehension,
representation and storage. On the other hand, it is also perfectly clear by
now that since stories are action discourses, they must also be organized
on the level of adequate action description. This means that structures are
assigned both at the local level of connections (reasons-consequences, *etc.*),
and at the global level of plans and ultimate goals in case of complex
action-sequence description. This global level is described in terms of
(semantic) macrostructures, which—if these are action macropropositions—
also require connection between (global) actions or action components,
such as motivations, decisions, aims, doings, and results. We conclude,
therefore, that both approaches to the structure and processing of stories
are necessary components of a theory, and it is pointless to mutually try to
refute the relevant observations made from different perspectives. So,
there is no adequate, *i.e.* complete, model of 'real' stories without some
kind of narrative categories and rules, and no sound story grammar with-

out a specification of the action structural 'content' of the narrative categories as it is represented by the story.

Regarding this last point, another (meta-)theoretical distinction is necessary. Most story grammars now in use in cognitive models analyze stories down to the level of action structure: motivations, attempts and outcomes, for instance, are terminal categories. Also, this kind of analysis links general *narrative* categories with the more general *semantic* structures of action or action description, I should think that this approach is both uneconomical and theoretically confusing. Such analyses will only be possible in very simple stories, *e.g.* in stories in which microstructures and macrostructures practically coincide. We have seen that narrative categories are mapped on semantic macrostructures, *i.e.* global content, of a discourse. This means that we cannot possibly go directly, by rules of formation or analysis, from a macrolevel to a microlevel by constituent analysis, or from narrative schemata to semantic structures. Given the proper conventional narrative categories, we may formulate constraints of a semantic nature upon the macropropositions which are finally *inserted* into the terminal narrative categories (which is a kind of transformation operation). Next, macropropositions thus inserted should be linked to the micro-level of actual action description by macrorules (which are another kind of mappings). Not only from this (meta-)theoretical point of view a direct link between narrative structures and local semantic structures may be confusing, but also the precise description of action sequences *need* not be taken up in a specific story grammar. Structures of actions may be specified in a more general semantics for action discourse. One could even make a stronger claim: the analysis of the structures of (inter-)action need not even be given in a more specific semantics for action discourse, but may be formulated in a more general *theory of (inter-)action,* which would be a possible basis for such a semantics (*cf.* van Dijk, 1976, 1977a). The same theory of action can be used as a basis for 'real' action production and understanding as well. Specific for a theory of action discourse, then, would be the theory of *action representation* in verbal or figural 'discourses.' Such a more specific theory would *e.g.* specify that not all actions of the sequence need be described, that some actions will be selected, that some actions will be described in greater detail and that, hence, there are levels and degrees of specificity or (over- and under-)completeness in description, and that, finally, actions may be described from different perspectives. Even more specific, this time not at the semantic level, would be a description of the particular styles of action discourses.

From my discussion it follows that it makes sense that important theoretical distinctions between kinds of structures, kinds of rules, levels, *etc.* be made, and that the set of theories involved in a complete description of stories should not be collapsed into an *ad hoc,* rather heterogeneous (or incomplete) model because some of these theories have a more general nature. Thus, the semantics of coherence holds for any discourse, and need not be specified for stories in particular; the theory of action is a more general basis of the semantics of action discourse, and a theory of action discourse is more general than a theory of stories.

REFERENCES

Abelson, Robert P. 1973. "The structure of belief system." In R. C. Schank and K. M. Colby, eds., *Computer models of thought and language.* San Francisco: Freeman, pp. 287–339.

Allport, G. W. and L. Postman. 1947. *The psychology of rumor.* New York: Holt.

Barthes, Roland. 1966. Introduction à l'analyse structurale des récits. *Communications* 8: 1–27.

Bartlett, F. C. 1932. *Remembering.* London: Cambridge University Press.

Bower, Gordon H. 1974. Selective facilitation and interference in retention of prose. *Journal of Experimental Psychology* 66: 1–8.

Bremond, Claude. 1973. *Logique du récit.* Paris: Seuil.

Charniak, Eugene. 1972. "Towards a model of children's story comprehension." Ph.D. Diss. MIT.

Colby, B.N. 1973. A partial grammar of Eskimo folktales. *American Anthropologist* 75: 645–662.

Communications 8. 1966. *L'analyse structurale du récit.* Paris: Seuil.

Culler, Jonathan. 1975. *Structuralist poetics.* London: Cambridge Univerity Press.

van Dijk, Teun A. 1972. *Some aspects of text grammars.* The Hague: Mouton.

van Dijk, Teun A. 1976. "Philosophy of action and theory of narrative" [1974]. *Poetics* 5: 287–338.

van Dijk, Teun A. 1977a. *Text and context.* London: Longman.

van Dijk, Teun A. 1977b. "Semantic macrostructures and knowledge frames in discourse comprehension." In M. Just and P. Carpenter, eds., *Cognitive processes in comprehension.* Hillsdale, New Jersey: Erlbaum.

van Dijk, Teun A. 1979. "Recalling and summarizing complex discourse" [1975]. In W. Burghardt and K. Hölker, eds., *Text processing.* Berlin/New York: de Gruyter.

van Dijk, Teun A. 1980. *Macrostructures. An interdisciplinary study of global structures in discourse, interaction and cognition.* Hillsdale, New Jersey: Erlbaum.

van Dijk, Teun A. and Walter Kintsch. 1977. "Cognitive psychology and discourse. Recalling and summarizing stories." In Dressler, ed. pp. 61–80.

van Dijk, Teun A. and János Petöfi. 1977. *Grammars and descriptions.* Berlin/ New York: de Gruyter.

Dressler, Wolfgang U., ed. 1977. *Current trends in textlinguistics.* Berlin/New York: de Gruyter.

Erlich, Victor. 1955. *Russian Formalism.* The Hague: Mouton (2nd revised edition, 1965.)

Forster, E. M. 1927. *Aspects of the novel.* New York: Harcourt, Brace and World, Inc.

Freedle, Roy O. and John B. Carroll, eds. 1972. *Language comprehension and the acquisition of knowledge.* Washington, D.C.: Winston.

Greimas, A. J. 1966. *Sémantique structurale.* Paris: Larousse.

Grimes, Joseph E. 1975. *The thread of discourse.* The Hague: Mouton.

Gülich, Elisabeth and Wolfgang Raible. 1977. *Linguistische Textmodelle.* München: Fink (UTB).

Halliday, M. A. K. and Ruqaiya Hasan. 1976. *Cohesion in English.* London: Longman.

Hamburger, Käte. 1968. *Die Logik der Dichtung* [1957]. Stuttgart: Klett (2nd revised edition).

James, Henry. 1934. *The art of the novel.* New York: Scribner's.

Kintsch, Walter. 1974. *The representation of meaning in memory.* Hillsdale, New Jersey: Erlbaum.

Kintsch, Walter and Teun A. van Dijk. 1978. "Toward a model of text comprehension and production." *Psychological Review* 85: 363–394.

Labov, William and Joshua Waletzky. 1967. "Narrative analysis: oral versions of personal experience." In J. Helm, eds., *Essays on the verbal and visual arts.* Seattle: Washington University Press, pp. 12–44.

Lakoff, George, 1972. "Structural complexity in fairy tales." *The Study of Man* 1: 128–150.

Lämmert, Eberhard, 1967. *Bauformen des Erzählens* [1955]. Stuttgart: Klett (2nd revised edition).

Longacre, Robert, ed. 1977. *Discourse grammar.* 3 vols. Dallas, Texas. Summer Institute of Linguistics.

Lubbock, Percy. 1965. *The craft of fiction* [1921]. London: Jonathan Cape.

Meyer, Bonnie F. 1975. *The organization of prose and its effects on memory.* Amsterdam: North-Holland.

Miller, George, Eugene Galanter and Karl Pribram. 1960. *Plans and the structure of behavior.* New York: Holt.

Minsky, Marvin. 1975. "A framework for representing knowledge." In P. Winston, ed., *The psychology of computer vision.* New York: McGraw Hill.

Neisser, Ulric. 1967. *Cognitive psychology.* New York: Appleton-Century-Crofts.

Newell, Allen and Herbert A. Simon. 1972. *Human problem solving.* Englewood Cliffs, New Jersey: Prentice Hall.

Petöfi, Jānos and Hannes Rieser, eds. 1973. *Studies in text grammar.* Dordrecht: Reidel.

Prince, Gerald. 1973. *A grammar of stories.* The Hague: Mouton.

Propp, Vladimir. 1968. *Morphology of the folktale* [1958]. Bloomington: Indiana University Press (second, revised edition).

Rumelhart, David. 1975. "Notes on a schema for stories." In D. Bobrow and A. Collins, eds., *Representation and understanding.* New York: Academic Press, pp. 237–72.

Schank, Roger. 1975. "The structure of episodes in memory." In D. Bobow and A. Collins, eds., *Representation and understanding.* New York: Academic Press, pp. 237–72.

Schank, Roger C. and Robert P. Abelson. 1977. *Scripts, plans, goals, and understanding.* Hillsdale, New Jersey: Erlbaum.

Stanzel, Frans K. 1964. *Typische Formen des Romans.* Tübingen: Vandenhoeck and Ruprecht.

Stevick, Philip, ed. 1967. *The theory of the novel.* New York: Free Press.

Thorndyke, Perry W. 1975. "Cognitive structures in human story comprehension and memory." Ph.D. Diss. Stanford.

Todorov, Tzvetan, ed. 1965. *Textes des formalistes russes.* Paris: Seuil.

Todorov, Tzvetan. 1969. *Grammaire du Décaméron.* The Hague: Mouton.

Woods, John and Thomas G. Pavel, eds. 1979. "Formal semantics and literary theory." Special issue of *Poetics* 8 (1/2).

von Wright, Georg Henrik. 1967. "The logic of action: a sketch." In N. Rescher, ed., *The logic of decision and action.* Pittsburgh: Pittsburgh University Press, pp. 121–136.

A Cognitive Approach
to Storyness

SUSAN LOHAFER

THERE IS A tradition of functionalism in short story criticism and theory, a tradition of saying what stories do.[1] What could be more practical than to measure one's span of attention by the seat of one's pants? The short story keeps us in our chair for about an hour, said Poe; it is prose under pressure. The short story speaks of and for submerged populations, said Frank O'Connor; it is humanity under pressure. Above all, though, the short story is the right size for teachers under pressure. Students can discuss one in about an hour. Stories are eminently *useable.*

On the other hand, they are strangely indescribable. In short story criticism, there is also a tradition of ineffability, of failing to say what stories *are.* "Every good story has mystery—not the puzzle kind, but the mystery of allurement," says Welty. Or Bowen: "The first necessity for the short story, at the set out, is *necessariness* . . . a vital fortuity."[2] These are gestures toward the source of story-power, what Charles May calls the mythic, primal, subjective, preconceptualized experience which the novel builds over but the story digs up.[3] If there *is* something primal in the experience of short storyness, can we get in touch with it? Can we use it to explain why the short story not only *does* but *is* something different?

In 1983, my own answers to these questions were based on a phenomenology of short-span reading experiences, wherein the reader's response to the sentence—its typical syntactic and lexical features, its tension between closural and anticlosural features—became the model for the experience of entering, moving through, and getting out of the story.[4] As it turns out, the most promising aspect of that argument was its emphasis on closure. There have since been many studies of the way stories end. But there has not been, within the discipline of literary studies, a way of moving from the analysis of closural features and effects, to a test of the primacy, the necessariness, the uniqueness of the short story in the family of genres. That is what I have been looking for these last few years.

However, it wasn't till I shifted my attention from the modifier "short" to the noun "story" that I was able to ask a different question: what is it that accounts for the perception of storyness in short stories? Thinking in those terms made me realize how very partial was my claim on the notion of "story." It belonged also to journalists, historians, cultural anthropologists, and—in the last decade—to discourse analysts, social psychologists, psycholinguists, and cognitive scientists. Researchers in these latter fields were already asking what storyness is.

Discourse analysts, in particular those of the Amsterdam School headed by Teun van Dijk, have studied the way readers—that is, human text processors—build the meaning of a whole discourse. According to Van Dijk, the serial propositions of the text are combined—by means of processing rules—into a smaller set of more general propositions, which he calls "macrostructures." The formation of these macrostructures is a cognitive strategy for processing the text, for making sense of it.[5] As we shall see later, van Dijk's model for text processing can suggest other ways in which readers "chunk" texts.

For over a decade, psychologists have been working with many of the same ideas, but from the other direction. They have been positing "story grammars," or systems of notation for the structure of storyness. In the eighties there have been ongoing debates about both the theoretical and the practical value of these grammars.[6] Some psychologists think processors recognize stories primarily for *other* reasons, for example, the difficulty and/or importance of goals for which human or humanlike agents strive, or, according to an increasingly important theory developed by William F. Brewer, by the affective states produced in human processors when they are reading a story as opposed to cuddling up with a good encyclopedia.

In general, there has been a shift away from the formal, culturally unmarked, linguistic models of story structure and story comprehension—that is, the story grammar approach—toward the more data-driven, culturally-determined, social science models of reader-response. There is much that is daunting for the literary scholar who peers into this territory. The models of inquiry, the rules of evidence, the very nature of what is regarded as knowledge—seem alien. It is, I believe, a matter of trading heuristics. Psychology, after all, has turned increasingly to the concept of "narrative" to explain human behavior. I will be arguing that short story critics can profitably turn to cognitive studies. At the very least, we gain an experimental approach to essentialist, honorific concepts inherited from Poe: "unity," "totality," and "single effect." Instead of asking how stories are composed, or even how stories "mean," we can ask how story-ness is recognized, by what cognitive strategies it is processed.

I have learned from the story grammarians that the perception of sto-ryness is a gestalt; each of us, as a human story processor, has internalized a story-scheme, a set of expectations about what stories offer. It is this story-schema, rather than any real stories, that the grammars represent. The question is, how are these schemas deployed? How can we watch them in action? Van Dijk's theory of macrostructures allows me to put the question another way. How do readers "chunk" a text into meaningful units above the sentence level? When do these chunks become story-size?

To find out, I began doing what I call "reader experiments" with my students. At the time, I was unaware that Bruer was using *his* students in reader-response tests of short story affects. He was dividing up stories into sections, asking questions after each section to determine how sur-prise, suspense, and curiosity "stage" a reader's response throughout a story. He was also looking at the way feelings of "completeness" and "out-come satisfaction" influence judgments about "story-liking" and "story-likeness."[7] However, my approach was different. I wanted to let readers do their own "chunking," in a way that would document, very pointedly, their sense of whole-storyness. Also, I remained convinced that the expe-rience of storyness is tied more directly to closure than to any set of story components or story affects.

The problem with studying the ends of stories is simply that the author is in control. He or she makes "chunking" at this point not only easy but inevitable. Therefore, I decided to study what I have been calling "preclo-sure," those points in a narrative where *readers* feel the story *could* end. By collecting intuitive preclosure choices from various groups of readers, I have been able to speculate about the influence of different kinds of train-ing and experiences on trends in preclosure choices. I have also learned a good deal about the features of the sentences that occur at preclosure points.

For the present experiment, I reversed the ratio of readers to stories: instead of having many readers read one story, I myself read forty-five well-known American short stories. Limiting myself to widely antholo-gized texts, I used fifteen from each of three major periods in the history of the genre: 1820–1850 ["Early"], 1920–1940 ["Modern"], and 1960–1980 ["Contemporary"]. I made my own preclosure choices, and finally, for each story, isolated three sentences: the preclosure point nearest the beginning of the story, which I called "anterior closure"; the preclosure point closest to the end of the story, i.e., "penultimate closure"; and the actual last sentence of the story, or "final closure." What I was doing was making explicit my own sense of storyness. Once I had collected the 135 closural sentences, I analyzed them in a variety of ways, cataloging their features, both global and local, syntactic and lexical. On another occasion, I used some of these findings to establish a generic model for closural staging in short stories.[8] In the present essay, I will discuss the staging of closure by historical period.

I found that sentences which triggered my sense of storyness in the "Early" period were more than twice as likely to come at the end of a paragraph as the closural sentences in either the "Modern" or the "Contemporary" periods. The higher coincidence of closural sentences and paragraph endings in the "Early" period certainly has to do with well-known features of nineteenth-century stories: the authors more managerial (and expository) treatment of information; the more prominent and clearly-jointed movement of plot. It also has something to do with the changing conventions of paragraphing itself: the trend has been away from the paragraph as a "block" of thought toward the paragraph as a stylistic variable. This is a change to which the text processor, whether human or artificial, must adapt: in twentieth-century stories, signals of closure are less reliably encoded in the visual structure of the story.

Does this shift hint at a general decrease in syntactic markers of closure, as we move through the history of the American short story? I did find that closural sentences in "Early" stories were more likely than "Modern" or "Contemporary" stories to have an inverted subject-verb order. The relative incidence was 4:20 (a notation system I will use from now on to indicate the number of occurrences of a given phenomenon in the three periods, in chronological order). The anterior closure sentence in "The Legend of Sleepy Hollow" is an example: "In one part of the road leading to the church was found the saddle trampled in the dirt; the tracks of horses' hoofs deeply dented in the road, and evidently at furious speed, were traced to the bridge, beyond which, on the bank of a broad part of the brook, where the water ran deep and black, was found the hat of the unfortunate Ichabod, and close beside it a shattered pumpkin" (this sentence, by the way, ends a paragraph). Closural sentences in "Early" stories were also more likely (17:1:12) to display alliteration (a phonemic rather than syntactic feature, but a form of structural patterning, nonetheless). Note that in the sentence just quoted, "d's" dominate, and a string of "b's" creates a striking—and braking-effect: "bridge," "beyond," "bank," "broad," "brook," "black." Triadic structures also appear more often in

"Early" than in "Modern" or "Contemporary" stories (13:0:7)—another predictable finding, given the association between tricolons and formal, "old-fashioned" prose style.

But let's slice the data another way, focussing on replication as a formal property within closural sentences. Let's look at it on all levels from individual letters (alliteration) to words to phrases to clauses; in all relations— syntax running into lexis—from identical ("dog," "dog") to coordinate ("dog," "cat") to disjunctive ("dog," "apple"); and to all degrees of repetition from double to triple to serial. We might expect to see an overall decline in replication as a formal device as we move into and through the twentieth century. However, that is not true for my sample. Instead, there is an overall drop in the "Modern" stories, followed by an overall—and equally dramatic—upswing in the "Contemporary" texts (31:13:33).

It's worth taking a moment to comment on what seems like the first surprising twist in the data. The high total in the "Contemporary" period includes an unusual number of repetitions at the serial degree, repetitions in the identical relation, and repetitions on the level of clauses. Here is an example of a word-level, coordinate-relation, serial-degree repetition in the final sentence of Cheever's "The Swimmer": "He *shouted, pounded* on the door, tried to force it with his shoulder, and then, looking in at the windows, *saw* that the place was empty." Here is a clause-level, coordinate doublet, with several word-level identities, in the anterior closural sentence of Ann Beattie's "A Clever Kid's Story": "He really thought *THAT HE WOULD ALWAYS BE* in control, *THAT HE WOULD ALWAYS BE* the storyteller."[9] Linguistically speaking, all of these features suggest a general shift to paratactic as opposed to hypotactic structures. Cognitively speaking, they suggest that closure in contemporary stories is less integrative and more interative.

Though less highly figured in conventional stylistic ways, closural sentences in the "Contemporary" period do seem more like their "Early" than like their "Modern" predecessors in relying on the surface structure of language to signal closure. But it is significant that "Early" stories rely more on doublets and triplets, as opposed to the serial repetitions found more often in "Contemporary" samples. Pairs and triads build relationships; serial repetition is a step toward what we might think of as cognitive entropy. The rising incidence of serial repetitions in the closural sentences of "Contemporary" stories may suggest modifications in the cognitive model for storyness, as we shall see later.

Let me turn, now, to the lexical features of closural sentences. I divide these into two main categories: closural words and keywords. Closural words are those that suggest a terminal status, either by naming such a

condition ("end," "final," "last," etc.), by posting an absolute degree of
some condition ("all," "nothing," "every," "none," etc.), by closing a logical relationship of either sequence or opposition ("then," "thus," "but,"
"however," etc.), or simply by marking a temporal shift ("then," "after,"
[in] future," etc.). Some words carry several of these markers. Poe's
"nevermore," for example, is particularly rich in closural force; it names a
final condition that is absolute, opposite to some previous state, and
extended through time—in this case indefinitely. The second group of
closural words are keywords. These include any words which have been
privileged in the text because of natural prominence (characters' names),
special "loading" (symbols), or significant repetition (recurrent images).
Most of them can be classified by what they refer to: a person, a thing, an
action, or an idea.

Overall, the highest incidence of lexical features occurred in the closural sentences of the "Early" period (78:59:57). There were slightly
more time-related closural words (10:3:6) and noticeably more face-value
closural words like "end" (18:8:10). We would expect these findings, for,
as we know, nineteenth-century stories tend toward greater resolution on
the level of plot. What would we expect of "Modern" stories? Thinking of
Hemingway, we would look for the highest incidence of "thing"-related
keywords. Interestingly enough, when coding keywords in this period, I
found myself often torn between the categories "think" and "idea." References to "things," pure and simple, occurred least often in the "Modern" period (11:4:12); however, references to things-as-ideas occurred
most often there (4:17:8). So, for example, in Anderson's "I Want to
Know Why," the penultimate closural sentence gives us a keyword, "[race]
tracks," that refers to as much to a complex of ideas (the previously idealized world of horses) as to a physical place: "At the tracks, the air don't
taste as good or smell as good [as it did before]." Maybe we've only confirmed the modernist dictum: "no ideas but in things." And yet, if we look
at keywords referring to ideas not in things—i.e., abstractions—we find
they occur nearly as often in the "Modern" as in the "Early" periods.
Where they decline is in the "Contemporary" period (45:43:26). This
datum, like the high incidence of syntactic replication in "Contemporary"
stories, may eventually lead us to a more precise understanding of the
"difficulty" of stories in this period—and of the cognitive adjustments
required.

It is time to move beyond local (sentence-level) features to global
(story-level) features that also allow us to target closural sentences. Every
closural sentence brackets a "story," one which begins with the first sentence of the text and ends with the chosen sentence. Since I have been

working with only three closural sentences—anterior, penultimate, and final—we can speak of three corresponding "stories," each concluding at one of the three closural sentences. We have, in other words an anterior story, a penultimate story, and a final story. The final story is, of course, the one we normally think of, the one designated by the title. The local features of the preclosural sentences may be enough to signal the end of an anterior or penultimate story; more often, however, these features reinforce the global signals, resulting in the cognitive chunking of the text into story units. We must therefore look at the closural sentences *in relation to the stories they terminate.*

I asked certain questions of each closural sentence: Did it refer to a specific action or idea, or did it summarize a state of affairs previously developed? Did it represent the point of view of an earlier-introduced character other than the narrator, a first-person narrator, an implied author speaking from a limited point of view, or an implied author speaking from an omniscient point of view? Did the sentence offer a return to an earlier action nor state of affairs, or an achieved equilibrium, or an unresolved paradox? Did it represent an obstacle removed, a problem solved, or a goal achieved—or the inverse of these outcomes—and for whom? Did it refer to a natural terminus like death, sleep, day's end—or to a conventional terminus like parting (the end of a visit) or [re]joining a (homecoming, a marriage)—or to a perceptual terminus like satisfaction-of-a-need (even a minimal one) or being-in-the-status-quo?[10]

Closural sentences in the "Early" period exhibited the highest incidence of references to death (13:3:6) and of problems solved (23:9:13)—as perceived by the reader rather than explicitly realized by a character or stated by a narrator (11:2:3). So, indeed, we'd expect of more "plotted" stories. The "Modern" period offered the highest number of inverse outcomes (0:9:5), the lowest incidence of omniscience in point of view (10:1:7), and the most frequent reliance on a character's perspective (13:19:13)—all suggesting the Hemingwayesque withdrawal of the narrator from a position of authority in a world where generations can be lost, and only individuals may, if lucky, survive. In the "Contemporary" period, terminals based on satisfaction (the weakest of the positive closural states) were most frequent (5:4:13). This finding is consistent with what we have discovered about "Contemporary" stories so far. It is no news that stories after 1960 often avoid the clear joining, logical progression, and neat resolution of conventionally "plotted" fiction; however, it is interesting to consider whether the processing intelligence comes to rely more on local than on global signals, or learns to detect more successfully the fewer, fainter signals we have noted. Or does it need to reconfigure itself in some primary way, so that it responds to different signals altogether? That is a question toward which I have been pointing throughout this discussion. More work needs to be done before it can be answered, but the present "experiment" allows us to take one more step.

We can look at the anterior, penultimate, and final closural sentences *as a sequence*. This is what I call the "staging" of closure. Describing this process means taking into account all of the features discussed above, and putting them into relationship as three stages of closure within a story. We've already seen that "Early" stories are more discursive, rhetorically and stylistically figured, and highly resolved than stories in the later periods. Looking at the anterior sentences in relation to the penultimate sentence in relation to the final sentence in story after story in this period, I asked myself whether I could identify a normative cognitive progression, a typical way in which closure was "staged." What these stories offered, it seemed to me, was a cognitive adjustment from wonder to wisdom: "has this really happened?"; "this is what's happened"; "this is the way things happen."

In the "Modern" group, anterior closure sentences tended to make simple, naive, declarations. Here are some examples from Anderson's "The Egg," Hemingway's "Indian Camp," and Fitzgerald's "Babylon Revisited": "The egg broke under his hand"; "He couldn't stand things, I guess"; "I lost everything I wanted in the boom."[11] Penultimate closural sentences tended to make statements of fact that were more "loaded," triggering a degree of cognitive processing hardly suggested by the surface features of the discourse. Here are the corresponding examples from the same stories: (Anderson) "the question got into my blood": (Hemingway) "The sun was coming up over the hills"; (Fitzgerald) ". . . they couldn't make him pay forever."

Final sentences in the "Modern" period were, as many people have noted, often tinged with irony on the part of either the narrator or the implied author: (Anderson) "And that, I conclude, is but another evidence of the complete and final triumph of the egg—at least as far as my family is concerned"; (Hemingway) "In the early morning on the lake sitting in the stern of the boat with his father rowing, he felt quite sure that he would never die"; (Fitzgerald) "He was absolutely sure Helen wouldn't have wanted him to be so alone." According to my sample and my preclosure choices, "Modern" stories often move the reader along from a naive world-view toward a skeptical one: "This is the way things are"; "this is the way they are if you read between the lines"; "this is the way he/she *thinks* they are, but they really aren't."

Now let's look at the "Contemporary" period. I'll illustrate with Oates's "Where are You Going, Where Have You Been?", Ursula LeGuin's "Schrodinger's Cat," and Raymond Carver's "Why Don't You Dance?" The anterior closure sentences were about four times more likely to be evaluative comments than statements of action: (Oates) ". . . they don't know a thing about you and never did and honey you're better than them because not a one of them would have done this for you"; (LeGuin) "'We used to think so,' I said, 'but really we should use larger boxes'"; (Carver) "'You must be desperate or something,' she said."[12] Penultimate sentences were more than twice as likely to offer a character's subjective reaction than a summary comment: (Oates) "She watched herself push the door slowly open as if she were safe back somewhere in the other doorway, watching this body and this head of long hair moving out into the sunlight where Arnold Friend waited"; (LeGuin) "He gazed about him in mute bewilderment, and did not flinch even when the roof of the house was lifted off just like the lid of a box, letting in the unconscionable, inordinate light of the stars"; (Carver) "There was more to it, and she was trying to get it talked out."

Final sentences were about four times more likely to show a character at-risk-but-adjusting in a strange world, rather than either fully integrated or truly embattled within it: (Oates) ". . . the vast sunlit reaches of the land behind him and on all sides of him, so much land that Connie had never seen before and did not recognize except to know that she was going to it"; (LeGuin) "I wonder if he found what it was we lost"; (Carver) "After a time she quit trying." In the "Contemporary" stories, the staging of closure reversed the direction taken in the "Early" period, now moving the reader away from, rather than toward, cognitive control: "This is the way things seem"; "this is the way they feel"; "this is the way it goes."

As I mentioned at the beginning, studies of closure helped turn short story criticism into short story theory. Studies of preclosure, as I have designed and performed them, push even further toward a theory of storyness. Those conducted with many readers of one story offer more objective evidence to work with, but in any case the training and sensibility of the investigator are necessarily in the picture. Happily so, I would argue, if we are interested in the value of these experiments to literary study.

That value, it seems to me, is at least three fold. Looking for preclosure is, first of all, a pedagogical strategy. It turns even the most naive student into a valued analyst—which is good for morale. Second, it is a critical tool; the collation of many readers' preclosure choices within and across stories turns intuitions into data. These data yield insight. On another occasion, I've shown how my own understanding of a story was enlightened by the preclosure choices of students baffled by the story.[13] Third and most important is a theoretical heuristic, prodding us to think about literary response as cognitive management. Storying is a way of processing experience in the interests of human well-being. The sense of storyness, whether derived form neurological patterns, perceptual gestalts, or cultural models, is a cognitive integer—and that accounts for the primacy of the short story as a narrative form. In both a functional *and* an essential way, the short story is that literary genre which activates, in order to modulate (both within stories and across periods), the sense of storyness.

NOTES

1. This essay is an expanded version of a talk given at the International Conference on Narrative, Madison, Wisconsin, May 1989.

2. Eudora Welty, "The Reading and Writing of Short Stories," and Elizabeth Bowen, "The Faber Book of Modern Short Stories," both in *Short Story Theories,* ed. Charles E. May (Athens, Ohio: Ohio Univ. Press, 1976), pp. 164; 156–57.

3. Charles E. May, "The Nature of knowledge in Short Fiction," *Studies in Short Fiction,* 21 (1984), pp. 327–38.

4. Susan Lohafer, *Coming to Terms With the Short Story* (Baton Rouge, Louisiana: Louisiana State Univ. Press, 1983), rpr. 1985.

5. Teun Van Dijk, *Macrostructures: An Interdisciplinary Study of Global Structures in Discourse, Interaction, and Cognition* (Hillsdale, New Jersey: Lawrence Erlbaum, 1980).

6. Robert Beaugrande, "The Story of Grammars and the Grammar of Stories," *The Journal of Pragmatics,* 6 (1982), pp. 383–422.

7. Robert F. Bruer and Keisuke Ohtsuka, "Story Structure, Characterization, Just World Organization, and Reader Affect in American and Hungarian Short Stories," *Poetics,* 17 (1988), pp. 395–415.

8. Susan Lohafer, "Preclosure in the American Short Story," *Visions Critiques* [Sorbonne], 5 (1989), pp. 297–304.

9. John Cheever, "The Swimmer" in The Stories of John Cheever (New York; Knopf, 1987); Ann Beattie, "A Clever-Kids Story," in *Secrets and Surprises* (New York: Random House, 1976). Emphases mine.

10. For a related discussion of closure signals on the global level, see John Gerlach, *Toward the End: Closure and Structure in the American Short Story* Tuscaloosa, Alabama: University of Alabama Press, 1985), pp. 8–16.

11. Sherwood Anderson, "The Egg," in *The Triumph of the Egg* (New York: B. W. Heubsch, 1921); Ernest Hemingway, "Indian Camp," in *Our Time* (New York: Scribner, 1930); F. Scott Fitzgerald, "Babylon Revisited," in *Taps at Reveille* (New York: Scribner, 1963).

12. Joyce Carol Oates, "Where Are Your Going, Where Have You Been?" *The Wheel of Love* (New York: Vanguard, 1970); Ursula LeGuin, "Schrodinger's Cat," in *The Compass Rose*; Raymond Carver, "Why Don't You Dance?" in *What We Talk About When We Talk About Love* (New York: Knopf, 1981).

13. In a talk given at the South Central Modern Language Association meeting, Houston, Texas, October 1987.

A Selected, Annotated Bibliography of the Short Story

Allen, Walter. *The Short Story in English*. Oxford: Clarendon Press, 1981.
An historical study of the development of the form in England and America.
Averill, Deborah. *The Irish Short Story from George Moore to Frank O'Connor*. Washington, D.C.: University Press of America, Inc, 1982.
An introductory study of the Irish short story for teachers and students.
Aycock, Wendell M., ed. *The Teller and the Tale: Aspects of the Short Story*. Lubbock: Texas Tech Press, 1982.
A collection of papers focusing on such aspects of short fiction as its oral roots, the use of silences in the text, and realism vs. anti-realism.
Backus, Joseph M. "'He Came into Her Line of Vision Walking Backward': Non-sequential Sequence-Signals in Short-Story Openings." *Language Learning* 15 (1956): 67–83.
A sequence signal is a word indicating that the sentence in which it appears follows another sentence on which it depends for its meaning. The short story makes frequent use of such signals out of context to plunge the reader *in media res* and to reflect the slow process of identification by which the reader confronts the new experience.
Baker, Falcon O. "Short Stories for the Millions." *Saturday Review* 19 (1953): 7–9, 48–49.
As a result of the formalist focus on form, the short-story writer has ignored entertainment value and the ordinary reader. Critics and editors have so disparaged the formula story that they have created a new formula—"the literary formula of the unresolved impasses."
Baldwin, Dean. "The English Short Story in the Fifties." In *The English Short Story, 1945–1980*, edited by Dennis Vanatta. Boston: Twayne, 1985, pp. 34–74.
Focuses on stories of social protest, especially those of Alan Sillitoe; super-natural stories of Sylvia Townsend Warner and Muriel Spark; mainstream

writers H. E. Bates, V. S. Pritchett, Rhys Davies; and major writers Doris Lessing, Roald Dahl, Angus Wilson, William Sansom, and Elizabeth Taylor.

Barzini, Luigi. "Italy." Translated by Helen Barolini. *Kenyon Review* 32 (1970): 95–97.

Modern Italian short stories follow the ancient pattern created by Boccaccio of being pithy, realistic, and slightly cynical.

Bates, H. E. *The Modern Short Story: A Critical Survey*. Boston: The Writer, Inc., 1941, 1972.

A history of the major short story writers since Poe and Gogol. Focuses more on English and European short-story writers than most histories of the form.

Bayley, John. *The Short Story: Henry James to Elizabeth Bowen*. New York: St. Martin's Press, 1988.

Discusses the "special effects" of the short story form, particularly its relationship to poetic techniques and devices. Contains analyses of stories by Henry James, Hemingway, Kipling, Chekhov, Lawrence, Joyce and Elizabeth Bowen.

Beachcroft, T. O. *The Modest Art: A Survey of the Short Story in English*. London: Oxford University Press, 1968.

An historical survey of the major figures of the English short story from Chaucer to Doris Lessing. The result of the basic difference between antique stories (listening) and modern stories (reading) is that the modern short-story writer attempts to portray rather than expound.

Beck, Warren. "Art and Formula in the Short Story." *College English* 5 (1943): 55–62.

Argues that there is no sharp technical difference between the popular short story and the literary short story. The literary story is the assertion of a different outlook—a protest against deceptive sentimentalizing of reality.

Bender, Hans. "West Germany." Translated by Peter Salm. *Kenyon Review* 31 (1969): 85–92.

Provides a brief survey of postwar German short story. Quotes several definitions of the form by German writers. Notes that although younger authors reject previous forms, in their prose texts the short story continues to live unrecognized.

Benjamin, Walter. "The Storyteller: Reflections on the Works of Nikolai Leskov." Rpt. in *Modern Literary Criticism: 1900–1970,* edited by Lawrence Lipking and A. Walton Litz. New York: Atheneum, 1972, pp. 442–55.

Benjamin claims that the art of storytelling is coming to an end because of the widespread dissemination of information and explanation. The compactness of story precludes analysis and appeals to readers by the rhythm of the work itself. For the storyteller the old religious chronicle is secularized into an ambiguous network in which the worldly and the eschatological are interwoven.

Bennett, E. K. *A History of the German Novelle*. 2d. ed. London: Cambridge University Press, 1965.

The final chapter of this standard study of German short fiction, written by
H. M. Waidson after Bennett's death, deals with the twentieth-century novelle.
Suggests that there is no way to distinguish the short story from the novelle.

Bettleheim, Bruno. *The Uses of Enchantment: The Meaning and Importance of
Fairy Tales.* New York: Alfred A. Knopf, 1976.

Psychoanalytic discussion of the therapeutic value of fairy tales with a
number of analyses of selected fairy tales.

Bierce, Ambrose. "The Short Story." *The Collected Works of Ambrose Bierce.*
1911; rpt. New York: Gordian Press, Inc., 1966, x, 234–48.

Criticizes William Dean Howells and the realistic school: "To them nothing
is probable outside the narrow domain of the commonplace man's most commonplace experience. . . . the truest eye is that which discerns the shadow
and the portent, the dead hands reaching, the light that is the heart of
darkness."

Black, John B. and Gordon H. Bower. "Story Understanding as Problem-Solving."
Poetics 9 (1980): 223–50.

Studies story grammars as theories of reader memory of stories and rejects
them as inadequate. Proposes an alternative approach based on the story as
problem-solving.

————, and Colleen M. Seifert. "The Psychological Study of Story Understanding." In *Researching Response to Literature and the Teaching of Literature,*
edited by Charles R. Cooper, Norwood, New Jersey: Ablex Publishing Corp,
1985, pp. 190–211.

Argues that when people read stories they use the same psychological processes to comprehend the events in the story that they use to comprehend life.
Cognitive research has shown that the knowledge of the world that we bring
to a story determines our understanding, whereas our memory of it is organized around schemas.

Bone, Robert. *Down Home: A History of Afro-American Short Fiction from Its
Beginnings to the End of the Harlem Renaissance.* New York: Capricorn
Books, 1975.

Provides a background for the African-American folktale, the Brer Rabbit
Tales, and the Local-Color writers; devotes a chapter each to Paul Dunbar,
Charles Chesnutt, Jean Toomer, Langston Hughes, Arna Bontemps, and the
Harlem Renaissance. Shows how the Afro-American short story is the child
of a mixed heritage.

Bonheim, Helmut. *The Narrative Modes: Techniques of the Short Story.* Cambridge, England: D. S. Brewer, 1982.

Statistical study focusing on basic short-story techniques, especially beginnings and endings. Argues that a limited set of techniques is used in story endings again and again. Discusses open and closed endings; argues that dynamic
modes are more apt to be open, while static are more apt to be closed.

Boulanger, Daniel. "On the Short Story." *Michigan Quarterly Review* 26 (Summer
1987): 510–14.

A highly metaphoric and impressionistic study of the form that focuses primarily on the detached nature of the short story; claims that there is a bit of Pontius Pilate in the short story writer, for he or she is always removed from the tragic outcome; points out how there are no class distinctions in the short story, no hierarchy.

Boyce, Benjamin. "English Short Fiction in the Eighteenth Century: A Preliminary View." *Studies in Short Fiction* 5 (1968): 95–112.

Discusses the types of short fiction found in eighteenth-century periodicals and inserted in novels: character sketch, oriental tale, stories of passion. Usually the purpose was didactic and the mode was either "hovering pathos" or "hovering irony." The most distinctive characteristic is the formal, even elegant, language.

Brickell, Herschel. "The Contemporary Short Story." *The University of Kansas City Review* 15 (1949): 267–70.

Makes several generalizations about the decline of quality magazines willing to publish fiction and about the trend of the short story to be more subjective, psychological, and poetic.

————. "What Happened to the Short Story?" *Atlantic Monthly* 116 (1915): 60–68.

Modern writers have succeeded in breaking the short story away from its formal frame and drawing it nearer to poetry, "making it a slice of the mind and spirit rather than the body."

Brown, Suzanne Hunter. "Discourse Analysis and the Short Story." In *Short Story Theory at a Crossroads,* edited by Susan Lohafer and Jo Ellyn Clarey. Baton Rouge: Louisiana State University Press, 1989, pp. 217–48.

A helpful analytical survey of the research currently being carried on by psychologists into the nature of discourse, storyness, and cognitive response to narrative.

Brushwood, John S. "The Spanish American Short Story from Quiroga to Borges." In *The Latin American Short Story: A Critical History,* edited by Margaret Sayers Peden. Boston: Twayne, 1983, pp. 35–70.

Late 1920s and early 1930s were characterized by innovative narration; movement to regionalism took place in the mid 1930s; return to innovation and cosmopolitanism characterized the early 1940s.

Burgess, Anthony. "Anthony Burgess on the Short Story," *Journal of the Short Story in English,* #2 (1984), pp. 31–47.

Says the novel presents an epoch, while the short story presents a revelation. Discusses different types of stories, distinguishing between the literary short story which is patterned and the commercial form which is anecdotal.

Canby, Henry S. "Free Fiction." *Atlantic Monthly* 116 (1915): 60–68.

Criticizes the well-made, formula story of the day because it is based more on convention than life. Claims the multitudinous situations, impressions, and incidents in modern life are incapable of being presented in a novel because of their very impermanence, but are "admirably adapted to the short story because of their vividness and their deep if narrow significance."

————. "On the Short Story." *Dial* 31 (1901): 271–73.

Argues that the novelist aims at a natural method of transcription while the short story adopts an artificial method of selecting only what bears on his or her narrow purpose—the conveying of vivid impressions of one phase of a situation or character.

_____. *The Short Story in English.* New York: Holt, Rinehart and Winston, Inc., 1909; reprinted 1932.

The romantic movement gave birth to the modern short story; Poe is the first important figure in the changing fashions of story-telling since Chaucer. The rest of the nineteenth century and the first of the twentieth century have applied Poe's theory of single effect to new subjects, primarily the contrasts of civilizations in flux.

Carens, James F. "In Quest of a New Impulse: George Moore's *The Untilled Field* and James Joyce's *Dubliners,*" In *The Irish Short Story: A Critical History,* edited by James F. Kilroy. Boston: Twayne, 1984, pp. 45–94.

Analyzes the major stories in these two most influential collections of Irish short fiction. Discusses the major contributions of Moore and Joyce in creating the modern Anglo-Irish short story.

Cassola, Carlo. "Italy." *Kenyon Review* 30 (1968): 486–90.

Discusses modern Italian short fiction as existentialist. What drives the modern Italian author to write is not psychological curiosity or social interest, but a metaphysical need.

Chatman, Seymour. "New Ways of Analyzing Narrative Structure, with an Example from Joyce's *Dubliners." Language and Style.* 2 (1969): 3–36.

A "test" of the narrative theories of Roland Barthes and Tzvetan Todorov, with a detailed analysis of Joyce's "Eveline." The story is considered both in terms of the internal relations of the narrative and the external relations between narrator and reader.

Clarke, John H. "Transition in the American Negro Short Story." *Phylon* 21 (1960), 360–66.

A shorter version of this article appears as the introduction to *American Negro Short Stories,* edited by John Henrik Clarke (New York: Hill and Wang, 1966). A brief historical survey of the African-American short story from Dunbar and Chesnutt at the turn of the century, through the Harlem literary renascence of the twenties, to the emergence of Richard Wright, who marked the end of the double standard for Black writers.

Connolly, Julian. "The Russian Short Story 1880–1917." In *The Russian Short Story: A Critical History,* edited by Charles A. Moser. Boston: Twayne, 1986, pp. 103–16.

Most of this essay focuses on Nikolay Leskov, Anton Chekhov, Maxim Gorky, Ivan Bunin, and Leonid Andreev. Briefly discusses the symbolist movement's influence on Russian literature at the turn of the century.

Corey, Herbert Ellsworth. "The Senility of the Short Story." *Dial* 62 (1917): 379–81.

Claims that the short story has become obsessed with unity that is abnormally artificial and intense. Seldom attaining high seriousness, it is a literature of feverish excitement, "the blood kinsman of the quick-lunch, the vaudeville, and the joy-ride."

Culler, Jonathan. "Story and Discourse in the Analysis of Narrative." *The Pursuit of Signs*. Ithaca: Cornell University Press, 1981.

Discusses the double logic of narrative by which plot is a sequence of events prior to a given perspective on the events, while at the same time the events are justified by their appropriateness to a thematic structure.

Current-García, Eugene. *The American Short Story, Before 1850*. Boston: Twayne, 1985.

Focuses on the types of magazine fiction before 1820. Devotes individual chapters to Washington Irving, Hawthorne, and Poe. Claims the shift toward realism in the form is largely due to the fiction of Melville.

————, and Walter R. Patrick. "Introduction." *American Short Stories*. Chicago: Scott, Foresman and Company. Rev. ed., 1964, pp. xi–liv.

An historical survey of the American short story through four periods: romanticism, realism, naturalism, and the modern period of both traditionalists (those who have carried on the Poe/De Maupassant/James tradition) and experimentalists (those who have focused more on the fragmented inner world of the mind).

————, eds. *What is the Short Story?* Rev. ed. New York: Scott, Foresman and Co., 1974.

Although this is primarily a short story anthology, it contains a generous selection of mostly American criticism on the short story arranged in chronological order.

Dollerup, Cay. "The Concepts of 'Tension,' 'Intensity,' and 'Suspense' in Short-Story Theory." *Orbis Litterarum* 25 (1970): 314–37.

Heavily documented survey of critical theory in German, Danish, and English on the concepts of intensity or tension in the short story and how these terms have been applied to linguistic rhythm, contrast, character, structure, and reader suspense in the form.

Duncan, Edgar Hill. "Short Fiction in Medieval English: A Survey." *Studies in Short Fiction* 9 (1972): 1–28.

A survey of short pieces in the Old English period, primarily in verse, which have in common the characteristic of "artfully telling a story in a relatively brief compass" and which focus on "singleness of character, of action, and/or impression."

————. "Short Fiction in Medieval English: II. The Middle English Period." *Studies in Short Fiction* 11 (1974): 227–41.

A brief sampling of short fiction elements in the "shorter romance" form, the exemplary narrative, the beast tale, and the fabliau introduced to Middle English by the French. Also noted are paraphrases of biblical stories, saints' lives, as well as the dream visions of *Pearl*, Chaucer's "The Book of Duchess," and the "Prologue to the Legend of Good Women."

Dunleavy, Janet Egleson. "Mary Lavin, Elizabeth Bowen, and a New Generation: The Irish Short Story at Mid-Century." In *The Irish Short Story: A Critical History,* edited by James F. Kilroy. Boston: Twayne, 1984, pp. 145–68.

    Discusses Lavin's art as economic, disciplined, and compressed; argues that she neither romanticizes nor trivializes Irish experience. Discusses the basic characteristics of the fiction of Elizabeth Bowen, Benedict Kiely, Michael McLaverty, and Bryan MacMahon.

Engstrom, Alfred G. "The Formal Short Story in France and its Development Before 1850." *Studies in Philology* 42 (1945): 627–39.

    After making distinctions between the *Nouvelle* and the *Conte* (a complex line of action vs. a compressed one), Engstrom points out the lack of any significant examples of *Conte* until Merimee's *Mateo Falcone* (1829), the first formal short story in French literature.

Evans, Walter. "The English Short Story in the Seventies." In *The English Short Story 1945–1980,* edited by Dennis Vanatta. Boston: Twayne, 1985, pp. 120–72.

    Focuses on new writers of the period, such as Susan Hill, Gabriel Josipovici, and Christine Brooke-Rose. The emphasis here is on different themes: personal crises, the individual in conflict in society; briefly discusses the Avant-Garde; claims the decade's finest collection of stories is *The Ebony Tower* (1974) by John Fowles.

Farrell, James T. "Nonsense and the Short Story." *The League of Frightened Philistines and Other Papers.* New York: Vanguard Press, Inc., 1945, 77–81.

    Ridicules the crop of short-story writing handbooks that sprang from Brander Matthews' *Philosophy of the Short–Story.* Their focus on form has made technical facility a value and has falsified the material of life.

Ferguson, Suzanne C. "The Rise of the Short Story in the Hierarchy of Genres." In *Short Story Theory at a Crossroads,* edited by Susan Lohafer and Jo Ellyn Clarey. Baton Rouge: Louisiana State University Press, 1989, pp. 176–92.

    A historical/critical survey of the development of the English short story, showing how social factors influence the rise and fall of the prestige of the form.

FitzGerald, Gregory. "The Satiric Short Story: A Definition." *Studies in Short Fiction* 5 (1968): 349–54.

    Defines the satiric short story as a sub-genre that sustains a reductive attack upon its objects and conveys to its readers a significance different from its apparent surface meaning.

Freundlieb, Dieter. "Understanding Poe's Tales: A Schema-Theoretical View." *Poetics* 11 (1982): 25–44.

    Argues that literary studies should shift to an explanatory analysis of reader comprehension processes. Applies schema theory derived from cognitive psychology to a number of Poe's tales.

Friedman, Norman. "Recent Short Story Theories: Problems in Definition." In

Short Story Theory at a Crossroads, edited by Susan Lohafer and Jo Ellyn Clarey. Baton Rouge: Louisiana State University Press, 1989, pp. 13–33.

A critical review of major short story critics, including Mary Rohrberger, Charles May, Susan Lohafer, and John Gerlach. Argues against those critics who support a deductive, single-term, mixed category approach to the form.

————. "What Makes a Short Story Short?" *Modern Fiction Studies* 4 (1958): 103–17.

Makes use of Neo-Aristotelian literary theory to determine the issue of the short story's shortness. To deal with the problem, Friedman says, we must ask the following questions: What is the size of the action? Is it composed of a speech, a scene, an episode, or a plot? Does the action involve a change? If so, is the change a major one or a minor one?

Flora, Joseph M., ed. *The English Short Story, 1880–1945.* Boston: Twayne, 1985.

Collection of essays on a number of British short story writers during the period, including Kipling, Lawrence, Virginia Woolf, Saki, A. E. Coppard, P. G. Woodehouse, and V. S. Pritchett.

Fonlon, Bernard. "The Philosophy, the Science, and the Art of the Short Story." *Abbia* 34 (1979): 429–38.

A discussion of the basic element of story, e.g., character, conflict, etc. Lists elements of intensity, detachment, skill, unity of effect. This is primarily a set of rules aimed at inexperienced writers.

Geismar, Maxwell. "The American Short Story Today." *Studies on the Left* 4 (1964): 21–27.

Criticizes the Salinger-Roth-Malamud-Updike coterie for their stress on craftsmanship of the well-made story and their ignoring of the social realities of the time.

Gerlach, John. "The Margins of Narrative: The Very Short Story, the Prose Poem, and the Lyric." In *Short Story Theory at a Crossroads,* edited by Susan Lohafer and Jo Ellyn Clarey. Baton Rouge: Louisiana State University Press, 1989, pp. 74–84.

Explores the basic requirements of story, focusing particularly on two minimalist stories by Enrique Anderson Imbert and Scott Sanders, as well as a short prose poem by W. S. Merwin. Argues that neither mere length nor fictionality are the constituents of story, but rather point.

————. *Toward the End: Closure and Structure in the American Short Story.* Tuscaloosa: University of Alabama Press, 1985.

A detailed study of the American short story, focusing particularly on the importance of closure, or the ending of the form; examines a number of stories in some detail in terms of the concept of closure.

Gullason, Thomas A. "The 'Lesser' Renaissance: The American Short Story in the 1920s." In *The American Short Story: 1900–1945,* edited by Philip Stevick. Boston: Twayne, 1984, pp. 71–101.

An historical survey of some of the major American short-story writers of the 1920s; analyzes briefly some of the best-known stories of Sherwood Anderson, F. Scott Fitzgerald, Ring Lardner, Ernest Hemingway, Dorothy Parker, Katherine Anne Porter. and William Faulkner.

————. "Revelation and Evolution: A Neglected Dimension of the Short Story." *Studies in Short Fiction* 10 (1973): 347–56.

Challenges Mark Schorer's distinction between the short story as an "art of moral revelation" and the novel as an "art of moral evolution." Analyzes Lawrence's "The Horse Dealer's Daughter" and Steinbeck's "The Chrysanthemums" to show the short story embodies both revelation and evolution.

————. "The Short Story: An Underrated Art." *Studies in Short Fiction* 2 (1964): 13–31.

Points out the lack of serious criticism on the short story, suggests some of the reasons for this neglect, and concludes with an analysis of Chekhov's "Gooseberries" and Nadine Gordimer's "The Train from Rhodesia" to disprove the charges that the short story is formulaic and lacks life.

Hanson, Clare. "Things out of Words: Towards a Poetics of Short Fiction." In *Re-reading the Short Story,* edited by Clare Hanson. New York: St. Martin's Press, 1989, pp. 22–33.

Argues that the short story is a more literary form than the novel; claims that short stories are framed to give them the sense of completeness that allows gaps and absences to remain in the story; thus we accept a degree of mystery or elision in the short story which we would not accept in the novel.

————, ed. *Re-reading the Short Story.* New York: St. Martin's Press, 1989. "Introduction," pp. 1–9.

Claims the short story is a vehicle for different *kinds* of knowledge, which may be in some way at odds with the 'story' of dominant culture. The formal properties of the short story—disjunction, inconclusiveness, obliquity—connect with its ideological marginality and with the fact that the form may be used to express something suppressed/repressed in the mainstream literature.

————. *Short Stories and Short Fictions, 1880–1980.* New. York: St. Martin's Press, 1985.

Argues that during this period the authority of the teller, usually a first-person 'framing' narrator who guaranteed the authenticity of the tale, was questioned by many modernist writers; argues that the movements from 'teller' to indirect free narration, and from 'tale' to 'text' were part of a more general movement from 'discourse' to 'image' in the art and literature of the period. Chapters on Kipling, Saki, Maugham, Joyce, Woolf, Mansfield, and Beckett.

Harris, Wendell V. "Beginnings of and for the True Short Story in England." *English Literature in Transition* 15, (1972): 269–76.

The true short story did not begin in England until Kipling discovered the means to control the reader's angle of vision and establish a self-contained world within the story that keeps the reader at a distance. The externality of the reader to the story's participants is a basic characteristic of the short story.

————. "English Short Fiction in the Nineteenth Century." *Studies in Short Fiction* 6 (1968): 1–93.

After distinguishing between "short fiction" appearing before 1880 and the "short story" after 1880, Harris surveys examples from both periods. The turning point was the definition posed by Brander Matthews which first appeared in *The Saturday Review* in 1884.

Harte, Bret. "The Rise of the Short Story." *Cornhill Magazine* 7 (1899): 1–8.

Harte's focus is on the rise of the local color story in America, which he says is the true American short story—as opposed to the earlier stories by Irving, which had English and German models.

Head, Dominic. *The Modernist Short Story*. Cambridge: Cambridge University Press, 1992.

After an introductory chapter that critiques the predominant formalist approach to modern short fiction theory, Head devotes separate chapters to Joyce, Virginia Woolf, Katherine Mansfield, Wyndham Lewis, and Malcolm Lowery to illustrate his own approach.

Hedberg, Johannes. "What is a 'Short Story'? And What is an 'Essay'?" *Moderna Sprak* 74 (1980): 113–20.

Reminds us of the distinction between the Chekhovian story (lack of plot) and the Maupassant story, (anecdotal and commercial); claims the essay and the short story are similar in that they are both a whole picture in miniature, not merely a detail of a larger picture—a complete work, not an extract.

Hesse, Douglas. "A Boundary Zone: First-Person Short Stories and Narrative Essays." In *Short Story Theory at a Crossroads,* edited by Susan Lohafer and Jo Ellyn Clarey. Baton Rouge: Louisiana State University Press, 1989, pp. 85–105.

Argues that the precise boundary point between essays and short stories does not exist. Analyzes George Orwell's essay "A Hanging" as a short story and William Carlos Williams' short story "Use of Force" as an essay. Also discusses essays and stories that fall in a boundary zone between essay and story.

Hogan, Robert. "Old Boys, Young Bucks, and New Women: The Contemporary Irish Short Story." In *The Irish Short Story: A Critical History,* edited by James F. Kilroy. Boston: Twayne, 1984, pp. 169–216.

General survey of contemporary Irish short-story writers such as old-guards Anthony C. West, James Plunkett, William Trevor, and Patrick Boyle; young buck writers Eugene McCabe, John Morrow, Bernard MacLaverty, Desmond Hogan, and Gillman Noonan; and women writers such as Edna O'Brien, Maeve Kelly, Emma Cooke, Kate Cruise O'Brien, and Juanita Casey.

Holloway, John. "Identity, Inversion, and Density Elements in Narrative: Three Tales by Chekhov, James, and Lawrence." In *Narrative and Structure: Exploratory Essays.* Cambridge: Cambridge University Press, 1979, pp. 53–73.

Holloway is concerned with looking at stories in which almost nothing happens. He says there is a distinctive kind of narrative episode which is

introduced by an item that is then followed by another item in inverse relationship to the first, which cancels it out and brings the reader back to where
he or she started.

Howe, Irving. "Tone in the Short Story." *Saturday Review*, 41 (1958): 16.

Because the short story lacks prolonged characterization and the independent momentum of the novel, it depends more on those technical devices or
inflections of style we call tone. "A novel written in one dominant tone
becomes intolerable; a story too often deviating from it risks chaos."

Howells, William Dean. "Some Anomalies of the Short Story." *North American
Review*, 173 (1901): 422–32.

The basic anomaly is that while readers seem to enjoy stories in the magazines, they do not read them when they are collected in a volume. Each story
requires so much of the reader's energy that several together are exhausting.
One of the basic defects of the short story is that it creates no memorable
characters.

Ingram, Forrest L., S.J. "The Dynamics of Short Story Cycles." *New Orleans
Review* 2 (1979): 7–12.

Historical and critical survey and analysis of short stories that form a single
unit, such as Joyce's *Dubliners,* Hemingway's *In Our Time,* Anderson's *Winesburg, Ohio*; suggests some of the basic devices used in such cycles.

János Szávai. "Towards a Theory of the Short Story." *Acta Litteraria Academiae
Scientiarum Hungariae, Tomus* 24 (1982): 203–24.

Discusses the Boccaccio story as a genre which gives the illusion of reflecting reality directly and spontaneously, whereas it is actually a complex, structured entity that both retains and enriches the basic structure of the story. The
enrichment resides, on the one hand, in the careful preparation of the *point*
and its attachment to a key motif and, on the other, in the introduction of a
new dimension in addition to the anecdote.

Joselyn, Sister Mary, O.S.B. "Edward Joseph O'Brien and the American Short
Story." *Studies in Short Fiction*, 3 (1965), 1–15.

Attempts a synthesis of O'Brien's philosophic and aesthetic attitudes which
may have determined his choices of "best stories"; discusses O'Brien's contribution to the history, theory, and growth of the American short story.

Jouve, Nicole Ward. "Too Short for a Book." In *Re-reading the Short Story,*
edited by Claire Hanson. New York: St. Martin's Press, 1989. pp. 34–44.

A impressionistic, non-critical essay about story length. Discusses *Thousand and One Nights* as archetypal model standing behind all stories, collections of stories, and story-telling. Makes a case for collections of stories that
stand together as organic wholes rather than single individual stories that
stand alone.

Kagan-Kans, Eva. "The Russian Short Story 1850–1880." In *The Russian Short
Story: A Critical History,* edited by Charles A. Moser. Boston: Twayne, 1986,
pp. 50–102.

Focuses primarily on Turgenev, Tolstoy, Dostoevski, and the radical, populist, and feminist writers of the period. Representative stories are analyzed in
terms of their contributions to the form and their relationship to, or reflection
of, Russian social life at the time.

Kenyon Review International Symposium on the Short Story.
    Part I, 30, Issue 4, 1968, pp. 443–90. Christina Stead (England), Herbert
    Gold (United States), Erin Kŏs (Yugoslavia), Nadine Gordimer (South Africa),
    Benedict Kiely (Ireland), Hugh Hood (Canada), Henrietta Drake-Brockman
    (Australia). Part II, 31, Issue I, 1969, pp. 58–94. William Saroyan (United
    States), Jun Eto (Japan), Maurice Shadbolt (New Zealand), Chanakya Sen
    (India), John Wain (England), Hans Bender (West Germany), and "An Agent's
    View" by James Oliver Brown. Part III, 31, Issue 4, 1969, pp. 450–502. Ana
    Maria Maute (Spain), Torborg Nedreaas (Norway), George Garett (United
    States), Elizabeth Taylor (England), Ezekiel Mphahlele (South Africa), Eliza-
    beth Harrower (Australia), Mario Picchi (Italy), Junzo Shono (Japan), Khush-
    want Singh (India). Part IV, 32, Issue I, 1970, pp. 78–108. Jack Cope (South
    Africa), James T. Farrell (United States), Edward Hyams (England), Luigi
    Barzini (Italy), David Ballantyne (New Zealand), H. E. Bates (England). Con-
    tributions from short-story writers from all over the world on the nature of
    the form, its current economic status, its history, and its significance.

Kilroy, James F. "Setting the Standards: Writers of the 1920s and 1930s." In *The
    Irish Short Story: A Critical History,* edited by James F. Kilroy. Boston: Twayne,
    1984, pp. 95–144.
    The major Irish writers who set the standards for short fiction in the 1920s
    and 1930s were Liam O'Flaherty, Frank O'Connor, and Sean O'Faolain; also
    includes brief discussions of Daniel Corkery and Seamus O'Kelley.

————. *The Irish Short Story: A Critical History,* edited by James F. Kilroy. Bos-
    ton: Twayne, 1984, "Introduction," pp. 1–19.
    An abbreviated survey of the Irish short story, from Marie Edgeworth's
    Castle Rackrent to the present. The focus is on the relationship between his-
    torical and social events and the development of fiction in Ireland, including
    political conflicts and upheavals and the rise of periodical publication.

Kimbel, Ellen. "The American Short Story: 1900–1920." In *The American Short
    Story, 1900–1945,* edited by Philip Stevick. Boston: Twayne, 1984, pp. 33–70.
    Historical survey of the development of the short story in the first two
    decades of the twentieth century; begins with Henry James and those writers
    such as Edith Wharton and Willa Cather who were strongly influenced by his
    work. Discusses the innovations of Sherwood Anderson and points out how
    he differs from earlier writers in developing the modern short story.

Kŏs, Erih. "Yugoslavia." *Kenyon Review* 30 (1968): 454–57.
    Argues that Yugoslavia is still under the influence of myths and only three
    generations removed from village life; thus the people tell stories to one
    another. The short story is the most frequently used form of literary expres-

sion in the country, although because of laziness the modern reader has begun to favor the novel at the expense of the short story.

Kostelanetz, Richard. "Notes on the American Short Story Today." *Minnesota Review* 5 (1966): 214–21.

Contemporary short-story writers focus on extreme rather than typical experiences and tend to emphasize the medium of language itself more than ever before. In a shift that pulls the genre farther away from narrative and pushes it closer to nonlinear forms of poetry, the contemporary short-story writer attempts to depict the workings of the mad mind, to simulate the feel of madness itself.

László, János. "Readers' Historical-Social Knowledge and Their Interpretation and Evaluation of a Short Story." *Poetics* 17 (1988): 461–81.

Examines a Hungarian short story to illustrate how interpretation of the short story depends on readers' historical knowledge of a particular epoch.

Leitch, Thomas M. "The Debunking Rhythm of the American Short Story." In *Short Story Theory at a Crossroads,* edited by Susan Lohafer and Jo Ellyn Clarey. Baton Rouge: Louisiana State University Press, 1989, pp. 130–47.

Argues that a particular kind of closure is typical of the American short story; uses the phrase "debunking rhythm" to characterize the kind of story in which a character realizes the falseness of one kind of knowledge but achieves no new kind of knowledge to take its place.

Lewis, C. S. "On Stories." In *Essays Presented to Charles Williams,* edited by C. S. Lewis, Grand Rapids, Michigan: William B. Eerdmans, 1966, pp. 90–105.

Although stories are series of events, this series, or what we call plot, is only a necessary means to capture something that has no sequence, something more like a state or quality. Thus, the means of "story" is always at war with its "end." However, this very tension constitues story's chief resemblance to life. "We grasp at a state and find only a succession of events in which the state is never quite embodied."

Lindstrom, Naomi. "The Spanish American Short Story from Echeverría to Quiroga." In *The Latin American Short Story: A Critical History,* edited by Margaret Sayers Peden. Boston: Twayne, 1983, pp. 35–70.

Discusses first Latin American short story, Estaban Echeverría's 1838 "The Slaughtering Grounds." Discusses movement from romanticism to realism and naturalism and then to modernism; notes that whereas Poe and de Maupassant were not taken so seriously elsewhere, Latin American readers see them as providing channels to alternate realms of experience.

Lohafer, Susan. *Coming to Terms with the Short Story.* Baton Rouge: Louisiana State University Press, 1983.

A highly suggestive theoretical study of the short story that focuses on the sentence unit of the form as a way of showing how it differs from the novel.

———. "Preclosure and Story Processing." In *Short Story: Theory at a Crossroads,* edited by Susan Lohafer and Jo Ellyn Clarey. Baton Rouge: Louisiana State University Press, 1989, pp. 249–75.

Analysis of the responses of 180 readers to a story by Kate Chopin in terms of identifying those sentences that "could" end the story but do not. This is a continuation of Lohafer's study of what she has defined as preclosure in short fiction.

Luscher, Robert M. "The Short Story Sequence: An Open Book." In *Short Story Theory at a Crossroads,* edited by Susan Lohafer and Jo Ellyn Clarey. Baton Rouge: Louisiana State University Press, 1989, pp. 148–67.

Discusses the need for readers of story cycles such as *Winesburg, Ohio* to extend their drive to find pattern to cover a number of individual sequences. Compares story cycles with mere aggregates of stories as well as with novelistic sequences.

McMurray, George R. "The Spanish American Short Story from Borges to the Present." In *The Latin American Short Story: A Critical History,* edited by Margaret Sayers Peden. Boston, Twayne, 1983, pp. 97–137.

Discusses Borges as a writer who ushers in a new literary era in South America; discusses the 1950s shift to political and social problems; argues that the most talented Spanish American writer since Borges is Julio Cortázar from Argentine. Also discusses José Donoso and Carlos Fuentes.

Marcus, Mordecai. "What is an Initiation Story?" *The Journal of Aesthetics and Art Criticism* 14 (1960): 221–27.

Distinguishes three types of initiation stories: those that lead the protagonists to the threshold of maturity only, those that take the protagonists across the threshold of maturity but leave them in a struggle for certainty, and decisive initiation stories that carry the protagonists firmly into maturity.

Martindale, Colin and Anne E. Martindale. "Historical Evolution of Content and Style in Nineteenth- and Twentieth-Century American Short Stories," *Poetics,* 17 (1988): 333–55.

Argues that the basic evolution of an art form is the result of the artist's continual necessary to produce novel works in order to counter effects of habituation. A series of American short stories written between 1820 and 1985 are examined to illustrate this increase in novelty and complexity.

Matson, Esther. "The Short Story." *Outlook,* 121 (1919): 406–9.

Instead of playing to our intellectual or spiritual natures, the short story plays on emotion. The danger of the short story is that the writer "must often be tempted to harp upon the emotions that depress and devitalize instead of invigorate."

Matthews, Brander. *The Philosophy of the Short-Story.* New York: Longmans, Green and Co., 1901.

An expansion of an 1882 article in which Matthews sets himself forth as the first critic (since Poe) to discuss the short-story (Matthews contributed the hyphen) as a genre.

Matute, Ana María. "Spain." Translated by William Fifield. *Kenyon Review* 31 (1969): 450–54.

Claims that the short story combines the mystery of poetry with the clarity of the novel and is thus the most apt narrative form; says the short story in Spain is of a higher quality than the novel.

Maugham, W. Somerset. "The Short Story." In *Points of View: Five Essays.* Garden City, New York: Doubleday and Co., Inc., 1958, pp. 163–212.

As might be expected, Maugham's preference is for the well-made story exemplified by De Maupassant's "The Necklace." However, most of the essay deals with Chekhov and Mansfield biographical material.

May, Charles E. "Artifice and Artificiality in the Short Story." *Story* 1 (Spring 1990), 72–82.

Discusses the artificial and formalized nature of the endings of short stories, arguing that the short story is the most aesthetic narrative form; discusses the ending of several representative stories.

———. "A Survey of Short Story Criticism in America." *Minnesota Review,* Spring 1973, pp. 163–69.

An analytical survey of criticism from Poe to the present, focusing on the short story's underlying vision and characteristic mode of understanding and confronting reality.

———. "The Unique Effect of the Short Story: A Reconsideration and an Example." *Studies in Short Fiction* 13 (1976), 289–97.

An attempt to redefine Poe's "unique effect" in the short story in terms of mythic perception. The short story demands intense compression and focussing because its essential subject is a manifestation of what philosopher Ernst Cassirer calls the "momentary deity." A detailed discussion of Stephen Crane's story "An Episode of War" illustrates the concept.

———. "Metaphoric Motivation in Short Fiction: In the Beginning Was the Story." In *Short Story at a Crossroads,* edited by Susan Lohafer and Jo Ellyn Clarey. Baton Rouge: Louisiana State University Press, pp. 62–73.

Discussion of how short fiction moves from the "tale" form to the "short story" form through motivation by metaphor in "Fall of the House of Usher," "Bartleby, the Scrivener," "The Legend of Sleepy Hollow," and "Young Goodman Brown."

———. "Teaching Narrative Literacy with Toolbook Short Story." *Technological Horizons in Education Journal,* Supplement, January, 1992, pp. 10–12.

Discussion of computer software application created by the author for teaching students how to transform narrative linearity into spatial meaning in the reading process.

———. "Why Did Detective Fiction Make Its Start in the Short Story." *Armchair Detective* 20 (1987): 77–81.

Discussion of the characteristics of the detective story of Poe and G. K. Chesterton; argues that they are more suitable to the short story than to the novel.

Menikoff, Barry. "The Problematics of Form: History and the Short Story." *Journal of the Short Story in English,* #2, 1984, pp. 129–46.

After a brief introduction on how the short story has been neglected, Menikoff comments briefly on the importance of Charles May's *Short Story Theories* (1976) and then discusses essays on the short story that appeared in *Critical Survey of Short Fiction* (Salem, 1981) and a special issue of *Modern Fiction Studies* (Spring, 1982).

Miall, David. "Text and Affect: A Model for Story Understanding." In *Re-reading the Short Story*, edited by Clare Hanson. New York: St. Martin's Press, 1989, pp. 10–21.

Discussion of what readers are doing in emotional terms when they read, using the defamiliarization model of the Russian formalists. Focuses on three aspects of emotion: self-reference, domain-crossing, and anticipation. Says that whereas literary texts constrain response by means of their shared frames and conventions, their affective response is highly divergent.

Mish, Charles C. "English Short Fiction in the Seventeenth Century." *Studies in Short Fiction,* 6 (1969), 223–330.

Divides the period into two parts: 1600–1660, in which short fiction declined into sterile imitation and preciousness, and 1600–1700, in which it was revitalized by the French influence of Mme. de Lafayette's *Princess de Cleves.* The French direction toward interiorization, psychological analysis and verisimilitude in action and setting, combined with the English style of the selfconscious narrator, moves fiction toward the novel of the eighteenth century.

Moffett, James. "Telling Stories: Methods of Abstraction in Fiction." *ETC.,* 21 (1964), 425–50.

Charts a sequence covering an "entire range" of ways in which stories can be told, from the most subjective and personal (interior monologue and dramatic monologue) to the most objective and impersonal (anonymous narration); includes examples of each type.

Moravia, Alberto. "The Short Story and the Novel." In *Man as End: A Defense of Humanism.* Translated by Bernard Wall. New York. Farrar, Straus & Giroux, Inc., 1969.

The basic difference between the novel and the short story is that the novel has a bone structure of ideological themes whereas the short story is made up of intuitions of feelings.

Moser, Charles A., ed. *The Russian Short Story: A Critical History.* Boston: Twayne, 1986. "Introduction: Pushkin and the Russian Short Story," pp. vii–xxiv.

Says that Pushkin reworked older tales, gave old plots a new twist, and "toyed with literary conventions." Focuses on Pushkin's contribution to the short story as a genre: brevity, surprise endings, and self-consciousness of narrative technique

Munson, Gorham. "The Recapture of the Storyable." *The University Review* 10 (1943): 37–44.

Says the best short-story writers are concerned with discovering a "story-able incident," a term he defines by quoting Henry James discussion of the writing finding a "tiny nugget" with "hard latent value."

Nedreaas, Torborg. "Norway." Translated by Orm Oeverland. *Kenyon Review* 31 (1969): 454–61.

Notes that although the short story is highly regarded by critics in Norway, it is not admired enough by the public for anyone to make a living writing short stories. Argues that the form often illuminates truth the way dreams do, for dreams may be truer than everyday truth.

Neuhauser, Rudolf. "The Russian Short Story 1917–1980." In *The Russian Short Story: A Critical History,* edited by Charles A. Moser. Boston: Twayne, 1986, pp. 147–90.

Discussion of post-revolution writers in Russia such as Evgeny Zamyatin, as well as the influence of the Russian formalist critics and writers such as Victor Shklovsky and B. M. Éjxenbaum. Separate sections are devoted to Russian literature and World War II, the thaw after the death of Stalin, the woman question, and science prose and village prose.

Newman, Frances. *The Short Story's Mutations: From Petronius to Paul Morand.* New York: B. W. Huebsch, Inc., 1924.

Although most of this book is story anthology, the interchapters chart the story's evolution from "The Matron of Ephesus" to Morand's "The Nordic Night"—an evolution of subtly changing techniques growing out of shifting philosophic attitudes. The broad movement is from the ironic mode to the impressionistic.

Oates, Joyce Carol. "The Short Story." *Southern Humanities Review* 5 (1971): 213–14.

The short story is a "dream verbalized," a manifestation of desire. Its most interesting aspect is its "mystery."

O'Brien, Edward J. *The Advance of the American Short Story.* Rev. ed. New York: Dodd, Mead and Co., 1931.

A survey of the development of the American short story from Irving to Sherwood Anderson. The focus is on contributions to the form by various authors: Irving's development of the story from the eighteenth-century essay, Hawthorne's discovery of the subjective method for psychological fiction, Poe's formalizing, Harte's caricaturing, James' development of the "central intelligence," and Anderson's freeing the story from O. Henry formalism.

————. *The Dance of the Machines: The American Short Story and the Industrial Age.* New York: The Macaulay Co., 1929.

Chapter four of this rambling polemic against machine-like standardization of the industrial age describes thirty characteristics that the short story ("the most typical American form") shares with the machine: e.g., it is patterned, impersonal, standardized, speeded-up, and cheap.

O'Connor, Flannery. "Writing Short Stories." *Mystery and Manners,* edited by

Sally and Robert Fitzgerald. New York: Farrar, Straus & Giroux, 1969, pp. 87–106.

In this lecture at a Southern Writers Conference, O'Connor discusses the two qualities necessary for the short story: "sense of manners," which one gets from the texture of his immediate surroundings; and "sense of mystery," which is always the mystery of personality—"showing how some specific folks *will* do, in spite of everything."

O'Connor, Frank. *The Lonely Voice: A Study of the Short Story.* Cleveland: The World Publishing Co., 1963.

The introductory chapter is extremely valuable "intuitive" criticism by an accomplished master of the short story. The basic difference between the novel and the short story is that in the latter we always find an intense awareness of human loneliness. O'Connor feels that the protagonist of the short story is less an individual with whom the reader can identify than a "submerged population group"; that is, someone outside the social mainstream. The remaining chapters treat this theme in Turgenev, Chekhov, Maupassant, Kipling, Joyce, Mansfield, Lawrence, Coppard, Babel, and Mary Lavin.

O'Faolain, Sean. *The Short Story.* New York: The Devin-Adair Co., 1951.

A book on the technique of the short story that claims that technique is the "least part of the business." O'Faolain illustrates his thesis that personality is the most important element by describing the personal struggles of Daudet, Chekhov, and de Maupassant. Also discusses the technical problems of convention, subject, construction, and language.

Orel, Harold. *The Victorian Short Story: Development and Triumph of a Literary Genre.* Cambridge: Cambridge University Press, 1969.

Chapters on Sheridan Le Fanu, Dickens, Trollope, Hardy, Stevenson, Kipling, H. G. Wells, and Conrad; focuses on the relevant biographical and sociocultural factors and says something about writers' relationship with editors and periodicals. Does not attempt a formal history of the evolution of the genre.

O'Rourke, William. "Morphological Metaphors for the Short Story: Matters of Production, Reproduction, and Consumption." In *Short Story Theory at a Crossroads,* edited by Susan Lohafer and Jo Ellyn Clarey. Baton Rouge: Louisiana State University Press, 1989, pp. 193–205.

Explores a number of analogies drawn from the social and natural sciences to suggest ways of seeing how the short story is different from the novel: the novel has a structure like a vertebrate, whereas the short story is like an exoskeletal animal; the novel is a macro form whereas the short story is a micro form.

O'Toole, L. Michael. *Structure, Style and Interpretation in the Russian Short Story.* New Haven: Yale University Press, 1982.

Analysis of a few major stories by Nikolai Leskov, Nikolai Gogol, Pushkin, Maxim Gorky, Ivan Turgenev, and Anton Chekhov in terms of the formalist theories of Victor Shklovsky, B. M. Éjxenbaum, Boris Tomashevsky, Mikhail Baktin, and Vladimir Propp, and the structuralist theories of Roland Barthes and Tzevetan Todorov. The introduction provides a general methodological introduction to interpretation through structural analysis.

Patrick, Walton R. "Poetic Style in the Contemporary Short Story." *College Composition and Communication* 18 (1957): 77–84.

The poetic style appears more consistently in the short story than in the novel because metaphorical dilations are essential to the writer who "strives to pack the utmost meaning into his restricted space."

Pattee, Fred Lewis. *The Development of the American Short Story.* New York: Harper and Row, 1923.

The most detailed and historically full survey of the American short story from Irving to O. Henry. Charts the changes in taste of the short-story reading public and indicates the major contributions to the form of such classic practitioners as Irving, Hawthorne, Poe, and Harte. Surveys the effect of the "Annuals," the "Ladies' Books," local color, Matthew's *Philosophy of the Short Story,* and the writing handbooks.

Peden, William. "The American Short Story During the Twenties." *Studies in Short Fiction* 10 (1973): 367–71.

Highly abbreviated account of the causes of the explosion of short stories during the Twenties, e.g., the new freedom from plotted stories, new emphasis on "now-ness," the boom of little magazines, and the influence of cinematic techniques.

———. *The American Short Story: Front Line in the National Defense of Literature.* Boston: Houghton Mifflin Co., 1964.

Discussion of major trends in the American short story since 1940. Contains chapters on those writers who focus on everyday life in contemporary society (Cheever, O'Hara, Peter Taylor, Updike, Powers, and Salinger) and those who are preoccupied with the grotesque, abnormal, and bizarre (McCullers, O'Connor, Purdy, Capote, and Tennessee Williams). An additional chapter surveys other short-story subjects such as the war, minorities, regions, and science fiction.

———. *The American Short Story: Continuity and Change, 1940–1975* 2nd. ed. Boston: Houghton Mifflin Co., 1975.

Includes chapters on publishing and the short story since 1940; stories of suburbia by Cheever, Updike, and others; stories of physical illness and abnormality by James Purdy, Tennessee Williams, Flannery O'Connor, Joyce Carol Oates; stories by Jewish writers such as Malamud, Bellow, Salinger, Grace Paley, Philip Roth, and I. B. Singer; stories by black writers such as Langston Hughes, Richard Wright, Ann Petry, Toni Cade Bambara.

Perry, Bliss. "The Short Story." *A Study of Prose Fiction.* Boston: Houghton Mifflin Co., 1902, 300–34.

Says the short story differs from the novel by presenting unique and original characters, by focussing on fragments of reality, and by making use of the poetic devices of impressionism and symbolism.

Picchi, Mario. "Italy." Translated by Adele Plotkin. *Kenyon Review* 31 (1969): 486–92.

Surveys the tradition of the short story in Italy and discusses the basic differences between the short story and the novel. Suggests that in the modern world, in a time of change and expectation, the short story has a greater reason for being than the novel does.

Pickering, Jean. "The English Short Story in the Sixties." In *The English Short Story, 1945–1980,* edited by Dennis Vanatta. Boston: Twayne, 1985, pp. 75–119.

Says that few of the cultural developments in England in the 1960s were reflected in the short story; claims the short story was in decline during the period; focuses on short story collections by Roald Dahl, William Sansom, Doris Lessing, V. S. Pritchett, and H. E. Bates.

———. "Time and the Short Story." In *Re-reading the Short Story,* edited by Clare Hanson. New York: St. Martin's Press, 1989, pp. 45–54.

A rehash of the old distinction between the short story as an art of revelation and the novel as an art of evolution. Structure, theme, characterization, language are influenced by the short story's particular relation to time as a moment of revelation.

Prince, Gerald. *A Grammar of Stories: An Introduction.* The Hague: Mouton, 1973.

An attempt to establish rules to account for the structure of all the syntactical sets that we intuitively recognize as stories. The model used is Noam Chomsky's theories of generative grammar.

Prichett, V. S. "Short Stories." *Harper's Bazaar* 87 (July 1953): 31, 113.

The short story is a hybrid, owing much to the quickness and objectivity of the cinema, much to the poet and the newspaper reporter, and everything to the "restlessness, the alert nerve, the scientific eye and the short breath of contemporary life." Pritchett makes an interesting point about the collapse of standards, conventions and values which has so bewildered the impersonal novelist but has been the making of the story-writer.

Propp, Vladimir. *Morphology of the Folktale,* edited by Svatava Pirkova-Jakovson. Translated by Laurence Scott. Bloomington: Indiana University Research Center, 1958.

All formalist and structuralist studies of narrative owe a debt to this pioneering early twentieth-century study. Using one hundred fairy tales, Propp defines the genre itself by analyzing the stories according to characteristic actions or functions.

Reid, Ian. *The Short Story.* London: Methuen & Co., Ltd., 1977.

A brief study in the Critical Idiom Series; deals with problems of definition, historical development, and related generic forms. Good introduction to the short story as a genre.

Rhode, Robert D. *Setting in the American Short Story of Local Color: 1865–1900.* The Hague: Mouton, 1975.

A study of the various functions that setting plays in the local color story in the late nineteenth-century, from setting as merely background to setting in relation to character and setting as personification.

Rohrberger, Mary. "Between Shadow and Act: Where Do We Go From Here?" In *Short Story Theory at a Crossroads,* edited by Susan Lohafer and Jo Ellyn Clarey. Baton Rouge: Louisiana State University Press, 1989, pp. 32–45.

A thought-provoking review of a number of modern short-story critics and theorists, largely by way or responding to and disagreeing with the strictly scientific and logical approach to definition of the form suggested by Norman Friedman.

———. *Hawthorne and the Modern Short Story: A Study in Genre.* The Hague: Mouton & Co., 1966.

Attempts a generic definition of the short story as a form which derives from the romantic metaphysical view that there is more to the world than can be apprehended through the senses. Hawthorne is the touchstone for her definition which she then applies to twentieth-century stories by Eudora Welty, Hemingway, Sherwood Anderson, Faulkner, and others.

———. "The Question of Regionalism: Limitation and Transcendence." In *The American Short Story, 1900–1945,* edited by Philip Stevick. Boston: Twayne, 1984, pp. 147–182.

Focus is on such writers as Ruth Suckow, Jesse Stuart, Langston Hughes, and Jean Toomer. Calls Toomer's *Cane* most significant work produced by the Harlem renaissance, compares it with Anderson's *Winesburg.* Also discusses Ellen Glasgow, Sinclair Lewis, James T. Farrell, Erskine Caldwell, John O'Hara, and John Steinbeck.

Ross, Danforth. *The American Short Story.* Minneapolis: University of Minnesota Press, 1961.

A sketchy survey that measures American stories since Poe against Aristotelian criteria of action, unity, tension, and irony. Ends with the Beat Generation writers who rebel against the Poe-Aristotle tradition by using shock tactics.

Ruthrof, Horst. "Bracketed World and Reader Construction in the Modern Short Story." In *The Reader's Construction of Narrative.* New York: Routledge & Kegan Paul, 1981, pp. 97–109.

Discusses the "boundary situation" as the basis for the modern short story. In the pure boundary situation, the reader's act of bracketing transforms the presented crisis into the existential experience of the reading act.

Schirmer, Gregory A. "Tales from Big House and Cabin: The Nineteenth Century." In *The Irish Short Story: A Critical History,* edited by James F. Kilroy. Boston: Twayne, 1984, pp. 21–44.

Survey of short fiction of Maria Edgeworth, William Carleton, Sheridan Le Fanu, and Somerville and Ross; emphasizes the ironic voice of Edgeworth's *Castle Rackrent,* the comic realism and the sophisticated use of narrative voice of Carleton, the use of the Gothic tradition and psychological complexity of Le Fanu, and the formal perfection of the stories of Somerset and Ross.

Schlauch, Margaret. "English Short Fiction in the 15th and 16th Centuries." *Studies in Short Fiction* 3 (1966): 393–434.

A survey of types of short fiction from the romantic *lai* to the *exemplum*, and from the bawdy *fabliau* to the *novella*. Schlauch's conclusions are that modern short story writers are heirs both in subject matter (e.g., internal psychological conflict) and technique (e.g., importance of dialogue) to a long tradition that antedates the seventeenth century, a tradition that is still worth studying.

Shah, Indries. "The Sufis." In *The Nature of Human Consciousness,* edited by Robert Ornstein. New York: The Viking Press, 1973, pp. 275–78.

Discussion of the therapeutic value of Sufi teaching stories.

Shaw, Valerie. *The Short Story: A Critical Introduction.* London: Longman, 1983.

This is a desultory discussion of the form, with little sympathy for a unified approach to the form. The focus is on British story writers, with one chapter on the transitional figure Robert Louis Stevenson. Other chapters deal with character, setting, and subject matter. Says the short story cannot be defined by unity of effect or by a history of its "favorite devices and eminent practitioners."

Smith, Horatio E. "The Development of Brief Narrative in Modern French Literature: A Statement of the Problem." *PMLA,* 32 (1917), 583–97.

Surveys the confusion between the *Conte* and *Nouvelle* and calls for a critical investigation of the practice and theory of the French forms similar to those published on the American short story and the German *Nouvelle.*

Stevenson, Lionel. "The Short Story in Embryo." *English Literature in Transition* 15 (1972): 261–68.

Discussion of the "agglomerative urge" in eighteenth- and nineteenth-century English fiction that contributed to the undervaluing of the short story. Not until 1880, when the fragmentation of the well-integrated view of society began in England, did the short story come into its own in that country.

Stevick, Philip, ed. "Introduction," *The American Short Story: 1900–1945.* Boston: Twayne, 1984, pp. 1–31.

Stevick's extensive introduction to this collection of essays by various critics is a helpful historical overview of the development of the twentieth-century short story. This is a good introduction to many of the features of the modern short story and how they came about at the beginning of the century.

―――――, ed. *Anti-Story: An Anthology of Experimental Fiction.* New York: The Free Press, 1971.

An influential collection of contemporary short fiction with a helpful introduction that characterizes anti-story as against mimesis, against reality, against event, against subject, against the middle range of experience, against analysis, and against meaning.

Stinson, John J. "The English Short Story, 1945–1950." In *The English Short Story, 1945–1980,* edited by Dennis Vanatta. Boston: Twayne, 1985, pp. 1–33.

Discusses some of the reasons that the short story was in decline in England during this period; claims there was no new direction in the form of the time; discusses Somerset Maugham, A. E. Coppard, Graham Greene, Sylvia Townsend Warner, V. S. Pritchett, and Angus Wilson.

Stroud, Theodore A. "A Critical Approach to the Short Story." *The Journal of General Education* 9 (1956): 91–100.

Makes use of American "New Criticism" to determine the pattern of the work; that is, why apparently irrelevant episodes are included, why some events are expanded and some excluded.

Sullivan, Walter. "Revelation in the Short Story: A Note on Methodology." *Vanderbilt Studies in Humanities,* vol. 1. edited by Richard C. Beatty, John Philip Hyatt, and Monroe K. Spears. Nashville: Vanderbilt University Press, 1951, pp. 106–12.

The fundamental methodological concept of the short story is a change of view from innocence to knowledge. The change can be either "logical" (coming at the end of the story), or "anticipated" (coming near the beginning); it can be either "intra-concatenate" (occurring within the main character) or "extra-concatenate" (occurring within a peripheral character).

Summers, Hollis. ed. *Discussions of the Short Story.* Boston: D. C. Heath and Co.; 1963.

Includes general pieces on the short story, such as Ray B. West's first chapter, Sean O'Faolain's chapter on "Convention," a chapter each from Percy Lubbock's *Craft of Fiction* and Kenneth Payson Kempton's *The Short Story,* Bret Harte's "The Rise of the Short Story," and excerpts from Brander Matthews' book. Also includes seven additional essays on specific short-story writers.

Terras, Victor, "The Russian Short Story: 1830–1850." In *The Russian Short Story: A Critical History,* edited by Charles A. Moser. Boston: Twayne, 1986, pp. 1–49.

Points out that 1830 marked the end of golden age of poetry and the shift to prose fiction, particularly short fiction, in Russia. Discusses the romantic origins of short fiction with Pushkin, the transition to psychological realism with Mikhail Lermontov, the significant contributions of the stories of Nikolai Gogol, the transition to the so-called natural school, and the early works of Dostoevski and Turgenev.

Thurston, Jarvis, O. B. Emmerson, Carl Hartman, and Elizabeth Wright, eds. *Short Fiction Criticism: A Checklist of Interpretation Since 1925 of Stories and Novelettes (American, British, Continental), 1800–1958.* Denver: Alan Swallow, 1960.

This checklist of interpretations of individual stories was brought up to date by Elizabeth Wright in the Summer, 1969 issue of *Studies in Short Fiction,* and has been supplemented by Ms. Wright, George Hendrick, and Warren Walker in each Summer issue since then.

Todorov, Tzvetan. "The Structural Analysis of Literature." In *Structuralism: An*

Introduction, edited by David Robey. London: Clarendon Press, 1973, pp. 73–103.

The "figure in the carpet" in James' stories is the quest for an absolute and absent cause. The cause is either a character, an event, or an object; its effect is the story we are told. Everything in the story owes its existence to this cause, but because it is absent the reader sets off in quest of it.

Tomashevsky, Boris. "Thematics." In *Russian Formalist Criticism: Four Essays.* Translated by Lee T. Lemon and Marion Reis. Lincoln: University of Nebraska Press, 1965, pp. 61–98.

Important early Russian formalist discussion on the relationship between thematic motifs and formal motivation in narrative.

Trask, Georgianne, and Charles Burkhart, ed. *Storytellers and Their Art.* New York: Doubleday Anchor, 1963.

A valuable collection of comments on the short story form by practitioners from Chekhov to Capote. See especially Part I: "Definitions of the Short Story" and "Short Story vs. Novel," pp. 3–30.

Voss, Arthur. *The American Short Story: A Critical Survey.* Norman: University of Oklahoma Press, 1973.

A comprehensive, but routine, survey of the major short-story writers in American Literature. Good for an overview of the stories and criticism, but nothing original.

Wain, John. "Remarks on the Short Story." *Journal of the Short Story in English* 2: 1984, pp. 49–66.

Wain agrees that it is a form of its own, with its own laws and logic, and that it is a modern form, beginning with Poe. Says the novel is like a painting whereas the short story is like a drawing, which catches a moment and is satisfying on its own grounds.

Ward, Alfred C. *Aspects of the Modern Short Story: English and American.* London: University of London Press, Ltd., 1924.

Brief discussions of representative stories of twenty-three different writers. In the introduction, Ward lists five rather simplistic characteristics of the parable form by which to judge the short story. However, he does note that the short story is ideally suited to the impressionistic effect and the territory of the unconscious.

Watson, James G. "The American Short Story: 1930–1945." In *The American Short Story, 1900–1945,* edited by Philip Stevick. Boston: Twayne, 1984, pp. 103–46.

Claims that the period between 1930 and 1945 is the most prolific outpouring of short fiction in the history of American literature; focuses on the importance of the little magazines; discusses the contributions of Hemingway, Faulkner, Fitzgerald.

Welty, Eudora. "The Reading and Writing of Short Stories." *The Atlantic Monthly,* February 1949, pp. 54–58; March 1949, pp. 46–49.

An impressionistic, but suggestive, essay in two installments that focuses on the mystery of story, on the fact that we cannot always see the solid outlines of story because of the atmosphere it generates.

West, Ray B. "The American Short Story." In *The Writer in the Room*. Detroit: Michigan State University Press, 1968, pp. 185–204.

Contrasts the short story's "microscopic" focus on inner motives with the novel's "telescopic" view from the outside. The novel is concerned with the human attempt to control nature through social institutions; the short story presents the individual's confrontation with nature as an indifferent force.

————. "The Modern Short Story and the Highest Forms of Art." *English Journal* 46 (1957): 531–39.

The rise of the short story in the nineteenth century is a result of the shift in narrative view from the "telescopic" (viewing nature and society from the outside) to the "microscopic" (viewing the unseen world of inner motives and impulses).

————. *The Short Story in America: 1900–1950*. Chicago: Henry Regnery, Co., 1952.

Takes up where Fred Lewis Pattee's book leaves off, but it lacks completeness or continuity. Chapter I is a short survey in itself of the development of the short story since Irving, Hawthorne and Poe. Chapter IV is devoted completely to Hemingway and Faulkner.

Williams, William Carlos. *A Beginning on the Short Story: Notes*. Yonkers, New York: The Alicat Bookshop Press, 1950.

In these "Notes" from a writers' workshop session, Williams makes several interesting remarks about the form: the short story, as contrasted with the novel, is a brush stroke instead of a picture; stressing virtuosity instead of story structure, it is "one single flight of the imagination, complete: up and down"; it is best suited to depicting the life of "briefness, brokenness and heterogeneity."

Wright, Austin. *The American Short Story in the Twenties*. Chicago: University of Chicago Press, 1961.

Using a canon of 220 stories—one set selected from the twenties and the other from the immediately preceding period—Wright examines differing themes and techniques to test the usual judgments of what the "modern short story" is.

————. "On Defining the Short Story: The Genre Question." In *Short Story Theory at a Crossroads,* edited by Susan Lohafer and Jo Ellyn Clarey. Baton Rouge: Louisiana State University Press, 1989, pp. 46–53.

Discusses some of the theoretical problems involved in defining the short story as a genre; argues for the formalist view of a genre definition as a cluster of conventions.

————. "Recalcitrance in the Short Story." In *Short Story Theory at a Crossroads,* edited by Susan Lohafer and Jo Ellyn Clarey. Baton Rouge: Louisiana State University Press, 1989, pp. 115–29.

A discussion of stories with endings that resist the reader's efforts to assimilate them and to make sense of them as a whole. Such final recalcitrance, Wright claims, is the extreme kind of resistance that the short story has developed to thwart closure and thus reduce the complexity of the story to a conceptual understanding.

A Note about the Editor

Charles E. May is professor of English at California State University, Long Beach. He is the author of *Edgar Allan Poe: A Study of the Short Fiction* and *The Short Story: A Study of the Genre* and editor of *Short Story Theories, Fiction's Many Worlds,* and *The Twentieth Century European Short Story.* He has published over a hundred and fifty articles, mostly on the short story, in a variety of journals, books, and reference works and has developed a software program, *HyperStory,* available from D. C. Heath Publishers, for short story instruction. In 1996–97, he was a Fulbright Fellow at University College, Dublin and Trinity College, lecturing on the short story.

DATE DUE